G000154439

The **AA** **KEY**Guide
Normandy
By Laurence Phillips

Contents

KEY TO SYMBOLS

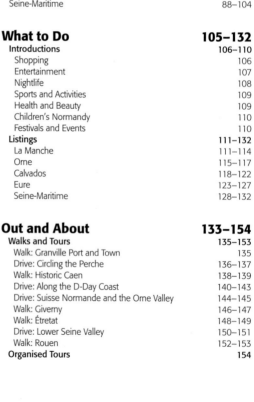

- Map reference
- Address
- Telephone number
- Opening times
- Admission prices
- Bus number
- Train station
- Ferry/boat
- Driving directions
- Tourist office
- Tours
- Guidebook
- Restaurant
- Café
- Shop
- Bar
- Toilets
- Number of rooms
- Parking
- No smoking
- Air conditioning
- Swimming pool
- Gym
- Other useful information
- Shopping
- Entertainment
- Nightlife
- Sports
- Activities
- Health and beauty
- For Children
- Cross reference
- Walk/tour start point

HOW TO USE THIS BOOK

Understanding Normandy is an introduction to the region, its geography, economy and people. **Living Normandy** gives an insight into Normandy today, while **The Story of Normandy** takes you through the country's past.

For detailed advice on getting to Normandy—and getting around once you are there—turn to **On the Move**. For useful practical information, from weather forecasts to emergency services, turn to **Planning**.

Out and About gives you the chance to explore Normandy through walks and tours.

The Sights, **What to Do** and **Eating and Staying** are divided geographically into five regions, which are shown on the map on the inside front cover. These regions always appear in the same order. Towns and places of interest are listed alphabetically within each region.

Map references for **The Sights** refer to the atlas at the end of this book or to the individual town plans. For example, Rouen has the reference ✚ 200 X4, indicating the page on which the map is found (200) and the grid square in which Rouen sits (X4).

UNDERSTANDING NORMANDY

This most peaceful of regions, with its seemingly endless coastline
and sleepy hinterland of half-timbered cottages, fast-flowing streams
and lush green fields, was born of centuries of conflict.
Every city of looming gables and turrets, each hamlet or village, and
almost every port and beach has a tale to tell. This may be a story of
knights and dukes, chivalry and kingship, it may be a seafarer's yarn of
exploration, discovery and piracy, or it may be a memory of more recent
battles and invasion from land, sea or air.
And each chapter in Normandy's story is illustrated, whether in
11th-century needlework at Bayeux, through stained glass in Rouen's
churches and cathedrals, or by the late 19th-century Impressionists
whose trail stretches from Honfleur to Le Havre and back to Giverny.

IDENTITY

Normandy has the patience to
tell its stories at a gentle pace.
Just far enough away from the
French capital, Paris, to retain a sense of
its own identity, this one-time dukedom—for
centuries foreign to France—has a quiet, self-
sufficient spirit. Although lacking the fiery
independence of neighbouring Celtic Brittany,
Normandy retains an awareness of its past and
its potential. A Viking land, colonised by
Norsemen from whom it took its name and spirit
of adventure, the region retains the self-reliance
of its colonial past.

Not long after the original Scandinavian settlers
claimed the land for themselves, Normandy
looked out to sea to make further conquests.
England was its most enduring trophy (Queen
Elizabeth II still retains title to the duchy of
Normandy), but the Norman empire stretched as
far as Sicily and southern Italy. Even after
Normandy became part of France at the end of
the Hundred Years War in 1453, its sea captains
pursued the path of colonisation, being among
the original settlers of Canada.

Traders, sailors, farmers and fighters: thanks to
centuries of outside influences, Normans can't be
pigeonholed. But when a patriotic Norman talks
of 'mon pays' (my land) he is more likely to be
referring to his region than to his country.

LANDSCAPE

Normandy has a
dramatic coastline, thrusting
symbolically through the English
Channel towards the Atlantic Ocean.
Even in this age of pan-European budget air
travel, this is still a region that regards seaports as
its principal gateways, just as when William
Shakespeare wrote of England's King Henry V
famously laying siege to Harfleur as the first step
in his invasion of France. Honfleur, Barfleur and
Dieppe are attractive enough to lure visitors as
destinations in their own right, while Le Havre,
Cherbourg and Rouen remain very much trading
posts. Between the ports are beaches of every
type and, at Étretat, some of Europe's most dramatic cliffs.

Inland, the pastoral nature of the region means
that agriculture continues to define the land.
Here, dairy farms and apple orchards dominate
the landscape, much as vineyards do in regions
further south. Rich forests in areas furthest from
the coast provide areas of unspoiled tranquillity.

While many towns—especially those in coastal
areas—suffered terribly from wartime bombings,
leaving a legacy of harsh concrete post-war
rebuilding, other areas were miraculously saved.
There are fine manor houses in a splendid range
of architectural styles, from Renaissance to the
traditional half-timbered houses of the Suisse

Normande, and the many chateaux and fortifications that survived the air raids are matched by the remarkable religious heritage of Gothic abbeys and cathedrals.

TOURISM AND THE ECONOMY

Those ports that once proved so lucrative as homes to privateers, pirates and adventurers continue to play a crucial role in France's transatlantic trade. Alongside the container ships at the docks are cruise liners and car ferries, a sign that the biggest modern boom is in tourism.

The traditional tourist lures of the French regions are augmented in Normandy by its World

capital. Once the region was adopted by the Impressionists, its success among the well-to-do was assured. Even today, a certain chic element defines several resorts, and the image of the playground of the wealthy is reinforced by casinos, spas and racecourses. Horses play a part in both tourism and business in the Orne, home of the Percheron breed and countless riding stables.

The agricultural legacy of a land of dairy farms supports a new style of gastronomic tourism that reflects a revived interest in traditional rather than faddish foods. Creamy sauces, full-flavoured cheeses, ciders and seafood are on menus in country inns and city-centre restaurants. Despite

Key attractions, left to right: Mont-St-Michel silhouetted at sunset; the British Military Cemetery in Ranville, the first town to be liberated after D-Day; the sandy beach near the resort Barneville-Carteret

War II sites, which attract visitors from the UK, the US and Canada, and increasingly from other European countries. Annual return visits by veterans themselves are declining, as is inevitable more than 60 years after D-Day, but interest in the sites and lessons learned from the war continues to grow as families and descendants of combatants come to pay their own respects.

Tourism flourished in Normandy in the mid-19th century, as Cabourg, Deauville and Trouville grew to meet the demands of fashionable Paris society needing a Riviera within easy reach of the

this interest, agriculture on its own has been affected by the politics of modern farming, with European Union (EU) quotas on milk production and regulations on the use of unpasteurised milk having put paid to many small, independent dairies. As a result, there is much rural unemployment in the heartland away from the cities and tourist resorts of the coast.

POLITICS

Normandy's long-time dependence on farming and fishing means that the influence of the

Heads of state commemorate the 60th anniversary of D-Day, which commenced on 5th June 1944

NORMANDY'S REGIONS

Officially, Normandy consists of two autonomous regions: Basse-Normandie (Lower Normandy) and Haute-Normandie (Upper Normandy), each subdivided into administrative *départements*. Essentially, Basse-Normandie is the western half of Normandy, containing the *départements* of Manche, Orne and Calvados; Haute-Normandie, meanwhile, is the region to the north and east, split between the *départements* of Eure and Seine-Maritime. In truth, however, modern-day Normans regard Normandy as one regional entity, and it is probably only the decision as to where a joint capital city would lie that presents the principal stumbling block to unification. Caen (William the Conqueror's city) is capital of Basse-Normandie, while Rouen (the more romantic city on the Seine, with its own legacy of dukes, kings and bishops) is capital of Haute-Normandie. Choosing between them would be difficult.

Normandy's *départements* are distinguished by the first two numbers of an address's post code (these also appear on car licence plates). These number pairs are as follows: Manche—50; Orne—61; Calvados—14; Eure—27; and Seine-Maritime—76. Each *département* also has its own well-defined character.

La Manche This coastal *département* is flanked on one side by the Cotentin beaches of World War II and on the other by Mont-St-Michel. Its seafaring past and present are represented in harbours as diverse as William the Conqueror's Barfleur and the resort of Granville. The principal port is Cherbourg, at the top of the peninsula, and the capital is St-Lô.

Orne The lush hinterland of Normandy is known as the country of the horse, and the main attractions for visitors are its stud farms and forests. It is an area known for good country food, and it has Alençon as its capital.

Calvados Sprawling out from its capital of Caen, Calvados includes the D-Day landing beaches and the picturesque inland regions of the Pays d'Auge and Suisse Normande. Here, country lanes are dotted with signs inviting passers-by to taste the eponymous apple brandy of the region's farmyard producers.

Eure Administered from the picturesque capital of Évreux, Eure was the frontier between old Normandy and France. It has a centuries-old legacy of abbeys and castles, and a newer artistic heritage thanks to Claude Monet's residence at Giverny.

Seine-Maritime Rouen, on the banks of the Seine, is the capital of this *département*. It's an area of historic ports, ranging from the rebuilt Le Havre to the picturesque towns and villages along the Côte d'Albâtre. Manor houses and abbeys, ruined and intact, are among the lures away from the coast and rivers.

European Union (EU) colours local politics, with views polarised between those who blame Europe for their woes and those dependent on subsidies. Voters move to the right and even the Front Nationale when fearing for their livelihoods, and tend towards the left, from socialism to communism, when remembering the wartime occupation. Whatever the individual leaning, politics plays a lively role in local life and conversations. Elected mayors have wide-ranging powers that often come as a shock to visitors from the UK or US, who are surprised at the large scale of local events and campaigns.

Political action is widespread, whether protests

SOCIETY

The native Norman reserve should not be taken as an anti-social sign. Good manners are valued and it is always worth making the effort to get to know the hosts at your inn or *chambre d'hôte* (bed-and-breakfast). A genuine interest in the local area and traditions will be rewarded with a very warm welcome, even an invitation to share a *goutte* (drop) of farmhouse Calvados, cider or Poiré. A sure indication of a welcome in winter is the offer of a *goutte* of Calva in your black coffee.

Outside the cities and university towns, Normans may not live the Latin late-night lifestyle, but for family occasions, confirmations and

Left to right: the fortress of Château Gaillard; the flag of Normandy; World War II gun at Arromanches

at ports by environmental campaigners or lorry drivers opposing a new EU directive. These can spill over to the days before and after the official industrial action. Since France has a long tradition of street-corner gatherings during political and social unrest, bystanders usually repair to the nearest café to pass the time.

Even when other parts of France are caught in a passing wave of nationalism or slight xenophobia, Normandy has affection for its visitors, especially those from the Allied liberating nations of D-Day. In commemoration season in June, newsagents sell thank you cards for locals to give to visiting veterans, and the British, American and Canadian flags fly in most villages. In recent years, however, in a lifting of earlier taboos, some commentators have debated the effects of the Allied bombings.

weddings, they do like to let their hair down. If you encounter a procession of cars with ribbons streaming from their door handles or aerials and their horns tooting incessantly, this is a traditional wedding parade travelling from the home town or village of the bride to that of the groom. The partying may continue for two or three days, as dispersed families unite around the table from Saturday afternoon until late on Sunday, irrigating the endless meal with shots of Calvados.

A more public form of merrymaking may be shared by visitors during Normandy's festivals, which often celebrate local produce. These food fairs, along with musical and other cultural events, provide excellent excuses for sharing a drink with locals, and are a good chance for outsiders to see the people of Normandy at their best.

Pointe du Grouin: Normandy is defined by its coast, which provides food, recreation and trade

LA MANCHE

Right: Gatteville lighthouse. Below: colourful fishing boats in Barfleur's busy harbour

Au P'tit Quinquin. (▷ 158) Dine on local Mont St Michel lamb in a simple country restaurant.

Avranches (▷ 39) With fabulous views out towards Mont-St-Michel, this town has a history entwined with that of the abbey itself.

Barfleur (▷ 40) A typical Cotentin fishing town with a fascinating history. The nearby Gatteville lighthouse is a must-see.

Cité de la Mer, Cherbourg (▷ 43) More than a mere aquarium, this is a celebration of Normandy's relationship with the sea.

Maison Gosselin Buy provisions and souvenirs at St Vaast-la-Hougue's legendary grocery (▷ 114).

Mont-St-Michel (▷ 46–48) Out of season, ideally in winter, is the best time to experience the amazing abbey and town perched on a granite rock in the bay.

Musée de Christian Dior, Granville (▷ 45 and 135) Visit the home of the man who devised post-war cool.

Patinoire Chantereyne Go late night ice skating in this complex in Cherbourg (▷ 112).

Tatihou, St-Vaast-la-Hougue (▷ 50) An island of timeless calm, just offshore from a bustling pleasure port.

A Percheron horse at the Haras du Pin stud

ORNE

Haras National du Pin (▷ 54) Anyone who loves horses should visit this elegant royal stud farm.

Jean-Claude Lebaron, Bagnoles-de-l'Orne (▷ 115) Another vice of the resort of Bagnoles—aside from spa pampering and casino gambling—is indulging in delicious chocolate swans from this shop.

Mortagne au Perche. (▷ 56) Taste the distinctive local *boudin noir* sausage.

Parc Naturel Régional Normandie-Maine (▷ 55) The flora and fauna of the park's four forests provide pure escapism for nature lovers.

La Poêlerie, Joué-du-Bois (▷ 12 and 116) Beer makes a refreshing alternative to cider at this farmhouse brewery.

Sées (▷ 56 and 117) Choosing turkeys at the December fair.

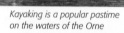

Kayaking is a popular pastime on the waters of the Orne

Café society at Deauville

CALVADOS

Au Repos des Chineurs Never mind the soap, at this hotel you can take your bedroom furniture home with you (▷ 170).

Bayeux Tapestry (▷ 58) No matter how many times you see it reproduced in print, the original needlework remains an impressive sight.

Beuvron-en-Auge (▷ 59) One of the prettiest corners of this picture-book region.

Norman knights triumph on Bayeux's tapestry

Deauville (▷ 68) Kicking off with its 'Swing In' festival in July and ending with the film festival in September, the chic resort becomes Paris-on-sea during the summer season.

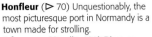

Honfleur (▷ 70) Unquestionably, the most picturesque port in Normandy is a town made for strolling.

Isigny-sur-Mer (▷ 121) Discover France's best-loved butter and cream at the world famous dairy.

Le Moulin du Vey (▷ 170) Stay in a watermill on the banks of the river Orne.

Mémorial de la Paix, Caen (▷ 62) This peace museum is a powerful indictment of the 20th century's rush to war.

Mulberry Harbour, Arromanches-les-Bains (▷ 58) The awe-inspiring remains of the floating harbour that launched the D-Day landings can still be seen.

Suisse Normande This area has the most rugged landscapes of Normandy and is a haven of adventure sports (▷ 121).

EURE

Abbaye du Bec-Hellouin (▷ 77) The calm of the abbey and its grounds exudes a powerful spirituality.

Auberge de la Truite. (▷ 163) Barrel-organs play as you dine on hearty fare at this typical *auberge* at Montreuil L'Argillé.

Château Gaillard, Les Andelys (▷ 78) Richard the Lionheart's final stronghold dominates Les Andelys and the surrounding countryside.

Val de Risle Pit yourself against the white waters of the river Risle in a kayak (▷ 126).

Évreux (▷ 77) Come here for waterside strolls along the river Iton and to admire the floral displays.

Grain de Café. The finest cup of tea in Normandy is served in this tiny cafe in Louviers (▷ 125).

Léry (▷ 125) Enjoy a day on the water at the lakeside leisure complex here.

Restaurant Baudy, Giverny (▷ 85) Before the crowds arrive or after they leave, dine in the restaurant that was the meeting place of Claude Monet and his fellow Impressionists.

SEINE-MARITIME

Abbaye de Jumièges (▷ 89) The perfect backdrop to a concert on a summer evening.

L'Auberge du Val au Cesne. (▷ 173) Ducks, chicks and cats greet arrivals at this charming inn.

Cathédrale de Notre-Dame, Rouen (▷ 99) The night-time summer light show projected on the cathedral's façade is spectacular.

Château du Champ-de-Bataille (▷ 90) The restoration of this castle and its grounds is a labour of love.

Église Jeanne-d'Arc, Rouen (▷ 102) Modern church architecture at its most inspiring.

Étretat (▷ 94) See magnificent cliffs and caves at one of France's most dramatic beaches.

Fêtes Jeanne d'Arc. Visit Rouen during the Joan of Arc festivities in May (▷ 132).

Musée des Beaux-Arts André Malraux, Le Havre (▷ 97) The natural light that inspired the Impressionists fills this modern art museum.

Palais Bénédictine, Fécamp (▷ 95) This distillery almost upstages the region's abbeys and cathedrals for sheer grandeur.

Abbaye de St-Wandrille Listen to the Gregorian chants at a service at this abbey (▷ 90).

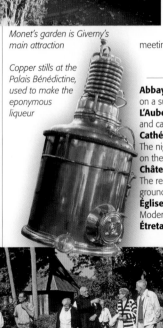

Playing a part: US Rangers in a D-Day re-enactment event. Inset: biking in Suisse Normande

Monet's garden is Giverny's main attraction

Copper stills at the Palais Bénédictine, used to make the eponymous liqueur

Left: Abbaye de St-Wandrille. Above: try local oysters

Drink apple juice in all its forms—Calvados, cider and Pommeau—down on the farm. Just stop the car when you see a sign for *Dégustation* (tastings) or visit Domaine Fougeray-Duclos (▷ 131) if you're in the vicinity.

Tour the D-Day beaches to experience the raw emotion of remembrance. Take a drive from Caen or Bayeux (▷ 140–143) or join an organised tour (▷ 154).

Explore ruined castles, the least restored of which provide a potent link with the past (Château de Pirou ▷ 42).

The ruins of Château de Pirou

Eat an omelette whisked in copper bowls on Mont-St-Michel (▷ 46–48); the generations-old recipe of Mère Poulard is generally believed to be the best in France.

Skip the diet and indulge in cream and cheese, especially Camembert, to get a real taste of Normandy.

Go to the market to buy food and craftwork direct from the producers. Every town will have one, each with its own flavour, but Rouen's Place St-Marc (▷ 130) and Honfleur's market (▷ 120) are worth a detour.

Visit a monastery at St-Wandrille (▷ 90) or Bec-Hellouin (▷ 77) to discover the serenity of the past today.

Above: a Sherman tank at D-Day's Utah beach. Left, an old bottle of Calvados. Right: a Camembert cheese. Below: market stalls

Buy the past as you go antiques hunting in the upmarket shops of Honfleur and Rouen, in bric-a-brac stalls and at auction sales.

Go fishing for trout and carp along the river Orne or put to sea with fishermen from coastal ports to land mackerel, herring, sole or bass (▷ 109).

Ride the rails and set off from Gare du Pont Erambourg (▷ 117) on a two- or four-man rail bike or on an historic scenic train to explore the hinterland.

Get festive at the region's numerous food (autumn's herring festival in Étretat, ▷ 132) and cultural events (the spring jazz festival in Countances, ▷ 114), the best times to meet locals.

Be pampered at a health spa by the coast (▷ 109).

Have a flutter one night at the gaming tables of the casinos in Deauville (▷ 120), Bagnoles-de-l'Orne (▷ 115) or Dieppe (▷ 129).

Relax on the beach, choosing from the sands of the Cotentin peninsula, les planches of Deauville or the pebble strands of the Côte d'Albâtre.

Go clubbing in Caen (New Club, ▷ 119) or Rouen (Le Chakra, ▷ 131) Evreux or Le Havre and be prepared to party until dawn.

Enjoy a round a golf at the Golf Club Dieppe-Pourville (▷ 129) or the Golf Barrière de Deauville (▷ 120).

Saddle up and explore the region on horseback. Village Équestre d'Étretat (▷ 129) or Village du Cheval de Bagnoles-de-l'Orne (▷ 117).

Get active on the beaches and have a go at sea-kayaking or sand yachting at Station de Voile de Granville (▷ 112).

Dance with the locals at a Sunday afternoon Guinguette at Jouy-sur-Eure (▷ 125).

Take a river cruise and explore the countryside as you eat a traditional Norman meal aboard the Val d'Orne or Guillaume le Conquérant (▷ 154).

Above right: beach tents at Cabourg. Right, cruising on the river Seine. Left: playing golf

Living Normandy

Left: tarte Normande is a dessert of glazed apples in a pastry case

Right: Norman chefs prefer to work with local produce

Below: *andouille de Vire*, a smoked sausage from Vire

Below: local woman with live crab

Food and Drink

Normandy remains fiercely proud of its culinary identity. And this is more than just a regional quality, as towns are defined by their particular specialities, such that a blindfolded diner could tell you his location by the dish of the day. In Caen, tripe is on every menu; Rouen has its tradition of preparing duck, complete with table-top rituals; in the villages that dot the bay of Mont-St-Michel, *gigot d'agneau* (leg of lamb) is prepared from the young sheep that graze on the salty grass of the reclaimed land; and on the Mount itself, restaurant walls are decked with shiny copper bowls for beating omelettes. Along the Cotentin, oysters from St-Vaast-la-Hougue are served at every table; in Dieppe, sole is the speciality; and in Mortagne-au-Perche, black *boudin* sausages are a local staple.

This is not a land of the one-course meal. Rich, creamy fare in hearty portions is standard, particularly in more rural areas. Wedding feasts routinely last days, the eating punctuated by a *trou normand*—a swig of Calvados that aids digestion and allows a diner to squeeze in more food. In chic restaurants, the glass of Calva may be replaced by an alcoholic sorbet. In a land of such fabulous cheeses, seafood and ciders, food fairs, festivals and markets are firmly part of Normandy's calendar.

Beer from Broken Apple Trees

What do you do when your apple orchard is ravaged by gales and you have no chance of a harvest for next year's cider? Steve and Jane Skews were working their 120-tree farm in Joué-du-Bois in December 1999 when devastating storms destroyed the orchards. Knowing that replanting the groves could take years, they looked for another solution and came up with the idea of brewing beer instead. They found some second-hand brewing equipment across the Channel and, with the help of villagers (including the mayor and his tractor), they dragged it onto the farm. In May 2001, Le Brewery Brasserie Artisanale opened (▷ 116). Its traditional ales are named Le Conquérant and Odo to celebrate local Norman heritage, the label designs were inspired by the Bayeux Tapestry, and bottles are sold in bars and shops across the region.

Le grande fromage: Camembert cheese originated in Normandy

Apples and pears: Normandy's orchards provide fruit for perry and cider

Right: a cheesemaker from Pays d'Auge displaying Pave and Pont l'Évêque cheeses

Top: sheep raised on salt marshes. Top left: if you don't like cider, you can still get a pint of beer here

POIRÉ

Disappearing Pears

It is easy to find cider in Normandy, and Calvados is the very essence of hospitality, but one of the great orchard tipples of the region is in danger of extinction. Poiré, or perry, brewed from pears, was once a popular alternative to cider, served in the farmhouses and taverns around Domfront and Mortain. Pear orchards were a common sight in the Perche, offering contrasting blossom in springtime to that of the ubiquitous apple trees. However, as countryfolk believe it takes 35 years to grow a pear tree suitable for making Poiré, farmers started to replace their pear trees with more lucrative apple trees, which yield fruit and profits in a fraction of the time. As the drink disappears from shops, visitors are most likely to find it in family-run guesthouses, where commercial farmers continue to make the drink for personal consumption.

Spring Butter is Good for You

Butter is often demonised by dieticians in natural foods versus cholesterol debates, but scientists have discovered that *beurre d'Isigny* churned in April and May could be good for your heart. Since AOC (*appellation d'origine contrôllée*) products are banned from using artificial additives, the cardiovascular and anti-stress benefits of the butter must come direct from the natural environment. It seems that Isigny's butters are boosted with iodine from pastures located close to the Cotentin coast, and are also a natural source of Omega 3, usually found in oily fish such as mackerel. The highest proportion of antioxidants is to be found in butter made in April and May, when the dairy product may be labelled as naturally rich in Omega 3. In other words, it's creamy yet guilt-free!

Swansong of a Duck

While many Normandy restaurants may acknowledge vegetarian diners, one table-top tradition strictly for hard-core carnivores has flourished since a 1980s revival: *caneton à la Rouennaise*. A sauce of Beaune red wine, veal stock, shallots, thyme and bay leaves is made up, while a suffocated duckling is cooked rare for less than 20 minutes. The bird's organs are added to the sauce and, at the table, cognac and port are poured in and flambéed. The final test of the true carnivore is watching the duck's bones being crushed in a silver press to squeeze the final drops of blood into the sauce. Not for the squeamish, this Rouen delicacy may be prepared only by a chef initiated into the Order of Canardiers, created in January 1986 by *maître canardier* Michel Gueret.

This Little Piggy

Normandy is proud of its cattle and treats its cows as bovine VIPs, but the region's pigs have long been the poor relations, with the pink-tinged white and black Cochon de Bayeux little more than a fleeting image in the memories of elderly farmers. The breed was virtually wiped out over decades of industry standardisation and the demands of productivity that made keeping free-range pigs for twice as long as usual uneconomical. Then, in 1998, the breed was rediscovered. A herby-flavoured cross between domestic Normand and Berkshire breeds, a true Bayeux pig must be born in the Bessin (straddling Calvados, Manche and Orne). Litters of piglets are weaned at seven weeks then raised in the open air on a diet of whey, barley and nettles. At eight months they're sacrificed to gastronomy. So successful has the revival been that the breed now has its own annual show in October.

Screen queens: Lauren Bacall and Nicole Kidman at Deauville film festival

Deauville's casino, left, looks out over the marina

Champagne flows in the hospitality tent at Deauville's Grand Prix

Jacques Garcia, right, interior designer extraordinaire

Society and
Fashion

Don't think of Normandy as a simple rural region, for high society has long been alive and well here. A strong ducal heritage led to a close relationship with the court, so, come the Revolution, Normandy became home to a hardcore royalist resistance. Even after the Terror had faded, aristocrats continued to live in the region. Generations of paternalistic concern for the workers on their estates meant that many Norman nobles retained the respect of their fellow citizens.

Various art movements grew up in Normandy and inevitably attracted fashionable salons of fellow artists and wealthy patrons: Impressionist Claude Monet's Giverny years saw the painter entertaining statesmen for lunch. The rise of the railways meant that the time taken to travel from Paris grew ever shorter. It was the railways that guaranteed the success of the seaside resorts, a mid-19th-century phenomenon that brought weekending Parisians to the coast and led to the building of grand hotels and *residences secondaires*. Casinos and partying, coupled with the fad for spas, kept the resorts in the society pages in the 20th century.

Air travel, motorways, and the fact that it is not on the high-speed TGV (Train à Grande Vitesse) network, changed Normandy's fortunes in the late 20th century, and may have saved areas from overdevelopment.

In the saddle: horse and rider at Deauville's Grand Prix horse race

Marianne Unfaithful

Marianne is the symbol of France. The bare-breasted figure featured on statues in every town, whose warrior-like pose is stamped on French coins and stamps is as much an image of France as the tricolour flag itself. For four memorable years, Marianne embodied the independent spirit of Normandy. Every few years a new model is chosen for Marianne. Previous inspirations had been Catherine Deneuve and Brigitte Bardot. In 1999, France chose 21 year-old supermodel Laetitia Casta, from Pont-Audemer. She proudly described her figure as 'made in Normandy from butter and cream' and promptly demonstrated her independence by leaving France for London in 2000. Her scandalous reign came to an end in 2003.

Busted: Norman model, Laetitia Casta, left France for Britain. She figures on the Euro coin, below left

Above: people-spotting in glitzy Deauville

The hot tip at Trouville-sur-Mer's donkey race, right

Fashion leader: a poster for the Christian Dior museum in Granville

Villa Les Rhumbs musée Christian Dior

A 21st-Century Sun King

Jacques Garcia, long France's golden boy of interior design and responsible for the grand luxury of such hotels as the Hôtel Royale in Deauville, bought the Château du Champ-de-Bataille, northeast of Évreux (▷ 83), in 1992 and set about restoring it. The interior is splendidly furnished throughout, but Garcia's creative masterpiece has been the reconstruction of the castle's gardens in the fashion of those at King Louis XIV's Versailles, which were designed by landscape architect Le Nôtre. With their chequerboard *parterres*, splendid architectural features and perfect perspectives of planting and waterways, the gardens at Champ-de-Bataille were completed in 2005. As befits Garcia's status as a modern-day arbiter of taste, the event was celebrated with a typically grand gesture—a production of Verdi's *La Traviata* in the chateau grounds.

Cannier than Cannes

The paparazzi may swarm over the stars at the Cannes Film Festival in May, but the first fortnight of September in Normandy sees a much more civilised Hollywood invasion of France. There may be fewer staged media moments and less in the way of velvet ropes, but there is certainly no reduction in glamour as Hollywood steps out on the famous Les Planches boardwalk at Deauville's American Film Festival, which famously rounds off the resort's summer season. Since 1984, the event has reflected the special relationship between America and the people of Normandy after the D-Day landings. Whereas other festivals attract ephemeral starlets, Deauville reels in the big names: The turn-of-the-millennium roll call included Kirk Douglas, Lauren Bacall, Steven Spielberg, Clint Eastwood and regular visitor Tom Hanks.

Donkeys Have Their Day

Normandy is a land of horses, and, from the studs of the Perche to the millionaires who mill around the racecourse of Deauville, horses are the regions's very symbol of high society. Thus, there is a pleasant irony in the fact that the resort of Trouville-sur-Mer (▷ 75), once a playground of the rich and famous but now eclipsed by its glitzier neighbours, holds a variation on the racing theme; here, donkeys take to the tracks rather than thoroughbred Arab stallions. Each August, Trouville's gambling fraternity eschews the expensive hats and tailcoats of rival race tracks across the estuary and makes its way to the beach, where carefully selected donkeys race along the sands. It may be an informal affair with free admission, but big money still changes hands, as cafés and bars are abuzz with rumours of favourites—all, of course, straight from the donkey's mouth.

Dior—the Sequel?

Could the inspiration for the next 'New Look' in fashion come from Christian Dior's home town of Granville (▷ 45)? It's a possibility. In 2005, to celebrate the centenary of Dior's birth, the designer's childhood home—the Villa les Rhumbs, now a museum dedicated to the couturier who shaped women's style through the 1940s and 1950s—launched an annual programme of weekly summer workshops on the art of couture, aimed at youngsters with an interest in fashion. The museum looks at the Norman and maritime influences on the young Christian Dior and how it affected his work in later life. In a different twist, the links between designing stylish clothes and creating attractive aromas are explored in the gardens of the Villa les Rhumbs, which are planted with fragrant flowers used by parfumiers.

Left: timber beams support this medieval building in Domfront

A view of Suisse Normande's landscape of rolling hills and fertile fields

The rose gardens of Angélique

Tourist attraction? Normans boast that Cap de la Hague nuclear power station is a safe, clean source of energy

The Norman
Landscape

Normandy is defined by its landscapes. The region takes particular pride in its blending of nature with domestic and rural architecture in a way that identifies each community. The region was scarred by wartime bombing, but this is the home of Norman architecture, with great monasteries, churches and castles.

The climate, with temperate summer sunshine and healthy rainfall, creates a land where pastures nurture the indigenous dairy and drinks traditions.

A post-war revival of traditional landscaping means that about 40 special gardens are now open to visitors, and a new concept in weekend breaks has emerged with the creation of *gîtes au jardins*, bed-and-breakfast or self-catering accommodation in private homes with beautiful gardens.

Sun, Sea and 18 Billion kWh

Normandy is surprisingly laid back in its attitude to nuclear power stations. Protests punctuate the political calendar (▷ 22), but the region regards the COGEMA reprocessing plant at Beaumont-Hague and the power station at Flamanville as assets to be proud of. Flamanville's plant, employing 680 people, is set into cliffs above popular beaches. Far from ignoring their presences, both atomic sites are marketed by the tourist boards as visitor attractions.

Flooding the Mont

It isn't easy to push an abbey into the sea, but by 2010 Mont-St-Michel should be surrounded by water once more. Over the centuries, the silting of the bay has led to the Mount becoming moored to the mainland.

The causeway often remains above the water at high tide. In 2005, a five-year project involving a dam and bridge was started to contain the sea around the abbey. A ban on cars within 2km (1 mile) of the Mount will also be put in place.

Roses of Remembrance

Love and grief may be measured in blooms and thorns in Normandy's most remarkable rose garden, a moving memorial to the death of a child. The Lebret family knew nothing of gardening when their beloved daughter Angélique died, but the planting of a rose in her memory grew into one of the most beautiful 'English' rose gardens in France. Since 1990, the rose garden at Les Jardins d'Angélique in Montmain, just outside Rouen, has evolved into a complex and lovingly landscaped estate around the manor house. Unlike the irises and water-lilies of Giverny, which are frozen forever to preserve a moment of time, Les Jardins d'Angélique are an ever-growing, vibrant, living testament to enduring love.

The Story of Normandy

The Rise of the
Normans

The region that we know today as Normandy was Celtic for 800 years, before the Romans conquered Amorica in 51–58BC. They linked the land with neighbouring Brittany and founded many ports and towns, including Rotomagus (Rouen), Mediolanum (Évreux) and Caracotinum (Harfleur). Christianity arrived in the second century AD, with the formation of the Bishopric of Rouen in AD206 by St. Nicaise. The region's reputation as a Christian heartland grew from the monasteries that were built in the seventh and eighth centuries AD.

From the second century AD, there were periodic invasions by Saxons, Franks and Norsemen, the latter arriving in force after AD800. In AD911, Normandy, the land of Norsemen, was established, with Rollo becoming the region's first duke. His successor, William Longsword, extended the dukedom to the Cotentin peninsula, and during the 11th century Norman armies conquered Sicily and southern Italy.

In 1027, William the Conqueror was born at Falaise. Invading England in 1066, William overcame King Harold at the Battle of Hastings to start a line of English kings. William Atheling, grandson of William and heir to the English crown, died when the *White Ship* sank off Barfleur's coast in 1120, leading to insecurities over English succession. From the 12th to the 15th centuries, England and France fought for control of Normandy. King Henry II of England married Eleanor of Aquitaine in 1152, claiming much of western France by the union, but the lands were regained by France in 1204. England's King Edward III invaded in 1346, sparking the Hundred Years War, which ended in 1453, when Normandy was returned to France for good.

Angelic Persuasion

Visitors often wonder what inspired the feat of engineering that is Mont-St-Michel (▷ 46–48). The original chapel may have been built by faith, yet its founder, Aubert, Bishop of Avranches, required a prod to get started. It is said that the Archangel St. Michael appeared to Aubert and ordered him to build the chapel. Aubert was sceptical about the vision and did not hurry to start the task. St. Michael returned once more, poking his finger into the bishop's head for emphasis. Aubin swiftly ordered construction to begin in AD709. The importance of listening to angels is seen only too clearly at Avranche's Église St-Gervais, where Aubin's skull is displayed, complete with the hole made by St. Michael's finger (▷ 39).

Before 1453

Gallo-Roman ruins in Jublains, near Alençon

A Viking Handshake

What do you get if you refrain from seizing power in France? The answer, if you are a Scandinavian ruler with a penchant for pillage, looting and compromise, is Normandy. The Vikings had spent most of a century attacking France's Channel coast and persecuting the region's Christians, when pagan raider Rolf the Walker led his forces along the Seine and into Paris at the turn of the 10th century. Rather than engage in long-term conventional battle, King Charles III of France decided to pay off the would-be invader by handing over the land known today as Normandy (after the Norsemen) following a simple handshake at the Treaty of St-Clair-sur-Epte in AD911. In return, Rolf agreed to Latinise his name to Rollo and run his newfound dukedom as a Christian.

Lion Heart, Achilles Heel

Richard the Lionheart, King of England and Duke of Normandy (1157–99), was feared across Europe as a bold crusading warrior. Yet his legacy in Normandy is a reminder that a lion's heart is no protection against an Achilles heel. At the end of his reign, this scourge of Saracens was less concerned with war in the Holy Land than in keeping France out of Normandy. Thus, in just one year from 1195 to 1196, he built the supposedly impenetrable Château Gaillard at Les Andelys to watch over the Seine and protect Normandy (▷ 78). Gaillard stood fast while Richard spent his last three years defending lands further south. But, after his death, French soldiers entered Gaillard by the sewers and, just a decade after the castle's construction, Rouen was in French hands.

Brand Leaders

Leaders' nicknames are like marketing brands. 'Lionheart' and 'Brave' are certainly invaluable political assets, but Duke William began his career with a less fortunate tag in 1035 when he inherited Normandy. Since his father, Robert the Magnificent, didn't marry William's mother, Herleva, William was dubbed 'The Bastard'. During his early years, William's nickname did seem a hindrance—he lacked support and faced assassination plots, which he survived only by forming an alliance with France's King Henri I. He wooed and wed his cousin Mathilde—albeit by dragging her around Lille by her hair—but the union courted controversy amid whispers of incest. Even the 1066 invasion risked negative spin, when William fell from his boat onto English soil. With a quip about seizing his new land with both hands, William went on to win the Battle of Hastings and the safer soubriquet of 'Conqueror'—and with it 21 years of peace.

The Wrong Trousers

Joan of Arc might have cheated the stake had prison guards not stolen her clothes. History tells of Joan's imprisonment and trial in Rouen, and how in 1431 she was sentenced to death as a heretic. On 24 May, in St-Ouen Abbey cemetery, Joan finally recanted, her death sentence commuted to life in prison. But English anger at her escape from execution led to devious attempts to reverse the decision. Having conceded that wearing men's clothes was heresy, Joan agreed to wear a dress, but on Trinity Sunday that dress mysteriously vanished. Leaving her cell, she was forced to don her masculine attire. As a result, she was accused by the English of rejecting her own recantation, and was led to the stake and martyrdom on 30 May, less than a week after her life had been spared.

Above and below: Joan of Arc was tricked to her death

Below: a re-enactment of the battle of Hastings and, inset, the seal of the victor, William

What's in a name? William the Conqueror, above, at Abbaye St-Étienne in Caen

Left: Richard the Lionheart at rest in Rouen cathedral

Centuries of War

By 1453 Normandy was French once more. In 1469, Charles of France, the last Duke of Normandy, relinquished the title.

Normandy's mercantile future was assured with the founding of Le Havre in 1517. Rouen, already the seat of Normandy's parliament since 1514, became a self-governing city in 1542. From 1562, France was torn by Wars of Religion. Protestant King Henri IV defeated the Catholics at Arques-la-Bataille (▷ 90) and Ivry-la-Bataille in 1589. The Edict of Nantes (1598) enshrined the civil rights of Protestants, until it was revoked by King Louis XIV in 1685, when pogroms led to the mass emigration of Huguenots from Norman ports. Other departures included that of explorer Samuel de Champlain, who sailed from Honfleur in the early 17th century to found Québec.

In 1789, thoughts turned to conflict again with the French Revolution. Most of Normandy, apart from Caen, sympathised with the Royalist cause in the struggle. In 1793, republican Girondins rose up against Chouan royalists at Granville.

The 19th century saw the rise in popularity of Normandy's seaside resorts, whose future was assured by the arrival of the Paris–Caen railway line. The first cross-Channel ferry service was established in 1825 between Newhaven and Dieppe. The area's popularity was given an extra boost in 1874, when artist Claude Monet exhibited the first Impressionist painting, of a sunrise at Le Havre. Monet lived in Giverny from 1883 until his death in 1926, and attracted many other artists to the region.

From 1940 Normandy fell under German occupation, until the Allied liberation of France began with the landings on the Cotentin beaches on D-Day, 6 June 1944.

1453

A landing craft with US soldiers arrives at the Norman coast in 1944. Inset: a D-Day veteran salutes at the 60th Anniversary

America's Norman Conquests

Just as the Normans had crossed the Channel to invade Britain, so the region's mariners sailed the Atlantic to reach North America in the 16th and 17th centuries. An Honfleur sailor, Jean Denis, found the mouth of the St. Lawrence river in 1506, a century before countryman Samuel de Champlain established Québec on behalf of the governor of Dieppe. It was from Dieppe that King François I's explorer Giovanni da Verrazano set sail for New France, discovering the site of New York in 1524. He also moored off what is now North Carolina, starting a tradition of Norman exploration of the Deep South. Réné de la Laudonnière tried to colonise Florida with Protestants from Dieppe and Le Havre in 1564. In 1682, Rouen's Cavalier de La Salle seized Louisiana for King Louis XIV.

Transatlantic race: Samuel de Champlain, who founded Québec

His last bath: *The Death of Marat* by Jean-Jacques Hauer (1793). See page 56

A Better Class of Pirate

In the 16th century, after centuries of battles with European neighbours, France realised a money-saving alternative to war was the use of self-employed pirates. Rather than declare outright war, King François I commissioned Dieppe's sailors to seize cargoes from the merchant ships of rivals. When Portugal declared sovereignty over African waters, François I issued letters of marque to Norman shipbuilder Jean Ango, a financier of expeditions. Ango's captains became privateers, looting Portuguese vessels, keeping a healthy commission for themselves and Ango, and giving the bulk of the plunder to the King. Ango flourished, becoming a patron of Renaissance art and entertaining royalty at his lavish manor house in Varengeville, which he built from his bounty (▷ 104). Not all privateers' cargo came from raids—the expeditions to North America brought tobacco to France.

Hollow Victory

The quick thinking of a village teacher saved France's two most unusual chapels from becoming a pile of firewood. The community of Allouville-Bellefoss, near Yvetot in Seine-Maritime, is famous for a remarkable 1,200-year-old oak tree with a grand girth measuring 10m (33ft). In 1696, the local parish priest built two chapels within the hollow trunk of the tree, the lower chapel dedicated to Notre Dame de La Paix and the upper room known as the hermit's chamber. The tree is topped with a steeple and an iron cross. During the French Revolution, when churches across the country were threatened with attack, verger and local schoolteacher Jean-Baptiste Bonheure placed a sign on the tree declaring it to be a Temple of Reason. His action spared the chapel-oak, which still hosts a Mass twice each year.

Walk on by: ladies with parasols on the promenade at Trouville-sur-Mer in 1910

Who's the Daddy?

The first Impressionist picture was painted at Le Havre, but its inspiration came further along the estuary in Honfleur. Claude Monet's iconic canvas of sunrise in Le Havre, *Impressions: Soleil Levant*, gave the name to the Impressionist movement when it was exhibited in 1874. Monet's haste to capture a particular moment of sunlight was the result of lessons learnt from his tutor, Eugène Boudin (1824–98), son of an Honfleur boatman. Boudin introduced Monet to the idea of painting outdoors, and a technique for adapting to the changing light and weather of the Normandy coast. Monet's tutor recorded not only the dates and times of his paintings, but prevailing wind speed and weather conditions as well. Although Boudin remained faithful to classical traditions of colour in his own work, his instinct for interpretation made this lesser known artist the true father of Impressionism.

The Highest Price

D-Day pioneers were able to transport huge military harbours across the sea and land silent gliders on target, next to Pegasus Bridge, but the best strategic brains of the 1940s were nearly outwitted by the modest hedge. The hedgerows that mark out the distinctive Norman landscape, known as *bocage*, proved the toughest obstacle for American forces fighting their way across the Cotentin peninsula in World War II. With lanes sunk below the level of fields, and bramble-thick hedges and trees surrounding each pasture, conventional vehicles and modern artillery proved ineffective, and progress could be made only by foot soldiers until tanks could be adapted with agricultural-style equipment. This quirk of the landscape cost one life for every metre advanced during the liberation of Lessay, and the lives of thousands of other soldiers across Normandy in 1944.

1945

Above: Monet in his garden. Left: his *Sunrise, Le Havre*, 1872

Into the Modern Age

Post-war Normandy entered the atomic age with the opening of a nuclear processing plant at la Hague. France's enthusiasm for nuclear power increased and power stations were built at Paluel and Flamanville in the early 1980s. *Le Redoutable*, the first French nuclear submarine, was launched at Cherbourg in 1971 (▷ 43). On a greener note, the Parc Naturel Régional Brotonne was created in 1974, with Normandie-Maine Natural Regional Park following in the next year. In 1991, the Cotentin and Bessin area also achieved nature park status. The second half of the 20th century saw yet another kind of achievement: the construction of majestic suspension bridges across the Seine estuary; the Pont de Tancarville opened in 1959.

Protesters Set Sail

While Normandy is proud of its power stations, even advertising them to tourists, the nuclear industry has also brought the region unwelcome international attention. In 1980, Greenpeace campaigners sailed into Cherbourg harbour to protest the transportation of nuclear waste. In the first skirmish in an ongoing battle between the nuclear industry and environmentalists, the Greenpeace boat was rammed by a naval vessel. Confrontations in 1997 centred on la Hague reprocessing plant and, in 2004, *gendarmes* took to inflatable dinghies to arrest French round-the-world yachtsman Eugène Riguidel, who had joined a flotilla trying to blockade Cherbourg.

Problem Port

It may have been the first regular Channel crossing, but in latter years the Newhaven–Dieppe ferry service suffered mixed fortunes, with the ports closed for long periods in the face of competition from rival short sea routes and the Channel Tunnel. This had a devastating effect on local economies. When the last private company left in 1999, Charles Revet, Conseil Général of Seine-Maritime, refused to allow the route to die. He led a collective of local councils to found Transmanche Ferries, which today continues to operate both the Normandy port and its English counterpart.

Norman Rule

It took several centuries, but after a succession of French rulers governing Normandy, on 23 December 1953 a Norman finally found himself in charge of France. Réné Coty was born in Le Havre in 1882 and held several key positions in local government before the outbreak of World War I. Between the two world wars, he served as both deputy and senator. During voting to pass political power to Marshal Pétain and his Vichy government in 1940, Coty refused to take on the position of Mayor of Dieppe under the German occupation. However, his finest hour came after World War II, when he became the second President of the Fourth Republic, a post he held for five years before handing power to Charles de Gaulle in 1958.

1945 – Today

Above: a high-speed ferry. Right: Greenpeace campaigners in Cherbourg. Left: helicopter carrier, Jeanne d'Arc, passes under Tancarville bridge

On the Move

ARRIVING

By Air

In recent years patterns of air travel to northwestern France have fluctuated. After a period of expansion, when low-cost operators began using small regional airports, the network suddenly contracted. This hit the short-break market and left many holiday-home owners unexpectedly stranded with no direct local flights. The picture is changing again as new operators fill the gaps.

There are some small airports in Normandy, but at present they handle few direct international flights. To get there by air from long-haul destinations such as North America or Australasia you have to route your journey via Paris, France's main air-gate, and take a connecting domestic flight. Lyon, Marseille, Nice and Nantes also have internal air-links with Normandy and Brittany. It may be cheaper to fly to London and continue your journey from there.

● There are no direct scheduled flights to Normandy from the UK. Low-cost airline Flybe currently flies to Brest and Rennes in Brittany. Beauvais Tillé airport (often billed as Paris) is 90km (56 miles) north of Paris and handy for travel to Rouen and Giverny (avoiding Paris). It is used by low-cost airlines, including Ryanair from Glasgow and Dublin.

● Paris has three airports. Busiest is Roissy–Charles de Gaulle, 23km (14 miles) from the city centre. It has three terminals, all connected with each other and with central Paris and its main railway stations by bus or train (RER Line B). The smaller Orly airport, 14km (8.5 miles) south of central Paris, takes mainly domestic but also some international flights. Its two terminals are linked by bus and train with Paris.

● At busy holiday periods (eg Christmas/New Year, Easter or July–August), flights into Paris get very booked up.

● From Paris, Air France provides domestic flights to Norman airports (Rouen, Caen, Le Havre) from Lyon. Independent airline Twin Jet has scheduled flights to Cherbourg from Paris-Orly.

● It is often more convenient, just as quick, and almost certainly cheaper to continue your onward journey to Normandy by train or rental car from a Parisian airport. From the Périphérique ring road, take the A13 motorway towards Caen for the D-Day beaches and the Cotentin. For Rouen, exit at junction for the D7 and N15.

● Flight prices usually increase the nearer you book to departure date, and are more expensive at weekends than mid-week. Book online to get the best deals.

Don't assume that 'no-frills' airlines are invariably cheaper.

● Exceptionally low fares imply some degree of inconvenience in terms of flight times, baggage allowances or airport location. Check whether prices quoted include departure tax, fuel surcharges and other charges, and what penalties are involved if you change your booking.

● Check newspaper ads and specialist agencies for bargains.

AIRLINE CONTACTS		
Aer Arann	06170 44 28 (Ireland)	www.aerarann.ie
Aer Lingus	0818 365 000 (Ireland)	www.aerlingus.com
Air France/Brit Air	0845 084 5111 (UK);	
	0820 820 820 (France)	www.airfrance.co.uk
American Airlines	1 800 433 7300 (US)	www.aa.com
Aurigny Air Services	0871 871 0717 (UK)	www.aurigny.com
British Airways	0870 850 9850 (UK)	www.ba.com
Bmibaby	0870 264 2229 (UK)	www.bmibaby.com
British Midland	0870 60 70 555 (UK)	www.flybmi.com
Continental	1 800 231 0856 (US)	www.continental.com
Delta	1 800 241 4141 (US)	www.delta.com
Easyjet	0871 750 0100 (UK)	www.easyjet.com
Flybe	0871 700 0123 (UK)	www.flybe.com
Twin Jet	00 33 892 707 737 (FR)	www.twinjet.net
United Airlines	1 800 538 2929 (US)	www.united.com

AIRPORT CONTACTS		
General airport information	www.worldairportguide.com	
Information on all French airports	www.aeroport.fr or www.french-airports.com	
PARIS		
Roissy-Charles de Gaulle	01 48 62 22 80	www.adp.fr
Paris-Orly	01 49 75 15 15	www.adp.fr
Beauvais Tillé	0892 682 066	www.aeroportbeauvais.com
Orlybus	01 40 02 32 94	
Paris Métro and RER information	0892 687 714	www.ratp.fr
Air France bus to Paris	0892 350 820	www.cars-airfrance.com
NORMANDY		
Caen-Carpiquet	02 31 71 20 10	www.caen.aeroport.fr
Cherbourg-Maupertus	02 33 88 57 60	www.aeroport-cherbourg.com
Deauville-St-Gatien	02 31 65 65 65	
Le Havre-Ste-Adresse	02 35 54 65 00	www.havre.aeroport.fr
Rouen-Boos	02 35 79 41 00	www.rouen.aeroport.fr

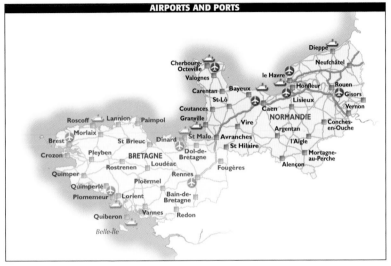

AIRPORTS AND PORTS

Dieppe
Neufchâtel
Cherbourg-Octeville
Valognes
le Havre
Honfleur
Rouen
Gisors
Vernon
Carentan
Bayeux
St-Lô
Lisieux
Coutances
Caen
NORMANDIE
Conches-en-Ouche
Roscoff
Lannion
Paimpol
Granville
Vire
Morlaix
Argentan
Brest
St Brieuc
Dinard
St Malo
Avranches
l'Aigle
Crozon
Pleyben
St Hilaire
Dol-de-Bretagne
Mortagne-au-Perche
BRETAGNE
Loudéac
Alençon
Quimper
Rostrenen
Fougères
Rennes
Quimperlé
Ploërmel
Plomemeur
Lorient
Bain-de-Bretagne
Quiberon
Vannes
Redon
Belle-Île

By Car

If you are taking your car from the UK to France you can either catch a ferry to a choice of ports on France's northwestern coast or take the Eurotunnel shuttle train through the Channel Tunnel. Driving to France from neighbouring countries on mainland Europe is straightforward on a comprehensive system of autoroutes (motorways).

FERRIES

Numerous cross-Channel ferries link France with the UK. To reach Normandy by sea, choose from a short crossing to Dunkirk, Calais or Boulogne, then a lengthy road journey down France, or a longer ferry route across the western Channel to a Norman port.

● It is generally cheaper to take a short crossing and drive down. Longer sea crossings are more expensive, but you save time and energy, as well as the cost of fuel and motorway tolls. From Calais, Dunkirk or Boulogne, allow 2–3 hours to reach Normandy.

● The cost of crossings varies depending on the time of travel, but fares are generally cheaper if you book in advance. You may get a discount by booking online.

● Look out for special offers, and good-value deals for short breaks. Expect to pay between £50–£100 standard return for a car plus up to five passengers on a short crossing and anywhere from £150 to £350 on a longer

crossing. On the short sea routes, Speed Ferries has introduced low-cost airline-style pricing, with one-way crossing from £25.

● Ferry Savers (0870 990 8492; www.ferrysavers.com) can book crossings with all the principal operators and has a best-price guarantee. You can also visit the website www.aferry.to.

● Confirm sailing times before setting off, as ferry brochures may not be up to date. Most companies require you to check in at least 45 minutes before departure. Don't fill your fuel tank to the brim just before boarding.

TRAVEL WEBSITES

Cheap Flights	www.cheapflights.co.uk
E Bookers	www.ebookers.com
Expedia	www.expedia.com
Flight Centre	www.flightcentre.com
Last Minute	www.lastminute.com
STA Travel	www.statravel.com
Trailfinders	www.trailfinders.com
Travel Cuts	www.travelcuts.com
Travelocity	www.travelocity.co.uk

● Modern ferries are stabilised for a smooth ride. All have on-board shops, bars, cafés or restaurants, exchange facilities, telephones and lounges. All carry vehicles as well as passengers, but LPG vehicles may be excluded for safety reasons.

● Access to the car decks is restricted during the crossing. Don't leave valuables in your car. Lock up with the car in gear and the handbrake on, but don't engage the alarm system. Before you leave your car, note which car deck you are parked on, and the closest door or stairway.

● Reserve a cabin on lengthy overnight crossings. A two-berth cabin costs about £40 extra.

● In 2005 LD Lines took over the Portsmouth to Le Havre crossing from P&O, which also axed its service from Portsmouth to Cherbourg. Brittany Ferries has taken up some of the slack for Cherbourg. LD Lines (0870 458 0401; www.ldlines.co.uk) will operate a daily, no-frills service.

ON THE MOVE

TAKING YOUR PET
UK visitors are allowed to take cats and dogs to France, subject to compliance with the DEFRA PETS scheme. You need the following documentation:
● Before setting off—a DEFRA-approved pet passport or veterinary certificate showing that your pet has been microchipped, vaccinated and blood-tested for rabies antibodies (allow 7 months before travel to arrange all this).
● On returning—a pet passport or certificate showing that your pet has been treated against ticks and fox tapeworm before re-entering the UK.
● It is your responsibility to ensure the welfare of your pet. Animals must remain in your vehicle. Escorted visits to the car deck may be organised.
● If documentation is not in order, your pet could be refused entry to the UK and placed in quarantine at your expense.
● If you are caught smuggling an animal, you risk severe penalties. The animal may be destroyed.

SAILING ROUTES
All timings are approximate and may take longer in bad weather.
● Norfolkline operates from Dover to Dunkirk (journey time 2 hours). If you don't mind the extra driving time and distance, this no-frills service is good value.
● P&O Ferries and SeaFrance sail from Dover to Calais (70–90 minutes). Hoverspeed's catamaran cuts the time to 50 minutes.
● SpeedFerries operates a fast-craft service between Dover and Boulogne (50 minutes), with very competitive fares.
● Transmanche Ferries runs a year-round service (4 hours) between Newhaven and Dieppe.
● Brittany Ferries sails from Portsmouth to Caen (6 hours); from Poole to Cherbourg (4 hours 15 mins; Fastcraft 2 hours 15 minutes, summer only).
● Condor Ferries has seasonal sailings from Weymouth/Poole to St-Malo (4 hours 30 minutes).
● Irish Ferries sails from Cork/Rosslare to Roscoff (12 hours).

The Eurostar service from London to Paris is quick and efficient

EUROTUNNEL
Eurotunnel is a shuttle train transporting vehicles and passengers along the Channel Tunnel.
● The UK Channel Tunnel terminal lies between Dover and Folkestone. Leave the M20 at junction 11A and follow the signs.
● Drive your vehicle on to the shuttle train as directed, and you will be whisked under the Channel in just 35 minutes to the French terminal at Coquelles, near Calais.
● Eurotunnel shuttle trains depart up to five times per hour, 24 hours a day, 365 days a year; the price is charged per vehicle (reserve ahead). LPG and CNG vehicles are not allowed for safety reasons.
● French border controls take place on the UK side, saving time when you arrive in Calais.
● You are advised to stay with your vehicle during the journey, although you can go to the lavatory or walk about within the air-conditioned carriage. During the journey you can listen to the on-board radio station. Staff are available if you need any help. If you want to sit inside your vehicle, open the windows to minimise the effects of pressure changes within the carriage.
● Eurotunnel contact details: 08705 35 35 35 (UK) www.eurotunnel.com.

ONWARD TRAVEL
● The quickest way to reach Normandy from Calais is to take the A16 via Boulogne and Le Touquet to Abbeville, then the A28 into Normandy. If you want to continue towards Lower Normandy, it is more straightforward to take the A29 towards Le Havre, avoiding Rouen. South of the Seine, the A13 takes you to Caen, and from here the A84 (known as the Autoroute des Estuaires) leads on to Rennes.
● You will have to pay autoroute charges (note the *Péage* sign). There is a hefty toll to cross the massive Pont de Normandie suspension bridge near Le Havre (have your euros ready; cards are not accepted). You can avoid motorway charges by sticking to alternative, and possibly more scenic, routes.

FERRY CONTACT DETAILS		
Brittany Ferries	08705 360 360	www.brittany-ferries.com
Condor Ferries	0845 345 2000	www.condorferries.co.uk
Hoverspeed	0870 524 0241	www.hoverspeed.com
LD Lines	0870 458 0401	www.ldlines.co.uk
Norfolkline	0870 870 1020	www.norfolkline.com
P&O Ferries	08705 20 20 20	www.poferries.com
SeaFrance	08705 711 711	www.seafrance.com
SpeedFerries	0871 222 7456	www.speedferries.com
Transmanche Ferries	0800 917 1201	www.transmancheferries.com

By Rail or Coach

France is justly proud of its railway system, particularly its world-renowned TGV (high-speed) service, which cuts overland journey times to ribbons. There are excellent train links between France and its European neighbours. Thalys, for example, operates high-tech rail services connecting Paris Gare du Nord with Brussels, Amsterdam and Cologne. Going to France by long-distance bus (coach) is worth considering if you're on a tight budget, and by no means as irksome as you might imagine. The main European operator from the UK is Eurolines.

BY TRAIN
The Channel Tunnel
The Channel Tunnel has revolutionised both road and rail travel between the UK and Continental Europe. The tunnel finally opened in 1994, almost 200 years after the first designs were submitted for a permanent link between England and France. It is the longest undersea tunnel in the world, with 39km (24 miles) of its 50km (31 miles) length under the Channel. It emerges on the British side near Folkestone, and meets the French coast at Sangatte (about 7km/4 miles southwest of Calais). Two separate rail systems operate through the tunnel, Eurostar and Eurotunnel (see below). Both the French and UK terminals link directly with the motorway system.

Eurostar
Eurostar is a sophisticated high-speed passenger train connecting London directly with Paris and Brussels.
● From London, up to 16 Eurostar trains per day pass through the Channel Tunnel into France. The introduction of upgraded track has cut the journey time to Paris to 2 hours 35 minutes on the fastest services.
● Some trains stop en route at Ashford International (UK), Calais–Fréthun (France) and Lille, where the line splits, one branch heading for Brussels, the other for Paris.
● Trains leaving London currently depart from Waterloo International, but a new Eurostar terminal will open at St. Pancras international in 2007.
● You can check in automatically with certain types of tickets, otherwise check in at the desks. You

must do this at least 30 minutes before your train is due to leave.
● Before you reach the departure lounge you must go through airport-style security checks and passport control (immigration procedures for your destination country are carried out at the Eurostar departure station). Once in the departure lounge there are newspaper and gift shops, cafés, lavatories, Internet points and a mail box.
● Boarding begins around 20 minutes before departure. Information screens tell you where and when to board. Each train has 18 carriages (cars) so you could face a long walk along the platform. Trolleys (carts) for luggage are available, although you need a £1 coin as a deposit. Once on board, large cases must be stored on the luggage racks at the end of each carriage, but you can put smaller bags in the racks above your seat.
● A buffet car serves drinks, snacks and light meals on board. Inform Eurostar of any special dietary requirements 48 hours before you travel. Upgrades are inexpensive, costing about £30. There are lavatories and a designated baby-changing area. The journey through the Channel Tunnel itself takes around 20 minutes; an announcement is made just before you enter it.

Onward Travel
● Calais or Lille are good starting points for non-TGV trains to north Normandy (Le Tréport or Dieppe). If Lower Normandy (Caen, Cherbourg) is your final destination, you may find it easier to enter Paris, where you will have to change stations from Gare du Nord to Gare St-Lazare (allow an hour to do this).

Ticket to ride: trains reach many parts of Normandy

● If you are planning to travel to Brittany, you can leave the Eurostar at Lille and catch a high-speed TGV Atlantique Ouest connection directly to Rennes (3 hours 50 minutes) or Quimper (6 hours 50 minutes). This will save you the bother and expense of crossing Paris.
● When you arrive at Paris's Gare du Nord station you do not need to go through passport control as immigration checks have already been carried out in London. Watch out for pickpockets at the stations in Paris.
● Trains for Normandy depart from Paris's Gare St-Lazare. From Gare du Nord, take Métro Line 4 (Porte d'Orléans) and change at Réaumur-Sébastopol to Métro Line 3 (Pont de Levallois-Bécon). Better still, take the high-speed underground express RER line E from Magenta (Gare du Nord) one stop to the terminus Haussmann St-Lazare. The Paris-Rouen intercity (Corail) service takes just over an hour from St-Lazare. The trip to Cherbourg takes around 3 hours.

Rail Passes

- Rail passes for visitors intending to travel extensively by train in France or Europe are good value, but they must be bought in advance in your home country. To buy certain passes you must have been resident in Europe for at least six months, and have a valid passport with you.
- If you are staying in France for a long time, you may want to buy an annual rail pass. This entitles you to a 50 per cent discount and is available to those aged 12 to 25 (Carte 12–25), those with a child under 12 (an Enfant+ card) and the over-60s (senior card).
- If your visit is confined simply to Brittany or Normandy, consider how much use you will make of a rail pass. The railway network is relatively limited in these regions.

In the UK and Ireland

- EuroDomino and InterRail passes give unlimited travel in France for specified periods to anyone resident in the EU for more than six months (available to any age group, but cheaper for under 26s). Both passes are available from Rail Europe UK.

In the US and Canada

- Eurail passes allow unlimited first-class travel within 17 European countries (excluding the UK).
- The France Railpass gives four days' travel in France within a one-month period.
- France Rail 'n' Drive gives 4 days' rail travel plus 2 days' car rental.

BY LONG-DISTANCE BUS

- Eurolines buses are modern and comfortable, with plenty of leg-room, safety belts, reclining seats, air conditioning and on-board washrooms (WCs). All services are non-smoking.
- Eurolines has introduced new services to Normandy from as little as £39 return. Approximate journey times from London Victoria are about 8 hours to Rouen, 10 hours to Caen. Several intermediate destinations are served, including Avranches.
- Cross-Channel travel is by P&O ferry from Dover, so you get a break from the bus.
- Book your ticket at least 30 days in advance for the least expensive fares. All ferry fares, motorway tolls and travel taxes are included in the price. Discounts are available for the over-60s, young people under 26 and children under 12. A booking fee of £3 is charged on all fares (check whether it is included in any price quoted).
- Through-tickets are easy to arrange from any National Express destination in the UK. A simple add-on fare of £15 (single or return) is charged for any connecting service to London.
- Check in at least one hour before the departure time; the Eurolines check-in desk is located near departure gate 19 at London's Victoria Coach Station.
- Luggage space is limited; you are allowed two suitcases per person plus hand luggage. Excess baggage cannot be carried.
- Eurolines buses arrive and depart from the city centre; you don't have to arrange transfers.

- Eurolines Contact Details
08705 143219 (UK)
www.nationalexpress.com/eurolines

TIPS

- You can book Eurostar tickets through Rail Europe. In central London, the Rail Europe Travel Centre shares premises with the French tourist office (Maison de la France, ▷ 186). Telephone bookings can be made every day including Sundays and Bank Holidays (Mon–Fri 8am–9pm, Sat 9am–6pm, Sun/hols 10am–5pm). Online reservations are generally cheaper, and include no booking fees.
- Eurostar Plus fares are a package deal including Eurostar and one journey within France. You can break your journey for 24 hours en route.
- You'll pay less for your Eurostar ticket if you reserve it in advance. It is highly recommended that you do this, since non-booked seats are limited. The train is split into Premium, First and Standard class. Premium and First class give you a meal, extra legroom, a reclining seat and free newspapers. Certain tickets also allow admission to business lounges at both ends of the journey.
- Remember that you need your passport to travel between Britain and France (see Visas, page 177).
- The official luggage allowance is two suitcases and one piece of hand luggage. Luggage must be clearly labelled with your name and seat number.
- Trolleys are available on the platforms in London and at Gare du Nord, but you need a £1 or €1 coin (refundable). If you have a heavy case a trolley is a good idea as the walk along the platform can be long if your carriage (car) happens to be the last of 18.

RAIL CONTACT DETAILS			
Eurostar	08705 186 186 (UK)		www.eurostar.com
Rail Europe			
(UK) 178 Piccadilly, London W1	08705 848 848		www.raileurope.com
			www.sncf.com
Rail Europe (US)			
226 Westchester Avenue,			
White Plains, NY 10064	1 877 257 2887		www.eurail.com
Thalys	0825 84 25 97 (France)		www.thalys.com
Lost luggage (Waterloo, UK)	020 7928 0660;		
(Gare du Nord, Paris)	01 55 31 58 40		

GETTING AROUND

Driving in Northwest France

Driving is the best way to tour rural areas of Normandy. It is less enjoyable in larger cities such as Caen or Rouen, where the traffic is heavy, the one-way systems confusing and parking sometimes difficult and expensive. Coastal resorts can also present driving problems in high season. The roads in France are always busy at the beginning of the summer school holidays (mid-July), and when the holidays end at the beginning of September (*la grande rentrée*).

BRINGING YOUR OWN CAR
Legal Requirements

● Private vehicles registered in another country can be taken into France for up to six months without customs formalities.

● You must always carry: a passport or national ID card, a full, valid national driver's licence (even if you have an International Driving Permit), a certificate of motor insurance, and the vehicle's registration document.

● Check your motor insurance is valid for driving in France, and against damage in transit, for example on the train or ferry. Third-party motor insurance is the minimum requirement in France but fully comprehensive cover is strongly advised.

● Display an international sticker or distinguishing sign plate as near as possible to the national registration plate at the rear of your car. If you don't, you risk an on-the-spot fine. Since March 2001, registration plates displaying the Euro-symbol of an EU country mean displaying a conventional sticker is unnecessary.

● To avoid dazzling oncoming drivers, adjust the headlights of left-hand-drive vehicles. On older cars, use simple headlamp beam converters that stick onto the glass. But don't use these on cars with halogen headlamps. If your vehicle has Xenon or High Intensity Discharge (HID) headlamps, your dealer may need to make the adjustment.

Breakdown Cover

If you are taking your own car, make sure you have adequate breakdown cover for your trip to France. For information on AA breakdown cover, call 0800 444 500 or visit www.theAA.com.

Renting a Car

● Most major car rental agencies have offices at airports, main railway stations and in large towns and cities throughout France.

● Renting a car in France can be expensive due to high taxes. Arranging a fly-drive package is generally a less expensive option. SNCF, the national railway firm, has inclusive train and car-rental deals from mainline stations.

● To be able to rent a car in France you must be at least 20 years old and have held a full driver's licence for at least a year. However, some companies either do not rent to, or else add a surcharge for, drivers under the age of 25. The maximum age limit varies, but the average is 70.

● Your rental agreement should include the following: unlimited mileage, insurance cover, theft protection, 24-hour emergency roadside assistance, a replacement vehicle if the one you have rented becomes unusable.

● Some agencies may charge extra above a certain mileage.

● Most international rental companies will let you return your car to other French cities, and even other countries, but there may be an extra charge for this. Always agree the drop-off point first.

● Make sure you have adequate insurance and that you are aware of what you are covered for in the event of an accident.

● Bear in mind that low-cost operators may have an extremely high excess charge for damage.

● Most companies supply vehicles with breakdown cover.

● If your car breaks down on an *autoroute*, look for emergency telephones on the roadside. You can contact the breakdown services from here.

Kilometres are used in France

GENERAL DRIVING
Roads

● The autoroute is the French counterpart of the British motorway and is marked by an 'A' on maps and road signs. Sections around cities or ports may be free of charge, but tolls are levied elsewhere (*autoroutes à péage*). Always have some cash available as foreign credit cards may not be accepted. For information on autoroute conditions throughout France call: 01 47 05 90 01 or look at www.autoroutes.fr.

● Other roads in Brittany and Normandy may be almost as fast as motorways. The next level in France's road hierarchy is occupied by *routes nationales* (code-marked N). The fastest of these key routes are dual carriageways called *voies express*, notably the N13 through Caen and up the Cotentin peninsula. The next grade of road is the *route départementale* (D), often surprisingly wide and fast. Minor rural lanes are labelled C roads.

● Beware of traffic-calming measures in built-up areas.

The Law
- In France you drive on the right *(serrez à droite)*.
- The legal age to drive is 18.
- In built-up areas vehicles should give way to traffic coming from the right *(Priorité à droite)*, unless signs advise otherwise. At roundabouts (traffic circles) with signs saying *Cédez le passage* or *Vous n'avez pas la priorité*, traffic already on the roundabout has priority. On roundabouts without signs, traffic entering has priority. A priority road can also be shown by a white diamond-shaped sign with a yellow diamond within it. A black line through the diamond indicates the end of priority. A red-bordered triangle with a black cross on a white background, with the words *passage protégé*, also shows priority.
- Holders of EU driver's licences who exceed the speed limit by more than 25kph (16mph) may have their licences confiscated by the police on the spot.
- You must wear a seatbelt. Children under 10 must travel in the back, with a booster seat, except babies under nine months with a rear-facing front seat.
- Do not overtake where there is a solid single central line on the road.
- There are harsh penalties if the level of alcohol in the blood is 0.05 per cent or more.
- Always stop completely at STOP signs, or you may be fined.

Road Signs
- Road signs are split into three categories. Triangular signs with a red border are warnings, circular signs are mandatory (such as speed limits or No Entry); square signs display text information.
- Common signs include: *déviation* (diversion), *attention travaux*

Pay as you go: a toll booth

(roadworks), *sortie* (exit), *gravillons* (loose chippings), *chaussée déformée* (uneven road and temporary surface) and *nids de poules* (potholes).
- Familiarise yourself with the French highway code on www.legifrance.gouv.fr.
- For more information on road signs: www.permisenligne.com.

Equipment
- Carry a red warning triangle in case you break down. Don't rely simply on hazard warning lights.
- Keep a spare-bulb kit, as it is illegal to drive with faulty lights.

Fuel
- Fuel *(essence)* comes as unleaded (95 and 98 octane), lead replacement petrol (LRP or *supercarburant*), diesel *(gasoil* or *gazole)* and LPG.
- Many filling stations close on Sundays and at 6pm the rest of the week. Some automatic dispensing machines may not accept foreign credit cards.
- Prices are highest at filling stations on autoroutes, and lowest at large chain supermarkets.
- Filling stations can be far apart in rural areas.

Parking
- Authorised parking spaces are indicated by road markings (white dotted lines). Blue markings, or those marked *Payant*, indicate a charge is due. Watch out for any signs indicating parking restrictions.
- Charges usually apply from about 9am to 6.30pm, Monday to Saturday. There may be a free period at lunchtime (12.30–2). Sundays and holidays are often free, but always check. In certain popular holiday areas or tourist attractions, parking charges are imposed only in high season.
- To pay for parking, buy a timed ticket from a meter *(horodateur)* at the side of the road and display it in your car. Some towns operate on an honesty system and allow you some free time, but you must display a 'clock' showing when you arrived. You can get one in local shops or *tabacs*—or ask in the tourist office.

Car Breakdown
- If your car breaks down on an autoroute, look for an emergency telephone along the roadside.
- If you break down on the Paris *Périphérique* or an *autoroute*, you must call the police or the area's official breakdown service.

Road Conditions
- To find out about traffic conditions, for example on the congested coastal routes in high season, visit www.bison-fute.equipement.gouv.fr (in French only). Queues can build up, particularly at weekends or towards the end of the day when people leave the beaches.
- For the National Road Information Centre (voice service in French) call 0836 682 000.
- For road conditions on autoroutes call 0892 681 077.
- For information on local road conditions, call 0826 022 022.
- Autoroute FM provides useful traffic bulletins on the radio.

Maps
The AA (UK) publishes four France atlases as well as a series

CAR RENTAL COMPANIES		
COMPANY	**TELEPHONE NUMBER**	**WEBSITE**
Avis	0820 050 505	www.avis.com
Budget	0825 003564	www.budget.com
Europcar	0825 352 352	www.europcar.com
Hertz	01 41 91 95 25	www.hertz.com
Sixt	0820 007 498	www.sixt.com

MOTORWAYS

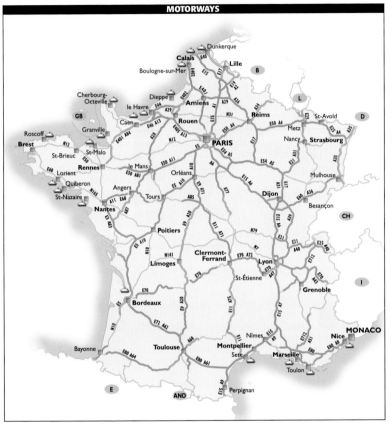

of France sheet maps. The AA website, www.theAA.com, has a helpful route planner. You can find town and city maps (plans) in France at newsagents like Maisons de la Presse, bookshops and some newspaper kiosks. Most towns and cities, and many villages too, have an *office de tourisme*, *syndicat d'initiative*, or town hall that can provide a local map, usually free of charge.

ROAD SIGNS

Allumez vos phares	Switch on your lights
Cédez le passage	Give way
Chantier	Road works
Péage	Toll
Priorité à droite/gauche	Priority to the right/left
Rappel	Reminder (continue with the previous instruction)
Route barre	Road closed
Sens interdit	No entry
Sens unique	One way
Serrez à droite/gauche	Keep to the right/left
Stationnement interdit	No parking
Travaux	Roadworks

SPEED LIMITS

Urban roads	50kph (31mph)
Outside built-up areas	90kph (56mph) 80kph (49mph) in wet weather
Dual carriageways (divided highways), and non-toll motorways	110kph (68mph) 100kph (62mph) in wet weather
Toll motorways (autoroutes)	130kph (80mph) 110kph (68mph) in wet weather

Visiting drivers who have held a licence for less than two years are not allowed to exceed the wet-weather limits, even in good weather

Other Ways to Get Around

Driving may be the most convenient way to tour Normandy, but if you are without a car there are other reliable ways to see at least the region's larger towns. Even if you have a car, you may sometimes wish to leave it at home and make a trip by train, bus or boat.

ON THE MOVE

France has a wide-ranging railway but small towns may miss out

TRAINS
In general, France has excellent trains—fast, comfortable and usually punctual. France's state railway, the Société Nationale des Chemins de Fer (SNCF), runs the services. These include *Grandes Lignes* (mainline routes) such as the ultra-modern, high-speed TGV (*Train à Grande Vitesse*) which can operate at speeds of up to 300kph/186mph, and Corail (fast intercity trains). TER trains (*Trains Express Régionaux*) operate on regional journeys. That said, the rail network in Normandy is not extensive, and while you can reach main towns easily by train, smaller places are served infrequently, if at all.

Tickets
● Most trains have first- and second-class carriages.
● Fares are split into blue (normal) and red (peak). Reduced-rate fares are generally available for normal travel on mainline routes, excluding TGV and *couchette* services.
● Ticket prices vary according to the level of comfort and departure time. First-class fares are roughly 50 per cent more expensive than second class.

● You can buy tickets in stations, at SNCF offices or *boutiques*, which you'll find in major cities like Rouen, and through some travel agents. Tickets for TGV trains must be reserved. You can do this up to a few minutes before departure, but in peak season book in advance. *Couchettes* must be booked at least 75 minutes before the train leaves its first station.
● Stamp your ticket *(composter)* in the orange machines on the platforms before you start your journey. You risk a fine if you forget to do this.
● If you are under 26, you can get a 25 per cent discount (called *Découverte 12–25*). Seniors also receive discounts (called *Découverte Senior*).
● When you travel second class, there are lower rates for booking more than eight days in advance (ask for *Découverte J8*) and more than 30 days in advance (ask for *Découverte J30*).
● Ticket machines accept notes, coins and credit cards. They can also be used to collect tickets you have ordered on the Internet, by telephone or Minitel.
● In France it may be difficult to change bookings made abroad.

Catering Service
● Catering facilities—ranging from sandwiches and salads to hot meals—are available on most TGV and mainline services, but can be quite expensive.
● A benefit of first-class travel is that you can have food served at your seat on most TGV trains. You'll need to reserve in advance.
● You can order meals when you buy your train ticket. Ticket machines dispense vouchers.
● Hot and cold drinks, sandwiches and snacks are served on most trains.

Station Assistance
● Larger stations will have an information kiosk.
● If you need assistance or a porter, look for a member of the station staff, identifiable by their red waistcoats.
● You need a €1 coin deposit to use the luggage trolleys (carts).
● Some stations have a left-luggage office or coin-operated lockers. Electronic locks issue a printed ticket with a code number, which you'll need to keep. Don't store valuables in lockers.

Understanding Railway Timetables
● You can pick up free timetables *(horaires)* at stations, at tourist offices, or at SNCF offices.
● SNCF timetables are published twice a year.
● There are two timetables: one for the *Grandes Lignes*, covering high-speed TGV and other mainline services, and another for the regional TER trains.
● On *Grandes Lignes* timetables, two rows of boxed numbers at the top refer to the *numéro de train* (train number) and to the *notes à consulter* (footnotes). In TER timetables, the train number is not listed.
● Footnotes explain when a particular train runs *(circule)*. *Tous*

les jours means it runs every day; *sauf dimanche et fêtes* means it doesn't run on Sundays and holidays. *Jusqu'au*, followed by a date, indicates the service runs only up until that date.

Timetable, Fare and other Information

● Timetable, fare and service information is available from SNCF train stations and travel agencies, by telephone (tel 08 91 67 68 69; 24 hours; 20.23c per minute), the Internet or Minitel.

● The relevant TGV brochure for northwestern France is Atlantique Ouest.

● *Train + Auto*, *Train + Vélo* and *Train + Hotel* schemes include car rental, bicycle transfer or accommodation bookings respectively in the price of your ticket. Ask for leaflets outlining these package deals.

● A booklet called *Le Guide du Voyageur* gives you the A–Z (in French) of all you need to know on French railway travel (available at rail agents, tourist offices, station booking offices).

BUSES

● Buses in Normandy cover a much wider network of destinations than the trains, but most individual routes are quite short. Long-distance bus travel is not very widespread in France; most people use the train for longer journeys. Buses are slightly less expensive than trains, and journey times are sometimes just as quick, but in rural parts of Normandy services may be infrequent, erratic or very seasonal.

● Buses are operated by a confusing number of different companies, some of which act as umbrella co-ordinators in certain areas. Since franchises may be up for renewal at any time it is not unusual for a new company to take over a route and sometimes change route numbers. Ask any tourist office for information, and you will be showered with little leaflets outlining separate routes.

● Bus or coach stations (*gares routières*) are often located close to railway stations, and some attempt is made to co-ordinate train and bus services. Smaller towns without train stations are often linked by bus to the nearest railway station. These buses may be operated by SNCF as a replacement for uneconomic rail services. Rail passes are valid on most SNCF buses, but check before you travel. For information on SNCF-run buses, telephone 0891 676 869 (24-hour premium-rate service).

● Bus transport within cities is generally excellent and cheap, whereas rural areas are much less well served. Many routes operate for schoolchildren or commuters rather than visitors, with long gaps during the day or complete breaks in holidays. But look out for market-day buses.

● You can generally buy tickets for short distances on board, but for longer journeys, buy tickets in advance at the bus station to reserve a seat.

● Few bus stations have a designated left-luggage office. Some have information desks that can double as luggage rooms.

TAXIS

● Taking a taxi is not the most cost-effective way of getting about but it may be the only convenient option.

● The fare consists of an initial pick-up charge plus a charge per kilometre, (0.6 mile), and any extra charges for luggage and journeys during the evening or on Sundays. All taxis use a meter (*compteur*).

● The best way to find a taxi is to head to a taxi stand, marked by a blue Taxis sign (often near railway stations, ferry terminals or main squares). You can phone for a taxi but this can be more expensive as the meter may start running as soon as the taxi sets off to collect you.

● Taxis taken from expensive hotels often charge more.

● Smoking is not allowed in some taxis—look for the sign.

● Always check the meter is reset before you set off.

● Some taxis accept bank cards, but it is best to have cash available. It is usual to give a tip of around 10 per cent.

● If you want a receipt, ask for *un reçu*.

BOATS

Normandy's offshore excursions are mostly limited to the Channel Islands and the Îles Chausey, accessible from Granville and one or two smaller ports on the Cherbourg peninsula.

● Compagnie Corsaire (08 25 13 80 50, www.compagniecorsaire.com): Excursions to Granville and Îles Chausey.

● Manche Iles Express (02 33 61 08 88, www.manche-iles-express.com): Trips to Jersey, Guernsey, Aurigny and Sark.

BY BICYCLE

France is an exceptionally attractive destination for keen cyclists, and nowhere more so than Normandy and Brittany, with plenty of glorious, diverse countryside, not too many mountains, and good facilities. Tourist offices supply maps and touring guides specifically for cyclists, and there are lots of places to rent or repair a bike. Bicycles can be taken on most trains, generally free of charge (check the SNCF website for details). Security is a problem, and there are high rates of theft, so check insurance cover.

Buses, taxis and bicycles only

Getting Around in Normandy's Cities

Even Normandy's largest cities are modest in size compared with, say, Paris or Lyon, but they can still be confusing and harassing for motorists. However, most have excellent bus and train links to other bases in the region, along with exemplary networks of internal public transport. The areas most visitors want to see are generally quite compact, and manageable on foot. In smaller cities, visit the Gare Routière bus depot near the train station to check out city bus routes, or look for local timetables at the main railway station or tourist office.

ON THE MOVE

CAEN

Taking the tram is an enjoyable way of seeing Caen

Caen has had an integrated public transport system since the mid-19th century, with two horse-drawn bus routes plying for trade in 1860. The first electric tramway was introduced in 1901, and the network continued to expand until it was totally destroyed by bombing in 1944. A post-war bus network was introduced and developed with video screens installed in modern buses in the 1980s. The 21st century saw the Twisto transport network extending to 24 communes between Caen and the coast and the inauguration of the next-generation Caen Tramway in 2002. Tickets are interchangeable between buses and trams, should be validated on boarding and are valid for an hour's travel. Simple one-way single tickets and day passes may be purchased aboard buses. Otherwise buy tickets from machines at stations or the two Twisto outlets.

Trams
Caen is proud of its tramway. Two routes, running north–south (Line A: Caen Campus 2–Ifs Jean Villar) and east–west (Line

B: Herouville St Clair–Caen Grâce de Dieu), each have a departure every 7 minutes. In the key central area around the main sites the lines run in tandem so tourists can expect to wait no longer than three and a half minutes for a tram. The tramway runs from 5.30–0.30 Mon–Sat, 9–midnight on Sundays. A single ticket costs €1.10 and a 10-trip ticket costs €9.30. Tourists should opt for the day pass at €2.90 per person, or €4 for a family.

Buses
The Twisto bus network is vast. Most visitors will find four routes particularly useful. Lines 1, 2 and 3 cover the city, along with the two tram routes. Bus number 2 goes out to the Mémorial Museum. Line 62 takes you to the beaches at the seaside resorts of Lion-sur-Mer and Hermanville-sur-Mer.

Information
The two Twisto shops sell tickets and offer free route maps (also available from the tourist office).
● Boutique Château
15, rue de Geôle
● Boutique Théâtre
Boulevard Maréchal Leclerc
Open Mon–Fri 7.15–6.30, Sat 10–4.45; Tel 02 31 15 55 55, www.twisto.fr.

Taxis
Taxis may be found at the city's two principal ranks at the main station and place de la République. Tel 02 31 52 17 89 (Abbeilles Taxis).

Bicycles
From 2005, the tourist office hires bikes at €10 for half a day and €15 for a full day.

LE HAVRE

Urban sprawl: you'll need public transport to cross Le Havre

The biggest city and seaport in the region is served by a network of buses running from 6am until as late as midnight on some key routes. Since nightlife may be located some distance from city-centre hotels, remember that taxis may be the only option in the small hours.

Buses
Bus Océane run services in the city centre, out to the modern port district and beyond to Harfleur and the suburbs. Tickets are available from the tourist office and newspaper and tobacco kiosks. However the two types of ticket most useful to tourists may be bought from the driver of the bus when you board. As soon as you step on the bus, you should validate your ticket in the machine by the door. A simple return ticket costs €1.40 and a Ticket Ville, day pass, costs €3.20 and is valid on all journeys until midnight on the day of purchase.
Information: 02 35 22 35 00; www.bus-oceane.com.

Taxis
You'll find 27 taxi ranks at various

convenient points around the city, including the station and seafront; call 02 35 25 81 81 (Radio Taxi). A taxi service for disabled visitors is available on 02 35 21 52 51.

Bicycles
Bike hire in Le Havre is excellent value: two hours for €2, a half day for €3 and a full day for €5. Hire bikes from the Hôtel de Ville (02 35 22 35 00) Mon–Sat 7–7 year round. In summer you may also hire cycles from the tourist office's outlet at the beach (02 35 43 18 59), open daily Jul–end Sep 11–7.

ROUEN
Rouen sprawls along the Seine and spills over into a network of suburbs. The main areas of interest to visitors however can be found within a 20-minute radius of the cathedral. Once in the city centre, everywhere may be visited on foot, and the inevitable tourist 'mini-train' works its way around the principal sites. The local Métro-Bus is run by the public transport network TCAR (*Transports en Commun de l'Agglomeration de Rouen*) with a principal metro line that runs north–south though the centre and buses to the rest of the city. Tickets may be used on both buses and metros. Each ticket is valid for one hour's travel, so you may change from bus to metro to complete a journey. Buy your ticket before boarding. Tickets are sold at the tourist office, tobacconists and from machines at metro stations.

Métro
Officially, Rouen has two metro lines. In fact it is a forked route with one northern terminus at Boulingrin and two southern termini, across the Seine, Georges Braques and Technopole. Most visitors will need just three stations, served by both 'lines': Théâtre des Arts, Palais de Justice and the Gare Rue Verte (for the mainline

Stick to the historic heart of Rouen because its suburbs stretch for miles. Commuters use the Métro and the eco-friendly buses

SNCF railway station).

All stations are to be found along the rue Jeanne d'Arc, between the Pont Jeanne d'Arc and the station. Leading artists have been invited to give each station its individual style. At Palais de Justice, train arrival indicators form part of Philippe Kauffmann's artwork *L'Horloge du Temps*, which plays with the concept of time itself. Rouen-born Jean-Pierre Bourquin is amongst several artists whose works are displayed at Théâtre des Arts.

The metro runs from 5am–11pm. Tickets cost €1.30 for a single journey, a Carte à 10 Voyages, 10-trip pass is €10.60. Visitors planning to explore further afield than the centre might consider buying a special pass. The Carte Découverte for one day is €3.60, 2 days €5.20 and 3 days €6.80

Buses
Smart, blue, energy-efficient buses in varying shapes and sizes serve the wider city and suburban area. Hop on and off, remembering to frank your ticket (prices as for the metro above)

for each journey. As well as its conventional buses, Rouen is proud of the TEOR (*Transport Est-Ouest Rouennais*), a concept midway between a bus and a tram without tramlines. The TEOR is an environmentally friendly vehicle which stops at 41 special platforms in the streets on three east–west routes across the city.
For more nformation call 02 35 52 52 52, or visit the website www.tcar.fr.

Taxis
Taxi ranks can be found at the railway station and on rue Général Leclerc. Or telephone 02 35 88 50 50.

Bicycles
Bike hire is not offered from Rouen's tourist office, but if you have not arranged cycles through SNCF, you can hire a bicycle for €14 per day from:
Atelier du Cycle Rouenais
47 rue d'Elboeuf,
76100 Rouen.
Tel 02 35 63 57 72
www.acr76.fr
Open Tue–Sat 9–12, 2.30–7
Metro: Honoré de Balzac

Visitors with a Disability

Getting around France is gradually becoming easier, thanks to the improved design of buses and trains. Any recently constructed public building, including airports and stations, will have facilities for people with disabilities and mobility problems. But you'll still find challenges when getting around Normandy, especially in historic towns with narrow, cobbled streets.

Before you travel, check what facilities are available, for example, at your arrival airport (www.aeroport.fr) and your hotel; many older buildings do not have an elevator. If you have mobility problems and may require help during a flight, tell your airline when you reserve your ticket. You may also find useful information on individual airline websites. The easiest way for visitors with disabilities to reach France from Britain is by using Eurotunnel, where you can remain in a vehicle for the whole journey. If you are taking a ferry, make sure you arrive early so that you can have help with boarding.

AIRPORTS

Caen and Le Havre airports have facilities for disabled travellers, including adapted WCs. In Paris, both Roissy–Charles de Gaulle and Orly airports are equipped for people with reduced mobility. Shuttle buses between terminals have ramps for wheelchairs, as well as voice announcements for people with visual impairments. The terminals have adapted lavatories, low-level telephones and reserved parking spaces. For details, ask for the leaflet *Guide—Passager à Mobilité Réduite* (fax requests to: 01 49 75 58 78 or email: DCCMP3@adp.fr). Various organisations offer special services from the airports into Paris, which you'll need to reserve in advance, such as Airhop (tel 01 41 29 01 29). The Orlyval train has wheelchair access.
● For information on facilities at airports in Normandy, contact Aeroguides (tel 01 46 55 93 43; www.aeroguide.fr).

TRAINS

Eurostar trains and terminals are wheelchair-friendly and wheelchair-users can also benefit from discounted tickets. France's long-distance trains are equipped for people with reduced mobility. On TGV and Corail trains, spaces for wheelchair-users are reserved in first class, although only a second-class fare is payable. Reserve at least 24 hours in advance. There are also adapted lavatories. Most large stations have elevators or ramps to the platform. If you need assistance, request it when you reserve your ticket. Facilities on regional trains tend to be more varied. It is always best to check before you travel. For more information, call 0800 154 753, look up SNCF's website (www.sncf.com), or see the pamphlet *Mémento du Voyageur à Mobilité Réduite*.

Further Information

See the French tourist office website, www.franceguide.com, for information on facilities for disabled visitors. The French volume of the Smooth Ride Guides series is available free of charge in English from the Maison de la France (▷ 186). This handbook has been compiled by many disability organisations and tourist boards throughout France. Various venues, including airports, ferries, railways, museums and accommodation, are rated for their user-friendliness.

Some historic towns are difficult for disabled visitors to access

USEFUL CONTACTS

Association des Paralysés de France
Tel 01 40 78 69 (Paris)
www.apf.asso.fr
This French organisation for the disabled is represented in each *département*. See the website for more information on local facilities.

Holiday Care Service
Tel 08451 249 971 (UK)
www.holidaycare.org.uk
Travel and holiday information for people with disabilities.

Mobile en Ville
www.mobile-en-ville.asso.fr
A website packed with information on disability access and related issues.

Mobility International USA
www.miusa.org
Promotes international travel and exchange schemes for people with disabilities.

RADAR (Royal Association for Disability and Rehabilitation)
Tel 020 7250 3222
www.radar.org.uk
Literature on travelling with disabilities.

Society for Accessible Travel and Hospitality (SATH)
Tel 212 447 7284 (from US)
www.sath.org
A US-based organisation offering advice for visitors with disabilities and promoting awareness of their travel requirements.

Tripscope
Tel 08457 585641 (UK)
www.tripscope.org.uk
Travel and transport information.

This chapter is divided into five regions, which are identified on the map on the inside front cover. Places of interest are listed alphabetically in each region. Major sights are listed on the contents page at the front of each regional section. To locate all the sights, turn to the Atlas on pages 195–207.

The Sights

LA MANCHE

This rugged peninsula thrusts into the western Channel, its history and geography determined by the winds and tides. But despite its ferry ports and bathing resorts, La Manche is old Normandy. The battleground of D-Day is also a land of ruined castles and old abbeys, testament to the days of dukes and kings, feudal lords and knights. Most famous of all the abbeys is Mont-St-Michel, which seems to rise from the sea in the early morning mist.

MAJOR SIGHTS

Still standing: the Benedictine abbey at Cerisy-la-Forêt

You can see Mont-St-Michel's bay from Avranches' botanical gardens; the town has kept the abbey's library since the French Revolution

ABBAYE DE CERISY-LA-FORÊT

197 Q5 • 50680 Cerisy-la-Forêt
02 33 56 10 36 Jul–end Aug daily 10.30–12.30, 2.30–6.30; Easter–end Jun, Sep, Oct Tue–Sun 10.30–12.30, 2.30–6.30 17km (10.5 miles) from St-Lô via the D6, D92 and D34

The well-maintained remains of a 12th-century Benedictine abbey stand at the edge of the Cerisy woods on a site that has been home to monks since the sixth century AD. The limestone abbey church was scaled down from its original grandeur in 1812, when it proved too large to serve as a parish church. The building nonetheless retains its original carved choir stalls as well as splendid vaulting. Fissures in the transept have led to a pro-gramme of reinforcement—similar projects date back to the 15th century. Visit the museum to see tiles and statuary from the original abbey. Between Easter and the end of October the buildings are illuminated at night-fall to beautiful effect.

ABBAYE DE HAMBYE

202 P6 • 50450 Hambye 02 33 61 76 92 Apr–end Oct daily 10–noon, 2–6 Adults €4, children (7–15) €1.60 From Villedieu-les-Poêles, take the D9 for 4.5km (3 miles), turn right onto the D51 for 9km (5.5 miles), then right again onto the D13

Second only to Mont-St-Michel (▷ 46–48), the Benedictine Abbey of Hambye, in the woods of the Sienne valley, is among Normandy's most complete monastic buildings. Despite the air of desolation and the crows nesting in the ruined church, the surrounding buildings are in good condition. The restoration of the sacristy, chapter house, parlour, scriptorium, kitchens and stables is now complete. The site offers a glimpse into the days of

the abbey's founding in 1145 by Guillaume Paysnel, without the detraction of the hordes of visi-tors at better known locations. Discover Norman tapestries, fres-coes, religious objects and paintings of the abbey from cen-turies past. But the most powerful image is of the ruined abbey church itself, its flying buttresses emerging from the woods and its tower poised against the sky.

ABBAYE DE LA LUCERNE

202 N7 • 50320 La Lucerne d'Outremer 02 33 48 83 56
Apr–end Sep daily 10–noon, 2–6.30; Oct–end Mar Wed–Mon 10–noon, 2–5. Closed Jan– mid-Feb Adults €4–5, youths (14–21) €3.10, children (7–14) €2.30 From La Haye-Pesnel, take the D309 to La Lucerne d'Outremer, then turn left onto the D35 for the abbey www.abbaye-lucerne.fr

The ruined 12th-century Abbey of Lucerne, set on the sandy soil of the Cotentin peninsula, has been undergoing restoration since 1959. On Sunday morn-ings, however, the stones echo to the sound of a traditional Mass, and on summer evenings music fills the air during concert season.

Lucerne was founded by William the Conqueror's nephew, Hasculfe de Subligny, in 1164, and in the intervening centuries the surrounding countryside has hardly changed. Highlights still to be seen include a Romanesque doorway and an 18th-century organ. There are traces of a 19th-century aqueduct, constructed to serve a watermill, along with the abbot's residence, a tithe barn and a section of the original clois-ters. A Romanesque lavatorium, a washing area with four small arches, is next to the entrance to the former refectory. Best of all is the traditional Norman *colombier* (dovecote), near the porter's lodge, a striking round tower with entrances for 1,500 birds.

AVRANCHES

202 P8 2 rue du Général de Gaulle, 50300 Avranches, tel 02 33 58 00 22; Jul, Aug Mon–Sat 9.30–12.30, 2–7, Sun 9.30–12.30, 2–6; May–end Jun, Sep Mon–Fri 9.30–12.30, 2–7, Sat 9.30– 12.30, 2–6; Oct–end Apr Mon–Fri 9.30– 12.30, 2–6, Sat 9.30–12.30, 2–5 Avranches www.ville-avranches.fr

This city of art and history is linked with Mont-St-Michel (▷ 46–48), a view of which can be had from the gardens at the top of the town. The town looks after the abbey's library of parchment manuscripts (some dating back to the eighth century AD) and 14,000 ancient books, stored at the Bibliothèque du Fonds Ancien in the town hall (tel 02 33 89 29 50; Jul, Aug daily 10–6; Jun, Sep daily 10–noon, 2–6).

Originally settled by the Gauls and Romans, it became a key citadel under the Normans. The main remnant of the Norman castle is the Tour St-Louis, a tower built in the 13th century and gar-landed with cannonballs from a 16th-century siege. Follow traces of the ramparts from the Jardins du Donjon for views across the Vallée de la Sée and the Baie du Mont-St-Michel.

Another restored site is the Palais Episcopal. The palace is testament to the power of the medieval bishops who controlled the city. The most famous was St. Aubert, who founded Mont-St-Michel in the eighth century AD (▷ 18). His skull is stored in the town's basilica, which attracted many influential churchmen. In the 11th century Avranches was a centre of study for disciples of Lanfranc and St. Anselm, both Archbishops of Canterbury.

Narrow cobbled streets have timbered house fronts from the 16th century. The Monument Patton commemorates the town's liberation on 31 July 1944.

THE SIGHTS

BARFLEUR

This pretty fishing port has excellent seafood and historical links with the kings of England.

Barfleur is a short drive from Cherbourg, on a stretch of the eastern side of the Cotentin peninsula popularly known as the Viking coast. The town has been putting boats to sea since the days of the Vikings and in the Middle Ages it was the peninsula's principal port. A plaque at the port entrance reminds visitors that the boat that took William the Conqueror to England in 1066 was built in Barfleur's shipyards. The town's tradition of shipping English monarchs continued in 1194, when Richard the Lionheart set sail from here to be crowned king.

DANGEROUS WATERS

In 1120, a royal tragedy occurred when the *White Ship* sank offshore with 300 members of the Anglo-Norman nobility aboard. William Atheling, heir to England's King Henry I and grandson of William the Conqueror, drowned in the treacherous currents that have claimed many ships over the centuries, an incident that led to fresh warring over the English succession. In 1348, King Edward III of England burnt Barfleur, and in the 15th and 16th centuries further attacks from the English and their allies destroyed the ramparts.

Today, the neat granite and slate buildings that stand around the port are modest and simple. The prettiest and oldest district is Cour Ste-Catherine, entered through a stone arch next to the harbour. A stroll around Barfleur's unpretentious harbour and on seaside paths takes in a couple of small lighthouses, these dwarfed by the massive Gatteville-le-Phare at Pointe de Barfleur, 4km (2.5 miles) north of the town. At 75m (246ft), it is the second-tallest lighthouse in France, and the light can be seen for 56km (35 miles). A museum at the foot of the tower recounts its history and explains modern lighthouse technology (closed mid-Nov–Jan). Barfleur is also home to France's first lifeboat station and there is a lifeboat museum in the harbour.

SAINTLY HEROINE

Before you leave Barfleur, visit the Bretonne quarter to pay homage to St. Marie-Madeleine Postel. Born in 1756, Julie Postel was a post-Revolution heroine who hid priests fleeing France in her schoolhouse. While she taught pupils in the kitchen, she persuaded fishermen to carry the fugitives across the Channel to England. Stained-glass windows in the local chapel depict scenes from her life.

Don't miss The Gatteville Lighthouse has stunning coastal views.

RATINGS

Historic interest	● ● ●
Photo stops	● ● ●
Walkability	● ● ●

BASICS

➕ 197 P3

ℹ️ 2 Rond-point Guillaume le Conquérant, 50760 Barfleur, tel 02 33 54 02 48; Jun–Sep daily 10–12.30, 2.30–6.30; Mar–May, Oct Mon–Sat 10–noon, 2–5; Nov–Feb Mon–Tue, Thu–Fri 10–noon, 2.30–4.30. Closed 2 weeks at Christmas

🚌 Regular service from Cherbourg
www.ville-barfleur.fr • Informative site linked to the town hall

TIPS

● Don't leave without trying the famous local mussels, known as *blondes de Barfleur*.
● Visit on Saturday mornings to enjoy the small market.

Above: kings and Vikings have set sail from Barfleur but today's seafarers are fishing boats.
Above inset: there are plenty of beach-based activities

Left: a plaque at the harbour noting William's departure for England in 1066

The clock tower of Bricquebec's Abbaye Notre-Dame-de-Grâce

BARNEVILLE CARTERET

🟦 196 M4 ℹ️ 10 rue des Écoles, 50270 Barneville-Carteret, tel 02 33 04 90 58; Mon–Sat 9–12.30, 2–6 ℹ️ Place Flandres Dunkerque, 50270 Barneville-Carteret, tel 02 33 04 94 54; Jul, Aug daily 10–12.30, 3–7 🚢 From Cherbourg www.barneville-carteret.net

This traditional resort, on the west coast of the Cotentin peninsula, is the union of the three towns of Barneville, Barneville-Plage and Carteret, and offers two styles of holiday within a mile of coastline. Barneville itself is the simpler option, a quiet residential town dominated by an austere 11th-century church. Restaurants are found here rather than along the neighbouring stretch of seaside. The beach at Barneville-Plage is a basic stretch of seafront. Carteret has a livelier beachfront, with shops, bars, seafood restaurants and a port. Cap Carteret's resort, to the west, still retains its Edwardian style. In summer, a ferry service operates between Carteret and the Channel Islands.

BRICQUEBEC

🟦 196 N4 ℹ️ Place Ste-Anne, 50260 Bricquebec, tel 02 33 52 21 65; Jul, Aug Mon–Sat 10–noon, 2–6; Sep, Oct, Mar–end Jun Mon–Sat 10–noon, 2.30–5 www.ville-bricquebec.fr

The pleasant market town of Bricquebec would probably have remained unnoticed by the outside world but for its legacy of monastic cheese-making. Named by Vikings as Brekkubekk, Norse for 'the brook of the slopes', it is topped by the ruins of a 14th-century chateau. The main street leads up to the gatehouse of the castle, whose 11-sided keep still stands. Visitors can explore the fortifications, walls and towers and step down into vaulted cellars and a 13th-century crypt.

The Abbaye Notre-Dame-de-Grâce, Bricquebec's Trappist

The shingle beach at Port Racine on Cap de la Hague

CAP DE LA HAGUE

Writers and artists have been inspired by a landscape of sandy beaches, lighthouses, stone walls and fishing boats.

This northwestern tip of the Cotentin peninsula is marked by landscaped parks and gardens, while windswept walks take you along rocky cliffs and through stone villages. The house in Gréville-Hague where painter Jean-François Millet was born in 1814 is open to visitors (tel 02 33 01 81 91; Jun–Sep daily 11–7; school holidays daily 1–6). A bust of the artist is all that remains of a complete statue after wartime bombings, although a new sculpture of Millet by Louis Derbré now stands in the village square. The 19th-century church at Gréville displays 15th-century statuary discovered during maintenance work.

RATINGS		
Cultural interest	●●●	
Outdoor pursuits	●●●	
Photo stops	●●●	

BASICS

🟦 196 M2

ℹ️ 45 rue Jallot, 50440 Beaumont-Hague, tel 02 33 52 74 94; Mon–Fri 10–noon, 1.30–5.30, Sat 10–1; also office at Goury: daily 10–1, 2–7

🚉 Cherbourg (20km/12 miles) www.lahague.org

TIP

● In July, a weekend hike of 95km (59 miles) is organised by La Hague's tourist office, consisting of four stages. Hikers can do a single stretch or the full tour, with accommodation and meals offered.

A POET'S PLACE

Poet Jacques Prévert fell in love with the area in the 1930s. In 1971, he bought a house in Omonville-la-Petite, where he lived until his death in 1977. He is buried alongside his wife and daughter in the village cemetery. Prévert's house hosts exhibitions on poetry and the arts (tel 02 33 52 72 38; Jun–Sep 11–7; Apr, May, Oct and school holidays 1–6). St-Germain-des-Vaux, north of Omonville-la-Petite and best known for its tiny Port Racine, the smallest harbour in France (complete with its own fishing fleet), has a waterfront garden named after Jacques Prévert (Jul, Aug daily 2–7; Sep, Oct, Easter–end Jun Sat–Thu 2–7).

The Château et Parc de Nacqueville, whose distinctive granite walls and stone roofs date from the 18th century, is listed as a national historic monument (tel 02 33 03 21 12; tours Easter–end Sep Wed–Thu, Sat–Mon 2, 3, 4, 5) and can be found at Urville Nacqueville, 5km (3 miles) west of Cherbourg. In 1830, Hippolyte de Tocqueville commissioned a romantic English garden here. Today, the ornamental trees, hydrangeas, azaleas and rhododendrons, waterfalls and a lake, liven up the chateau's grey façade.

Beach huts on the promenade at Carolles

Geese, ballet and Shakespeare: find out how they are all connected at the Château de Pirou, a 12th-century fort on the Cotentin coast

monastery (tel 02 33 87 56 12; services daily 8.15, 2.15, 6, 8), was founded in 1824 by Dom Augustin Onfroy and is the town's main claim to fame. The second abbot, Dom Germain, decreed that the monks' self-sufficiency would best be guaranteed by cheese production, as in other Trappist communities such as Port Salut and Mont des Cats. So successful was the idea that the monks signed an agreement with the Maison de la Providence society to sell their cheese across France. The Providence brand became a national favourite and by World War II the monks were collecting milk from around 230 Cotentin farmers. Competition from industrial cheese factories resulted in the monks selling the brand in 1961 to a commercial operation in Valognes. Today, you can see a slide show on the life of the monks and on the cheese-making (on request, afternoons only), then buy some of the holy cheese from the abbey shop.

CAROLLES

➕ 202 N7 ℹ️ 2 rue de la Poste, 50740 Carolles, tel 02 33 61 92 88; Easter–mid-Jun Sat, Sun 10–12.30; mid-Jun–mid-Sep daily 10–12.30, 2.30–5 www.ville-carolles.fr

A low-key alternative to busier holiday resorts in Granville and Avranches, Carolles-Plage has summer bathing huts and beach bars, yet outside peak months it retains the peace and quiet of a simple coastal village. Walk from the centre of Carolles through woodland and along the Vallée du Lude to reach the seashore. The best view of the Baie de Mont-St-Michel is from Le Pignon Butor. From here you can walk along the cliffs or follow a Grand Randonnée trail into the Vallée des Peintres, which was found by amateur artists in the 1860s, as bathers embraced the seaside.

CHÂTEAU DE GRATOT

➕ 202 N6 • Centre d'Animation du Château de Gratot, 50200 Gratot ☎ 02 33 45 18 49 ◐ Daily 10–7 💷 Adults €3, children (10–18) €1.50, under-10s free 🚗 Coutances (4km/2.5 miles)

The romantic ruins of a castle where a knight is said to have wooed, won and wed a fairy are being rescued from centuries of neglect and an army of weeds. Seat of the Argouges family for 500 years, the chateau is most famous for its Tour de la Fée (Fairy Tower). Legend has it that a knight came to drink at the waters of Gratot and saw a beautiful fairy, who disappeared when she caught sight of him looking at her. He returned each night and on the fifth visit saw her again. He proposed, and she agreed to marry him on the condition that he never spoke the word 'death'. Years later, at a tournament, the knight uttered the fatal word and his wife fell from the window of the Fairy Tower, never to be seen again, although locals say you can hear her whispering the word '*mort*' (death) on stormy nights.

The octagonal Fairy Tower, with it square bedroom, spiral staircase and balustraded walkways, is among the most ambitious of the restoration projects now being carried out. The castle's four towers date from the 14th and 15th centuries, while a 17th-century lodge and mansarded house are also being renovated.

A baker's sign in Carolles

CHÂTEAU DE PIROU

➕ 196 N5 • 50770 Pirou ☎ 02 33 46 34 71 ◐ Jul, Aug Thu 10–noon, 2–6.30; Sep–end Jun daily 10–noon, 2–5 💷 Adults €3.10–4, children (7–14) €2.30 🍴 Pirou village and Plage (2km/1 mile) 🚗 Coutances (20min drive) www.chateau-pirou.org

Normandy's oldest fortified castle gave its name to the most graceful move in ballet, the pirouette, and also provided a hero of the Norman Conquest and a Shakespearean character. During a Viking siege of the original wooden fortress, the defenders of the castle were said to have magically turned themselves into geese and flown away. For centuries, geese nested there each spring and were fed by locals, who named the birds after the castle. The spinning and twisiting of the geese as they launched themselves into flight gave rise to the title of the dance move.

The stone fort, near Cotentin's sand dunes, dates from the 12th century. A knight from Pirou took part in the Norman Conquest of England in 1066, and was rewarded with Stoke-Pirou, an estate in Somerset. One of the lords of Pirou in the 15th century was English knight Jehan Falstoff, later caricatured by William Shakespeare as Sir John Falstaff, hero of the plays *King Henry IV* and *Merry Wives of Windsor*.

By the 19th century, the castle was a modest farm. However, in 1968 it was listed as an historic monument by the State and work began on restoring the building, which now stands on an island in an artificial lake. The original 12th- and 14th-century ramparts remain, protected by five fortified gates. Later additions, including a chapel, kitchens and living quarters, are also open to visitors. **Don't miss** Son et lumière shows with a medieval theme are held in July and August.

CHERBOURG

The ferry port, with a maritime history museum, leads directly to the D-Day beaches trail.

Flattened by air raids and unimaginatively reconstructed after World War II, Cherbourg has never been an obvious visitor destination. King Louis XIV's architect, the Marquis de Vauban, planned a major naval base here in the 17th century, although the navy did not establish itself at the port until 1858, nor did it play an important military role until Liberation on 27 June 1944, three weeks after D-Day. Allied divers cleared the port of wrecks and mines in order that Cherbourg could replace the makeshift Mulberry Harbour at Arromanches.

The town's main claim to fame since 1969 has been as an Atlantic gateway, where passengers have boarded the greatest oceangoing liners of the modern age. Funnels of the *SS France* and Cunard's *Queen Elizabeth* and *QE2* were once familiar features on the Cherbourg skyline, even if today's port mostly welcomes the more humble cross-Channel ferries.

CITÉ DE LA MER
✉ Gare Maritime Transatlantique, 50100 Cherbourg ☎ 08 25 33 50 50
🕐 Jun–mid-Sep daily 9.30–7; mid-Sep–end May daily 10–6 💶 Adults €14, children (6–17) €10, under-6s free
The art deco Gare Maritime Transatlantique terminal has been reinvented as the Cité de la Mer, a celebration of man's conquest of the deep. Besides the museum of naval history, the main attraction in the port is *Le Redoutable*, France's first nuclear submarine, launched here in 1967. It is the largest submarine in the world open to the public.

BEYOND THE SEA
The Musée d'Ethnographie 'Emmanuel Liais' (tel 02 33 53 51 61; May–end Sep Tue–Sat 10–noon, 2–6, Sun, Mon 2–6; Oct–end Apr Wed–Sun 2–6), has exhibitions on Inuit life. Or admire the works of Jean-François Millet (1814–75) at the Musée Thomas-Henry (tel 02 33 23 39 30; May–end Sep Tue–Sat 10–noon, 2–6, Sun, Mon 2–6; Oct–end Apr Wed–Sun 2–6), near the port. Historians can see World War II exhibits at Fort du Roule (tel 02 33 20 14 12; Jun–Aug daily 11–6; May and Sep daily 10–12, 2–6; rest of year Sun, Mon 10–12, Wed–Sun 2–6). There are markets at place de Gaulle (Tue, Sat morning, Thu all day) and Octeville's avenue de Normandy (Sun morning).

Don't miss The amazing 'undersea' trail at the Cité de la Mer brings the visitor face to face with marine life at Europe's largest aquarium.

Catch of the day: fishing boats lined up in Cherbourg's harbour. Inset: an advert on the side of a building in Cherbourg

RATINGS	
Cultural interest	●●●
Chainstore shopping	●●●
Good for kids	●●●●

BASICS
🗺 196 N3
ℹ 2 quai Alexandre III, 50100 Cherbourg, tel 02 33 93 52 02; Jul–Aug Mon–Sat 9–6.30, Sun 10–12.30; Sep–May Mon–Sat 9–12.30, 2–6; Jun Mon–Sat 9–12.30, 2–6.30
🚉 Cherbourg
www.ot-cherbourg-cotentin.fr • French-language site

Two fishing boats at the quai Alexandre III in Cherbourg

On top of the world: the view from the top of Gatteville Lighthouse on the east coast of the Cotentin peninsula sweeps across Veys Bay, an important area for migrating marine birdlife

THE SIGHTS

COTENTIN

🔲 196 N4 🚹 2 quai Alexandre III, 50100 Cherbourg, tel 02 33 93 52 02; Jul–Aug Mon–Sat 9–6.30, Sun 10–12.30; Sep–May 9–12.30, 2–6; Jun Mon–Sat 9–12.30, 2–6.30

🚇 Cherbourg, Valognes
www.ot-cherbourg-cotentin.fr

The unspoilt landscape of the Cotentin peninsula suggests a remote region far removed from Normandy's commercial towns and the more gentle beauty of the hinterland. Cotentin offers an authentic glimpse of French rural life, with farming and fishing very much to the fore. On the west of the peninsula, the stark rugged coastline around Cap de La Hague (▷ 41) and Nez de Jobourg is almost Breton in its craggy majesty, perfect for windswept walks and views out to the Channel Islands. In contrast, the eastern side has a lusher, more verdant landscape, where green fields and rich woodland mark the countryside around the Val de Saire stretch to the dunes of the D-Day beaches. The hedgerows of the man-made Cotentin *bocage* landscape proved a serious obstacle to liberating Allied troops in 1944, and provided cover for guerrilla resistance.

Neither as glitzy or sophisticated as such popular coastal destinations as Deauville, as picturesque as the Suisse Normande region, nor as established on the tourist trail as Étretat and Honfleur, Cotentin offers a simpler glimpse of country life by the sea. The bathing may be excellent around Flamanville on the west coast, but, safety assurances aside, some holidaymakers may feel uncomfortable about swimming in the shadow of a nuclear power plant. Highlights of the region include the views from the top of Gatteville Lighthouse

by Barfleur (▷ 40); and La Pernelle, with a panoramic observation point overlooking the Val de Saire and a tiny *mairie* (town hall), claimed by locals to be the smallest in France.

COUTANCES

🔲 202 N6 🚹 Place Georges Leclerc, 50200 Coutances, tel 02 33 19 08 10; Jul–Aug Mon–Fri 9.30–6.30, Sat 10–12.30, 2–6, Sun 10–1; rest of year Mon–Fri 9.30–12.30; 2–6, Sat 10–12.30, 2–5 🚇 Coutances
www.ville-coutances.fr

Hailed as a masterpiece of Norman Gothic architecture, the cathedral at Coutances is cunningly grafted onto the remains of an earlier Romanesque church. The 13th-century construction is beautifully proportioned, with strong buttresses anchoring it to the ground, elegant spires and an octagonal lantern tower. Stained-glass windows tell the story of Archbishop of Canterbury Thomas Becket (c1118–70); King Henry II of England, who was responsible for Becket's murder, did penance for his crime in Normandy.

The origin of the town lies in the third century AD, when a settlement here was dubbed Constantia, after the Roman Emperor Constantius-Chlorus (cAD250–306). The name Constantia subsequently evolved into both Coutances and Cotentin (see above). The seat of a bishop and a political centre until the French Revolution, Coutances is sleepier today than in times past. It is essentially a peaceful and well-to-do town, away from the seaside tourist trail. Among other traces of the town's glory days are three arches, all that remains of the original 14th-century aqueduct. The Musée Quesnel-Morinière (tel 02 33 45 11 92; Jul, Aug

Mon, Wed–Sat 10–noon, 2–6, Sun 2–6; Sep–end Jun Mon, Wed–Sat 10–noon, 2–5, Sun 2–5. Closed public holidays and mornings Nov–Mar), housed in the former Hôtel Poupinel, has a collection of local art, crafts and clothes, although these are gloriously outshone by the splendid *Lions and Dogs Fighting* by painter Peter Paul Rubens (1577–1640). The nearby Jardin des Plantes is a pleasant spot for a walk or picnic on a summer's day. If you're here in spring, catch the Jazz Sous les Pommiers festival (▷ 114).

GENÊTS

🔲 202 N8 🚹 Relais de Genêts, La Maison du Guide Decouverte de la Baie du Mont-St-Michel, 1 rue Montoise, 50530 Genêts, tel 02 33 70 83 49; Apr–end Oct daily 9–12.30, 1.30–6.30; Nov–Apr Mon–Fri 2–6 🚌 From Avranches
www.decouvertebaie.com

Dominated on misty mornings by the emerging silhouette of Mont-St-Michel, this former fishing port shares its modest history with the monastery across the bay. Nowadays, flocks of sheep, prized for their meat, graze on the salt marshes here, except during the great seasonal tides. Yet, until the bay silted up after the 15th century and the rival town of Granville (see below) found favour, Genêts was Normandy's most prosperous port. As gateway to the Mount, Genêts sent food, wine, clothes and even building materials to the inhabitants of Mont-St-Michel. Today, visitors gather by the bridge next to the 12th-century church to take guided walks across the treacherous sands to the abbey, and the town is also home to one of the Maisons de la Baie (▷ 48). Opposite the village is the island of Tombelaine, a staging post for the escorted pilgrimage and a bird sanctuary,

The slate roofs of Granville encircle the town's harbour. The resort, in the bay of Mont-St-Michel, comes alive in the summer season

The Romanesque abbey of Lessay, rebuilt in 1945–58

home to gulls and egrets. The granite rock was used by England's King Henry V as a fortress in his unsuccessful campaign to take over the Mount following his victory over the French at Agincourt in 1415.

GRANVILLE

🔲 202 N7 ⓘ 4 cours Jonville, 50406 Granville, tel 02 33 91 30 03; Mon–Sat 9.15–12.30, 2–6, Sun 10.30–12.30 🚉 Granville
www.ville-granville.fr

This busy port and lively summer resort, on the bay of Mont-St-Michel, retains its 15th-century battlements, built by Englishman Thomas Scales. The main entrance to the upper town is still via the original drawbridge of the Grand'Porte. Climb to the Musée du Vieux Granville (tel 02 33 50 44 10; Apr–Sep Wed–Mon 10–noon, 2–6; Oct–end Mar Wed, Sat–Sun 2–6) to see local crafts and learn about the history of the fishing port. Modern art at the Musée Richard Anacréon (tel 02 33 51 02 94; late Jul–end Sep Tue–Sun 11–6; rest of year Tue–Sun 2–6) includes works by Pablo Picasso (1881–1973). **Don't miss** The Musée Christian Dior is in the fashion designer's childhood home (tel 02 33 61 48 21; late May–end Sep daily 10–6.30; ▷ 135).

LA HAYE-PESNEL

🔲 202 N7 ⓘ Rue de la Libération, 50320 La Haye-Pesnel, tel 02 33 90 75 02; Jul, Aug Tue–Sat 8.30–noon, 2.30–6; Sep–end Jun Tue 8.30–noon, Wed 10–12.30, 2–6, Fri 8.30–noon, 1.30–5, Sat 10–noon 🚉 Foligny (4km/2.5 miles)

Within half an hour of Mont-St-Michel, between Avranches and Granville, is La Haye-Pesnel, the perfect base for a couple of days'

exploration on horseback. The pretty little market town in the *bocage* landscape of fields and hedgerows is celebrated for its flowers, which spill out onto the streets from window boxes, pots and tubs set outside the brick and stone cottages. On 1 May, La Haye-Pesnel holds its flower market, and every third August (next date 2007) the summer Triennale Fleurie festival sees flowers on every spare ledge, wall and street corner.

In the summer months, artists open the doors to their workshops and galleries to sell their creations to visitors, and many set up stall during the Wednesday morning market. Visit the church of Ste-Madeleine, whose bell dates back to 1793. The Ecu-Musée du Cidre (tel 02 33 61 31 51; Easter–end Sep Mon–Fri 2–6), at the Ferme l'Hermitière in St-Jean-des-Champs, north of the town, offers

cider tastings and demonstrations of farmhouse skills.

LESSAY

🔲 196 N5 ⓘ 11 place St-Cloud, 50430 Lessay, tel 02 33 45 14 34; Jul, Aug Mon–Fri 9–12.15, 1.30–6, Sat 10–12.15, 2.30–6; Sep–end Jun Mon–Fri 9–12.15, 1.30–5.30 🚉 From Cherbourg
www.canton-lessay.com

Lessay is famous for its abbey (daily 9–7), which was founded by Baron Turstin Haldup of La Haye-au-Puits in 1056. The Benedictine monks and abbot came to the small town just north of Coutances from the Abbaye du Bec-Hellouin (▷ 77). The original 12th-century abbey buildings that once surrounded the church fell victim to religious conflicts and the Hundred Years War (1337–1453). They were completely rebuilt in the 18th century, but totally destroyed in the bombings of 1944. The church itself was also seriously damaged by the bombardments of the Battle of Normandy. However, it was reconstructed to its original design between 1945 to 1958 using traditional local building materials, and is now regarded as a typical example of Normandy's Romanesque style. The honey-toned limestone walls and lichen-coated roof slates from La Hague seem as mellow and timeless as ever. The three-tiered nave has a gallery connecting the topmost windows. Light shining through the simple stained-glass windows provides a contemplative and cool atmosphere inside. **Don't miss** The Foire de Sainte-Croix (Holy Cross Fair) is held in the town of Lessay in September.

The World War I memorial in La Haye-Pesnel's town centre

Mont-St-Michel

The silhouette of Mont-St-Michel rising from the mists is one of the symbols of France itself. The UNESCO World Heritage Site attracts more visitors than any other provincial attraction in the country.

Holy water: Mont-St-Michel is surrounded by sea at high tide

A waxwork displayed outside the Grevin Museum

Inside a side-chapel of the abbey, with an open Bible

SEEING MONT-ST-MICHEL

This fortified religious community, separated from the mainland by quicksands and racing tides, is a surreal sight, especially when glimpsed through the early morning sea mists. Reached via a causeway just north of Pontorson, the Mount was originally an island in the sea between Normandy and Brittany.

Although Mont-St-Michel, now a UNESCO World Heritage Site, is one of the most crowded visitor attractions in the country during peak season, it is still well worth making the effort to cross the causeway from the mainland. In summer, aim to arrive at around 8am or after 5pm to miss the crowds, and don't venture onto the mudflats unless you are part of a guided walk, as tides can sweep in quickly.

Once you are at the summit of the Mount, ignore your aching calf muscles and continue climbing the steps of the abbey—the views of the protected Baie de Mont-St-Michel from the very top are stunning.

HIGHLIGHTS

ABBAYE

✉ 50170 Le Mont-St-Michel ☎ 02 33 89 80 00 🕐 May–end Aug daily 9–7 (last entry 6pm); Sep–end Apr daily 9.30–6 (last entry 5pm) 💶 Adults €8, youths (18–25) €5, under-18s free
www.monum.fr

You can join a guided tour around the abbey and discover the huge treadmill in which prisoners once trudged to work a system of pulleys to haul building materials up the side of the Mount. The original name of the rock island beneath the abbey was Mont Tombé, suggesting it was used as a burial ground.

The abbey is often referred to as *La Merveille* (the Wonder), but this epithet actually applies to a Gothic extension commissioned by King Philippe Auguste of France in the 13th century to celebrate his conquest of Normandy. The name reflected the amazing feat of the architects and builders who created it in just 20 years. The Merveille, with its three floors of dining rooms for pilgrims, nobles and monks, is topped by a tranquil cloister garden, with a window looking out to sea.

BASICS

➕ 202 N8
ℹ️ 50170 Le Mont-St-Michel, tel 02 33 60 14 30; Jul, Aug daily 9–7; Apr–end Jun, Sep Mon–Sat 9–12.30, 2–6.30, Sun 9–noon, 2–6; Oct–end Mar Mon–Sat 9–12, 2–6, Sun 10–noon, 2–5

🍴 La Mère Poulard, on the Mount, serves world-famous omelettes beaten in age-old copper bowls that have fortified pilgrims and visitors alike for years (tel 02 33 89 68 68)

🚌 From Rennes, St-Malo

🚆 TGV to Rennes, then morning bus link to the Mount. Pontorson station, 9km (6 miles) away, has bus services

🅿️ The visitors' car park alongside the present causeway is to be replaced with parking for 4,200 cars in 2007, 2km (1 mile) south of the coast road on the mainland. Parking will cost €4, but a free shuttle-bus (eventually to be replaced with a railway line) will take visitors from their vehicles to the Mount

🚻 €0.35

📖 Free English-language leaflets; illustrated guidebook €4.50
www.ot-montsaintmichel.com • Good factual site, with tidal information

Crowning glory: Mont-St-Michel's abbey overlooks the village

TIPS

- If the main street is packed with people, climb the steps to the less crowded ramparts to look down on the village and across the sea.
- Rather than pay €8 to visit the abbey, you could time your visit to coincide with the mid-day Mass, when tickets are free. You can take your time walking through the monument after the service.
- *Son et lumière* shows are staged in the summer.

Mont-St-Michel is one of France's most popular tourist attractions

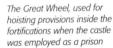

Sunlight streams through the double row of marble arches in the cloisters of the abbey

The Great Wheel, used for hoisting provisions inside the fortifications when the castle was employed as a prison

MAISONS DE LA BAIE

✉ Courtils ☎ 02 33 89 66 00 ✉ Le-Vivier-sur-Mer ☎ 02 99 48 84 38 ✉ St-Léonard ☎ 02 33 89 06 06 🕐 Jul, Aug daily 10–7; Apr–May daily 2–6; Jun, Sep 10–6; school holidays daily 2–6
www.maison-baie.com

Back on the mainland, you can enjoy wonderful views of the Mount from the Maison de la Baie vantage points at Le-Vivier-sur-Mer, Courtils and St-Léonard. These individually themed mini-museums offer a perspective on the daily life of the abbey in times past, along with excellent displays of local wildlife. They also organise escorted treks across the sands to the Mount, on foot and on horseback.

BACKGROUND

The Mount has drawn pilgrims since AD708, when St. Aubert, Bishop of Avranches, built a modest chapel on the 79m (260ft) granite Mont Tombé after seeing a vision of the Archangel Michael. Benedictine monks settled here and a village soon formed around them. A Romanesque church was constructed on the site in the 11th century, and work continued on other buildings over the following years. The Mount was fortified against the English during the Hundred Years War (1337–1453) and managed to resist attack. Work continued on the abbey between the 15th to the 17th centuries, and the site was also used as a prison after the French Revolution. It opened to visitors as a national monument in 1874, and in 1897 Emmanuel Frémiet's gilded statue of St. Michael was placed on top of a new steeple, 157m (515ft) high. A monastic community returned to the site in 1969, and monks and nuns continue to provide a spiritual anchor today within what might otherwise be merely a hub of tourism and history. Although 3.5 million visitors come to Mont-St-Michel each year, the resident population is just 35.

A project (due to finish in 2007) to replace the causeway with a footbridge will ensure the Mount is surrounded by sea at high tide to combat the build-up of silt, now 5m (16ft) deep.

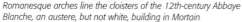
Romanesque arches line the cloisters of the 12th-century Abbaye Blanche, an austere, but not white, building in Mortain

Dropping in: the Parachute Museum of Ste-Mère-Église

THE SIGHTS

MORTAIN

➕ 202 Q8 ℹ️ La Collegiale, 50140 Mortain, tel 02 33 59 19 74; Apr–end Oct Mon–Sat 9.30–12.30, 1.30–6.30; Sun 9.30–12.30, 1.30–5; Nov–end Mar Tue–Sat 9.30–12.30, 2–6
www.ville-mortain.fr

Churches and waterfalls bring visitors to this town on a high ridge overlooking the Sélune valley and the Mortain forest. To reach the Grand Cascade, follow signs out of town and park on the roadside; here, the waters of the Cance tumble 20m (65ft), and in early summer the scene is coloured by rhododendrons. The Petit Cascade, closer to the town, is an easy walk from Mortain's architectural attractions. The latter include the 12th-century Abbaye Blanche and the Église St-Evroult, in the centre of Mortain, dating from the 11th century (tours Jul–Aug, Tue, Fri afternoon). The church's treasure is the Chrismale reliquary, an eighth-century AD casket. Mortain's Petite Chapelle has painted biblical scenes and commands views to Mont-St-Michel. The chapel has a tourist information desk (Jul, Aug daily 3–7; May, Jun Sat–Sun 3–7).

ST-LÔ

➕ 197 Q6 ✉️ Place Général de Gaulle, 50010 St-Lô, tel 02 33 77 60 35; Jul, Aug Mon–Fri 9.30–12.30, 2–6, Sat 9.30–1; rest of year Mon 2–6, Tue–Fri 9.30–12.30, Sat 9.30–1
www.saint-lo.fr

St-Lô was razed to the ground on 6 June 1944, four years after its occupation by the Germans. The Grande Brûlerie (Great Burning) began at 8pm and continued all night, destroying 95 percent of the town and killing 500 of its 1,200 inhabitants. Despite calls to leave the town in ruins as a memorial and create a new city elsewhere, the citizens insisted on rebuilding St-Lô around the

enclos, or hilltop fortification. The destruction had revealed the foundations of the original Gaul castrum (military camp), on which the new town was laid out.

Vestiges of the old ramparts remain today. The Tour des Beaux Regards lookout tower has views over the Vire. The only surviving relic of the citadel is La Poudrière (Powder Magazine), with a thick fragment of the city wall at one side. The Église Notre-Dame has modern bronze doors, although one bomb-damaged façade has been left as testament to the wartime devastation.

A museum within the Centre Culturel Jean Lurçat on place Champ-de-Mars (tel 02 33 72 52 55; Wed–Mon 10–noon, 2–6. Closed Jan–end Mar, school holidays and public holidays) houses the municipal art collection; there are also some fine tapestries dating from the 16th century. The Musée du Bocage Normand (tel 02 33 56 26 98; Jun–end Sep Wed–Fri 10–noon, 2–6, Sat–Sun 2–6; Oct, Mar–end May Wed–Sun 2–6; Nov–end Feb Thu–Sun 2–6) is a grand farmyard ringed by 17th- and 19th-century stone farm buildings, with stables, a bakery and cider press illustrating traditional Normandy farming life.

STE-MÈRE-ÉGLISE

➕ 196 P4 ℹ️ 6 rue Eisenhower, 50480 Ste-Mère-Église, tel 02 33 21 00 33; Apr–end Sep Mon–Sat 9–1, 2–6, Sun 2–6; Oct–end Mar Mon–Fri 9–12.30, 1–4; closed mid-Dec–mid-Jan
🚌 From Cherbourg
www.sainte-mere-eglise.info

A mannequin of a parachutist hanging from the town's church tower recalls D-Day and acts as a reminder that this corner of the Cotentin has a history of conflict. During the Hundred Years War (1337–1453), fortified farms witnessed fighting between France and England, and through

the 16th- and 17th-century Wars of Religion Ste-Mère became a Protestant fiefdom. During the French Revolution, the town was renamed as Mère Libre.

Occupied by the Germans from 18 June 1940 during World War II, Ste-Mère was liberated at midnight on 5 June 1944, when an American parachutist was left dangling from the church tower by his parachute; he survived the battle and spent the rest of his life in the town. D-Day memorials dominate the church square, with the Musée des Troupes Aéroportées (tel 02 33 41 41 35; Feb–Dec) home to a Douglas C-47 aircraft. The church dates from the 11th–15th centuries but a stained-glass window shows the Virgin Mary surrounded by aeroplanes and parachutists. Another window was donated by veterans of the 505th Regiment of the US 82nd Airborne Division. The statue of Iron Mike erected in 1997, named for the patron saint of parachutists, is 2.5km (1 mile) out of town. On D-Day, American troops captured the bridge over the Merderet stream, a scene depicted in a map on the excellent, parachute-shaped bronze memorial table.

Ste-Mère has peaceful stories, too. The Fontaine St-Méen, next to the church, is dedicated to the English-born St. Méen, who struck the ground with his staff to bring forth healing waters. There is also a museum of farming, Ferme-Musée du Cotentin (tel 02 33 95 40 20).

Working copper in the Atelier du Cuivre in Villedieu-les-Poêles

VALOGNES

🗺 196 N3 ℹ 6 Allée de la Poste, 50700 Valognes, tel 02 33 40 35 89; Jul, Aug daily 10–noon, 2–6.30; Sep–end Jun Mon–Sat 10–noon, 3–6 🚉 Valognes

Although Valognes was seriously damaged during wartime air raids, its centre harbours some architectural delights. The Hôtel de Beaumont re-creates 18th-century life in a splendidly decorated merchant's house of the period (tel 02 33 40 12 30; Jul–mid-Sep daily 2.30– 6.30; and Tue 10.30–noon). The interesting Musée Régional de Cidre (tel 02 33 40 22 73) is dedicated to cider-making, and the Musée de l'Eau-de-Vie et des Vieux Métiers (02 33 40 26 25), has displays on Calvados.

VILLEDIEU-LES-POÊLES

🗺 202 P7 ℹ Place des Costils, 50800 Villedieu-les-Poêles, tel 02 33 61 05 69; Apr–end Sep, daily 9–12.30, 2–6.30; Oct–end Mar Mon–Sat 9–noon, 2–6 🚉 Villedieu-les-Poêles www.ot-villedieu.fr

Don't let the name fool you: They make more than *poêles* (pots and pans) at Villedieu. The town still manufactures church bells in the traditional manner, yet it was the workshops beating out kitchen implements that gave it its name. At the Musée de la Poeslerie (tel 02 33 90 20 92) you can learn how copper workshops were first established in the 12th century by the Knights of the Order of St. John of Jerusalem. One of the world's last surviving bell foundries, the Fonderie de Cloches, is open to the public (tel 02 33 61 00 56). Other museums in town are the Maison de l'Étain, with pewterwork (tel 02 33 51 05 08) and the Musée du Meuble Normand (tel 02 33 61 11 78), where you can admire a collection of traditional Norman furniture.

St-Vaast-la-Hougue's harbour has a dramatic history

ST-VAAST-LA-HOUGUE

This smart little harbour is famous for its oysters.

This modest port sits at the top of the Cotentin peninsula a half-hour drive from Cherbourg, and makes an ideal base for those wishing to explore offshore Normandy. At the tip of the natural southern causeway linking St-Vaast with the former island of La Hougue is the distinctive silhouette of architect Marquis de Vauban's fort and a mariners' chapel of local stone.

ISLAND OF LEGENDS

Just offshore lies St-Vaast's key attraction, the tiny island of Tatihou, which played its part in the town's most famous hours.

RATINGS	
Good for food	●●●●
Outdoor pursuits	●●●
Walkability	●●●

BASICS
🗺 197 P3 ℹ 1 place du Général de Gaulle, 50550 St-Vaast-la-Hougue, tel 02 33 23 19 32; Jul, Aug Mon–Sat 9.30–12.30, 2.30–6.30, Sun 2.30–6; Sep Mon–Sat 9.30–noon, 2.30–6; Oct–end Mar Mon–Sat 10–noon, 2.30–5; Apr–end Jun Mon–Sat 10–noon, 2.30–6, Sun 2.30–6 🚍 From Cherbourg 🚉 Valognes (18km/11miles) www.saint-vaast-reville.com

In 1346, the English King Edward II landed here to claim the French throne, then in 1692 King James II gathered a fleet at La Hougue in order to invade England and regain the crown from William and Mary. Overwhelmed first by the Anglo-Dutch fleet at Barfleur, then by treacherous currents at Cap de la Hague, James II's ships retreated, only to be set alight by the English off Tatihou. More recently, in an act of D-Day heroism, two local men, Charles Moncuit and Auguste Contamine, defied German gunfire and swam from St-Vaast to the island. There they raised the French flag to welcome the Allies, thus saving Tatihou from bombing.

Today, no more than 500 visitors a day may cross to Tatihou, due to strict environmental-protection rules. The trip can be made on foot at low tide or on an amphibious boat, the price of which is included in the admission charges to the island's fort and maritime heritage museum. The best time to visit St-Vaast is August for the international open-air music festival, with free fringe entertainment on the quayside and music in the port bars until late.

The former pirate haunts of the St-Marcouf islands, l'Ile de Terre and l'Ile du Large are now home to thousands of gulls, cormorants and herons, perching on derelict military buildings. During summer months, local fishermen and lifeboat crews take visitors out to sea for a closer view of these uninhabited sea-bird sanctuaries.

Don't miss Maison Gosselin (▷ 114) is a famed Norman grocer.

ORNE

This greenest of Normandy's hinterlands is the kingdom of the horse. It is a countryside of rich woodland, manor houses and noble families. The legacy of this aristocratic history is a province of large estates and equestrian centres, such as the royal stud farm of Haras National du Pin. The ciders, perries and Calvados brandies produced here are listed in the national register of *Sites Remarquables du Goût* (Areas of Outstanding Taste).

MAJOR SIGHTS

Market day in Argentan in front of the church of St-Germain

Copper bottomed: pots and pans in the kitchens of Château de Carrouges prove how seriously the French take cuisine

ALENÇON

✚ 204 T9 🚻 Maison d'Ozé, place de la Magdeleine, 61000 Alençon, tel 02 33 80 66 33; Jul, Aug Mon–Sat 9.30–7, Sun, public holidays 10–12.30, 3–6.30; Apr– end Jun, Sep Mon–Sat 9.30–noon, 2–6.30; Oct–end Mar Mon–Sat 9.30–noon, 2–6 🚉 Alençon
www.paysdalencontourisme.com

Normandy's southern gateway is a handsome old market town, the heart of the region's lace-making industry. Royal laceworks were introduced here in the 17th century by Jean Baptiste Colbert, King Louis XIV's finance minister. A museum, the Musée des Beaux-Arts et de la Dentelle (tel 02 33 32 40 07; Jul, Aug daily 10–noon, 2–6; Sep–end Jun Tue–Sun 10–noon, 2–6), is in a former Jesuit college in the Cour Carrée de la Dentelle.

There is lots to see in Alençon, including the 19th-century Halle au Blé (Corn Exchange), opposite the town hall. Its religious heritage includes St. Thérèse of Lisieux's birthplace at 50 rue St-Blaise and the Gothic Église Notre-Dame in place de la Magdeleine. The tourist office is in the Maison d'Ozé, a 16th-century house. Alençon's oldest building is the medieval Café des Sept Colonnes, in Grande Rue, a timbered building that was once home to the town's executioner.

Don't miss
The library of the Musée des Beaux-Arts et de la Dentelle is a former chapel, with a wooden boat-shaped roof.

A display of lacemaking in Alençon

ARGENTAN

✚ 204 T8 🚻 6 place du Marché, Chapelle St-Nicolas, 61205 Argentan, tel 02 33 67 12 48; Jul, Aug Mon, Sat 9–1, 2–7; Tue–Fri 9–7; Sep–end Jun Mon–Fri 9.30–12.30, 2–6, Sat 9.30–12.30, 1.30–5.30 🚉 Argentan
www.argentan.fr

This historic town on the banks of the river Orne has a royal and industrial heritage and makes a good base for touring the Suisse Normande area. Argentan was home to Eleanor of Aquitaine (c1122–1204), wife of both King Louis VII of France and then King Henry II of England, and was visited by her son Richard the Lionheart. Negotiations were held here in an attempt to reconcile Henry II with Archbishop Thomas Becket, but the talks failed and the king's knights departed from the town on their murderous mission to Canterbury Cathedral in 1170.

Between 1134 and 1618, the city was ringed by two walls with 20 turrets dominating the skyline; of these, today's visitors can still see the 12th-century keep and the Tour Marguerite. The 14th-century chateau now houses law courts, and the castle's Chapelle St-Nicolas is used as the tourist office. In the 18th century, the town was an administrative headquarters for the region and a home to nobility. After the French Revolution Argentan was able to maintain its influence, as its riverside location and the advent of the railways made it a key industrial centre during the 19th and 20th centuries.

CHÂTEAU DE CARROUGES

✚ 204 T9 • 61320 Carrouges ☎ 02 33 27 20 32 🕐 Mid-Jun–end Aug daily 9.30– noon, 2–6.30; Sep, Apr–mid-Jun daily 10–noon, 2–6; Oct–end Mar daily 10– noon, 2–4.30. Closed public holidays 🚻 Access for visitors with disabilities 🚉 From Alençon, follow the D112 and N12 towards Domfront, then take the D909 to Carrouges
www.monum.fr

This moated chateau, with its beautiful grounds, is the principal lure to Carrouges. For five centuries, the red-brick, granite and slate edifice was home to the Le Veneur family, until it was purchased by the State in 1936. Today's chateau evolved from the 14th to the 17th centuries. It is a testament to the age of gracious living, with furnishings dating from the Renaissance to Restoration periods. The Le Veneur family were lavish hosts—the 1473 guest list included King Louis XI of France. No less interesting to visitors is life below stairs; don't miss the impressive battery of copper pans and mixing bowls in the kitchens.

The well-maintained gardens and estate are set between the two forests of Écouves and Andaines, themselves containing some of the most dramatic landscapes in the area and forming part of the Normandy-Maine Natural Regional Park (▷ 53). The chateau's immaculately restored outbuildings house the park's offices and information centre. Of particular note in the grounds is the renovated miniature chateau, its conical towers serving as a flamboyant gatehouse to the estate.

Some claim that Carrouges castle is named for Karl le Rouge, whose blemished face bore witness to a confrontation between his jealous mother, unfaithful father (the lord of the manor) and a fairy temptress. A more likely origin of the name is a corruption of the word carrefour, meaning 'crossroads'.
Don't miss Tour the 11th-century church of Ste-Marguerite de Carrouges in the village.

High-pitched roofs and the plain, Norman façade highlight the Renaissance origins of the Château d'O. Inset, a detail of the exterior

CHÂTEAU D'O

Visit a moated fairy-tale castle that seems to float on water.

Home to a family that included some canny royal courtiers, this Gothic castle was built in 1484 on the site of an 11th-century fort for Jean d'O, chamberlain to France's King Charles VII. Jean's descendant François d'O (c1551–94) was something of a political chameleon, managing to stay in favour with each of the ever-changing power-houses of the period. Among his useful political appointments, he was finance adviser to King Henri III and, later, counsellor to King Henri IV. François's fickle alliances during the Wars of Religion led to accusations that he was siphoning off royal funds to pay for the chateau's west wing, added in 1590.

The chateau's pale gold and grey stone façade, decorated with red and black brick patterns, is reflected in the still waters of the moat. Carved on the south wing is the O family emblem, the ermine. The old gatehouse is adorned with elaborate carvings and François's west wing has an arcade and windows with ornate grilles. Although the castle is a private residence, the interior is open to the public. Its rooms are furnished in 18th-century style; highlights include a series of trompe l'oeil paintings of the Greek god Apollo and the nine muses, who are depicted as eagles in flight. These frescoes were discovered during renovation works.

RATINGS

Photo stops	●●●●
Cultural interest	●●●
Walkability	●●●●

BASICS

⊞ 204 T8 • 61570 Mortrée
☎ 02 33 28 88 71
⊙ Jul–Sep on selected days
🍴 La Ferme du Château
🚉 Surdon (6km/4 miles)
🚍 From Caen, follow the N158 towards Sées until you reach Mortrée
❓ Access for visitors with disabilities restricted to grounds only

Trompe l'oeil marbling in the Salon des Muses

IN THE GARDEN

The grounds may be upstaged by the majesty of the chateau itself, but they are stunning in their own right. Close to the house, a walkway across the moat leads to a tranquil courtyard and simple gardens give way to woodland. These walks from the main house lead past a chapel and an orangery, which often hosts temporary exhibitions. The wealth of the gardens does not lie in its lovely old rose bushes, but rather in its classic potager. Here are fruit trees and herb beds, as well as an impressive range of traditional vegetables, including almost 200 varieties of marrows, cucumbers and gourds. Visitors can dine in the former farm buildings, once home to estate workers and now housing a restaurant.

The church of Notre-Dame-sur-l'Eau in Domfront

Percheron horses paraded at an open day at Haras National du Pin. The breed originates in Normandy and was revived at the stud

CHÂTEAU DE SASSY

✚ 204 T8 • 61570 St-Christophe-le-Jajolet ☎ 02 33 35 32 66
◉ Mid-Jun–mid-Sep daily 10.30–12.30, 2–6; mid-Sep–end Sep, mid-Mar–mid-Jun Sat–Sun, public holidays 3–6
🚌 From Alençon

A sturdy red-brick castle, with tall chimneys and neat formal gardens, stands by the hamlet of St-Christophe-le-Jajolet in farming country outside Argentan (▷ 52). The hilltop house was built in 1760, and in 1850 the estate became home to the dukes of Audriffet-Pasquier. Gaston d'Audiffret, ex-mayor of St-Christophe-le-Jajolet and destined to become President of the French Senate, married the niece and heir of the Duc Pasquier, *préfet* (chief admin officer) of the Paris police, uniting the two distinguished families. Their descendants still live here today.

On display in the house are some fine tapestries and a lock of hair cut from the head of King Louis XVI before he went to the guillotine in 1792. This was presented to a member of the Pasquier family who had acted as the monarch's defence counsel during his trial. In 1925, the family commissioned garden restorer Achille Duchêne to design and build a classical terraced garden to replace the original vegetable garden in front of the chateau.

DOMFRONT

✚ 203 R8 ℹ 12 place de la Roirie, 61700 Domfront, tel 02 33 38 53 97; Tue–Fri 9.30–12.30, 2–6, Sat 9.30–12.30, 1.30–5.30 🚉 Flers (23km/14 miles), then bus to Domfront www.domfront.com

Unrivalled views over the landscape of Lower Normandy make pretty Domfront an essential stop on a clear day. Dominated by the remnants of an 11th-century fortress perched high on the hilltop overlooking the Varenne river, the town has clusters of typical stone and timber houses lining its cobbled streets. At the foot of the hill stands the church of Notre-Dame-sur-l'Eau, where Archbishop of Canterbury Thomas Becket is said to have celebrated Mass in 1166.

In spring and summer, brick-bordered flowerbeds, pots and hanging baskets justify Domfront's reputation as one of Normandy's Villes Fleuries (Flower Towns). The town is equally renowned for its produce—it lies in the heart of Camembert country, and also makes the brandy Calvados Domfrontais (from apples and pears), Pommeau (a fortified apple drink) and Poiré (perry). In spring, the white blossom of the pear orchards outside Domfront provides an unforgettable sight and scent.

Don't miss In early August the town stages a medieval fair, with music, markets and feasting.

HARAS NATIONAL DU PIN

✚ 204 U8 • 61310 Le Pin-au-Haras ☎ 02 33 36 68 68 ◉ Apr–mid-Oct daily 9.30–6; mid-Oct–end Mar daily 2–5 💶 Adults €4, students €2.50, children €1.50 ♿ Access to the stud for

visitors with disabilities 🚌 From Argentan, take the N26 to Nonant-le-Pin and then Le Haras du Pin

Known as the Versailles of the Horse, the Haras National du Pin is the oldest of 23 national stud farms, having been commissioned by King Louis XIV and built between 1715 and 1730. A palatial estate comprising 1,100ha (2,500 acres) of landscaped grounds adorned with imposing buildings is home to 10 breeds of thoroughbreds. Some 60 stallions live on the estate from July to February, with 20 in residence year-round.

The best day to visit is a Thursday between June and September, when each afternoon the stallions and horse-drawn carriages are seen in the main courtyard during the musical parade. Also on Thursdays and during school holidays, the chateau itself opens its galleries of tapestries, paintings and period furniture to the public. Stable, tack-room and forge tours include displays of traditional skills and crafts, while the Bergerie racecourse sees meetings in September and October and is the setting for a three-day event in spring.

Not all local legends involve heroes with four legs. Alphonsine Plessis, on whose life the heroines of Alexandre Dumas's *La Dame aux Camélias* and Giuseppe Verdi's *La Traviata* were based, was born at Nonant-le-Pin nearby in 1824. At Gacé, meanwhile, you can visit a permanent exhibition celebrating legendary stars, from Greta Garbo to Maria Callas, who have played the role of Alphonsine on stage and screen.

A gilded horse head decorates the wrought-iron gates of the Haras National du Pin stud, France's top horse breeder

Bridge over the river Sarthe: St-Céneri-le-Gérei, population 120, in the Alpes Mancelles region, is one of the prettiest villages in France

PARC NATUREL RÉGIONAL NORMANDIE-MAINE

This vast natural park has hiking, climbing and canoeing opportunities galore, plus there are picturesque villages to explore and gastronomic treats to try.

The huge Normandy-Maine Regional Natural Park is one of 32 such parks that preserve 10 per cent of France's countryside from the ravages of modern life. Straddling two regions, Normandy and the western Loire, the 134,000ha (331,000-acre) protected zone is home to 160,000 people as well as numerous winged and four-legged inhabitants. The forests of Écouves, Andaines, Perseigne and Sillé, covering 60,000ha (148,000 acres), shelter deer and boar.

Tributaries of the Orne river flow north through the park towards the English Channel, while the waters of the Sarthe, Mayenne, Egrenne and Varenne head west to the Atlantic. In some places these seem little more than brooks; elsewhere, such as at Villiers, the natural gorges are dramatic.

For height, head to the Mancelles Alps and the loftiest point in western France, Mont des Avaloirs (417m/1,368ft). On lower ground is the Passais country, lush farmland covered with apple and pear orchards, where the still of the night is punctuated by the sounds of hunting owls. Forest rangers take escorted groups on nature rambles, mushroom hunts and deerstalking expeditions here, and anglers have dozens of rivers and streams to discover.

A TASTE OF NORMANDY

With several of Normandy's 10 listed gourmet products hailing from Domfront, there is every reason to make a detour to the pretty hilltop town (▷ 54). The Maison de la Pomme et de la Poire (tel 02 33 59 56 22; Apr–end Sep daily 9.30–12.30, 2–7), a museum and orchard in Barenton, west of Domfront, promotes the history of local fruits and demonstrates techniques of making cider and the less common *poiré*. Visitors looking for themed breaks in the region, be they gastronomic or sporting, can choose to stay in any of the park's various towns, villages and hamlets. The spa towns of Bagnoles-de-l'Orne and belle époque Tessé-la-Madeleine both make excellent bases for exploring the park, as do Alençon (▷ 52), Sées (▷ 56), Carrouges (▷ 52), La Ferté-Macé and Domfront (▷ 54).

RATINGS

Activities	●●●○
Good for kids	●●●○
Photo stops	●●●○

BASICS

✚ 203 R8 ℹ Maison du Parc, 61320 Carrouges, tel 02 33 81 75 75; Mon–Fri 9–noon, 2–6
www.parc-naturel-normandie-maine.fr
• A comprehensive French site with excellent listings of events and sites, and even a quiz

TIP

● The Château de Carrouges (▷ 52), in Carrouges village, is home to the park information centre.

Walk up an appetite for the tasty specialities of the region

Knights of the Black Sausage roam Mortagne-au-Perche

Mind the edge: the Roche d'Oëtre rocky outcrop, where the ground can be slippery and the winds strong in winter

MORTAGNE-AU-PERCHE

➕ 205 V9 ℹ️ La Halle au Grains, 61400 Mortagne-au-Perche, tel 02 33 85 11 18; mid–May–Oct Tue–Sat 9.30–12.30, 2.30–6 ; mid–Jun–mid–Sep Mon 10–12.30, 2.30–6, Sun 10–12.30; Oct–mid–May Tue–Sat 10–12.30, 3–6 🚌 Alençon www.cdc-mortagne-au-perche.com

This slumbering hilltop town of sausages and sundials was once a regional capital. But since the province of Perche, established in 1114, was abolished after the French Revolution, Mortagne has had little need for civil servants. Instead, this fortified town now spends its energies on gastronomy, particularly on producing *boudin*. Up to 5km (3 miles) of the black sausage are consumed at the annual Festival du Boudin Noir held in March, attended by the world's leading pork butchers, when new members are inducted into the Brotherhood of the Knights of the Black Sausage. The Saturday morning farmers' market is the best place to find both *boudin* and local ciders.

Mortagne's streets are lined with 18th-century townhouses, including several elegant hotels along the rue St-Croix. Look out for the palatial home of the local tax collector. The first floor of the Maison des Comtes du Perche, on rue de la Porte St-Denis, is a museum (tel 02 33 25 25 87; Tue–Sat 3–6) devoted to the philosopher Alain (1868–1951).

The peaceful cloisters of the 16th-century hospital and the 13th-century crypt of St. André have been restored. The town also has two dozen sundials. In the public gardens behind the town hall is a reminder that this is a region of fine bloodstock. The equestrian statue here is of a local Percheron horse.

Don't miss On the first weekend of September, Mortagne holds an annual horse fair. The August donkey festival is biennial.

ROCHE D'OËTRE

➕ 203 S7

The high point of a drive through Suisse Normande, the Roche d'Oëtre is a 118m (387ft) rock face with unrivalled views over the Orne valley and the Rouvre gorge. From the road, take a signposted track to the cliff top. An observation point indicates the landmarks to be seen. But there is no barrier, so keep well back from the edge. Stop off at nearby Pont d'Ouilly to visit St. Roch chapel, scene of the St. Roch pardon ceremonies in August. The church is decorated with frescoes of the saint's life.

SÉES

➕ 204 U8 ℹ️ Place du Général de Gaulle, 61500 Sées, tel 02 33 28 74 79; Jun–end Sep Mon–Sat 9.30–12.30, 2–6; Oct–end May Mon 2–6, Tue–Fri 9.30–12.30, 2.30–6, Sat 9–1 🚌 From Alençon

A major religious centre on the banks of the river Orne, Sées is famous for its magnificent Gothic cathedral (daily 9–7). In AD400, St. Latuin became the first Bishop of Sées, although the cathedral that stands today, a blend of both Norman and Île-de-France Gothic styles, was constructed in the 13th and 14th centuries. With much of the original stained glass intact, the transept is bathed in light, which, along with its music, has been a hallmark of Sées. On Fridays and Saturdays in July and August, enjoy the celebrated *son et lumière* show. In summer, the building's exterior, with its 16th-century buttresses and spires, is illuminated. Musical entertainment is held on the Orne's riverbanks on Sundays in August.

The great religious heritage of Sées extends beyond the cathedral. Former 14th–18th-century canonical lodgings house the Musée Départementale d'Art Religieux (tel 02 33 81 23 00;

Jul–end Sep Wed–Mon 10–6), a collection that includes paintings, sculptures and religious regalia.

VIMOUTIERS

➕ 204 U7 ℹ️ 21 place de Mackau, 61120 Vimoutiers, tel 02 33 39 30 29; Apr–end Oct Tue–Sat 9–noon, Sun 10–noon, 2.30–6, Mon 2–6; Nov–Mar Mon 2–5.30, Tue–Sat 10–12, 2–5.30 🚉 Lisieux (30km/19 miles)

Vimoutiers hosts an apple fair on the third weekend in October, but for most of the year the fruit is eclipsed by Normandy's most celebrated cheese. The Musée du Camembert (opening hours as for the tourist office) is the most important attraction here, and two statues in the town pay homage to the dairy tradition. One depicts the Normande breed of cow, while the other commemorates Marie Harel (1761–1812), who lived in the village of Camembert 5km (3 miles) away. Marie sheltered a priest during the Revolution, and in return for her kindness he gave her the monastic recipe for Camembert cheese. While you are in town, admire the stained-glass windows of the Église Notre-Dame and visit the 16th-century Maison de Charlotte Corday (not open to the public), home of the woman who, on 13 July 1793, assassinated Revolutionary leader Jean-Paul Marat in his bath.

Cheesemaker extraordinaire: a statue of Marie Harel in Vimoutiers

CALVADOS

Calvados is a land of both kings and farmers, where the Suisse Normande is bisected by fast-flowing rivers and the Pays d'Auge is characterised by ancient churches and half-timbered houses. Before the D-Day landings on 6 June 1944, this sleepy countryside remained unchanged for centuries. It was the home of William the Conqueror; today it is renowned for orchards and apple presses, which create ciders and the famous Calvados brandy.

MAJOR SIGHTS

RUE
THE DEVONSHIRE RÉGIMENT

ARROMANCHES-LES-BAINS

The countryside surrounding this peaceful holiday resort is still dominated by reminders of the 1944 D-Day landings.

British Prime Minister Winston Churchill and US President Franklin Roosevelt had been planning Operation Overlord, the Allied invasion of Normandy, for a year before D-Day itself and Arromanches was its hub. While this stretch of coast was not as well fortified as the most likely invasion point near Calais to the north, Gold Beach lacked a port large enough for the military equipment required. So, the Allies created portable harbours, one for the Americans at Omaha Beach, the other, Mulberry Harbour, to be installed overnight at Arromanches.

After dark on 5 June 1944, some 2,000 landing craft set sail from England, the fleet towing the harbours in small sections across the Channel. These temporary jetties were set up at right angles to the beach. From the cliff tops above the beach at Arromanches, visitors can see the remains of the harbour's vast arc, one of the most vivid images of the battle still in existence. Over a period of three months, 2.5 million troops and 4 million tonnes of equipment landed here.

RATINGS

Historic interest	● ● ● ●
Photo stops	● ● ●
Good for kids	● ● ●

BASICS

☐ 198 R4

🛈 2 rue du Mal Joffre, 14117 Arromanches-les-Bains, tel 02 31 22 36 45; daily 10–noon, 2–5; longer hours Jul–Aug; closed Sun in Dec, weekends in Jan

🚌 From Bayeux

www.arromanches.com • A basic website with good D-Day links

TIP

● Don't be put off by the garish advertisements for Arromanches 360, as the film is both powerful and effective.

Top: Arromanches, now a modest resort, was a centrepiece of the D-Day landings
Inset: there are local clues that British forces landed at Arromanches
Below: a field gun

MUSÉE DU DÉBARQUEMENT

✉ Place du 6 Juin, 14117 Arromanches-les-Bains ☎ 02 31 22 34 31 🕐 May–end Aug daily 9–7; Sep daily 9–6; Oct, Mar daily 9.30–12.30, 1.30–5.30; Nov, Dec, Feb daily 10–12.30, 1.30–5; Apr daily 9–12.30, 1.30–6. Closed 24, 25 and 31 Dec, Jan 💶 Adults €6.50, children €4.50
www.normandy1944.com

The official D-Day Landing Museum, on the beach site of the harbour itself, uses a bombardment of images to evoke the events of D-Day to forceful effect. It displays a model of the scene in 1944 and has a collection of personal memorabilia donated by soldiers who took part in the invasion. Photographs and film clips may also be seen.

ARROMANCHES 360

✉ Chemin du Calvaire, 14117 Arromanches-les-Bains ☎ 02 31 22 30 30 🕐 Jun–end Aug daily 9.40–6.40; Sep, Oct, Apr, May daily 10.10–5.40; Nov, Mar daily 10.10–5.10; Dec, Feb daily 10.10–4.40. Closed Jan 💶 Adults €4, children/seniors €3.50, under-10s and World War II veterans free
www.arromanches360.com

The circular cinema on the cliff top screens a powerful 20-minute, wordless, documentary, which is an excellent evocation of the day itself and a superb introduction to the story for older children. The experience helps them appreciate less animated exhibitions along the coast.

Even the grocer shop signs look good in Beuvron-en-Auge

Seeking shade: holidaymakers pitch striped tents on Cabourg's sandy beach, scene of the first topless sunbathing in France

, of Caen

BAYEUX

See pages 60–61.

BEUVRON-EN-AUGE

🔒 199 T5 ℹ️ 14 Les Halles, 14430 Beuvron-en-Auge, tel 02 31 39 59 14; Jul, Aug daily 10.30–1, 2–6.30; May Sat–Sun 10.30–1, 2–6.30. Out of season, contact the tourist office at rue Pasteur, 14340 Cambremer, tel 02 31 63 08 87 🚂 From Lisieux www.cambremer.com

Cited as one of the prettiest villages in France, Beuvron-en-Auge is probably Normandy's top photo opportunity. There are picturesque tableaux at every turn, the timbered houses brightened up with tubs of geraniums that crowd every windowsill and spare inch of pavement. The floral abundance reaches its peak in early May, when crowds flock to the annual geranium festival.

Between the timbering, gables and wattle and daub of the artists' cottages and the steep-roofed covered market, you will catch a glimpse of a spire or two, one the dainty steeple of the 17th-century Église St-Martin and the other belonging to the medieval chapel St-Michel de Clermont. Little remains of the ancient seat of the chateau of the dukes of Harcourt, but the village's 15th-century manor house is an impressive example of typical Pays d'Auge architecture. Despite Beuvron's chocolate-box prettiness, the authentic character of the region may still be found here, as the village is on the official cider route. Some 20 cider-makers offer tastings and visits to apple presses within an easy drive of the village. With so many towns closer to the coast blighted by wartime bombing, Beuvron is an unscathed reminder of the beauty of Camembert and Calvados country and of the traditional rural way of life.

CABOURG

🔒 198 T5 ℹ️ Jardins du Casino, 14390 Cabourg, tel 02 31 91 20 00; Jul, Aug daily 9.30–7; school holidays Sep–end Jun Mon–Sat 9.30–12.30, 2–6, Sun 10–noon, 2–6; school terms Sep–end Jun Mon–Sat 9.30–noon, 2–5.30, Sun 10–noon, 2–4. Closed Tue Nov–end Mar 🚂 From Caen 🚂 From Lisieux in peak season www.cabourg.net

Gamblers, golfers, philosophers and exhibitionists changed a fishing port from a backwater to a haunt of the rich and famous when Cabourg became a playground of Parisians in the 1850s. In 1853, lawyer Henri Durand-Morimbau, in partnership with local architect Paul Leroux, turned a sleepy harbour of sand dunes and fishing boats into the resort of Cabourg-les-Bains. Its original casino and Grand Hôtel (▷ 169) were joined by a second casino and 2,500-seat theatre, and by 1884 the railway line from Paris had been extended to Cabourg and neighbouring Dives (▷ 69) and Normandy's new seaside towns were linked by a waterfront tramway from Deauville (▷ 68). In the early 20th century, new golf courses and luxury summer homes gave Cabourg a reputation for exclusivity. French President Raymond Poincaré (1860–1934) came here to unwind and automobile tycoon Louis Renault (1877–1944) found it a haven from the world of business. Most famously, novelist Marcel Proust (1871–1922) fictionalised the resort as Balbec in *À la Recherche des Temps Perdu*, where he compared watching the wealthy hotel guests dining in restaurant windows to an aquarium.

In World War II, the gentility of the grand buildings was shattered when the Nazis took over much of town and established brothels for officers and soldiers. One former bordello became a

A bust of Marcel Proust in Cabourg's Grand Hotel

girls' school after the Liberation. Post-war saw the jet set returning in the 1950s and *chanteuse* Edith Piaf topping the bill at the casino's stage. In the following decade, the pioneering spirit saw France's first topless sunbathing. Today, Cabourg's casino still attracts high rollers, with movie buffs hitting town for the summer film festival.

CAEN

See pages 62–63.

CANAPVILLE

🔒 199 U5 ℹ️ Place de la Mairie, 14804 Deauville, tel 02 31 14 40 00; Jul–mid-Sep Mon–Sat 9–7, Sun 10–1, 3–6; mid-Sep–end Jun Mon–Sat 9–12.30, 2–6.30, Sun 10–1, 2–5 🚂 From Lisieux

Nestling in an unlikely setting between the peaceful river Toques and a busy road is Canapville's Manoir des Evêques de Lisieux (tel 02 31 65 24 75; Jul, Aug Wed–Mon 2–7), once the country seat of the bishops of Lisieux's diocese (▷ 69). A smart timber-framed building dating back to the 13th century and decorated in the Pays d'Auge style during the 15th century, the manor house is notable for its tiled roof and some interesting woodcarvings, including a bishop's head on the gatepost. Inside, the ground-floor rooms are furnished in 18th-century style and there are displays of Chinese porcelain. Visitors can walk through the gardens, stopping off at the apple store and traditional cider press.

Bayeux

The world's most famous piece of embroidery, the 11th-century tapestry depicting the Battle of Hastings, lives in this medieval town.

Bayeux's war cemetery and the town's copper-domed cathedral

Lighting up: the cathedral's huge stained-glass window

Bayeux, with shops and cafés, offers more than just a tapestry

Clean streets, timbered buildings and the gentle sound of watermills in the medieval quarter make Bayeux a welcome diversion on the Battle of Normandy route. The 11th–15th-century cathedral (Jul–end Sep daily 8.30–7; Oct–end Jun daily 8.30–6), with its predominantly 13th-century Gothic architecture, sports a carved fresco over the south entrance depicting the murder of Archbishop Thomas Becket in Canterbury in 1170 by soldiers of England's King Henry II. The cathedral was the original home to the Bayeux Tapestry, which is now housed in its own building nearby (see below).

The principal lure of Bayeux is, of course, its tapestry, but the place has more recent historical significance, being the first town liberated from German occupation after D-Day. The Musée Mémorial de la Bataille de Normandie (tel 02 31 51 46 90; mid-May–end Sep daily 9.30–6.30) focuses on the 1944 battle. Bayeux's less violent heritage is displayed in the beautifully timbered and gabled Hôtel du Doyen (tel 02 31 92 14 21; mid-May–Sep daily 9.30–6.30), where you can see an ever-changing programme of art, porcelain and lace-making exhibitions.

BAYEUX TAPESTRY

✉ Centre Guillaume le Conquérant, 13 bis rue de Nesmond ☎ 02 31 51 28 28
🕐 May–end Aug daily 9–7; Sep, Oct, mid-Mar–end Apr daily 9–6.30; Nov–mid-Mar daily 9.30–12.30, 2–6; closed second week of Jan 💶 Adults €7.50, children (10–18) €3, under-10s free

The tapestry, measuring 70m (230ft) long but only 50cm (20in) high, is a masterpiece of political propaganda and cartoon storytelling and was commissioned by William the Conqueror's half-brother, Odo, Bishop of Bayeux. Although popular legend has it that William's wife, Queen Mathilde, was the creative force behind the work, it was in fact stitched by English nuns over a period of 10 years, between 1070 and 1080. The frame-by-frame drama of how William, Duke of Normandy, won the crown of England in 1066 is punctuated by Latin captions, and by dramatic scenes of Halley's comet, shipwrecks and banquets. Multilingual audio guides provide a running commentary and an exhibition explains the needlecraft. Arrive early to see the tapestry, since coach parties tend to crowd the place out from mid-morning onwards and spoil the view.

RATINGS

Historic interest	● ● ● ● ●
Specialist shopping	● ● ●
Eating out	● ● ●

BASICS

➕ 197 R5
ℹ Pont St-Jean, 14400 Bayeux, tel 02 31 51 28 28; Jun–Aug Mon–Sat 9–7, Sun 9–1, 2–6; Apr, May, Sep, Oct daily 9.30–12.30, 2–6; Nov–end Mar Mon–Sat 9.30–12.30, 2–5.30
🚆 From Caen
🚌 From Cherbourg and Caen
www.bayeux-tourism.com • A practical site about Bayeux and the D-Day beaches, with English-language option

TIP

● Your entry ticket to the tapestry also grants you free admission to the exhibitions at the Hôtel du Doyen.

Left: a medieval-themed parade through Bayeux

Caen

The base of William the Conqueror in the 11th century.
The setting for the Mémorial de Caen, a poignant peace museum.

*D-Day landmark: Pegasus
bridge in the Bassin St-Pierre*

*Above: William the Conqueror;
top, flags at the war memorial*

*Al fresco eating on rue du
Vaugeux in central Caen*

RATINGS	
Historic interest	●●●●
Photo stops	●●●
Shopping	●●●

BASICS

✚ 198 S5

🛈 Place St-Pierre, 14000 Caen, tel 02
31 27 14 14; Jul, Aug Mon–Sat 9–7, Sun
10–1, 2–5; Sep–end Jun Mon–Sat
9.30–1, 2–6, Sun 10–1

🚌 Caen

www.caen.fr/tourisme • A detailed website with English-language information
on events and sights

TIPS

● If you are pressed for time
when touring Normandy, but
do not want to miss out on the
Mémorial de Caen, stay on the
city's Périphérique ring road
and follow signs for the
museum rather than going into
the centre itself.

● The 24-hour city bus pass is
great value at €2.90 per person
or €4 for a family of up to five
people.

SEEING CAEN

Caen is a working city with a busy port on the river Orne and
several top-class attractions, these inevitably associated with
tumultuous moments in history. After the massive bombardments of 1944, it rebuilt itself as a business hub; sadly, the
unimaginative concrete estates that now circle the centre
threaten to overpower the older architecture there. It is, however,
worth making the effort to get past this modern ring to find the
city's historic core. Once there, a good network of buses and
trams links the sights, although most central attractions may be
visited on foot. An unexpected marina and the canal linking Caen
to Ouistreham (▷ 73) are surprising reminders that the seemingly landlocked city is in fact a seaport. As a result, the
restaurants of the Vaugeux quarter are known for their excellent
seafood dishes.

HIGHLIGHTS

MÉMORIAL DE CAEN

✉ Esplanade Eisenhower, 14000 Caen ☎ 02 31 06 06 44 🕐 Jul, Aug daily 9–8;
Sep, Oct, Feb–end Jun daily 9–7; Nov–end Jan 9–6. Closed two weeks in Jan
🚌 Town bus 2

The museum displays start with the post-World War I peace pledges
of 1919, and then move through newsreels and scenes of daily life to
the horrors of the Holocaust and Nazi occupation during World War II.
Multi-screen special effects recount the Battle of Normandy, and a
harrowing film, *Espérance* (*Hope*), hammers home the empty truth
of post-World War peace II, with painful images of conflicts in Europe,
Africa and the Middle East. Sections of the Berlin Wall mark out a
huge new Cold War exhibit, and an observatory reveals current
locations of global disorder and suffering.

MUSÉE DES BEAUX-ARTS

✉ Le Château, 14000 Caen ☎ 02 31 30 47 70 🕐 Wed–Mon 9.30–6 🚌 Town bus
2, 8, 9; tramway A, B to St-Pierre or Université

The restored ramparts of the 11th-century ducal castle, founded by
William the Conqueror in 1060, provide a pleasant walk and enclose

the Musée des Beaux-Arts, a splendid collection of works by Dutch, Italian and French artists from the Renaissance to the 20th century. Look out in particular for the street scene by Pieter Bruegel the Younger (1564–1638) and the 16th-century *Madonna and Child* triptych by Cima da Conegliano (c1459–1517).

MORE TO SEE
LE PLAN DE ROME
✉ Campus 1, Université de Caen, Esplanade de la Paix, 14032 Caen
☎ 02 31 56 62 00 🕐 Appointment only, Sep–Jun 🎟 Free

The glory that was Rome—at a scale of 1:400! This plaster model of the city of Rome at the time of Emperor Constantine (cAD280–337) measures

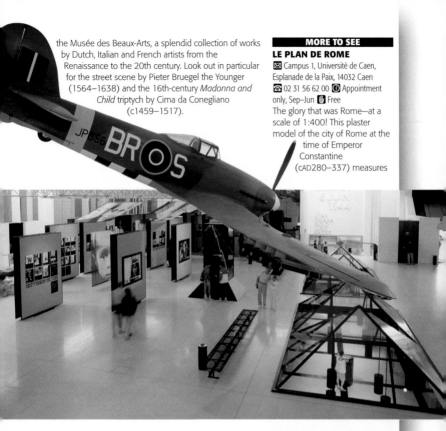

'Museum for Peace': an exhibition at the Mémorial de Caen

MUSÉE DE NORMANDIE
✉ Le Château, 14000 Caen ☎ 02 31 30 47 60 🕐 Wed–Mon 9.30–6. Closed 1 Jan, Easter Sunday, 1 May, 11 Nov, 25 Dec 🚌 Town bus 2, 8, 9; and tramway A, B to St-Pierre or Université

Also in the chateau is the Museum of Normandy, which fills in many of the gaps in the region's history between the better known dates of 1066 and 1944.

The castle is flanked by two abbeys: St-Étienne, attended by men and hence also called Abbaye-aux-Hommes; and La Trinité, for women and so also known as the Abbaye-aux-Dames.

ABBAYE ST-ÉTIENNE
✉ Esplanade Jean-Marie Louvel, 14000 Caen ☎ 02 31 30 42 81 🕐 Mon–Thu 8–6, Fri 8–5, Sat–Sun, public holidays 9.15–1, 2–5.45 🎟 Adults €2, under-18s free, students/seniors €1 Mon–Sat and free on Sun 🚌 Town bus 1, 2, 3, 4, 5, 8, 11, 14 and 18 🎧 Guided tours 9.30, 11, 2.30, 4

The so-called Men's Abbey (see above) was constructed in 1066 and restored during the 18th century. Inside, limed oak-panelled rooms are adorned with paintings from the 17th–19th centuries. You can see William the Conqueror's tomb at the Renaissance-Gothic abbey church of St-Étienne, although only his thigh bone remains after a raid by Huguenots in the 16th century. The abbey itself is now Caen's Hôtel de Ville (Town Hall).

ABBAYE DE LA TRINITÉ
✉ Place Reine Mathilde, 14000 Caen ☎ 02 31 06 98 98 🕐 Daily 2.30–4. Closed 1 Jan, 1 May, 25 Dec 🚌 Town bus 4

Today, the Women's Abbey (see above) also serves as a public building—it is now home to the Conseil Regional de Basse-

70sq m (750sq ft) and was built by architect Paul Bigot. A *son et lumière* presentation (€2.50) should appeal to the more theatrical historian.

COLLINE AUX OISEAUX
✉ Avenue Mountbatten

The 50th anniversary of D-Day in 1994 saw the municipal rubbish tip near the Mémorial de Caen reinvented as a glorious floral park, dedicated to peace. The 17ha (41-acre) site has terraced flower beds, a 15,000-bloom rose garden and paths accessible to wheelchair-users. Other gardens near the museum honour the US, the UK and Canada.

Stone gargoyles adorn the rooftops of Caen's older buildings

Normandy (Lower Normandy Regional Council). The severe Romanesque architecture remains typically Norman in design, and guided tours allow you to see the tomb of Mathilde, William the Conqueror's queen (1032–83), the grand staircase and the cloister. In good weather, the abbey grounds provide a memorable stroll. Formerly known as the Parc St-Louis, the Parc Michel d'Ornano is an elegant 18th-century garden adjoining the Abbaye de la Trinité, with the requisite dainty flowerbeds, shady avenues of lime trees, a sprawling cedar and a maze.

BACKGROUND

The city's importance and power derive from its role as the formal seat of William the Bastard, King of England and Duke of Normandy (c1027–87), and his cousin-bride, Mathilde. In addition to its ducal castle, Caen's twin abbeys were founded by the King and Queen to regain admission to the Church (the couple had been excommunicated following their incestuous marriage). When William left Normandy for the conquest of England in 1066, he appointed Mathilde as regent of the duchy and she governed from Caen in his stead as he established his new kingdom across the Channel. Mathilde was crowned Queen in 1068, but it was as Duchess of Normandy that she was buried in her favoured city of Caen in 1083.

Over the centuries, Caen's wealth grew from its merchant class, as trading allowed its leading citizens to prosper. The Hôtel d'Escoville, on place St-Pierre, is a beautiful mansion in the heart of town that was built in the 16th century by Caen merchant Nicolas le Valois d'Escoville; today, it is home to the tourist office and Artothèque contemporary art gallery.

Head for the shops and cafés of the Vaugeux district for food

William the Conqueror's tomb in the Abbaye St-Étienne

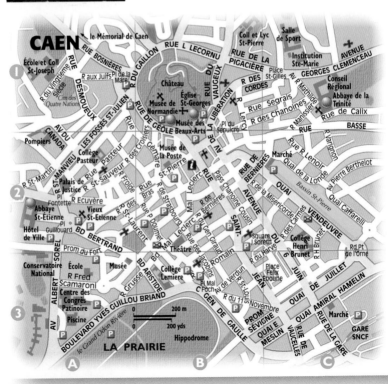

Balleroy's balloons: the study is decorated with hot-air balloons

CHÂTEAU DE BALLEROY

197 Q5 • 14490 Balleroy
02 31 21 60 61 Jul, Aug daily 10–6; Sep–mid-Oct, mid-Mar–end Jun Wed–Mon 10–6 Adults €6.86, children €5.35 From Bayeux
www.chateau-balleroy.com

This elegant, symmetrical pink and grey chateau was built by the legendary architect François Mansart for Jean de Choisy in 1636. Standing at the end of a long avenue of trees, it provides a spectacular backdrop to the hot-air balloon meetings that are held here. The ballooning connection dates to the castle's acquisition in 1970 by American publishing magnate, senator and record-breaking balloonist Malcolm Forbes, who established the world's first balloon museum in a converted stable block here. The museum covers the history of the sport from the Montgolfier brothers' pioneering flight in 1783 to the first successful crossing of the Atlantic in 1978.

Forbes continued a tradition of high-profile masters of Balleroy displaying their passions at the chateau. Count Albert de Balleroy (1828–72) was an acclaimed artist, known for his studies of hunting hounds. He famously shared a Paris studio with the Impressionist Édouard Manet, and was a friend of the poet Charles Baudelaire and painter Camille Pissarro. Albert de Balleroy's paintings adorn the oak-panelled Salon Louis XIII at the chateau. In contrast, the Salon d'Honneur is graced by a selection of royal portraits by Charles de la Fosse, Claude Vignon and Juste d'Egmont. But the chateau's true treasure is its remarkable cantilevered stairway, designed by Mansart himself.
Don't miss The remarkable two-storey 17th-century *colombier* (dovecote) was considered a status symbol in feudal Normandy.

Sleep well: luxurious bedrooms have tapestry and brocade

CHÂTEAU DE FONTAINE-HENRY

This splendid, privately owned chateau offers a glimpse of gracious living.

198 S5 • 14610 Fontaine Henry
02 31 80 00 42
Mid-Jun–mid-Sep Wed–Mon 2.30–6.30; mid-Sep–end Oct, Easter–mid-Jun Sat–Sun 2.30–6.30. Closed Nov–Easter
Adults €8, children (12–16) €5.50 From Caen
www.chateau-de-fontaine-henry.com

RATINGS			
Cultural interest	●	●	●
Historic interest	●	●	●
Photo stops	●	●	●

Magnificently emerging above the treetops in the unlikely setting of the Mue valley between Caen and the coast, the Château de Fontaine-Henry dominates its peaceful hamlet of stone houses. The original part of the castle was built for the influential Harcourt family at the end of the 15th century, and has carved Gothic stone walls. The later wing, added around 1550, is completely different in style. It's an extravagant palatial confection with an exaggerated soaring slate roof that overshadows even the pointed Renaissance spires. The neo-classical elements were added during the reign of France's King Henri II (1519–59).

A FINE COLLECTION
Today, the chateau provides an imposing setting for many high-profile exhibitions, and its permanent art collection is an attraction in its own right. Furniture dating from the Louis XV period to the 19th century and a beautiful selection of porcelain gathered from across Europe and the Far East is testament to generations of collectors. Paintings span 300 years of fine artists, with canvases from the Renaissance to the 19th century, including a study of nymphs and satyrs by French painter Nicolas Poussin (1594–1665).

The oldest building on the estate is the late medieval chapel, dating from the mid-13th century. It has an elegant square tower and small narrow windows in the lancet style. The nave was adapted to suit the fashions of the 16th century. Of note inside are the stone choir stalls lining the walls.

Unlike many chateaux open to the public by day, Fontaine-Henry also allows a few visitors to stay the night, albeit in the stable block. The former saddlery has been converted into a *gîte* (holiday home), sleeping up to four people.

Don't miss Musical tours of the castle, led by costumed guides, are held on Friday evenings in summer.

Messing about on the river Orne under Clécy's viaduct

Viewed across its moat, the Château St-Germain-de-Livet

CHÂTEAU ST-GERMAIN-DE-LIVET

Find the beauty of the Loire's chateaux in Normandy. This castle is a treasure trove of paintings and furniture.

🔳 199 U6 • 14100 St-Germain-de-Livet ☎ 02 31 31 00 03 🕐 Feb–end Sep, late Oct–mid-Dec Wed–Mon 10–12, 2–6. Closed early–late Oct, mid-Dec– end Jan 🎫 Adults €6.15, under-18s free 🚌 From Lisieux www.ville-lisieux.fr

RATINGS	
Cultural interest	● ● ●
Historical interest	● ●
Photo stops	● ● ●

TIPS

● It is forbidden to take pictures inside the chateau.
● Lisieux and other towns often hold exhibitions of art by Delacroix and Reisener, the last Romantics before the age of the Impressionists.

Just 7km (4 miles) from the town of Lisieux (▷ 69) in the heart of the Pays d'Auge is the Château de St-Germain-de-Livet, a veritable fairy-tale palace of round towers and colourful brick and stone walls reflected in the waters of a hidden tributary of the river Touques. With peacocks strutting on the lawns and ducks quacking in the river that wraps itself around the base of the towers, St-Germain-de-Livet is part pleasure palace, part fortress. The castle dates from the 15th century, its two remaining wings meeting at a turreted gatehouse. The earliest section is a traditional Norman half-timbered manor house, which connects with a romantic 16th-century patchwork of chequered white stone, green-glazed tiles and red bricks. Superbly renovated by Julien Pillaut in the 1950s, the building is the property of Lisieux town.

The first room you come to is the grand Salle des Gardes, which is in the oldest part of the castle and is dominated by an enormous fireplace. The Louis XIII and Louis XIV chairs here are among the earliest items of the furniture collection, but the main attraction in this first room are the frescoes depicting chivalric tableaux, slightly damaged, but redolent of the room's history.

ARTISTIC COUSINS

You will see furniture from the Louis XV and Louis XVI periods and an 18th-century sedan chair as you walk through the chateau. On the first floor are reminders of St-Germain-de-Livet's association with the arts: Caricatures and a painted screen here are signed by the poster artist Leonetto Cappielo (1875–1942). Tiled salons lead to the castle's famous Chambre Delacroix, furnished with items bequeathed by the artist Eugène Delacroix (1798–1863) to his cousin Léon Reisener, the castle's owner in the 19th century.

CLÉCY

🔳 203 S7 🔳 Place du Tripot, 14570 Clécy, tel 02 31 69 79 95; Jul, Aug Mon–Sat 10–12.30, 2.30–6.30, Sun 10–12.30; early–mid-Sep, May, Jun Tue–Sat 10–12.30, 2.30–6.30, Sun 10–12.30; mid-Sep–Apr Tue–Fri 10–12.30, Sat 10–12.30, 2.30–5, Sun 10–12.30 www.suisse-normande.com

Clécy sits on the banks of the river Orne and is an easy drive from the outskirts of Caen (▷ 62–64). For visitors on a photo-opportunity tour through the improbably pretty Suisse Normande, this is a great spot to stop for lunch and then stroll off the effects of good food. Waterfront restaurants, *buvette* (refreshment) bars and picnic spots line the riverbanks near the Pont de Vay, with its fast mill race and houseboats, while high up in the town itself traditional inns are sheltered by storybook gables. Even the 19th-century church looks like an unlikely marriage between a dovecote and a collection of cuckoo clocks.

The Ecomuseé de l'Abeille, or Museum of Beekeeping (mid-Jun–mid-Sep Tue–Sun 3–6), provides the opportunity to taste honey flavoured by the local flora, while on the edge of town is the Musée du Chemin de Fer Miniature (Model Railway Museum, tel 02 31 69 07 13; Jul, Aug daily 10–noon, 2–6.30; Sep Tue–Sun 10–noon, 2–6; Oct Sun 2–5; Mar–Easter Sun 2–5.30; Easter–end Jun daily 10–noon, 2–6. Closed Nov–end Feb), complete with a miniature Suisse Normande landscape through which the tiny trains travel. Discover paintings of the local area by Impressionist André Hardy (1897–1986) at the Musée Hardy (tel 02 31 69 79 95; Jul, Aug Mon–Sat 10–12.30, 2.30–6.30, Sun 10–12.30; early Sep–mid-Sep, Apr Tue–Fri 10–12.30, Sat 10–12.30, 2.30–5;

Steam power: the model railway museum at Clecy

May–mid-Sep Tue–Sat 10–12.30, 2.30–6.30, Sun 10–12.30). To experience these very views, hike through the hills on well-marked paths to such popular lookouts as the Pain de Sucre, with its vistas across the Orne valley.

CRÈVECOEUR-EN-AUGE

➕ 199 T6 ℹ️ 11 rue d'Alençon, 14100 Lisieux, tel 02 31 48 18 10; mid-Jun–end Sep Mon–Sat 8.30–6.30, Sun 10–12.30, 2–5; Oct–mid-Jun Mon–Sat 8.30–noon, 1.30–6 🚉 Lisieux during school term www.chateau-de-crevecoeur.com

Like Beuvron (▷ 57), the village of Crèvecoeur is an essential element of any exploration of the beautiful Pays d'Auge hinterland of the Côte Fleurie. At the moated 15th-century Château de Crèvecoeur manor house (tel 02 31 63 02 45; Jul, Aug daily 11–7; Sep, Apr–end Jun daily 11–6; Oct Sun 2–6. Closed Nov–end Mar), you can see the remains of the original 11th-century keep, plus the 16th-century gatehouse and the 12th-century chapel, which in more recent times has been used as a farm building. Such a complete ensemble of seignorial buildings is unique in the region. Also make sure you see the lovely timbered dovecote. During the summer season, the chateau stages exhibitions and re-enactments of scenes of medieval life, when visitors can dine with costumed characters from the manor's colourful past.

An unlikely additional exhibition, displayed next to the historic presentations, is centred on the oil industry and the work of the Schlumberger Foundation in sponsoring science education programmes. The Schlumberger brothers, both involved in the petrochemical industry in the first half of the 20th century, financed the restoration of the chateau's original timber-framed and stone buildings.

The design of the chateau's gardens is based on family history

CHÂTEAU DE VENDEUVRE

A museum of miscellany provides an insight into the intimacies of 18th-century Norman aristocratic life.

➕ 198 T6 • 14170 Vendeuvre
☎ 02 31 40 93 83 🅲 May–Sep daily 11–6; Apr, Oct–Nov, Sun and public holidays 2–6. Closed Dec–end Mar
💶 Adults €7–8, children €5–6.30 (price depends on number of sights visited) ☕ Tearoom on site www.vendeuvre.com

RATINGS			
Cultural interest	●	●	●
Historic interest	●	●	●
Good for kids	●	●	●

TIP

● Visitors in summer appreciate the refreshing splashes of the 'surprise' fountains in the water gardens. Two mazes are also worth exploring.

Vendeuvre lies on the river Dives between the Pays d'Auge and Suisse Normande. Building started on the chateau in 1750, when architect Jacques-François Blondel was commissioned to create a summer house for Alexandre de Vendeuvre. Today, this home is a cabinet of curiosities and provides a rare glimpse into the life of the Norman nobility of the 18th century. Listed as an historic monument, the airy house provides a backdrop for displays of the minutiae of country living. Visitors buy tickets allowing admission to as many of the attractions in the chateau and its grounds as they wish.

In the state bedroom, there are wig-stands, powders and potions as the room is set for a lady's preparation for an evening's entertainment. Across in the smoking room, you'll find the paraphernalia of tobacco and snuff, along with a pipe-smoking automaton. The Salon de Compagnie, meanwhile, is where ladies would play cards as their lap dogs reclined in elegant kennels.

CANINE COMFORT

Accommodation for four-legged companions is a speciality of the house. One of the most popular attractions is a miniature bed, complete with authentic hangings, made for the pet cat of King Louis XV's daughter. Dog kennels are a theme of mini-exhibitions, which display a large collection of royal and aristocratic dwellings and carrying cases for pampered pets.

The Musée du Mobilier Miniature (Museum of Furniture Miniatures), in the castle's orangery, showcases exquisite masterpieces, minuscule scale-model desks, chairs and even staircases. These tiny works of art were made by master craftsmen during their apprenticeships as cabinet makers and carpenters.

Don't miss The stone vaulted kitchens have an animated cook.

Famous neighbours: Hollywood stars on Deauville's promenade. Inset: crossing the finishing line at August's Grand Prix

DEAUVILLE

The fashionable summer playground of the rich and famous is the setting of an exclusive film festival.

This famous resort on Normandy's north coast is characterised by huge mock-Norman hotels and the weekend homes of rich Parisians. Popular pastimes here include looking stylish on the seafront, betting on the races, gambling at the casino and taking in a cabaret show. If it is all very artificial, then that is the point—the resort is essentially an upmarket beach party.

It is hard to imagine that glittering Deauville is something of a newcomer to the holiday business. Until 1910, neighbouring Trouville (▷ 75) was the glamorous watering hole of choice for Parisians, then Eugène Conuché built a rival casino and racecourse at Deauville. Suddenly, Deauville became the chic place to play and to stay. It was here in 1916 that the former musical hall artiste and companion to an English aristocrat, Gabrielle 'Coco' Chanel, reinvented herself as a couturière. She created her first trademark jersey dress from traditional Normandy fishermen's sweaters.

THE SEASON
Deauville comes alive in July and August, when the season begins with the 'Swing In' jazz festival and continues with a summer of horse racing. The season ends with the American Film Festival in September, which—as those in the know will tell you—is far more glamorous than Cannes, since the stars wander around town and there are far fewer bodyguards and velvet ropes to keep ordinary people at bay. Don't visit too far out of season, since without bright sunshine and glittering glamour the place can feel very empty.

In summer, regular holidaymakers are offered a glimpse of the luxury lifestyle enjoyed by the wealthy greats of the past. The Villa Strassburger (tours Aug Wed, Thu afternoons), originally built for the Rothschild family, was bought in the 1920s by an American millionaire. The Ancien Presbytere and Vieille École (both 1730), next to the church at the top of the town, are also fine buildings, and are used as occasional exhibition venues by the tourist office.

Don't miss Beach huts on Deauville's boardwalk are inscribed with the names of Hollywood legends who have graced its promenade.

RATINGS

Good for food	●●●
Cultural interest (film festival)	●●●
Good for pampering	●●●●

BASICS

✚ 199 U5

🛈 Place de la Mairie, 14804 Deauville, tel 02 31 14 40 00; Jul–mid-Sep Mon–Sat 9–7, Sun 10–1, 3–6; mid-Sep–end Jun Mon–Sat 9–12.30, 2–6.30, Sun 10–1, 2–5

🚉 From Caen and Le Havre

🚌 From Lisieux in season

www.deauville.org • Site of the local tourist office, with information and tips in English

TIPS

● Deauville is very much a summer resort; out of season, there is little to do.
● Bring smart clothes with you, as the casino and race track are places to dress up and be seen.

Courtyard crafts at the antiques centre of Dives-sur-Mer

The view over Falaise's rooftops from the castle where William the Conqueror was conceived

DIVES-SUR-MER

🔳 198 T5 ⓘ Rue du Général de Gaulle, 14160 Dives-sur-Mer, tel 02 31 91 24 66; mid-Jun–mid-Sep Mon–Sat 10–noon, 2–6
www.dives-sur-mer.com

William the Conqueror is celebrated in this one-time river port, from which he set sail in 1066 for England. He endowed the town with a church, Notre-Dame, which was expanded over the next 400 years, and was known locally as the Église St-Sauveur, thanks to the story told in one of its stained-glass windows about a statue of Christ the Saviour found in the sea. Halles, the wooden market hall, was constructed by monks in order to claim rents from traders; a typical local market is held here every Saturday morning, with an extra midweek market taking place on Tuesdays in July and August.

From July to mid-September, guided tours leave the market halls at 5pm to visit other historic sites around Dives-sur-Mer. Among these is the Hostellerie Guillaume le Conquérant, a post house that was once favoured by a visit from French writer Madame de Sévigné (1626–98), and the 16th- and 17th-century Manoir du Bois Hibout. Bicycles may also be hired to explore the countryside outside the town, while less energetic visitors may prefer to visit the various craft shops and restaurants near the marina, known as the Village Guillaume le Conquérant.

FALAISE

🔳 204 T7
ⓘ Boulevard de la Libération, 14700 Falaise, tel 02 31 90 17 26; Jul, Aug Mon–Sat 9.30–12.30, 1.30–5.30, Sun 10–12, 3–5; Sep–end Jun Mon–Sat 9.30–12.30, 1.30–5.30
www.otsifalaise.com
www.chateau-guillaume-leconquerant.fr

The town of Falaise was largely destroyed during World War II, but the Château Guillaume le Conquérant remains, a crucial site in the history of Normandy and England (tel 02 31 41 61 44; Jul, Aug daily 10–7; Sep–end Dec, mid-Feb–end Jun 10–6. Closed Jan–mid-Feb). It was here that Duke Robert of Normandy had an assignation with Arlette, daughter of a local tanner, which resulted in the birth of his illegitimate son William the Conqueror in c1027. A history of controversy continues into the modern era. Today's debate rages over Bruno Decaris's contemporary restoration of the 12th-century keep and chapel and the 13th-century Tour Talbot in concrete and steel. The works incorporate a glass floor through which the foundations of the original castle may be seen, and a walk on the ramparts gives views of the Ante valley. Elsewhere in town, stop by the Hôtel Dieu hospital and old Fontaine d'Arlette.

The Musée Août 1944 (tel 02 31 90 37 19; Apr–mid-Nov 10–noon, 2–6) tells the story of the World War II fighting that took place around Falaise and has a model of Canadian soldiers liberating the town. A less sombre diversion is found at Musées des Automates on the boulevard de la Libération (tel 02 31 90 02 43; Apr–end Sep daily 10–12.30, 1.30–6; Oct–mid-Jan, mid-Feb–end Mar Mon–Sat 10–12.30, 2–6, Sun 2–6. Closed mid-Jan–mid-Feb). Children will enjoy the collection of clockwork figures and caricatures at this museum of animated department store window displays dating from the 1920s to the 1950s. Included here are mechanical tableaux of Christmas scenes, the Tour de France and fairylands that once graced the shop fronts of such Parisian institutions as the Galeries Lafayettes.

LISIEUX

🔳 199 U6 ⓘ 11 rue d'Alençon, 14100 Lisieux, tel 02 31 48 18 10; mid-Jun–end Sep Mon–Sat 8.30–6.30, Sun 10–12.30, 2–5; Oct–mid-Jun Mon–Sat 8.30–noon, 1.30–6 🚆 From Rouen 🚌 From Rouen and Évreux
www.lisieux-tourisme.com

Pilgrims flock here in summer to pay homage to St. Thérèse of Lisieux, whose touching autobiography proved particularly popular during the hard days of World War I. Born Thérèse Martin in 1873, she moved with her family to Lisieux at the age of four. Throughout her childhood she begged her father to allow her to enter the Carmelite convent with her sister; aged only 15, Thérèse received papal dispensation to do so.

Always a frail young woman, Thérèse developed tuberculosis in the draughty convent. She died in 1897, aged just 24, shortly after completing her memoirs, *History of a Soul*. She was canonised in 1925 and her relics are displayed in the Carmelite chapel. In summer, a mini-train shuttles visitors between the chapel, Thérèse's family home at Les Buissonnets, and the domed basilica of Ste-Thérèse.

Also in Lisieux is the Gothic cathedral of St-Pierre, which contains the tomb of Bishop Cauchon, who executed Joan of Arc in 1431; it is also said to be where Eleanor of Aquitaine married England's King Henry II in 1152. The town itself provides a pause for reflection during a drive through the surrounding countryside, which is divided by old hedgerows and dotted with timbered farms and venerable manor houses.
Don't miss On Saturday mornings (and Wednesdays too in summer) you can buy delicious cheeses and cider at the market.

THE SIGHTS

Honfleur

One of France's most attractive working ports is a familiar sight in art galleries across the world.

Enjoy the sights of handsome Honfleur from a café table

SEEING HONFLEUR

This much-painted fishing harbour has been captured on canvas by such famous artists as J. M. W. Turner (1775–1851) and local man Eugène Boudin (1824–98). Today, it continues to attract painters seeking seascape inspiration, as well as visitors in search of a seafood supper at the quayside. If you arrive by car, follow signs to one of the larger car parks (smaller parking areas will invariably be full up) and prepare to explore the improbably picturesque narrow streets and lively quaysides on foot. Temptation awaits at each corner, and the lures of the port and town, the antiques and art shops, the delicious fresh food and the ever-changing exhibitions make nonsense of any prepared itinerary.

RATINGS	
Cultural interest	● ● ● ○
Historic interest	● ● ● ○
Photo stops	● ● ● ● ●

BASICS

✚ 199 U4

🛈 Quai Lepaulmier, 14602 Honfleur, tel 02 31 89 23 30; Jul, Aug Mon–Sat 10–7, Sun 10–5; Sep–end Jun Mon–Sat 10–12.30, 2–6, Sun 10–5;

🚌 From Pont-l'Évêque

www.ot-honfleur.fr • In French and English; displays photos of the town and supplies practical information

TIP

● Unless you can visit out of season, arrive early to avoid the crowds of day-trippers.

HIGHLIGHTS

MUSÉE EUGÈNE BOUDIN

✉ Place Erik Satie, 14602 Honfleur ☎ 02 31 89 54 00 🅖 Mid-Mar–end Sep Wed–Mon 10–noon, 2–6; Oct– Dec, mid-Feb–mid-Mar Mon, Wed–Fri 2.30–5, Sat–Sun 10–noon, 2.30–5. Closed Jan–mid-Feb 🎫 Adults €5.20, children and students €3.70

Here, works by French Impressionist and local painter Eugène Boudin (1824–98) hang alongside pieces by Jean Baptiste Corot, Raoul Dufy and one of Boudin's student, Claude Monet.

Main picture: sitting on a dock at Honfleur watching the ships roll in
Below: French Impressionism at Musée Eugène Boudin

MAISONS SATIE

✉ Boulevard Charles V, 14602 Honfleur ☎ 02 31 89 11 11 🅖 May–end Sep Wed–Mon 10–7; Oct–end Dec, mid-Feb–end Apr Wed–Mon 11–6. Closed Jan–mid-Feb 🎫 Adults €5.10, children and students €3.60, under-10s free

This modern museum experience is less conventional than the Musée Eugène Boudin (see above), but it is highly stimulating. It cele-brates the life and work of another son of Honfleur, the eccentric composer and artist Erik Satie (1866–1925). Art and music join forces as you walk past surreal images while listening to Satie's music playing through headphones.

VIEUX BASSIN

Jean-Baptiste Colbert (1619–83), King Louis XIV's finance minister, commissioned the Vieux Bassin (Old Dock) in 1681, ordering the demolition of part of the ramparts to open Honfleur out to its harbour and so realise its full trading potential. The only remnant of those orig-inal town walls is the 16th-century Lieutenance, a quirky-looking building at the entrance to the harbour, adapted from the former Caen gateway of the medieval fortress. The building's name dates

CHAPELLE DE NOTRE-DAME DE GRÂCE

✉ Côte de Grâce, 14602 Honfleur
🕐 Jun–end Aug daily 8–8; Sep–end May daily 8–7

The original Romanesque chapel here was built around 1023 by Richard II, Duke of Normandy, but was destroyed by a landslide in 1575; townsfolk erected the present chapel in the early 17th century. Hilltop Notre-Dame is worth visiting for the scores of votive offerings, plaques, paintings and model ships donated by sailors and pilgrims. Among the worshippers who have stopped here to pray are Napoleon I, King Louis XIII, St. Thérèse of Lisieux (▷ 69) and explorer Samuel de Champlain. At Whitsun, the sailors of Honfleur return here for their annual pilgrimage.

Ready for action: fishing boats moored at St-Étienne quay

from its original role as the home of the king's lieutenant. The arms of Honfleur are carved on the watch turrets and a statue of Our Lady of the Harbour perches in a niche. To prevent boats going in or out of the Vieux Bassin at night in order to avoid paying taxes, a chain was strung between the Lieutenance and a tower that once stood opposite the present bridge.

Tall, slate-fronted, oak-tiled and timber-framed buildings dating from the 16th to 18th centuries surround the Vieux Bassin. They may look alike but each is unique in size and shape. What they have in common is the strange fact that each has two ground floors, one opening onto the quayside (today usually housing ship's chandlers, art galleries or restaurants), and a second, halfway up the house, opening onto a street on the hill behind the port. Thus each building boasts two different householders.

The 15th-century church of Ste-Catherine, constructed by shipbuilders, has an 18th-century bell tower across the square as a precaution against fire. Buskers and craft stalls inhabit the pedestrian-only streets nearby.

The town's famous salt warehouses, in the rue de la Ville, were among the greatest salt stores of the region (see Background). Built

in 1670 under the authority of Colbert, they had walls of stone taken from the ramparts and were topped with remarkable oak roofs. Originally, Honfleur had three stores that could hold 10,000 tonnes of salt, but one was destroyed by fire in 1892. The remaining two warehouses are listed buildings owned by the town and are now used as venues for concerts and exhibitions, when visitors have the opportunity to admire their magnificent oak beams.

BACKGROUND

Honfleur's two greatest gifts to the world were Canada and the Impressionist movement. If was from this port that Jean Denis set off to discover the St. Lawrence river estuary in 1506, and Samuel de Champlain departed a century later to found Canada. It was also under these Normandy skies that the 19th-century artist Eugène Boudin experimented with painting weather conditions, later passing on his skills to Claude Monet and the Impressionists.

Although its name evokes images of great adventurers and sailors, Honfleur's wealth was actually built on salt. For generations, fishing had been a local affair, with daily catches delivered to the seaside. However, as fishermen explored territories further afield, they needed a method of keeping the fish fresh on the return trip to France. From the 16th century, salt was used to preserve the massive hauls of cod brought back from Newfoundland and the St. Lawrence estuary, and as such it became a precious commodity and the basis of Honfleur's prosperity.

Music on the move: an old-fashioned organ grinder on the streets of Honfleur

The Allies landed here on D-Day at Sword Beach in Ouistreham, to be met by gun placements such as this one

The big cheese: Pont l'Évêque is famous for its soft cheese

ORBEC

⊞ 199 V6 🚹 6 rue Grande, 14290 Orbec, tel 02 31 32 56 68; Jul, Aug Mon–Sat 9.30–12.30, 2–7, Sun 10–1; Sep–end Jun Mon–Fri 9.30–12.30, 2.30–5.30, Sat 10–12.30, 3–5.30 🚌 From Lisieux www.mairie-orbec.fr

The fast-flowing river Orbiquet runs through Orbec in the valleys of the Pays d'Auge. The town, with its grand mansions and rows of attractive timber-fronted houses, owes its earliest wealth to the river, although the water-mills gave way to textile mills in the 19th century. The later indus-tries of cider- and cheese-making continue, and the town is home to the Lanquetot cheese-makers.

The 16th-century Vieux Manoir in rue Grande is now a municipal museum with paintings, ceramics and Pays d'Auge artefacts (tel 02 31 32 58 89). The town's Église Notre-Dame (daily) was origi-nally built in the 13th century and reconstructed in the 14th century after it was set ablaze by the English. A tower was added in the 15th century and a century later the building was remodelled in Renaissance style. Finally, in the 19th century, the church was given a Gothic Revival makeover. **Don't miss** In school holidays, Orbec stages pottery classes for children (call the tourist office).

OUISTREHAM

⊞ 198 S5 🚹 Jardins du Casino, 14150 Ouistreham, tel 02 31 97 18 63; Jul, Aug daily 10–1, 2–7; Sep, Apr–end Jun daily 10–12.30, 2–6.30; Oct–end Mar Mon–Sat 10–12.30, 2.30–6, Sun 10–12.30 🚌 From Caen www.ville-ouistreham.fr

Best known as Caen's ferry port, Ouistreham also boasts the tradi-tional lures of a seaside town: the beach resort of Riva Bella has a casino and marina. Ouistreham was the site of D-Day's Sword Beach and is an obvious starting point for D-Day driving tours. The Musée de Débarquement no. 4 Commando, opposite the casino, contains many military exhibits (tel 02 31 96 63 10; Mar–end Oct daily 10.30–6), while the Musée du Mur de l'Atlantique is housed in a German bunker (tel 02 31 97 28 69; Apr–end Sep daily 9–7; Feb–mid-Nov daily 10–6; closed mid-Nov–Jan).

MUSÉE DU N°4 COMMANDO

OUISTREHAM · RIVA-BELLA

Riva Bella's Commando museum

One survivor of the Battle of Normandy is the 11th-century Église St-Samson (daily 8.30–7). The church was built by Norman lords and served not only as a religious sanctuary but also as an army lookout post. Ouistreham's lighthouse (Jul, Aug Fri–Sun 3–6) is another vantage point.

POINTE DU HOC

⊞ 197 Q4 🚹 118 rue A. Briand, 14450 Grandcamp-Maisy, tel 02 31 22 62 44; Tue–Sat 10–noon, 2–6

This 30m (100ft) cliff symbolises D-Day's challenge. High above the American landing point at Omaha Beach, the German look-out point, its five artillery guns defended by the 352nd Infantry Division, was bombarded to allow US Rangers to climb the steep rocks of the Cotentin head-land. The legacy of the Battle of Normandy is to be found in craters and chunks of concrete, now reclaimed by the landscape itself. From the viewing station and memorial, the vast theatre of the Omaha and Utah beach campaigns may be seen. The story of the assault and of how the Rangers held out against the odds is retold at the Musée des Rangers, 5km (3 miles) west of the Pointe du Hoc at Grandcamp-Maisy (tel 02 31 92 33 51; daily 9.30–1, 2.30–6.30; closed Mon morning and Dec–Jan).

PONT-L'ÉVÊQUE

⊞ 199 U5 🚹 16 bis, rue St-Michel, 14130 Pont-l'Évêque, tel 02 31 64 12 77; Jul, Aug Mon–Sat 10–1, 2.30–6.30, Sun 10–2; Sep–end Feb Mon–Sat 10.30–12.30, 3–5; Mar–end Jun 10–12.30, 2.30–5.30. Easter, Whitsun 10–2 🚌 Lisieux www.pontleveque.com

The town named after a bishop's bridge is famous for its creamy cheese, first produced here in the 12th century. Locally made Calvados brandy is another source of income for the town. Its timber-framed buildings typify the Pays d'Auge; the 17th-century Hôtel Montpensier, with its painted frontage (now a library), and the brick and stone Hôtel de Brilly, today's town hall, are out-standing examples. At the Musée du Calvados et des Métiers Anciens (tel 02 31 64 30 31; Easter–mid-Nov daily 10–12.30, 2–6.30), learn about distilling. The Musée de la Belle Époque et de l'Automobile (tel 02 31 65 05 02; Feb–mid-Nov daily 9–noon, 2–6), at Château de Betteville south of town, has a collection of more than 100 classic cars. Pont-l'Évêque's flam-boyant Église St-Michel houses Franco-Prussian war memorials. May is the best time to visit, when there is a vintage car rally and a national cheese fair. **Don't miss** A farmer's market is held on Sundays June to October.

The market is the heart of the community of Les Halles. Traders sit down for a beer or Calvados after the morning's business is done

Trimmed lawns in the grounds of Château d'Harcourt

x

THE SIGHTS

ST-PIERRE-SUR-DIVES

✚ 199 T6　ℹ Rue St-Benoist, 14170 St-Pierre-sur-Dives, tel 02 31 20 97 90; Jul, Aug Mon–Sat 9.30–12.30, 1–5.30, Sun 10–noon; Sep–end Jun Mon–Sat 9.30–12.30, 1–5.30
www.mairie-saint-pierre-sur-dives.fr

Gastronomic tradition is as much a part of this typical country town as the stones of its abbey church, and never more so than on Monday mornings when the rafters of Les Halles, the market hall, echo to the sounds

Traditional joinery in the market hall of St-Pierre-sur-Dives

of poultry and traders vying for attention. This beamed barn of a market building is the very hub of the community and traders sell their chickens and ducks, cheese and pains d'épices gingerbread cakes until lunchtime. The present market is a reconstruction of the 13th-century building, which was bombed during World War II. The renovations relied on traditional methods, not one nail was used; instead, the cavernous temple to consumerism and community is held together with 290,000 wooden dowels. The market hall is open to visitors daily from Easter to the end of October, and on the first Sunday of each month throughout the year it hosts an antiques market.

Jardin Conservatoire des Fleurs et des Légumes du Pays d'Auge, is a 600sq m (6,500sq ft) garden preserving flowers and vegetables traditionally grown throughout the Pays d'Auge. While the colourful plants and shrubs from the windowboxes of the region might be more photogenic, the diversity of cabbages, broccolis and asparagus here is nothing short of impressive.

St-Pierre's Benedictine abbey is one of the best-preserved ensembles of monastic buildings in Normandy. The abbey church dates from the 11th, 13th and 18th centuries, and has a meridian line carved across its nave that indicates the position of the sun at noon. In a building that once formed part of the abbey, an exhibition of cheese-making is open to visitors (Mon–Sat). **Don't miss** The cloisters of the abbey are both tranquil and understated.

THURY-HARCOURT

✚ 203 S6　ℹ 2 place St-Sauveur, 14220 Thury-Harcourt, tel 02 31 79 70 45; Jul, Aug Mon–Sat 10–12.30, 2.30–6.30, Sun 10–12.30; Sep, May, Jun Tue–Sat 10–12.30, 2.30–6.30, Sun 10–12.30; Oct–end Apr Mon 2.30–5, Tue–Fri 10–12.30, 2.30–5, Sat 10–12.30
🚌 From Caen
www.suisse-normande.com

Thury-Harcourt, the gateway to the Suisse Normande region, has a ruined, moated castle, the Château d'Harcourt, originally dating from the 18th century and set in a large park (tel 02 31 79 72 05; May–end Sep daily 2.30–6.30; Apr Sun 2.30–6.30). Two gatehouses with strange beehive-shaped roofs, one wing and a bricked-up façade are all that remain of the building, although a ruined chapel in the grounds may also be visited. The single reminder that this is modern Normandy, rather than some central European utopia, is the plaque on the park wall paying tribute to the British forces who fought in the area during World War II. In the town is the Romanesque Église St-Sauveur, with a 12th-century door and 15th-century nave.

VIRE

✚ 203 Q7　ℹ Square de la Résistance, 14500 Vire, tel 02 31 66 28 50; Jul, Aug Mon–Sat 9.30–6.30; Sep–end Jun Mon–Sat 9.30–12.15, 1.45–5.30 🚌 From Caen 🚌 From Granville and Argentan
www.vire-tourisme.com

Vire is a traffic bottleneck on a busy through road, but if you park your car and wander around town you will find a few treasures that survived wartime bombing. The most important of these old buildings is the Porte-Horloge clock tower on the place du 6 Juin. The original 13th-century fortified gateway to the town was capped by its belfry and turret in the 15th century and adorned with a clock in 1840. The building hosts summer exhibitions.

Not much remains of Vire's original fortifications, most of which were destroyed well before the Battle of Normandy. The town once had a castle, which played an important role in the Hundred Years War between France and England (1337–1453). In 1630, Cardinal Richelieu, chief minister to King Louis XIII, ordered the fortress to be razed to the ground; the sole surviving relic was the Norman keep, two sides of which still stand on the place du Château.

Notre-Dame church is an amalgam of styles, its Romanesque chapel having been reinterpreted in the Gothic style in the 13th century. In 1948, the church was restored following the inevitable damage of D-Day.

The 18th-century Hôtel-Dieu hospital on place Ste-Anne is now a museum of art and local traditions, including displays of Norman costume and crafts (tel 02 31 68 10 49). At nearby Vassy, a command post of the Knights Templar of Courval dates from 1140. You can view the privately owned manor house from the outside.

x

You can stretch your legs on the promenade of this seaside resort and, right, the town-centre cafés are perfect for a refreshing drink

TROUVILLE-SUR-MER

The classic 19th-century French seaside resort still offers beachfront fun, shopping and donkey races.

Well before Deauville became the haunt of the Parisian party set (▷ 68), it was Trouville, just across the estuary of the Touques river, that lured the well-to-do to the Côte Fleurie as seaside holidays first came into fashion. Landscape artist Charles Mozin 'discovered' the resort in 1825, and his works, exhibited in Paris, soon drew painters Claude Monet and Jean Baptiste Corot, and writers Alexandre Dumas and Gustave Flaubert, to the coast in search of artistic and literary inspiration. By the heyday of the Second Empire (1852–70), the promise of casinos and the seaside proved a magnet to the fashionable Paris set. Consequently, Trouville established itself as very much the destination of choice in those heady days and was dubbed the Reine des Plages (Queen of Beaches).

CONTEMPORARY LIFE

The Villa Montebello, one of many private houses of the period, is today home to a municipal museum housing art treasures of this golden age (tel 02 31 88 16 26; Apr–end Sep Wed–Mon 2–6.30). Many similar 19th-century seafront villas near the wooden promenade still claim prime position alongside the casino, aquarium and seafood restaurants.

If Trouville seems a little less glamorous than today's glitzier neighbour Deauville, it nonetheless has a year-round life, with its own community thriving even outside the peak tourist season. There is a working fishing port, and behind the livelier resort you will find attractive shopping streets; these two worlds collide at the daily fish market next to the port, itself a listed building. On Wednesday and Sunday mornings a bustling quayside market sells a range of regional foods. In May, the town holds a jazz festival, while July sees older traditions celebrated at the annual Fête de la Mer (Festival of the Sea), testament to Trouville's origins as a quiet fishing port.

RATINGS

Good for kids	●●○
Outdoor pursuits	●●●○
Walkability	●●○

BASICS

✚ 199 U4 🚹 32 quai Fernand Moureaux, 14360 Trouville-sur-Mer, tel 02 31 14 60 70; Jul, Aug Mon–Sat 9.30–7, Sun 10–4; Sep, Oct, Apr–end Jun Mon–Sat 9.30–noon, 2–6.30, Sun 10–1; Nov–end Mar Mon–Sat 9.30–noon, 1.30–6, Sun 10–1 🚊 From Lisieux and Caen 🚉 From Lisieux www.trouvillesurmer.org

TIP

● Come in August for donkey races on the beach (▷ 15).

Tents line Trouville's beach

EURE

Normandy's frontier with the kingdom of France was a key battleground between the French and English, and the countryside around is punctuated by fortresses and churches whose fortunes have been entwined with those of kings and power brokers. The area is laced with waterways whose own history is told by watermills and wash houses, painted by the 19th-century artists who followed Impressionist Claude Monet to Normandy.

MAJOR SIGHTS

A street lined with half-timbered town houses leads to the abbey.
Right: the Tour St-Nicholas, the abbey's only medieval building

ABBAYE DU BEC-HELLOUIN

This working abbey provides a haven of quiet reflection. It has been a historic seat of learning for 1,000 years.

The walled Abbey of Bec-Hellouin has the air of a venerable centre of learning, one whose history has been intertwined with that of England for a millennium. Some come for guided tours, others for academic research in the library, and the resident monks welcome travellers seeking a religious retreat. But even an hour spent in the tranquil grounds, with birdsong the only sound to be heard, is revitalising.

POLITICAL INFLUENCE

The abbey was founded in the Middle Ages as a place of learning, but it soon established itself as a major influence on politics. Lanfranc (c1005–89), an adviser to William the Conqueror and later Archbishop of Canterbury, taught here. The abbey continued to maintain strong links with England through the turbulent years surrounding the murder of Archbishop of Canterbury Thomas Becket in 1170, and even beyond King Henry VIII's break with Rome in the 16th century.

During the French Revolution, the monks were expelled, books and tapestries were looted and the 13th-century church and chapter house were demolished. Even the bells were melted down. In 1948, the state acquired the abbey, and monks returned the following year.

Today, a smart village street leads to the abbey grounds. The tall Tour St-Nicolas, the only surviving medieval building, is separate from the rest of the abbey, which sits in the Risle valley 45km (28 miles) southwest of Rouen. The original church no longer exists, and today's services are held in the newer 17th- and 18th-century buildings (visitors welcome; Matins 7am). The central cloisters, dating from the 17th century, remain a particularly spiritual place, while the waterside Cour de France garden is another location for reflection. Since the abbey remains a place of learning, the library is open to visitors only by prior arrangement with the abbey librarian (tel 02 32 43 72 64).

INSPIRED CREATIVITY

Unlike the cheeses and alcoholic drinks produced by other religious communities, the monks' workshop at Le Bec is famous for its stylish tableware. The plates, bowls and vases are on sale in the abbey shop. The workshop itself, Les Ateliers du Bec, is open to visitors (▷ 123).

RATINGS

Cultural interest	● ● ●
Historic interest	● ● ●
Specialist shopping	● ● ● ●

BASICS

✚ 206 W5 • 27800 Le Bec-Hellouin
☎ 02 32 43 72 60
🕐 Guided tours of interior: Wed–Mon 10–noon, 3–4. Grounds only: daily 8am–9pm. Les Ateliers du Bec: Mon–Sat 11–11.45, 2.45–5.45
💶 Adults €4, children €3.10, under-12s free
🚉 Brionne (7km/4.5 miles)
🍴 Restaurants in the village
♿ Access for visitors with disabilities: grounds accessible, one or two low steps to each of the buildings, toilets not wheelchair-friendly
🅿 Free parking in village centre
www.abbayedubec.com • A well-ordered and comprehensive French-language website with an online shop

TIPS

● Check out times of religious services before you visit—the shop is manned entirely by members of the monastic community, so it closes during prayers.
● When a coach party arrives, stay away from the buildings. The grounds are large enough to allow you to find tranquillity away from the crowds.
● The pretty village of Le Bec-Hellouin is worth a stroll.

Les Andelys

The legends and defences of Château Gaillard dominate this small settlement on the Seine. Richard the Lionheart of England may have put Les Andelys on the map, but painters and writers added an artistic flourish to its story.

Les Andelys hugs a river bend. Below: a statue of St-Sauveur

The church of St-Sauveur, built by Richard the Lionheart

Rays from the setting sun reflect off the river Seine

RATINGS

Historic interest	● ● ●
Cultural interest	● ● ●
Photo stops	● ● ● ●

BASICS

✚ 207 Y5

🛈 Rue Philippe Auguste, 27702 Les Andelys, tel 02 32 54 41 93; Jun–end Sep Mon–Fri 10–noon, 2–6, Sun 10–noon, 2–5; Oct–mid-Dec, Mar Mon–Fri 2–6, Sun 10–1; mid-Dec–end Dec, mid-Jan–end Feb Mon–Fri 2–6; Apr–end May Mon–Fri 10–noon, 2–6, Sun 10–1. Closed early Jan–mid-Jan

🚌 From Évreux (marked 'Les Andelys')

🚉 Gaillon Aubevoye (12km/8 miles)

www.ville-andelys.fr • A lively English-language site with gossipy historical notes

SEEING LES ANDELYS

Here are the ruins of one of the most important castles of the Middle Ages. The town itself was once a favourite haunt of artists and writers, such as Victor Hugo and Nicolas Poussin. Despite its rich artistic and industrial heritage, Les Andelys, midway between Paris and Rouen, and once a bordertown between France and England, remains for most visitors one of the final chapters in the romantic legend of Richard the Lionheart. He built Château Gaillard, which dominates the skyline. But Les Andelys has never been defined by war alone; for centuries it was a centre of culture and religious activity. Andely le Jeune, today dubbed Petit Andely, flourished from modest beginnings as a fishing port on the Seine.

HIGHLIGHTS

CHÂTEAU GAILLARD

✉ 27702 Les Andelys ☎ 02 32 54 17 48 🕐 Mid-Mar–mid-Nov, Wed–Mon 10–1, 2–6 💶 Adults €3, children (10–16) €2.50, under-10s free

High on a chalky hilltop overlooking a loop of the river Seine, the ruins of the Château Gaillard were the heart of Anglo-French politics in the Middle Ages. This once-majestic fortress was built in 1196 by Richard the Lionheart (1157–99), King of England and Duke of Normandy, to defend Rouen from the French King Philippe Auguste (1165–1223). The castle took 12 months to build, leading Richard to refer to it as 'My beautiful one-year-old'. French troops seized the fortress in 1204 (▷ 19). Today, one tower, several walls and a keep remain.

LES ANDELYS

Below Château Gaillard is Les Andelys, once two separate settlements, Petit Andely and Grand Andely. Petit Andely, on the banks of the river and once a small fishing village, has historic stone and timber houses and shops. On its cobbled square stands the 12th-century church of St-Sauveur, used by pilgrims going to Santiago de Compostela in Spain.

Grand Andely, once called Andely-Le-Vieux, was a royal favourite in Gallo-Roman times. Notre-Dame church, with its lovely stained glass, is built on the site of a convent founded by Clothilde (cAD474–545), wife of Clovis I, King of the Franks. St. Clothilde is credited with a

miracle: According to local legend, exhausted workmen constructing the church called on her for help, and her prayers turned the waters of the nearby fountain into a fortifying wine. Pilgrims later came to drink the miraculous waters for their strength-giving powers.

THE A-LIST

The waterside position of Les Andelys strengthened its wool trade and for many years it was a leading textile town. Eventually, farming boosted the local economy and its role in the grain trade led to the building of several grand hotels. Novelist Victor Hugo (1802–85) was among the literary guests to stay at the Hôtel le Grand Cerf. He wrote the line 'The wide fireplace with its proud shield devours an entire oak tree to heat us' in the visitor book. Another visitor was the playwright Pierre Corneille (1606–84), who was married in the town.

Many buildings dating from the 16th to 19th centuries were ruined in World War II, but one, near the fountain, is now the Musée Nicolas Poussin (tel 02 32 54 31 78), which pays homage to the eponymous 17th-century artist, the town's most famous son. Musée Normandie-Niémen tells the story of the Normandie-Niémen air squadron, which was created by Charles de Gaulle in 1942 (tel 02 32 54 49 76).

BACKGROUND

In the 13th century, as the chateau was being constructed, so the church and hospital became popular halts for pilgrims trekking from northern to southern Europe. The castle's fortunes fluctuated until Henry IV (1553–1610) and then Cardinal Richelieu (1585–1642) decided on its partial demolition. Civic life flourished outside the city walls. The suburb La Madeleine became a centre of weaving, while watermills and vineyards added to the prosperity.

The wool trade gained a fine reputation with clothmaker Louis Flavigny holding a royal warrant. Silkworks were established to widen the range of textiles. By the 19th century, wine merchants joined middle-class mill owners. In the mid-19th century, as the town was being discovered by a generation of writers and artists, the usually canny business community made its biggest mistake by rejecting the offer to have a railway station. Thus, Les Andelys did not get the crucial rail links that boosted trade in rival towns.

Top: Château Gaillard in the morning light, occupying a key defensive position above the Seine. Inset: you can see the castle's formidable fortifications from above, but the French entered through the sewers

TIP

● Visit during the four horse-racing days in spring and summer, when traditional trotting events are staged on an old race track below the chateau.

Bernay's Musée des Beaux-Arts has a thousand ceramic items

Before he conquered England in 1066, William, Duke of Normandy, vanquished rebels from Brionne; this is the view from his fortress

BEAUMONT-LE-ROGER

⊞ 206 W6 ✉ 1 rue de Belgique, 27170 Beaumont-le-Roger, tel 02 32 44 05 79; May–end Oct Wed–Sat 10–6, Sun 10– noon 🚌 Évreux–Louviers service 🚆 From Évreux

The gleaming white ruins of the Prieuré de la Ste-Trinité greet visitors to this town on the outskirts of the Beaumont forest. To discover the town of Beaumont-le-Roger is to discover Roger de Beaumont, who turned a simple settlement into a powerful town.

Originally it was a peaceful Roman village in the green Risle valley, land that came to be owned by Norman dukes. In 1017, Judith, wife of Duke Richard II, established an abbey at nearby Bernay (see below), and the estate passed into the hands of Onfroy de Vieilles. His son was Roger de Vieilles, later known as Roger de Beaumont (c1022–94), who became a powerful adviser to William the Conqueror. It was Roger who acted as counsellor to Queen Mathilde, helping her govern Normandy while her husband was invading England. After the success of the Norman Conquest, Roger built a chateau, fortified the village and founded the church of St-Nicolas and the priory. The estate later passed into the hands of Robert d'Artois (1287–1343), adviser to England's King Edward III.

The original priory was built by Roger in 1070. The remains visible today date from the 13th century. After the French Revolution, the priory was abandoned and its relics moved to the Église St-Nicolas. The flying buttresses of the priory line the roadside as you climb the hill to the nave.

Today's Beaumont is a pleasant country town, a good base for visiting nearby chateaux and hiking in the forest. The church of St-Nicolas is still standing, albeit with 17th-century additions, and has some excellent 16th-century stained-glass windows. Its clock tower sports an animated Roman soldier who chimes the hours.

BERNAY

⊞ 206 V6 ℹ 29 rue Thiers, 27300 Bernay, tel 02 32 44 60 58; Apr–Sep Mon–Sat 9.30–7, Sun 10–1; Oct–Mar Mon–Sat 9–5.30 🚌 From Pont-Audemer 🚆 From Lisieux and Évreux www.bernay27.fr

Bernay is best known for its abbey, which was founded in the 11th century by Judith of Brittany, wife of Richard II, Duke of Normandy. Springtime pilgrims still make their way to Bernay for the Whit Monday services at the Basilique Notre-Dame de la Couture (Our Lady of the Fields). The oldest part of today's church dates back to the 13th century, when the 11th-century building was expanded for the seasonal visitors. In the 16th and 19th centuries it was enlarged again. The only remaining part of the original sanctuary is the crypt, but there are carved capitals in the choir in the Romanesque part of the church. Stained glass, from the 15th to 19th centuries, fills the naves with dappled light. Construction work started on Bernay's other church, the Église Ste-Croix, in 1374 and was completed at the end of the 19th century. Its interior owes A gargoyle on St-much to the former abbey church Nicolas's church of Bec-Hellouin (▷ 77), and it harbours a 17th-century nativity scene and 16 statues of the Apostles and Evangelists that were carved in the 14th century. The church organ, restored in 1998, is often played in concerts.

The Musée des Beaux-Arts (tel 02 32 46 63 23; open mid-Jun–mid-Sep Tue–Sun 10–noon, 2–7; mid-Sep–mid-Jun Tue–Sun 2–5.30), in an old abbey building on the place Guillaume de Volpiano, contains examples of ceramics and tableware from the 16th–19th centuries, concentrating on the blue and white faïence of Rouen (▷ 99).

BRIONNE

⊞ 206 W5 ℹ 1 rue du Général de Gaulle, 27800 Brionne, tel 02 32 45 70 51; May–Sep Mon–Sat 9.30–12.30, 2–6.30, Sun 10.30–12.30; Oct–end Apr Tue–Sat 9.30–12.30, 2–6, Sun 10.30–12.30 🚌 From Évreux 🚆 Brionne

The remains of a square-sided keep perch high above the lovely town of Brionne and the trout-rich river Risle. The climb to the top is worth it, if only for the impressive views over the waterway and its valley. The fortress harks back to the days when Brionne was annexed by William, Duke of Normandy, in 1050 after a three-year siege, which wrested control of the area from the dukes of Burgundy. Much of the 11th-century fort was dismantled in the 18th century, but several broad stone walls remain as a symbol of William's power.

Such signs of machismo and military might are not the only image of Brionne. Visitors can enjoy a collection of vintage toys at Au Pays de la Poupée, a doll museum (tel 02 32 45 76 24; May–end Sep daily on request); wander around the 15th-century Église St-Martin, with its slate steeple; and enjoy the local delicacy, truite fumée (smoked trout), in traditional taverns.

At the end of its drive, Château de Beaumesnil is a breathtakingly grand house, with an ornately carved exterior

16th-century glasswork at Église Ste-Foy in Conches-en-Ouche

BROGLIE

✚ 199 V6 🚇 place des 3 Maréchaux, 27270 Broglie, tel 02 32 46 27 52; mid-May–mid-Sep Mon–Sat 9.30–12.30, 2–7, Sun 10–1; mid-Sep–mid-May Mon–Sat 9.30–12.30, 2–6 🚉 Bernay www.bernay27.fr

Among the beech groves of the Charentonne valley, the Château de Broglie dominates this small town. A private residence, the chateau is said to have been built on the site of a Roman fort by William the Conqueror in the 11th century. John Lackland, England's King John (c1167–1216), stayed here several times. During the Hundred Years War (1337–1453), the chateau was taken from the English by Jean d'Orléans, companion of Joan of Arc. Although the chateau is not open to the public, the town's 11th-century church, which has Romanesque and Renaissance styles, may be visited (daily 9–7).

Behind the church, the 15th-century Maison de la Léproserie (Leprosarium), on whose wood beams grotesque faces are carved, is a fine photo opportunity. Also near the church, find the birthplace of celebrated civil engineer Auguste Fresnel (1788–1827); in front of the house is a bronze bust of the scientist, by David d'Angers (c1788–1856). Fresnel designed lenses to magnify the power of lighthouses and was elected to the Académie des Sciences in 1823. Even more famous was his cousin, Prosper Merimée (1803–1870), the author of Carmen, whose work to preserve national monuments saved many great treasures.

Broglie's water garden, the Jardin Aquatique (tel 02 32 44 60 58), has lawns and marshlands along its canal banks. Bamboo and willow trees flourish among the water-loving grasses, with ornamental rhubarbs and lobelia adding flashes of colour.

CHÂTEAU DE BEAUMESNIL

✚ 206 W6 ✉ 27400 Beaumesnil ☎ 02 32 44 40 09 🕐 Jul, Aug daily 10–12, 2–6; Easter–end Sep Wed–Mon 2–6 💶 Adults €7, children (12–21) €3.50, under-12s free 🚉 Bernay www.office-du-tourisme-beaumesnil-eure.com

The splendid 17th-century Château de Beaumesnil, known as Le Mesnil Royal, stands in 80ha (200 acres) of woodland and flamboyantly landscaped gardens. These grounds, dating from the 17th century, were laid out in the fashion of the royal gardener André le Nôtre by his protégé La Quintiniue, and host an antiques fair on August's first weekend. During the summer months, when the house and grounds are open to the public, children are drawn to the challenge of the maze, while others explore the Louis XIII castle itself.

Beaumesnil village, surrounded by the Pays d'Ouche, has castles, manor houses, grand estates and cider presses nearby. At St-Pierre-de-Mesnil, a traditional moated castle, the Château du Blanc Buisson (1290), is open year-round. Also worth seeing are the red-brick dovecote at the 16th-century Manoir de Val and the 15th-century Tour de Thevray.

CHÂTEAU DU CHAMP-DE-BATAILLE

✚ 206 W6 • 27110 Le Neubourg ☎ 02 32 34 84 34 🕐 Gardens: mid-Jun–Aug daily 2–6; Sep–Oct, Sat–Sun, public holidays 2–6. Chateau: days as above, 3.30– 5.30. Admission all year to pre-booked groups 🚉 From Évreux www.duchampdebataille.com

Noted for its remarkable gardens, this wonderful brick and stone residence dates from the 17th century. Recent owners have lavished design, research and generous budgets on the building to ensure that it is once again worthy of its grounds.

Originally constructed by Alexandre de Créqui, the chateau was home to the influential Harcourt family until just before the French Revolution. Its most recent history saw it serving as a prisoner of war camp and women's prison before being repurchased by the Duke of Harcourt after World War II. The Duke began a restoration project that was completed by France's leading contemporary designer, Jacques Garcia, who bought the estate in 1992. The library, salons and bedrooms are furnished with impeccable taste and respect for tradition, while original 16th- and 17th-century furnishings, clocks, porcelain and fabrics make each room a glimpse of a lost world. It is remarkable that such a recent private collection can give so authentic a view of the past, from the regal splendour of the salons down to the kitchens. The courtyards and grounds are equally unmissable. While the full tour is expensive, it does make visitors feel like privileged guests.

CONCHES-EN-OUCHE

✚ 206 W7 🚇 Place A. Briand, 27190 Conches-en-Ouche, tel 02 32 30 76 42; Tue–Sat 10–12.30, 2–5.30 and Sun 10–12.30 Jul–Aug 🚉 From Évreux 🚉 From Évreux www.conches-en-ouches.fr

The town of Conches, in the Pays d'Ouche, is between the forest of Conches and the Rouloir valley. Originally a Celtic settlement that was later seized by the Romans, it became Norman in 1034 when the lords of Tosny, descendants of Rollon I, Duke of Normandy, inherited the fiefdom of Châtillon. During this golden age of pilgrimage, the Tosny nobility would join the greatest of all religious treks, the long march to the shrine of Santiago de Compostela in Spain.

Standing tall: the twin towers of the church of Écouis

The castle keep and grounds at Gisors. The castle and the town were possessed by both the English and the French

On their return from one journey, they stopped at Conques-en-Rouergue in southwest France, where they witnessed the cult of St. Foy, the martyr of Agen. Roger de Tosny then transported St. Foy's relics to Châtillon, where he built a church dedicated to the martyr, and so Châtillon became known as the Conques (later Conches) of the Pays d'Ouche.

The present Gothic Église Ste-Foy dates from the 15th century. Its 56m (184ft) spire dominates the town, although this is a copy of the original, which collapsed during a storm in 1842. The tomb of 11th-century theologian and philosopher Guillaume de Conches is housed in the church, which is noted for its stained-glass windows, among the best examples of 16th-century Norman glasswork in existence. A description of the windows may be obtained from the tourist office.

Glasswork is one of Conches' great claims to fame. The Musée du Verre et de la Pierre (tel 02 32 30 90 41; Jun–mid-Sep Wed–Sat 10–noon, 2–5, Sun 2–5), on the route de Ste-Marguerite, has three stunning windows by François Décorchemont (1880–1971), a local artist who is credited with reviving the medieval style of glasswork. On rue Paul Guilbaud, everyday Norman life through the ages is celebrated at

Sign of the swan at Le Cygne hotel in Conches-en-Ouche

the Musée du Terroir Normand (tel 02 32 37 92 16; Jun–mid-Sep Wed–Sat 10–noon, 2–5, Sun 2–5). Tools and ephemera from homes and workshops evoke local trades and crafts.

However, the most vivid image of Conches is the ruined 12th-century fort built by the Tosny family. Photogenic ivy-covered towers and a circular keep dominate the neat gardens.

ÉCOUIS

➕ 207 Z6 ℹ️ 4 rue du Général de Gaulle, 27140 Gisors, tel 02 32 27 60 75; Apr–end Sep Mon–Sat 10–12.30, 1.30–6.30, Sun 10–12.30; Oct–end Mar Mon–Fri 9–noon, 2–6 🚌 From Évreux

A royal passion for hunting may be the reason for the unexpected appearance of the magnificent church of Écouis (tel 02 32 69 43 08 to organise a visit) in such an undistinguished setting. The twin towers of the façade are a sign of the architectural harmony of the church, which was created in just three years (1310–13).

At the time, Écouis was a prosperous market town. Its position close to the royal hunting grounds of the Forêt de Lyons (▷ 86) and the fact that its parish church of St-Aubin came under the authority of Bec-Hellouin Abbey (▷ 77) led to its fortunes being favoured by the court. King Philippe IV's finance minister, Enguerrand of Marigny (1260–1315), commissioned the town's hospital and won royal and papal permission to upgrade St-Aubin to a grander institution to be run by a college of 10 canons.

In September 1313, the new church was consecrated in the presence of the papal legate. This was the crowning moment of Enguerrand's career. So influential had he been at court, that 18 months later he was hanged for sorcery. King Louis XI and Louis XII both visited the church,

and its most famous canon, St. Vincent de Paul (1581–1660), is remembered on a bronze medal in the choir. After the French Revolution, Enguerrand's tomb was destroyed and the church looted; few of the 52 statues commissioned by him remain. From 1996 to 1999, stained-glass windows were created in the period style by Sylvie Gaudin.

GISORS

➕ 207 Z5 ℹ️ 4 rue du Général de Gaulle, 27140 Gisors, tel 02 32 27 60 75; Apr–end Sep Mon–Sat 10–12.30, 1.30–6.30, Sun 10–12.30; Oct–end Mar Mon–Fri 9–noon, 2–6 🚌 From Évreux

Gisors is the capital of the Vexin Normand region and crowns a rare hill in an otherwise flat landscape. This is the crossroads of the historic Plantagenet, Vexin and seaward trails, and the junction of three provinces: Picardy, Normandy and Île-de-France. Here, men play boules on what was once the moat of a fortress established by William Rufus, King of England and Duke of Normandy (1056–1100). The ruins of the castle are a few steps away from the town centre.

In the Plantagenet era (1154–1399), the fort and town passed from English to French hands, so that Gisors became a prized possession of England's King Henry II (1133–89) then King Philippe Auguste of France (1165–1223). The resulting French and English military architecture is an interesting hybrid. The Tour du Prisonnier was the town gaol in the 16th century; graffiti scratched by prisoners can be seen on the walls.

St-Gervais-et-St-Protrais, the parish church of Gisors, dates from the 12th–16th centuries and includes Renaissance features as well as Gothic flourishes. Its imposing dimensions bear comparison with some of France's great cathedrals.

ÉVREUX

This well-preserved historic centre is renowned for its arts scene, while waterways wind through plains and forests.

Standing on the banks of the river Iton, Évreux was the ancient capital of the Eure. It has a remarkable collection of buildings that have survived centuries of siege and battle, from the ages of Vikings and Plantagenets up until World War II. Fortunately, the centre of town also managed to avoid the concrete patch-up style that blighted so many cities in the second half of the 20th century. With a friendly atmosphere and lively arts scene, Évreux makes a good choice for an overnight stay if you want more than just dinner and bed.

TOWN SIGHTS

The ultimate symbol of the spirit of survival is surely Évreux's Cathédrale Notre-Dame, which largely escaped the Allied bombardments of 1940, its replacement spire topped with a golden rooster that was installed in 1973. Parts of the church date back to the reign of King Henry II of England (ruled 1154–89), and the blend of early and flamboyant Gothic styles is testament to the town's stoic rebuilding plans following each fresh battle. The splendid stained-glass windows, dating from the 13th–17th centuries, are well worth seeing.

The free-standing bell tower, the ornate Gothic Tour de l'Horloge, was built between 1490 and 1497 and is one of the last vestiges of the town's medieval fortifications. It is home to the Louyse bell, cast in 1406, which still chimes the hour.

Next to the cathedral is the 15th-century bishop's palace, now the Musée de l'Ancien Évêché (tel 02 32 31 81 90; Tue–Sun 10–noon, 2–6), a local history museum. Look out for its splendid collection of bronzes. Another local treasure may be found in the 12th-century Église St-Taurin on the western side of town. Here, in what was once an abbey church, is a fine 13th-century gold-plated and enamelled silver chest containing relics of St. Taurin, who was first Bishop of Évreux in the fourth century AD.

Évreux's Italianate theatre, built at the start of the 20th century, replaced an earlier playhouse that had served the town for most of the 19th century. In the foyer, admire Charles Denet's paintings of scenes from the works of playwrights Molière and William Shakespeare.

Don't miss Visit the old public and private wash houses along the banks of the river and its many arms and canals. Continue the water theme by taking a trip out of town to see working watermills.

Top: cafés have Cathédrale Notre-Dame as a backdrop. Inset: statues and a bell tower in a town-centre square

RATINGS	
Cultural interest	● ● ●
Historic interest	● ● ●
Photo stops	● ● ●
Walkability	● ● ● ●

BASICS

✚ 207 X6

🛈 Place du Général de Gaulle, 27000 Évreux, tel 02 32 24 04 43; Jun–end Sep Mon–Sat 9.30–12.30, 1.30–6.15, Sun 10–12.30

🚉 Évreux

www.ot-pays-evreux.fr • Informative English-language site about the area

TIPS

● Hear stories of the town from private taxi drivers, who offer commentated tours of the city (from €40 for six people; book in the tourist office).
● One Saturday each month, the tourist office organises a heritage walking tour.

Giverny

In this small town is the home of Impressionist painter Claude Monet and the gardens that inspired his famous water lilies series. Although well aware of its tourist appeal, Giverny is a rewarding daytrip.

Left to right: inside the Monet museum, flowers in the garden, the creeper-covered verandah

RATINGS	
Cultural interest	●●●○
Photo stops	●●●●
Specialist shopping	●●●○

BASICS

✚ 207 Y6

ℹ 36 rue Carnot, 27201 Vernon, tel 02 32 51 39 60; May–Aug Tue–Sat 9.30–12.15, 2.15–6.30; rest of year Tue–Sat 10–12, 2–5

🚌 From Évreux

🚆 Vernon, then taxi or bicycle the 5km (3 miles) to Giverny

www.giverny.org • In French and English; see photos of Monet's gardens and find out what's on in the area

Monet, surrounded by flowers in his garden

SEEING GIVERNY

Thousands of visitors leave Normandy's main sightseeing trail to visit this modest town in the Seine valley. Ironically, there are no original works by Monet (1840–1926) in the pretty pink and green house where he lived until his death, although plenty of prints and copies adorn the rooms. The crowds are lured by the garden, the lily pond and its famous Japanese bridge, which are kept as close as possible to the way they were in Monet's day.

HIGHLIGHTS

MAISON DE CLAUDE MONET

✉ Fondation Claude Monet, rue Claude Monet, 27620 Giverny ☎ 02 32 51 28 21 🕐 Apr–end Oct Tue–Sun 9.30–6 💶 Adults €5.50, children €3, under-7s free www.fondation-monet.com

Monet bought this house, with a vegetable garden and an orchard, in 1895, having rented it as a family home since 1883 for himself, his two sons, and Alice Hoschedé and her six children. The story goes that the artist first saw Giverny through a train window in 1833 and fell in love with it, although the railway line has since closed. Monet painted the irises and lily pond scenes that were his final obsessions here.

The interior of the house is laid out as it was in Monet's day, but there is no time to linger: Tour guides are not allowed to talk to their groups inside the building and visitors are hustled through to avoid gridlock. Once outside, you can take time to explore the walled garden—Le Clos Normand, in front of the house—and the lily pond across the road. The Clos Normand contains 100,000 plants that are replaced each year and another 100,000 perennials, while the famous lily pond was created by the artist by diverting a branch of the river Epte into his garden. A main road divides the gardens, but an underpass takes visitors to the pond. Wonderful though the gardens are, the crowds mean they are not a place for contemplation. The art trail spills over onto the nearby streets; rue Claude Monet is filled with artists' workshops and galleries.

MUSÉE D'ART AMÉRICAIN

✉ 99 rue Claude Monet, 27620 Giverny ☎ 02 32 51 94 65 🕐 Apr–end Oct Tue–Sun 10–6 💶 Adults €5.50, children (12–18) €3, under-12s free; also free first Sun of every month
www.maag.org

Once Monet began exhibiting his work in Paris, Giverny became a popular subject for aspiring artists. Four years after his arrival in 1883, a stream of painters descended on the village. Willard Metcalf, Louis Ritter and Theodore Wendel were among the first Americans to arrive, and they were soon followed by a succession of lesser known artists, who took rooms at the town's Hôtel Baudy (see below). Monet himself, while welcoming some of the initial arrivals, soon distanced himself from the others and did not encourage a salon or Giverny movement. The museum today houses a collection of around 100 works by these visitors, as well as both permanent and temporary exhibitions of paintings of other parts of France by American artists.

RESTAURANT BAUDY

✉ 81 rue Claude Monet, 27620 Giverny ☎ 02 32 21 10 03 ⊘ Apr–end Oct Tue–Sat 10–9, Sun 10–7
Once known as the Hôtel Baudy, this former boarding house and bar in rue Claude Monet is where Monet met up with Auguste Renoir, Alfred Sisley, Camille Pissarro and Auguste Rodin. Now a restaurant and café, the place preserves much of its 19th-century style. Stop here for a drink, snack or meal, and then explore the bar where the artists would meet, the rose garden and Giverny's first artists' studio.

Top and inset: you've seen the bridge over the lily pond in art galleries, now cross the real thing in Monet's garden

BACKGROUND

The village of Giverny itself existed quietly long before Monet arrived. Here, under weeping willow trees, the Seine meets the river Epte, and the two principal hillside streets are lined with low pink and green houses with slate roofs, their walls covered with wisteria. While today's visitors recognise Giverny for its irises and water lilies, the area was once celebrated for its grapes rather than its flowers. Back in the heyday of St. Wandrille Abbey (▷ 90), the monks owned several vineyards in Giverny.

Although it was undoubtedly art that put Giverny on the map, the village dates back to neolithic and Roman times—in 1838, Gallo-Roman graves were discovered here, and as the churchyard was being restored in 1860, workmen discovered more plaster coffins dating to the earliest centuries of the Christian era. Not far from the church is the grave of St. Radegonde, a ruined monument that testifies to a neolithic settlement. The church is dedicated to the saint, who was said to have healing powers.

TIPS

● Arrive early to see the lily pond without the crowds.
● Visit in early summer to see the gardens at their very best.
● Wheelchair-users can cross the main road between the gardens as an alternative to the underpass.
● The neighbouring town of Vernon (▷ 87) is well worth a visit, as it is the closest place to find actual work by Monet.

Quiet, tree-lined roads lead the way to the pretty village of Lyons-la-Forêt, with its half-timbered houses

RATINGS

Good for food	● ● ●
Outdoor pursuits	● ● ●
Photo stops	● ● ●

BASICS

✚ 207 Y5

ℹ 20 rue de l'Hôtel-de-Ville, 27480 Lyons-la-Forêt, tel 02 32 49 31 65; Tue–Sun 10–noon, 2–5

🚃 Gisors (30km/19km)

www.lyons.tourisme.free.fr • The local tourist office's French-language site

Flower baskets adorn the timber roof of the marketplace

LYONS-LA-FORÊT

The ancient forest surrounding one of France's most beautiful villages is home to abbeys and chateaux.

Surrounded by the Forêt de Lyons, with its acres of tall beech trees, the village of Lyons-la-Forêt is a lovely cluster of 17th-century timber-framed houses set around a 13th-century wooden market hall. Lyons was built on the site of a 12th-century fortress and grew up along the perimeter of the feudal moat. Its church, Église St-Denis, also dates from the 12th century. The tourist office is on the ground floor of the Hôtel de Ville, with its splendid 18th-century décor. The area is famed for its farmhouse meats, with some farms open to visitors.

As well as being a popular base for rural holidays, Lyons is where Maurice Ravel (1875–1937) composed *Le Tombeau de Couperin* in 1917. The house where he stayed is marked with a plaque. If the Lyons seems strangely familiar, that is probably because of its popularity with French film directors; Jean Renoir (son of Impressionist painter Auguste), in 1932, and Claude Chabrol, in 1990, chose the village as a backdrop for their versions of *Madame Bovary*.

LAND OF ABBEYS AND CASTLES

The 10,600ha (26,200-acre) Forêt de Lyons, once a royal hunting ground, is the setting for an abbey, a convent and two castles. The ruined Cistercian Abbaye de Mortemer (tel 02 32 49 54 34) dates from the 12th–13th centuries, and over the years the beauty of its buildings has attracted many distinguished visitors, among them King Richard the Lionheart (1157–99). The abbey contains a museum of monastic life that also includes displays on ghost stories and folk legends of the region. In season, visitors can tour the abbey grounds in a little train. Some 11km (7 miles) southwest of Lyons-la-Forêt is the 12th-century Cistercian Abbaye Notre-Dame de Fontaine-Guérard (tel 02 32 49 03 82), a convent with a medicinal garden.

The Château de Fleury-la-Forêt (tel 02 32 49 63 91), an easy drive from Lyons-la-Forêt, has a toy and doll museum and an animal ark in its grounds. Visitors can stay overnight and breakfast in the old kitchens. Nearby, on the edge of the forest, is the 16th–17th-century Château de Vascoeuil (tel 02 35 23 62 35), which hosts modern art exhibitions. There is a 17th-century dovecote in the grounds.

Turn back time: half-timbered houses in Verneuil-sur-Avre

Escape the tourists of Giverny at the riverside town of Vernon, which boasts a collection of original works by Monet

THE SIGHTS

PONT-AUDEMER

✚ 199 V5 🚹 Place Maubert, 27500 Pont-Audemer, tel 02 32 41 08 21; Jun–end Sep Mon–Sat 9–12.30, 2–6, Sun 10–noon; Oct–end May Mon–Sat 9–12.30, 2–5.30 🚉 Pont-Audemer

Known as the Little Venice of Normandy, as it is wrapped and lapped by two branches of the river Risle, Pont-Audemer was once a town of tanners. The trade flourished by the waterside, and any trip through the narrow alleyways and canals of the old centre passes former tanneries where animal skins were hung out to dry. Today, the town's timbered and gabled buildings are adorned with hanging baskets and antique cast-iron and copper lanterns. Small wooden bridges and unexpected waterways, with floral displays, have gained Pont-Audemer recognition as one of the prettiest detours in France.

Sights include the church of St-Ouen, where austere Romanesque and extravagant Renaissance styles sit side by side. Inside, the light is filtered through stained glass dating from the 16th and 20th centuries. On Mondays, a market offers a good range of food and crafts. In winter, the stalls shut down at the end of the morning, but in peak season traders stay into the afternoon. Also in summer, a 1950s vintage railway train runs thrice daily on Sundays between Pont-Audemer and Honfleur (▷ 126).

VERNEUIL-SUR-AVRE

✚ 206 W8 🚹 Mairie, 27130 Verneuil-sur-Avre, tel 02 32 32 10 81; Mon–Fri 8.30–noon, 2–5.30, Sat 9–noon 🚉 From Évreux

Another fortified stronghold guarding the border between France and Normandy, Verneuil was once a strategic military settlement ringed by ramparts and moats. The town was founded in 1120 by King Henry I of England (1068–1135). Today, many of the fortified walls remain and the surviving outer moats provide an interesting walk. A severe and brooding tower, the Tour Grise, was built as a keep or dungeon by King Philippe Auguste (1165–1223) when the town was taken by the French in 1204. The Hundred Years War saw Verneuil in the firing line again as France fought England.

Verneuil has a religious as well as a military heritage. An ornate yet rather chunky 15th-century Gothic tower stands on top of the 12th-century Église de la Madeleine. Inside, bright colours mark out the vaulting and are mirrored in the stained-glass windows and statuary. The church is surrounded by 15th- and 16th-century stone and half-timbered houses. The original church of the town, Notre-Dame, dates from the 12th century. Also worth a visit is the chapel in the 17th-century former Benedictine Abbaye de St-Nicolas.

VERNON

✚ 207 Y6 🚹 36 rue Carnot, 27201 Vernon, tel 02 32 51 39 60; May–end Aug Tue–Sat 9–12.30, 2–6; rest of year Tue–Sat 10–12, 2–5 🚉 From Évreux

Although neighbouring Giverny (▷ 84–85) has long been overtaken by the crush of tourism, the town of Vernon, unsaddled by the brand of a famous artist, has retained its own identity. But while most tourists ignore it in favour of Giverny, Vernon's Musée Alphonse-Georges Poulain (tel 02 32 21 28 09; Apr–end Sep Tue–Fri 10.30–12.30, 2–6, Sat–Sun 2–6; Oct–end Mar Tue–Sun 2–5.30) actually owns original works by Impressionist Claude Monet (1840–1926), whereas none may be seen in the artist's home town. Housed in an interesting stone and timber building with beautifully carved exterior beams, the museum was established to display a donated collection of stuffed birds. However, thanks to the generosity of Monet and his family, the gallery is now home to a circular study of water lilies by the master himself, as well as a view of the cliffs of Pourville at sunset. Two paintings of Giverny by Monet's stepdaughter Blanche may also be seen, along with several works by American artists.

Many typical Norman buildings in the town survived the air raids of World War II. The lovely Maison du Temps Jadis is one of these, the oldest building in town and now home to the tourist office. Walking through the town, look out for faces carved into the timbers of the old houses. Vernon also has some interesting fortifications, built to protect it in its role as a border town between the kingdom of France and the duchy of Normandy. Included among these is a circular keep, all that remains of a 12th-century building; it is not open to the public. Another fortification that may be admired from the outside only is the medieval Château des Tourelles, built by King Philippe Auguste of France (1165–1223). Three of its original towers have survived, while the fourth is being restored after World War II bomb damage.

Finally, visit Vernon's church of Notre-Dame to see its abstract stained glass, and stop by the 18th-century Château de Bizy, 4km (2 miles) outside town, to admire its fine tapestries. Most surprising for visitors who come to Vernon initially to see Monet's water lilies paintings is the range of entertainment and dining on offer in the town after dark. **Don't miss** The picturesque timbered Vieux Moulin, a remnant of a long-forgotten bridge, balances above the river on stone stilts.

SEINE-MARITIME

This region, from the river Seine along the Côte d'Albâtre, is the cradle of Impressionism. The name says it all: The fast-running Seine passes through towns and villages associated with legendary French figures, from Joan of Arc to Victor Hugo, and flows out to greet the seas of maritime legend, of pirates and privateers, and of fishing boats and great transatlantic liners, where stark white cliffs rise above the waves.

MAJOR SIGHTS

The abbey's main chruch, Notre-Dame, was consecrated in 1067 in the presence of William the Conqueror. Inset: looking stoney faced

ABBAYE DE JUMIÈGES

The abbey that can be regarded as the blueprint for the great Norman churches of France and England.

Let your imagination fill in the gaps between the stones when you visit the impressive ruins of the Abbey of Jumièges within their park. Although much of the buildings was destroyed in the 18th century, you can still sense their majesty. The roofless ruins of the 11th-century church of Notre-Dame and its earlier 10th-century neighbour, the Église St-Pierre, are the perfect backdrop to a romantic stroll.

Founded in AD654 by St. Philibert, then burnt down by the Vikings, the Benedictine abbey rose to its first period of greatness under the dukes of Normandy with the construction of the Église St-Pierre around AD940. Jumièges grew until the Hundred Years War, when it began to decline; by 1792, just seven monks remained and the abbey was looted. In 1852, the Lepel-Cointet family began restoration work and Jumièges became a state-owned national monument in 1947.

Today, the imposing bone-white abbey ruins, standing among centuries-old trees, still dominate the village of Jumièges. Although open to the skies, the Notre-Dame church buildings remain stunning examples of Norman church architecture, the lack of vaulting seeming to illuminate the detail of the stone and woodwork of the walls, arcades and towers. While the west of the church is well preserved, smaller chapels have long gone; beyond the transept some 13th-century Gothic restorations of older Romanesque features hint at what might once have been. The west wall of the lantern tower survives and the south transept leads to the Passage Charles VII between Notre-Dame and the Église St-Pierre. Some painted decorations remain in the older church, while the choir is decorated with *culots* (carvings).

MYTHS AND MISTRESSES

Hear about the abbey's myths and legends on the guided tour. One of these concerns the lime-tree avenue in the gardens between the abbey and 17th-century house of Abbot François de Harlay. Allegedly, the avenue is named after Agnès Sorel, mistress of Charles VII (1403–61), who used it as a trysting place to meet the king.

Don't miss Admire the illuminated white stone buildings against the midnight sky during evening nocturnes (May–Sep, selected Sats).

RATINGS

Cultural interest	● ● ●
Historical interest	● ● ● ●
Photo stops	● ● ●

TIPS

● Wear comfortable shoes, for despite the fact that the entrance is solid enough, a visit to the abbey is essentially a country walk.
● Bring a blanket and sweater with you when attending concerts, as it can get very chilly.

BASICS

✚ 200 W4 • 24 rue Guillaume-le-Conquérant, 76480 Jumièges
☎ 02 35 37 28 97
🕐 Apr–Sep daily 9–7; rest of year daily 9.30–1, 2.30–5.30
💷 Adults €4.60, under-18s free. Guided tours included in admission price
🚆 Rouen (28km/17.5 miles)
🍴 No café on site, but food and drink are available in the village
🎁 Shop with an excellent range of monastic and regional gifts, as well as a good selection of reference books in French and English
♿ Shop has wide aisles for wheelchair-users; the grounds are not flat, so the park offers a strenuous wheelchair ride; toilets in the shop (at the main entrance) are well equipped for visitors with a disability
www.jumieges.fr
www.monum.fr • The national state monument site

Still standing: the north transept of the Abbaye de St-Wandrille is the only element of the original abbey remaining

You can't miss the front door of Caudebec-en-Caux's church

ABBAYE DE ST-WANDRILLE

✚ 200 W4 • 76490 St-Wandrille-Rançon ☎ 02 35 96 23 11 ◷ Mon–Sat 9–12.30, 1.30–6.30; Sun, public holidays 11.30–12.30, 2.30–6.30 ◷ Guided tour of interior and outside cloister: €3.50 ▣ Yvetot (16km/10 miles) www.st-wandrille.com

Behind a grand gateway copied from that at the royal Château of Fontainebleau near Paris, today's Abbaye de St-Wandrille is a bewildering architectural cluster. Founded in AD649 by Count Wandrille as a study centre, the abbey's original buildings were destroyed by the Vikings. Rebuilt in the 13th–16th centuries, the abbey passed into secular hands after the French Revolution, becoming first a working mill and then a private home. In 1931, it began its latest religious incarnation as a Benedictine monastery.

This confusing history explains the juxtaposition of styles of the surviving buildings: The 17th-century library and Louis XIV staircase, for example, are a

Benedictine monks at the Abbaye de St-Wandrille

luxurious contrast to the simple ruins of the older cloister. Be sure to see the restored refectory and former bookbinding workshop.

The 20th century has also left its architectural legacy: the Chapel le Notre-Dame, which was built by the monks between 1952 and 1968 and consecrated in 1977 (the previous chapel was bombed in 1944). The modern abbey church, rebuilt in 1967–69, was converted from a tithe barn that was transported here from Neuville-du-Bosc. The monks sell their homemade jam at the abbey shop, and religious services held here are noted for their evocative Gregorian chants at morning Mass and vespers.

ARQUES-LA-BATAILLE

✚ 201 X2 ℹ Pont d'Ango, 76204 Dieppe, tel 02 32 14 40 60; Jul–Aug daily 9–7; Oct–end Apr Mon–Sat 9–noon, 2–6; May, Jun, Sep Mon–Sat 9–1, 2–7, Sun 10–1, 3–6 ▣ From Rouen ▣ Arques-la-Bataille

The Battle of Arques may have been fought and won more than 400 years ago, but the brooding grey-stone ruins of the chateau loom above the town as a reminder of the conflict that gave the place its name. Where the river Varenne meets the Béthune, so on 21 September 1589 did the Catholic Duke of Mayenne come to meet Protestant King Henri IV in battle over the King's succession at the royal castle (▷ 20), which was said to be able to withstand any cannonball. At the end of the day, the strong walls and weather brought victory to the King.

The main part of the castle was built during the 11th and 12th centuries and was added to until the 16th century. Atop a rocky hill, and with a rigged square keep, the chateau

is reached via a steep meandering road from the *mairie* (town hall) in the main square below. Splendid views of the countryside can be had from its walls, and the last of the three doors leading into the castle has a carved image of the Battle of Arques. Another homage to Henri IV and the battle can be found in the contemporary woodwork of a chapel within the 16th-century church of Notre-Dame de l'Assomption.

CAUDEBEC-EN-CAUX

✚ 200 W4 ℹ Place du Général de Gaulle, 76490 Caudebec-en-Caux, tel 02 32 70 46 32; Apr–end Nov daily 10–12.30, 1.30–6.30; Dec–end Mar Mon–Sat 10–12.30, 1.30–6 ▣ From Rouen www.caudebec-en-caux.com

The southern part of the Pays de Caux region borders the river Seine, and among the attractive resorts on this pretty stretch of the river is Caudebec-en-Caux, which has held a lively Saturday market in the square for more than 600 years. The scene is dominated by the exquisite late-Gothic church of Notre-Dame, with its fine stained-glass rose window. A century in the building, the church was completed in 1539, when it was hailed by King Henri IV as the most beautiful in his kingdom. Note the main western doorway, which is carved with more than 300 figures. The church and a handful of neighbouring houses survived a fire in 1940, which destroyed much of the historic core of Caudebec.

There is plenty more to see in town, including the 14th-century ramparts with their integral prison and the Musée Briochet-Brechot (Fri 3–6), a local history museum housed in the Maison des Templars. Here, alongside reminders of the turbulent days of the 16th-century Wars of Religion, are images of natural

Sheep keep the lawns of Château de Miromesnil tidy. A small chapel is hidden in the beech forest surrounding the estate

Wild at heart: wallabies roam the grounds of Château Clères

THE SIGHTS

threats to the town, including devastation by fire and flooding from tidal surges, or bores, washing up the Seine, which once made sightseeing along the river a dangerous occupation. Today, safe and attractive views of the Seine can be enjoyed from waterfront terraces. Along the river is Villequier, where, in 1842, a treacherous tidal bore claimed the lives of the daughter and son-in-law of writer Victor Hugo. The Musée Départemental Victor Hugo (tel 02 35 56 78 31) here is housed in the family home of Charles Vacquerie, Hugo's son-in-law, and details the author's life.

CHÂTEAU DE MARTAINVILLE

🔟 201 Y4 • 76116 Martainville-Épreville ☎ 02 35 23 44 70 🕐 Apr–end Sep Mon–Sat 10–12.30, 2–6, Sun 2–6.30; Oct–end Mar Mon–Sat 10–12.30, 2–5, Sun 2–5.30 💷 Adults €3, under-18s free www.cg76.fr

The 15th-century Château de Martainville is home to a heritage centre that preserves regional traditions. Called the Musée des Traditions et Arts Normande, the centre is perfectly suited to the style of the chateau, which has retained many original features, with Gothic brick chimneystacks outside and imposing fireplaces within. Some 400 years of domestic furnishings, tableware and artefacts are displayed in the grand reception rooms, with old Rouen and Pays de Caux chairs and buffets, and plenty of blue and white crockery and copper pans. In the grounds is a very photogenic 18th-century cart shed with traditional timbering and a dovecote dating from the 16th century.

CHÂTEAU DE MIROMESNIL

🔟 201 X2 • 76550 Tourville-sur-Arques ☎ 02 35 85 02 80 🕐 Apr–end Oct

daily 2–6 💷 Adults €6, children (10–17) €4, under-10s free 🚇 Arques-la-Bataille (5km/3 miles) www.chateaumiromesnil.com

The home of the third Marquis de Miromesnil (1723–96), chancellor to King Louis XVI, is more famous as the birthplace of a literary lodger. The author Guy de Maupassant was born in this 16th-century red-brick and stone chateau, south of Dieppe, on 5 August 1850. Maupassant's parents rented the castle from 1849 to 1853, and the works of the great short-storywriter now have pride of place in the library.

Today, the chateau attracts many visitors to its well-tended grounds (Jul–Aug 10–1, 2–6, €4), which are dominated by a sprawling cedar tree. The park itself is an excellent example of 18th-century landscaping, walls of Varengeville brick and white stone marking out each distinct area. Of particular note are the kitchen gardens, a traditional French potager with rows of vegetables separated by lines of blue delphiniums.

Little remains of an earlier house, built some way from the present site, except for the chapel of St-Antoine, which was once linked with Fécamp Abbey. The chapel was renovated in the 16th and 18th centuries and in 1950 received three new stained-glass windows, designed by Guy de Vogüé. The current owner of the estate is the Comte de Vogüé, who may often be seen guiding summer visitors around the house and its park.

CLÈRES

🔟 201 X3 🚩 59 avenue du Parc, 76690 Clères, tel 02 35 33 38 64; Apr–late Sep Mon 2–5, Tue–Fri 10–noon, 2–5.30, Sat–Sun, public holidays 2–6; late Sep–end Mar Mon 2–5, Tue–Fri 10–noon, 2–5.30 🚉 From Rouen www.ot-cleres.fr

For a century, Clères' appeal has not been its 15th-century chateau but the Parc Zoologique de Clères Jean Delacour (tel 02 35 33 23 08; Apr–end Sep daily 10–7; Oct daily 9–12, 1.30–5; closed Nov–Mar) that lies in the grounds. On neat lawns and around well-tended lakes lives an incongruous community of antelopes, kangaroos, gibbons, deer, flamingoes and peacocks, which roam in semi-liberty through the park as imagined by the zoo's creator, naturalist Jean Delacour.

CÔTE D'ALBÂTRE

🔟 200 V2 🚩 Pont d'Ango, 76204 Dieppe, tel 02 32 14 40 60; Jul–Aug Mon–Sat 9–1, 2–8; May, Jun, Sep Mon–Sat 9–1, 2–7, Sun 10–1, 3–6; Oct–Apr Mon–Sat 9–12, 2–6 🚉 Dieppe, Fécamp, Le Tréport, Le Havre

The Alabaster Coast consists of 120km (75 miles) of cliffs, coves, peaks and green valleys between Le Tréport and Le Havre. Named for the alabaster hues of the rock faces, the white-chalk and grey-flint headlands and crags have been steadily eroded by the wind and waves. The original limits of the Normandy shore now stand as pillars in the sea at such spots as Étretat (▷ 94), and the combination of fast-changing skies, white cliffs and verdant plateaux led to this spot becoming the cradle of Impressionism. The advent of the railways brought artists Eugène Boudin, Camille Pissarro and Alfred Sisley to the coast, while the light and natural forms at Étretat and Le Havre inspired Monet. The Alabaster Coast's villages are charming, the towns of Étretat, Eu (▷ 95) and Fécamp (▷ 95) are distinctive, and the coastline rewards walkers. Some coves are inaccessible by land and others reached by ladders. Dieppe is the biggest draw (▷ 92–93), but Le Tréport is the prettiest diversion (▷ 104).

Dieppe

A lively working port with a colourful maritime history, Dieppe deserves further exploration and is much more than a gateway to Normandy.

RATINGS

Cultural interest	● ● ●
Good for food	● ● ● ●
Historic interest	● ● ● ●
Walkability	● ● ● ●

BASICS

✚ 200 X2

🛈 Pont d'Ango, 76204 Dieppe, tel 02 32 14 40 60; Jul–Aug Mon–Sat 9–1, 2–8; May, Jun, Sep Mon–Sat 9–1, 2–7, Sun 10–1, 3–6; Oct–Apr Mon–Sat 9–12, 2–6
🚆 From Rouen 🚢 From Newhaven
www.dieppetourisme.com • Useful site with regularly updated events listings

TIPS

• A tour of Dieppe's memorials takes in Abraham Duquesne, scourge of pirates (place National), the founders of Québec, Canadian war heroes and the inventor of the coffee filter (square du Canada).
• The old fishermen's houses along the quai du Hâble make great photographic subjects.
• Seafood restaurants can be found along quai Henri IV.
• Dieppe's centre is easily managed on foot with a map from the tourist office.

SEEING DIEPPE

Dieppe is a cheery harbour town with a bustling market and a waterfront café scene. It offers day-trippers a welcome alternative to the industrial feel of other ports. The pulse of the place is best taken just across the port from the ferry terminal. Bounded by two roads, the boulevard Maréchal Foch is a promenade running the length of the shingle beach seafront, parallel to the Grande Rue, a pedestrianised shopping street. There is no escaping the port's seafaring past: The Globe Café was the home of Balidar, a notorious pirate, and many of the town's white-brick buildings were built after Dieppe was bombarded by British ships in 1694.

HIGHLIGHTS

HARBOUR AND SEAFRONT

Dieppe's main sights can be found by the waterfront. The Avant Port is packed with working boats and pleasure craft, and is reached via the twin Pont d'Ango and Pont Colbert bridges, designed by Gustave Eiffel (1822–1923). Between the pleasure ports and modern ferry terminal is the historic seafarers' district of Le Pollet.

Parallel to the main seafront promenade is the boulevard de Verdun, which runs southwest to the 15th-century Les Tourelles, the last remaining gate from the town's original fortifications. Further inland, along Grande Rue, find the place du Puits Salé, whose original salt-water well was replaced by a fountain. Artists Claude Monet, Auguste Renoir and Raoul Dufy shopped for their art supplies in the square.

CHÂTEAU MUSÉE

✉ Rue de Chastes, 76200 Dieppe ☎ 02 35 06 61 99 🕐 Jun–end Sep daily 10–noon, 2–6; Oct–end May Wed–Mon 10–noon, 2–5. Closed 1 May, 1 Nov, 25 Dec 🎫 Adults €3, children €1.50, under-12s free
www.mairie-dieppe.fr

Above: Dieppe has retained an attractive working harbour

The round-turreted 15th-century chateau is now a museum displaying paintings by Auguste Renoir, Eugène Boudin and Camille Pissarro, as well as a noted ivory collection—a reminder of Dieppe's 17th-century ivory-carving industry and the town's strong links with Africa. In addition to the painting and seafaring legacies of the town, the museum also celebrates Dieppe's musical heritage with a gallery devoted to the composer Camille Saint-Saëns (1835–1921).

NOTRE-DAME DE BON SECOURS
✉ Chemin de Falaise, 76200 Dieppe 🕐 Daily 10–6
This cliff-top church, which was constructed in 1876 in memory of victims of the sea, watches over maritime traffic entering the port on one side and the shingle beaches of the Alabaster Coast on the other.

CITÉ DE LA MER
✉ 37 rue de l'Asile Thomas, 76200 Dieppe ☎ 02 35 06 93 20 🕐 Daily 10–noon, 2–6 👤 Adults €5, children (4–16) €3, under-4s free
At this maritime museum and aquarium in the centre of the fishing quarter, history meets ecology in displays on the English Channel.

BACKGROUND

Dieppe was a haunt of pirates and privateers. Most famously, in the 16th century, King François I's shipbuilder, Jean Ango, organised expeditions to capture Portuguese ships and their cargoes. Links with the sea continued into the 17th century, when Dieppe was a merchant port and hub of the African ivory trade. Since Roman times it had been a spa resort and in the 19th century Dieppe found favour with fashionable bathing parties and became France's first seaside resort.

The ferry service to and from Newhaven on the south coast of England has had a chequered history, as various shipping lines abandoned the route. Today, the French have solved that problem by buying the English port to guarantee a flow of visitors (▷ 22). Throughout its many incarnations, Dieppe has also been home to a fishing fleet, and the morning catch still scents the sea air and lures visitors to lunch. Sadly, the quayside seafood stalls have moved inland to a less attractive market hall.

Above: shoppers crowd the pedestrianised Grand Rue

Above: carved ivory in the Château Musée

Hole in the wall: the chalk cliffs close to Étretat offer superb views over the sea and town. Inset: heroic aviators Nungesser and Coli

ÉTRETAT

Dramatic blue-grey cliffs have been spectacularly moulded by the elements at the jewel of the Alabaster Coast.

RATINGS	
Photo stops	●●●●●
Beaches	●●●●
Walkability	●●●

BASICS

✚ 199 U3

🛈 Place Maurice Guillard, 76790 Étretat, tel 02 35 27 05 21; mid-Jun–mid-Sep daily 9–7; mid-Sep–mid-Jun daily 10–noon, 2–6

🚆 From Bréauté at weekends and from Le Havre

🚉 Bréauté (19km/12 miles)

www.etretat.net • Local history and information

TIPS

● Take the cliff walk at sunset, when the chalk changes colour with the fading light. At nightfall, the cliffs shine dramatically thanks to dazzling illuminations that reflect their stark white grandeur above the dark sea.

● Check weather reports before taking the cliff walk off-season, as winds may be very strong and steps slippery.

● Hardy visitors can join locals for the New Year's Day swim!

● Pack your golf clubs; one of France's most spectacular golf courses is on the cliff top.

Étretat is best enjoyed out of season, when its bay is deserted and the arches of the magnificent chalk headlands seem to straddle the ocean. The effect of the cliffs here is that of a grand cathedral carved out of France itself, its flying buttresses arching into the sea. At low tide a vast cave in the cliff face appears on the pebbled beach. On the Falaise d'Amont cliff, visitors stop by the sailor's chapel of Notre-Dame de la Garde (closed to the public) to admire views across the bay to the Falaise d'Aval and its adjacent 70m-high (230ft) rock stack, known as the Aiguille d'Étretat (Étretat Needle).

In town, visit the place du Maréchal Foch, with a reconstructed wooden covered market (built in 1926) amid a cluster of attractive 16th-century townhouses. Étretat's church of Notre-Dame dates back as far as the 11th century and has been listed as an historic monument since the mid-19th century.

ARTISTIC EXPOSURE

A modest fishing village for most of its life, Étretat nestled in obscurity until the mid-19th century, when writers Guy de Maupassant and Alexandre Dumas discovered the charms of its cliff-enveloped pebble beach. Chic visitors arrived from Paris, lured by the paintings of Jean Baptiste Corot, Eugène Boudin, Eugène Delacroix and Claude Monet. The composer Jacques Offenbach (1819–80) bought a house here, which he dubbed Villa Orphée in honour of his greatest musical triumph and whose 10 rooms he named after his compositions.

Étretat remembers its heroes as well as its artists. A plaque in the main square recalls a World War I hospital and liberation by Scottish troops in World War II. High on the eastern cliffs next to Notre-Dame de la Garde, a monument honours the aviators Charles Nungesser and François Coli, whose plane *l'Oiseau Blanc* was last seen crossing these cliffs in 1927 on its ill-fated bid to fly from Paris to New York. Their bodies were never recovered, presumed drowned in the Atlantic.

At the Manoir de Cateuil on the Le Havre road, is the dairy farm of Le Valeine (tel 02 35 27 14 02; Jul–Aug Sat–Wed 9–12.30, 2–7), which demonstrates traditional crafts. Here, you can see how farmers make cheeses, ice cream and cider, and enjoy a tasting or two.

Eu, and its chateau, hosted royal guests and marriages

DIEPPE

See pages 92–93.

EU

🔲 201 Y1 ℹ️ 41 rue Paul Bignon, 76260 Eu, tel 02 35 86 04 68; May–mid-Nov Mon–Sat 9.30–12.30, 2–7, Sun 10–1; mid-Nov–Apr Mon–Sat 9.30–12, 2–6.30 (closed Sun, public holidays) 🚉 Eu www.ville-eu.fr

Of all the varied diversions on the Alabaster Coast, Eu has the most regal history. It was here in 1050 that the notorious nuptials between William, Duke of Normandy and future King of England, and his cousin Mathilde of Flanders took place, a marriage that had a profound effect on Norman history. As penance for the incestuous marriage, William and Mathilde founded Abbaye St-Étienne and Abbaye de la Trinité in Caen (▷ 62–64).

The town's association with royalty continued in the 19th century, when King Louis-Philippe (1773–1850) entertained England's Queen Victoria (1819–1901) here during the state visit of 1843. Louis-Philippe was very fond of Eu's chateau, a building dating from 1578 and built on the site of William's original castle. In the late 19th century, France's leading architect, Viollet-le-Duc, remodelled the castle as a family home for Louis-Philippe's grandson, the Comte de Paris. Now a municipal building, the castle houses the Musée Louis-Philippe (tel 02 35 86 44 00; mid-Mar–early Nov Sat–Mon, Wed–Thu 10–noon, 2–6, Fri 2–6), which showcases the stunning regal apartments and suites, including the bedroom used by Queen Victoria and Prince Albert.

Eu was the birthplace of François and Michel Anguier, France's great 17th-century baroque sculptors. The brothers went on to work on the Palais du Louvre in Paris.

Beneficial Bénédictine: copper stills in the palace's museum

FÉCAMP

Art and liqueur meet in Fécamp's Palais Bénédictine.

RATINGS	
Cultural interest	● ● ●
Historic interest	● ● ●
Photo stops	● ● ●

PALAIS BÉNÉDICTINE

✉️ 110 rue Alexandre le Grand, 76400
☎️ 02 35 10 26 10 ⏰ Mid-Jul–mid-Sep daily 10–6; mid-Sep–mid-Oct, mid-Apr–mid-Jul daily 10–noon, 2–5.30; mid-Oct–end Dec, early Feb–mid-April daily 10.30–11.45, 2–5. Closed 25 Dec, Jan–early Feb, 1 May 💰 Adults €5.60, children (12–18) €2.80, under-12s free

🔲 199 V3 ℹ️ 113 rue Alexandre le Grand, 76403 Fécamp, tel 02 35 28 51 01; Jul, Aug daily 9–6.30; Sep–end Mar Mon–Fri 9–6, Sat 9.30–12.30, 2–6, Sun 9.30–12.30; Apr–end Jun Mon–Fri 9–6, Sat–Sun, public holidays 10–6 ℹ️ Point d'Informations Plage, boulevard Albert 1er, tel 02 35 28 51 01; Jul, Aug daily 10–1, 2–6.30; May–end Jun Sat–Sun, public holidays 10–1, 2–6.30 🚉 Fécamp www.fecamptourisme.com • Mainly French-language site

On the Alabaster Coast is a flamboyant palace, where the liqueur Bénédictine is made (not, contrary to myth, by monks). Alexandre le Grand obtained the 16th-century elixir's recipe from a Venetian monastery and started a distillery in 1863, commissioning Camille Albert to create the neo-Gothic and neo-Renaissance palace.

The project was shrewd marketing rather than an eccentric folly. Artworks perpetuated the myth of a monastic drink as well as keeping a tradition of religious art in the town. In the Gothic Room are treasures from Fécamp's Abbey; other rooms contain the works of Flemish, French and Italian masters. Before leaving, visit the Espace Contemporain, famous for its modern art exhibitions.

ÉGLISE DE LA TRINITÉ

✉️ Abbatiale de la Trinité, 76400 Fécamp ⏰ Daily 8–8
The 12th-century Holy Trinity Church was part of Fécamp's abbey and harbours a relic said to be the blood of Christ. Also inside the church is the Angel's Footprint. According to legend, as bishops met in AD943 to discuss which saint should be patron of the new church, an angel appeared and commanded that it be dedicated to the Holy Trinity. Before leaving, he left his footprint on a stone.

MARITIME HERITAGE

Fécamp is also a major fishing port. Some of the tales from 400 years of cod fishing are retold in the Musée des Terre Neuvas (tel 02 35 28 31 99; Jul, Aug daily 10–7; Sep–end Jun Wed–Mon 10–noon, 2–5.30). The museum has a splendid reconstruction of a shipwreck, and displays on the sea, its beaches and cliffs; it also has an excellent section devoted to shipbuilding.

Le Havre

Le Havre inspired a generation of Impressionist painters and today it is home to Normandy's finest art collection.

Le Havre's seafront is close to the centre of the city

A new light: there are eye-catching modern buildings in Le Havre, which was the subject of most post-war reconstruction in France

RATINGS	
Cultural interest	●●●●
Walkability	●●●
Outdoor pursuits	●●●

Far right: Le Havre's modernist Cultural Centre was designed by Oscar Niemeyer. Below: the clock at the railway station

SEEING LE HAVRE

Only the most imaginative passenger arriving in Le Havre on the ferry could conceive that such a modern concrete conurbation of housing blocks, goods yards and oil refineries might ever have inspired one of the most influential art movements of the past 150 years. Of course, it was not today's industrial port of Le Havre, bounded by the English Channel and Seine estuary, that seduced painter Claude Monet and his followers.

In November 1944, 80 per cent of the town was destroyed by bombing, and after the war architect Auguste Perret (1875–1954) was commissioned to create a new city. The 150ha (370-acre) site of his bold redesign—the largest post-war rebuilding project in France—attempts to make use of the light that influenced the Impressionists. On grey and rainy days, the weather is less than kind to the harsh, modern materials of Perret's brave new city, but when the sun shines or the evening's artificial lighting kicks in, Le Havre has a definite contemporary style. By night, the buzz in Normandy's largest city moves from the superb museums and galleries to the city's six theatres, its cafés and its numerous bars, clubs and cinemas. Even if Le Havre lacks the romantic charm maintained by Honfleur, another magnet for great artists (▷ 70–72), the beach is just 500m (550yd) from the tourist office in the town centre and is worth visiting.

HIGHLIGHTS

SEAFRONT

Some 2km (1 mile) of seafront within an easy walk of the city centre provide all the facilities of a modern resort, with gardens, sand and pebble beaches, playgrounds, hot showers, changing rooms and even bicycle paths. The Blue Flag beach has a safety zone, manned by lifeguards from mid-June until mid-September, as well as special floating beach wheelchairs to provide easy access to the sea for visitors with disabilities. Sailing is another option, available from the city's marina.

Between the beach and the city is Perret's new district, with a spacious main square in front of the town hall and a tree-lined boulevard, avenue Foch, which is best explored on sunny afternoons.

MUSÉE DES BEAUX-ARTS ANDRÉ MALRAUX

✉ 2 boulevard Clemenceau, 76600 Le Havre ☎ 02 35 19 62 62 🕐 Mon, Wed–
Fri 11–6, Sat–Sun 11–7. Closed public holidays 💶 Adults €3.80, under-18s free
www.lehavretourisme.com

The cultural lighthouse of Le Havre is undoubtedly the finest art
gallery in Normandy. Named after a celebrated art critic, this show-
piece glass building is as close as an indoor space can get to bathing
in the natural light that launched a whole artistic movement. If you
spend a long afternoon here in autumn, the changing colours of the
sky affect the mood of the museum. The two local heroes are, of
course, Le Havre's own home-grown fauvist, Raoul Dufy
(1877–1953), and Honfleur's most famous son, Eugène Boudin
(1824–98). Choose to start your visit with a walk by the works of this
pair, or take the more conventional route, passing paintings by
17th–20th-century masters and stopping along the way to admire
Jean-Honoré Fragonard's *Tête de Jeune Homme* (c1760–80) and
one of Claude Monet's celebrated water lilies studies alongside canvases by Alfred Sisley and Auguste Renoir.

ÉGLISE ST-JOSEPH

✉ 76600 Le Havre ☎ 02 32 74 04 04 🕐 Mid-Jun–Sep Sat, Sun 🎧 Free guided
tours at 4.30

The most successful of Perret's innovations, with a 106m (348ft)
tower made from 13,000 shards of stained glass, this concrete building was completed in 1957. It is best enjoyed within, the coloured
glass making kaleidoscopic patterns on the walls and floor.

LE VOLCAN

✉ Espace Oscar Niemeyer, 76063 Le Havre ☎ 02 35 19 10 20
www.levolcan.com

Le Havre's dramatic cultural centre, created by Oscar Niemeyer, the
designer of Brasilia, is the focal point of the commercial docks in the
modern town, its sweeping concrete curves offering a liberating contrast to the more rectangular buildings that lie between the port and
beach. The building itself houses a national theatre and concert halls,
as well as a cinema. The varied programme of events is published on
the venue's website.

Above: a buoy guides ferries

BASICS

➕ 199 U4

🏠 186 boulevard Clémenceau, 76059
Le Havre, tel 02 32 74 04 04;
Easter–end Oct Mon–Sat 9–7, Sun,
public holidays 10–12.30, 2.30–6;
Nov–Easter Mon–Sat 9–6.30, Sun,
public holidays 10–1

🚌 From Lisieux, Caen and Caudebec-
en-Caux (connection with Rouen)

🚆 Le Havre (trains from Rouen)
www.lehavretourisme.com • Good
overview of the city, plus events guides

The tower of Église St-Joseph, designed by Auguste Perret

CATHÉDRALE NOTRE-DAME

✉ Rue de Paris, 76600 Le Havre ☎ 02 32 74 04 04 ⏱ Daily during daytime

A 16th- and 17th-century confection of Gothic and Renaissance styles, Le Havre's cathedral sports reptilian gargoyles and flying buttresses. There is a rose window above the north entrance, which is known as the Ave Maria door after the inscription on the façade. The coat of arms of Cardinal Richelieu (1585–1642), chief minister to King Louis XIII, adorn an organ donated by the *éminence grise* in 1637.

MUSÉE DE PRIEURÉ

✉ 50 rue de la République, 76700 Harfleur ☎ 02 35 45 40 62 ⏱ Jun–end Sep Wed–Sun 3–6; Oct–end May Wed, Sat–Sun 3–6 💶 Adults €1.50, under-16s free

Displayed within this old inn is the story of Harfleur, the forgotten precursor to Le Havre. Moving from prehistoric and Roman remains to images of the town in its medieval heyday, including the ramparts stormed in William Shakespeare's play *Henry V*, the displays allow visitors to imagine the past and see exhibitions by contemporary artists.

BACKGROUND

As far as most visitors are concerned, Le Havre's history began in the 19th century. Artist Claude Monet (1840–1926) grew up in the town, and his sunrise painting of the boats here, entitled *Impression—Soleil Levant* (c1873), gave Impressionism its name. But this great seaport has a heritage that pre-dates Monet. King François I (1495–1547) created the old town in 1517, when the former port of Harfleur (as featured in the lines of Shakespeare's *Henry V*, 'Once more unto the breach') silted up. Harfleur is now hidden in an industrial quarter of greater Le Havre.

The new port, originally named Havre de Grâce, was built on estuary marshland that benefited from long, high tides. The royal naval shipyard developed into a commercial port, its transatlantic trade supplying goods to rebels in America's War of Independence and receiving tobacco and coffee in return. From the 1850s, Le Havre was Europe's gateway to New York, the sailing vessels and steamships eventually giving way to the great ocean liners.

TIPS

● Boat trips around the port, or rented audio guides for solo strolls by the waterside, give lively introductions to the city.

● A day pass for the bus network costs €3.20 and is the quickest way to get around town.

● If you are visiting at a weekend, take advantage of the Bon Weekend en Ville promotion, offering two nights' hotel accommodation for the price of one. There are similar deals at Le Havre's museums.

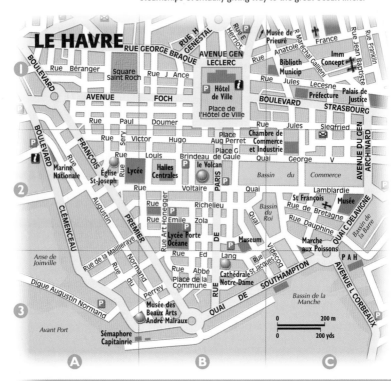

Rouen

History pervades Normandy's capital, a city of cobbled streets, tall timbered houses and Gothic churches. It is the resting place of the heart of King Richard the Lionheart and where Joan of Arc was executed.

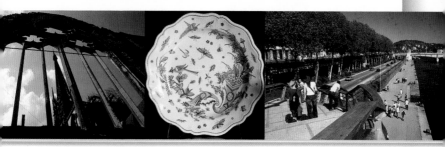

France's tallest spire, framed by the ruins of the Bishop's Palace

An 18th-century plate in Rouen's Museum of Ceramics

Street life in the historic core of the Norman capital

SEEING ROUEN

Rouen rises on the horizon as a blur of steeples above the grandly Gothic Notre-Dame Cathedral and nearby Abbey of St-Ouen. This makes for a memorable first view, especially if you are lucky enough to arrive at dawn or dusk. Don't be misled by the sprawling perimeter—the historic core is quite compact. Although there are bus and Métro systems, the city is best explored on foot, as all the major sights are walkable from the main station. Any trip should begin opposite the cathedral with a visit to the tourist office, which is housed in Rouen's oldest Renaissance building, the former tax collector's office (1509).

RATINGS	
Cultural interest	●●●
Historic interest	●●●●
Shopping	●●●●
Walkability	●●●

Local heroine: a statue of Joan of Arc on the spot where she died in place du Vieux Marché

HIGHLIGHTS

CATHÉDRALE DE NOTRE-DAME
✉ Place de la Cathédrale, 76000 Rouen ◷ Tue–Sun 8–6, Mon, public holidays 2–6
Rouen Cathedral is one of the great churches of France, known across the world thanks to Impressionist painter Claude Monet's *Cathédrales de Rouen* series (1892–93). Monet worked on the paintings from the second floor of what is now the tourist office. The cathedral's Gothic architecture spans 400 years, from the mid-12th to early 16th centuries. The dark, shadowy interior is offset by flashes of bright blue light through the stained-glass windows, which date from the 13th century. The choir contains tombs of many dukes of Normandy, while the crypt holds the heart of King Richard I (the Lionheart) of England. The 151m (495ft) spire, the tallest in France, was built in the 19th century. In summer months a spectacular light show projects images, inspired by the paintings of Monet, onto the cathedral façade.

AÎTRE ST-MACLOU
✉ Rue Martainville, 76000 Rouen ◷ Courtyard: daily 8–8 💶 Free 🚌 Palais de Justice 🚋 3, 13
A short walk from the Gothic Église St-Maclou (mid-Mar–Oct daily 9–7; rest of year 9–6) in place Barthélemy is its unusual annexe, the Aître St-Maclou. This pretty courtyard of timbered buildings is now home to the city's School of Fine Arts. A more macabre history is

hinted at by the skulls that adorn the woodwork. This was a plague cemetery, built to house the remains of the victims of the Great Plague of 1348, which claimed the lives of 75 per cent of Rouen's population.

GROS HORLOGE
⊠ Rue du Gros-Horloge

No visit to Rouen is complete without a stroll under the 14th-century Gros Horloge, a huge, one-handed, ornamental clock mounted on a sumptuously carved Renaissance arch straddling the road of the same name. Once part of a nearby belfry, the remarkable timepiece was moved to its present position in the 16th century, after locals complained that it was impossible to see the clock face in the old town's narrow streets.

BASICS

🚇 200 X4

🛈 25 place de la Cathédrale, 76000 Rouen, tel 02 32 08 32 40; Mon–Sat 9–12.30–1.30–6

🚉 Rouen (good connections to Paris) **www**.rouentourisme.com • Information about the city and its attractions, as well as photos

High time: Rouen's clock tower. Above: enjoying the café scene

Red flowers, black and white walls in historic rue Martainville

Urban sprawl: stick to the heart of Rouen and avoid the rest

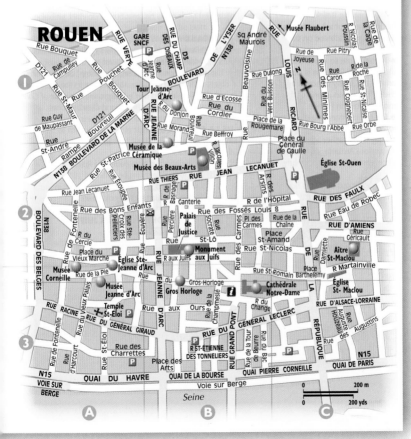

Le Tréport's seafront and quayside is the focal point for visitors to this traditional, low-key resort on the Alabaster Coast

Look through the windows of Varengeville-sur-Mer's church

THE SIGHTS

ST-MARTIN-DE-BOSCHERVILLE

⊞ 200 X4 🚹 25 place de la Cathédrale 76000 Rouen, tel 02 32 08 32 40; Mon–Sat 9–12.30–1.30–6 🚉 Rouen (12km/8 miles), then bus 🚌 Rouen www.abbaye-saint-georges.com

The 12th-century abbey church of St-Georges (tel 02 35 32 10 82; Apr–end Oct daily 9–6.30; Nov–end Mar daily 2–5), which dominates the village square of St-Martin-de-Boscherville, is among the best-preserved Romanesque churches in Upper Normandy. In 1114, Guillaume de Tancarville commissioned an abbey to be built on a former pagan site of worship. A religious community had already been established in the grounds of Boscherville manor by an earlier Tancarville, Raoul, who had once been tutor to the young William the Conqueror and later fought alongside him at the Battle of Hastings. Under William's patronage, the estate eventually settled on the religious community.

St-Georges' stark façade is typical of the string of pearly white churches that once adorned the Normandy landscape. Inside, the airy interior has surprisingly secular capitals displaying medieval jousting scenes. Visitors can tour the cloisters and chapter house, as well as gardens that follow the original 17th-century plans. The orchard, kitchen garden and herb gardens are open to the public, and the estate has impressive panoramic views across the abbey lands and the Seine valley.

LE TRÉPORT

⊞ 201 Y1 🚹 Quai Sadi Carnot, 76470 Le Tréport, tel 02 35 86 05 69; Jul, Aug daily 9.30–7; Sep–end Mar Mon–Thu 10–noon, 3–6, Fri–Sat 10–12.30, 2.30–6.30; Apr–end Jun, Sep Sun and public holidays 10–1, 3–5 🚉 Le Tréport 🚢 From Dieppe www.ville-le-treport.fr

From springtime, Le Tréport has a lively weekend buzz as Parisians let their hair down at the fishing port on the river Bresle, where Normandy meets Picardy. Just as in summer months, the bustling harbourside and shingle beaches below the Alabaster Coast cliffs are a magnet for holidaymakers who have discovered this modest alternative to Dieppe, along the coast (▷ 92–93).

The attraction of the resort is obvious. Old houses huddle together along the picturesque streets of Le Cordiers Cordant fishermen's quarter, while the steep 378-step climb to the Calvaire des Terrasses, a cross high above the port, offers views across the slate roofs of the town and along the coast towards the Somme *département*.

VALMONT

⊞ 200 V3 🚹 113 rue Alexandre le Grand, 76403 Fécamp, tel 02 35 28 51 01; Jul, Aug daily 9–6.30; Sep–end Mar Mon–Fri 9–6, Sat 9.30–12.30, 2–6, Sun 9.30–12.30; Apr–end Jun Mon–Fri 9–6, Sat–Sun, public holidays 10–6 🚉 Fécamp (12km/7.5 miles), then taxi

Valmont's chateau and abbey, a 11km (7-mile) drive inland from Fécamp, where the Alabaster Coast blends into the Pays de Caux, offer a glimpse into the age imaginatively invented by the faux-religious Palais Bénédictine (▷ 95). The vestiges of the Abbeye de Valmont (tel 02 35 27 34 92) are 16th- and 17th-century amendments to a 14th-century building. After the French Revolution, when the community's monks left the site, the abbey became a private home to which the artist Eugène Delacroix (1798–1863) was a frequent visitor. While the main church and most of the buildings are roofless ruins, the smaller Chapelle de la Vierge remains intact. Inside the chapel, 15th-century stained-glass windows tell the story of the Virgin Mary.

The Château de Valmont (tel 02 35 27 38 06; mid-Jul–early Sep Mon–Fri 9–noon, 2–5) was home to the Estouteville family, allies of William the Conqueror. The Romanesque keep contrasts with the 11th–15th-century styles of the main fortress.

VARENGEVILLE-SUR-MER

⊞ 200 X2 🚹 Pont d'Ango, 76204 Dieppe, tel 02 32 14 40 60; Jul–Aug Mon–Sat 9–1, 2–8; May, Jun, Sep Mon–Sat 9–1, 2–7, Sun 10–1, 3–6; Oct–Apr Mon–Sat 9–12, 2–6 🚢 From Dieppe

Varengeville is less a town than a cluster of villages in the woods that line the coast road south of Dieppe, a pretty drive or bicycle ride from the port that is punctuated by plenty of distractions. The highlight is the extravagant and lavishly decorated Manoir d'Ango, built in 1530 by privateer and master of politics Jean Ango (▷ 93) as a summer residence. Ango commissioned the fashionable Italian artists of the day to create grand artworks to adorn his holiday home, from sculpture to (long gone) frescoes, and in the Renaissance house he would entertain such wealthy and influential guests as King François I. Nearer the sea is the Parc Floral du Bois des Moustiers (tel 02 35 85 10 02; mid-Mar–mid-Nov daily 10–noon, 2–6), which is best visited between Easter and June when the magnolias and rhododendrons are in flower. The gardens surround a lovely house built at the end of the 19th century by the great English architect Sir Edwin Lutyens. Both the church and Chapelle St-Dominique in Varengeville boast stained-glass windows by the Cubist Georges Braque, who, like artist Joan Miró and film director Jean Cocteau, discovered the resort in the early 20th century.

This chapter gives information on things to do in Normandy other than sightseeing. It is divided into five regions, which are identified on the map on the inside front cover. Within each region, towns are listed alphabetically.

What to Do

SHOPPING

Normandy is a great destination for modest self-indulgence. Comfort foods are local staples, while the cities and seaside resorts are home to boutiques that sell the top names in fashion to sophisticated holidaymakers.

FOOD AND DRINK

With agriculture ruling much of its countryside, Normandy produces classic fare that has inspired restaurant menus and family meals for centuries. The pastures of Basse-Normandie yield some of the best dairy produce in the world. Cheeses, such as Camembert, Pont-l'Évêque and Livarot, are found in shops across the region. At farm shops and dairies you may be able to find cheese

Buy a pan in Villedieu-les-Poêles

made with unpasteurised milk and taste the product before you buy. Normandy has some little-known goat's cheeses, from the Seine-Maritime, while the region's rich cow's milk is used to make France's finest butter at Isigny-sur-Mer.

Farm shops and farmers' markets are the best places to pick up other speciality foods, such as the *boudin noir* black sausages of the Perche area (▷ 56). Here, you can buy a variety of pâtés. Sées is famous for corn-fed poultry (▷ 56).

Normandy's orchards and apple presses mean that cider is on sale everywhere, along with Calvados (apple brandy) and Pommeau (apple juice fortified with Calvados). The

best buys are to be found by following signposts to local producers or by taking official tours of major manufacturers.

In town centres, an '*épicerie fine*' is a quality grocer's store, usually selling food from small producers. A *boulangerie* is a bakery, where *baguettes* are baked several times a day and best eaten straight away. *Brasillés* are loaves made with the local salted butter. A *pâtisserie* is a cake shop and a *chocolatière* makes chocolates. A *boucherie* is a butcher, a *charcuterie* is a delicatessen and a *poissonerie* sells fish; local favourites include mackerel, herring and oysters.

MODERN STORES

Supermarkets (*hypermarchés*) are found on the outskirts of big towns and cities. Here you find a boulangerie, boucherie, charcuterie and poissonerie under one roof, alongside clothes, electrical and household goods. The best-known names are Carrefour, Auchan and E. Leclerc. Smaller supermarkets, such as Intermarché, can be found on the roads leading to minor towns.

MARKETS

The market (*marché*) is a French institution. Large cities have at least one daily market as well as a weekly event, and even the smallest town has a market day, with traders and shoppers coming from outlying villages. These usually start between 7 and 9am and continue until noon, and are good places to find local farm produce. Apple and cheese fairs are held across Normandy, while a *foire artisanale* is a craft fair selling anything from wool to handmade jewellery.

CLOTHES

Knitwear is a Norman tradition. All ports have boutiques selling tailored woollens that appeal to both the boardwalk and catwalk markets. Cotentin even has its own label, the Tricoterie du Val de Saire, which has outlets across the region.

Many individual boutiques survive, selling fashion (*prêt-à-porter*), lingerie and shoes. The fashionable resorts have plenty of designer outlets. Department

Shopping at Dieppe's market

stores (*grands magasins*) include the big Parisian names, Printemps and Galeries Lafayette.

ART AND ANTIQUES

From roadside junk shops (*brocantes*) to weekend flea markets (*marchés aux puces*), you can still find bargains, such as embroidered vintage bed linen. Antiques shops in larger towns are good for Rouen's blue and white crockery and copper utensils. Galleries, especially in the Impressionist country around Honfleur and the Alabaster Coast, promote works by up-and-coming French artists. Country auction houses provide a day's entertainment in their own right.

ENTERTAINMENT

Normandy may be best known for its rural pleasures, but it also celebrates the arts. Shows range from *café-théâtre* in Caen to *son et lumière* in remote ruined abbeys, summer arts festivals by the sea and opera in chateau gardens. Pick up a free local listings guide.

THEATRE AND CINEMA

You will find theatres in most major cities, as well as in a surprising number of smaller towns. Normandy has several *scènes nationale* (national theatre stages), ranging from 19th-century Italianate playhouses to modern arts centres. Programmes vary from touring productions to in-house pieces, and from classical works to experimental performance art. A diverse mix of music, dance

Many towns hold recitals

and children's entertainment may all be enjoyed. As well as a main playhouse, university towns host a number of alternative venues, from *café-théâtre* to outdoor spaces, where fringe shows are staged throughout the year. In rural areas, principal theatres often double as cinemas.

Most cities have a choice of traditional cinemas in their centre and modern multiplex options on their outskirts. The majority of foreign films will be dubbed into French (marked as 'VF' in listings), but in university towns you will often find American or British movies screened in the original language, with French subtitles ('VO' in listings).

MUSIC

Normandy has a constant musical soundtrack. From the springtime jazz festival in the orchards of the Cotentin to the mellow sounds of a city-centre jazz club in winter, you can find music wherever you go. Large-scale dance productions and big-name rock concerts are staged at arenas such as Caen's Zénith, while lesser-known musicians can be discovered performing in bars everywhere. At seaside resorts, casinos have cabaret.

The former railway station at Louviers, in Eure, is now La Gare aux Musiques, a venue for performances by up-and-coming musicians, while the Brasserie Hotteterre in La Couture-Boussey, Eure, is a great spot for enjoying live music and tasting the local brew at the same time. The opening of the gardens at Champ-de-Bataille in summer 2005 saw grand opera staged in the grounds of the chateau.

Festivals provide the ideal opportunity to enjoy music in characteristic places. Deauville's swing season in July is among the biggest events, but even country food fairs provide an excuse for live music in the open air. On 21 June (or the nearest Saturday night to that date), France's national music day inspires concerts, informal jam sessions and busking in towns and villages. For a weekly waterside party, discover the tradition of the *guinguette*: On Sundays, lunch segues into evening with families taking to the dance floor, as accordions or bands play favourite tunes in a bar on the banks of the Eure, the Orne or the Seine. Some *guinguettes* open for evenings during the week.

BOOKING TICKETS

Theatre box offices are open during normal working hours through the week, and should take credit card bookings. Fnac music shops in Caen, Le Havre and Rouen (www.fnac.com) and the Virgin Megastore in Rouen (www.virginmega.fr) have in-store and on-line booking agencies handling all high-profile events. For festival information and bookings, enquire at local tourist offices.

Cherbourg's grand theatre

ETIQUETTE

The French dress smartly for the theatre, even though formal wear is rarely seen outside opera premieres. Festivals are informal, but beach attire is frowned upon at evening events. Women and men should dress appropriately for concerts held in a church.

In theatres and cinemas, if an attendant escorts you to your seat, a *pourboire* (tip) of small change is expected.

SMOKING

Theatres and cinemas operate a non-smoking policy but smaller venues may be smoky. Music venues, bars and clubs may have a non-smoking zone, but it may be a token gesture.

NIGHTLIFE

Nightlife in Normandy invariably involves a drink, and so tends to blossom around the café and bar culture. Since clubs, concerts, cabarets and casinos don't get going until late, it is customary to start any evening, whether sporting or cultural, with a visit to a local bar.

CAFÉ-BAR

Night and day, the café-bar is the hub of French social life. Even the smallest village will have at least one bar where the locals gather to gossip, watch sport on TV, and have a few drinks. In the country, a single bar will be the hang-out for pool-playing teenagers, a rendezvous for cloth-capped pensioners and a refuge for farmers sharing conspiracy theories about politicians.

Nightclubs are found in the cities

In cities, each crowd chooses its own bar, and there are favourite places for an early-morning coffee, an aperitif or a late-night tipple. A PMU bar is part of the French tote system, where television screens show horse-racing and the barman will take bets on the race. In contrast, cafés come into their own with the pleasures of a well-chosen table on the terrace. Drinks are sometimes slightly more expensive when served outside rather than at the bar—notices in the window will indicate both prices.

While the country café may switch on a mirror ball and disco lights for an evening's karaoke, the scene in town is much more varied. In many cases, the line between bar and club culture is blurred. Latin and salsa venues in Le Havre attract the tequila, tapas and tango set, while bars in Évreux offer a round-midnight choice of live music or a DJ.

Bars in cities may open early at around 7am for breakfast and may close as late as 2am. In the countryside and the off-season, however, they may close by 9pm. The legal age for drinking is 16 and unaccompanied minors are not allowed in bars. Youngsters aged 14–16 may drink wine or beer if accompanied by an adult.

NIGHTCLUBS

Most cities and resorts have a busy club scene, with several establishments to suit different tastes. In the more rural areas, you may find just one venue, often with a choice of dance floors to cater for the young crowd and the over-30s. While retro nights are very popular, hip-hop and techno tend to be played more commonly.

Clubs open sometime after 10.30pm, but they do not fill up until the bars close after 1am. Most venues stay open until dawn. Midweek admission is often free, while weekends usually bring a door charge of €10–15. Many offer discounted or free entry to women and students, but when there is a charge the ticket usually includes your first drink at the bar. Drinks in clubs are expensive compared to café-bars. In Rouen and Caen, 'after clubs' open at weekends from around 6 or 7am until 9.30am and offer a mellower music policy to round off the night. You will find flyers advertising these venues in boutiques, trendy bars and tourist offices.

GAY AND LESBIAN CLUBS

There is a lively gay club scene in Le Havre and Rouen, with venues proving just as popular with young straight partygoers. Caen and Cherbourg have a choice of gay bars and Caen's Club Escapades offers gay sporting and social events. There are also gay-friendly venues in Alençon and Évreux. Monthly listings are posted at www.gaynormandie.com.

CASINOS

Casinos are venues for various entertainment, from cabaret to good dining. You should dress well, but there is no need to lose your shirt; the price of admission gains you a handful of non-refundable chips. Some casinos offer a choice of English or American roulette; the odds are slightly better at the English table. Doors tend to open around 10pm and close in the small hours.

CABARET

The sequinned showgirl revue is staple entertainment at the dinner theatre rooms of the seaside casinos. Do not expect the scale of Parisian shows, but few conclude without the traditional cancan. Smaller piano bars at casinos offer more intimate entertainment.

BOWLING

Ten-pin bowling is a popular night out in Normandy. Most bowling alleys offer dinner then a session on the lanes. Book ahead at weekends.

SMOKING

Smoking is still part of the French social scene. Some smart bars have a no-smoking corner, but people will light up around you in most venues.

SPORTS AND ACTIVITIES

Normandy has a great deal to offer outdoors. The coastline provides an excellent setting for wind and water sports, and horse-riding and cycling are ideal ways of seeing the countryside. Leisure options ranging from ice-skating to go-karting burn up excess energy, while municipal sports centres in most towns house swimming pools (*piscines*), tennis courts and other facilities at reasonable prices. For more information, visit a local tourist office (▷ 186). Free guides listing sporting activities are published in each district.

HIKING AND CYCLING

Normandy's countryside is ideal for walkers, who can hike along sections of the coastline or explore such regions as the Parc Naturel Régional Normandie-Maine (▷ 55). The region is marked with a wide range of Sentiers de Grandes Randonnées (long-distance) and Petites Randonnées (shorter) hiking trails, which are indicated on dedicated maps published by the Institut Géographique National (www.ign.fr). You can also find topographical guides at tourist offices and in park bookstores. In addition to these routes for serious walkers, local *mairies* (town halls) and tourist offices can provide information on their own marked trails along cliffs and through woodland. The Comité Régional de la Randonnée Pédestre in Oisel (tel 02 34 65 47 89) and the Fédération Française de Randonnée Pédestre (www.ffrp.asso.fr) produce specific updated information for walkers. You can also opt to *randonnée avec âne*—travel with a donkey, loading your kit in the panniers; for more information, check with the local tourist office.

Details of VTT (mountain bike) trails are available from all tourist offices, many of which can also arrange bicycle hire. In July, France's leading sporting event, the Tour de France, often passes through the region—discover the route in advance at www.letour.fr and find a spot by the roadside to watch the race and enjoy the associated carnival-style roadshow.

FISHING

Hire a boat to fish the Cotentin seaboard and Côte d'Albâtre, or enjoy angling from the river banks. You need a permit from a tackle shop to fish privately owned stretches of rivers and *étangs* (lakes). *Départements* produce free guides to fishing.

GOLF

Normandy has an ideal climate for golf, and there are courses across the region, some with fitness centres, clifftop views, and chateaux; 37 courses are open year-round, 23 of them with 18 holes. In Calvados, you can buy a pass accessing all the region's courses.

HORSE-RIDING

Le Haras National du Pin (▷ 54) and Le Haras de Préaux are two breeding stables that have won Normandy world-wide fame. Many stables are open to the public, and riding lessons and hacks are widely offered. Information can be obtained through the website of the Fédération Française d'Equitation (www.ffe.com).

WATER SPORTS

Sailing can be enjoyed from the ports and marinas along the Norman coastline—there are sailing schools (*écoles de voile*) and boatyards hiring dinghies and motorboats from Le Havre to Granville. Inland, you can go boating on the lakes of the Léry-Poses basin, southeast of Rouen in Eure, and canoe or kayak on rivers. For simpler routes, canoes or kayaks may be hired by the hour or half-day; longer itineraries often require a guide.

ADVENTURE SPORTS

Acrobranching (swinging through the trees) and paint-balling are among the treats on offer in the region's forests. There are also go-karting tracks outside major towns, and air and wind sports, such as sand yachting, can be tried along the beaches. Rock climbing and abseiling is also organised.

Sand yachting on Vauville beach

HEALTH AND BEAUTY

The French adore spas and health treatments derived from mineral springs and sea water. The belle époque Bagnoles-de-l'Orne, in a lakeside setting, is the biggest spa in western France, attracting 12,000 visitors a year to the spring, with its 24°C (75°F) waters. The spa season runs from mid-March to the end of October, while the winter months herald 'get back into shape' deals. Thalassotherapy sea-water treatments at resort hotels use the natural minerals in mud and seaweed. Resorts create a package centred around the basic treatment, with massage, water jets, sauna and steam baths as standard.

CHILDREN'S NORMANDY

Normandy has plenty to keep children entertained, whether the traditional treats of the seaside or the option of activity centres and theme parks. There are also plenty of outdoor choices, from horse-riding to bicycle trails. The emphasis throughout is on having fun as a family, rather than segregating kids and adults.

FAMILY ACTIVITIES

A lot of family fun may be had on Normandy's railways. Vintage trains run through scenic countryside in high season, miniature trains tour local country circuits and rail bike four-seater contraptions can be pedalled along genuine railway track through the Suisse Normande area. Normandy's agricultural tradition ensures that there are plenty of farms where children can observe cheese-making and other techniques and often meet the animals at the same time. Go-karting tracks, Cherbourg's ice-skating rink, water parks and ten-pin bowling are also all bound to keep the active family happy.

ADVENTURE PARKS, THEME PARKS AND ZOOS

Woodland adventure parks have discovery and activity trails adapted for various age groups and abilities, so that teenagers and younger children are able to explore according to their own abilities. Normandy's theme park, Festyland, at Bretteville-sur-Odon on the outskirts of Caen, has the roller-coasters and side-shows that children expect, but the theme here is Normandy's heritage, with William the Conqueror, the Vikings and other periods of local history marking out the rides and restaurants. There are also several zoos and animal parks in the region, whose occupants range from local farm breeds to more exotic species from abroad.

WHAT TO DO

FESTIVALS AND EVENTS

Hundreds of events fill Normandy's festive calendar, many of them centred around food. Even the first major jazz event of the year, Jazz Sous les Pommiers, is scented with the springtime apple blossom of the Calvados orchards of Coutances.

TRADITION AND RELIGION

Joan of Arc is remembered each May in Rouen, the city of her trial and martyrdom. Every five years, the city also hosts its famous l'Armada, a gathering of tall ships and their crews from around the world as the Seine relives the golden age of sail; the next l'Armada is planned for summer 2008. Also on a nautical theme, spring and summer each year bring traditional blessing ceremonies for smaller boats in fishing ports such as Honfleur and Étretat.

Christmas sees markets in the old town of Rouen and in smaller centres around the region, some of them staging nativity scenes, with villagers and farm animals re-creating Bethlehem. December brings the annual poultry fair to Sées, where people choose their Christmas turkey.

ARTS

Normandy has a love of film, and several small festivals dedicated to the medium are staged during the year. Various events celebrate Asian and British cinema, but best known is Deauville's September American Film Festival, which attracts the

See traditional country dances at a Normandy festival

biggest names in Hollywood to the Norman seaside. Summer music events range from July's celebration of the big-band sound at Deauville to the concerts on the island of Tatihou in August.

FOOD AND DRINK

Cheese fairs in spring and summer, and grand apple and cider festivals throughout the autumn harvest season, are Normandy's best-known food events. The *boudin blanc* sausage is honoured in Mortagne-au-Perche and herrings and scallops are fêted along the coast. The second weekend of September sees the Automne Gourmande gathering of chefs and farmers at Bagnoles-de-l'Orne, with gourmet workshops and tastings as the town becomes a *bistrot des chefs* (tourist office tel 02 33 37 85 66).

LA MANCHE

Fair sailing: yachts in Cherbourg's marina share the water with cross-Channel passenger ferries

Cherbourg and the Cotentin peninsula both promise lively nightlife, with clubs open until the small hours. In the daytime, a range of country and seaside activities at the farm or marina are on offer, along with vintage and miniature railway rides for all the family. As elsewhere in Normandy, food is rarely off the agenda—there are shopping opportunities, dairy and farmyard tours, and demonstrations of traditional culinary techniques that range from harvesting oysters to preparing the most famous omelette in France.

KEY TO SYMBOLS	
Shopping	
Entertainment	
Nightlife	
Sports	
Activities	
Health and Beauty	
For Children	

BARNEVILLE-CARTERET

✪ LA MAISON DU BISCUIT

Sortosville-en-Beaumont, 50270 Barneville-Carteret
Tel 02 33 04 09 04
www.maisondubiscuit.fr
The Burnouf family has been baking traditional biscuits for more than 100 years. The old bakery in La Haye-du-Puits has been surpassed by this new factory, whose shop stocks other local delicacies.
🕐 Tue–Sat 9–noon, 2–6.30, closed Jan
🎟 Free guided tour 🔧

✪ LE TRAIN TOURISTIQUE DU COTENTIN

Clos St-Jean, St-Jean-de-la-Rivière, 50270 Barneville-Carteret
Tel 02 33 04 70 08
www.trains-fr.org/unecto/ttc

The vintage diesel locomotive runs along 10km (6 miles) of track between Carteret and Portbail. The summer Sunday service is augmented by Tuesday and Thursday runs between local market towns.
🕐 End Jun–early Sep Sun, Tue, Thu departing Carteret or Portbail at 10 or 3
🎟 Adults €6, children (4–12) €4

CHAMPREPUS

✪ ZOO DE CHAMPREPUS

Parc Zoologique, 50800 Champreprus
Tel 02 33 61 30 74
www.zoo-champreprus.com
Wild animals roam in these gardens, between Villedieu-les-Poêles and Granville, with flamingos on the marshlands and ostriches on the savannah. Feeding time for the lemurs is a highlight of this zoo, whose collection of the Madagascan primates is famed across France. The big cats include lions, cheetahs and leopards.
🕐 Jul, Aug daily 10–7; Oct, mid-Feb–end Feb daily 1.30–6; Mar Sat–Sun 1.30–6; Apr–end Jun, Sep daily 10–6. Closed Nov–mid-Feb 🎟 Adults €11, children (3–12) €6

CHERBOURG

⊕ ESPACE JACQUES FEREY

7–17 rue au Blé, 50100 Cherbourg
Tel 02 33 53 14 18
This corner site is home to a huge showroom where you can find popular menswear and women's fashion labels. The sportswear, leisurewear and formal outfits are from designer houses such as Burberry and Marlboro Classic.
🕐 Mon–Sat 10–noon, 2–7

⊕ MARCHÉ AUX PUCES

Town centre, 50100 Cherbourg
Everything from antiques to old toys, books, second-hand clothes, china and glassware can be found at the sprawling flea market in Cherbourg's centre. Traders set up stalls on the place de la Révolution, rue d'Espagne and the parvis de la Basilique Ste-Trinité.
🕐 First Sat of month 8–6

🎭 LE BAYOU

5 rue Tour Carré, 50100 Cherbourg
Tel 02 33 53 04 55
Despite the traditional New Orleans frontage, this is a good

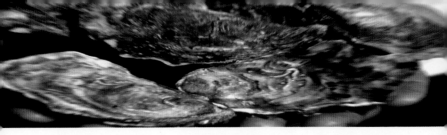

place to hang out at the weekend and hear new bands perform live. On hot summer nights, try to find a table in the little courtyard for a breath of fresh air. It's not too expensive either, with beers around the €1.20 mark.

🕐 Tue–Sat 3pm–1am

🎭 LE TRIDENT

B.P. 807, 50108 Cherbourg
Tel 02 33 88 55 55
www.trident-sn.com

Cherbourg's national theatre is a union of three separate venues in the city. The Classic Théâtre à l'Italienne, on place du Général de Gaulle, is a traditional 600-seat 19th-century playhouse. Le Théâtre de la Butte, on place René Cassin, was built in 1986 and has 400 unreserved places, so arrive early to choose your seat. Both of these theatres stage a vibrant programme of new and classic performance. On avenue de Paris is Le Vox, which was renovated in 2000 and has free seating for 240. This venue hosts jazz cabaret evenings. The Trident operates a car-pool scheme and theatregoers staying outside Cherbourg may be asked to offer a lift to other out-of-town customers.

🕐 Times vary according to performance schedule 💷 Admission varies depending on performance

🍷 L'ANTIDOTE

41 rue au Blé, 50100 Cherbourg
Tel 02 33 78 01 28

You can try wine by the glass from one of this bistro's hundreds of vintages. The bright designer interior is all wood and brass, and there's a pleasant terrace, open in fine weather.

🕐 Summer daily 8–midnight; rest of year Tue–Sat 8–midnight

🍷 ART'S CAFÉ

69 rue du Blé, 50100 Cherbourg
Tel 02 33 53 55 11

Reggae and rock are pumped through the sound system

here and there are live bands too. The walls are hung with works by young artists, there are theme nights on Fridays and Saturdays, and the house punch is the drink of choice. Although open all day, the hip crowd arrives after 11pm.

🕐 Mon–Sat 11am–1am

🍷 LE CRABE-TAMBOUR

5 rue de l'Union, 50100 Cherbourg
Tel 02 33 15 74

Don't line up outside the garish murals of this popular discothèque on the pedestrianised rue de l'Union much before 1am, as the party crowd doesn't arrive until the neighbouring bars have shut up for

Café culture in Cherbourg

the night. But the mood is lively, with the mixture of pop and rock attacting a mixed group who bop until dawn.

🕐 Wed–Sun midnight–5am

🍷 FIFTY'S DINER

Place de Gaulle, 50100 Cherbourg
Tel 02 33 43 58 20

Go back to the future with this retro 1950s American-style diner. Most evenings the television screens live sport, but on Friday nights this is the place for karaoke, with cheerful clusters of friends taking the mike to sing American pop classics in French accents.

🕐 Mon–Sat 8am–1am, Sun 10am–1am (food served noon–2.30, 7–11) 💷 Burger, coffee and drink: €9

🍷 LE FREEDOM CAFÉ

9 rue Charles-Blondeau, 50100 Cherbourg
Tel 02 33 94 08 88

The essential gay rendezvous in Cherbourg, a scene stalwart, attracts a mixed crowd of men and women of all ages.

🕐 Daily 5pm–2am

⛸ PATINOIRE CHANTEREYNE

Port Chantereyne, 50100 Cherbourg
Tel 02 33 53 60 50

Cherbourg's ice-skating rink welcomes families in the afternoon, while evening sessions appeal to couples. The rink is part of a sports complex with a dance hall and swimming pool. No credit cards.

🕐 Sep–end May Tue eve, Wed afternoon, Fri eve, Sat afternoon, Sun eve, all afternoons in school holidays
💷 Adults €4.70 afternoons, €5.20 evenings; children €3.40 afternoons, €3.60 evenings, including skate hire

GRANVILLE

🏛 ANTIQUITÉS BROCANTE DE LA FORGE CORNON

Route de Villedieu, 50400 Granville
Tel 02 33 51 53 76

Re-create a rustic Norman garden at home thanks to this second-hand shop. It sells Norman artefacts, including farm carts, water pumps and urns, 19th-century farm tools and pre-war milk churns.

🕐 Daily 9–7

⛵ STATION DE VOILE DE GRANVILLE

260 boulevard des Amiraux, 50400 Granville
Tel 02 33 91 83 72
www.station-nautique-granville.com

The water and beach sports on offer here include windsurfing, catamaran sailing, sea kayaking and sand yachting, but be warned that the bay of Granville has some of Europe's strongest tides. You may also hire or charter a sailing boat and set off for the Channel Islands, or visit the health spa.

🕐 Reserve ahead 💷 €18.50–21 per session of catamaran sailing, windsurfing or kayaking

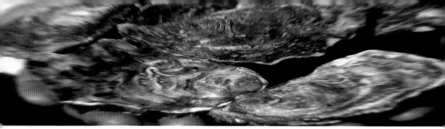

GRATOT

Ⓨ LA SOIFFERIE
117 rue Argouges, 50200 Gratot
Tel 02 33 47 88 34
For a great night out in the Coutances area, this nightclub appeals to those who prefer to sit around the swimming pool sipping the house gin fizz as much as to the young crowd shaking their stuff on the dance floor. It is lively, without the intensity of city clubs.
🕐 Fri–Sat and eve of public holidays 11pm–5am

HAMBYE

🏛 ANTIQUITÉS FARRADECHE CHRISTIAN
Route de Granville, 50450 Hambye
Tel 02 33 90 40 36
Best known for its displays of antique Norman furniture, cherrywood grandfather clocks, 19th-century chestnut dressers and Louis XV oak wardrobes, this antiques shop and furniture restoration centre also does a nice line in smaller *bibelots* (curiosities and ornaments) from across the region.
🕐 Mon–Sat 9–7, Sun 2–7

LESSAY

Ⓨ LE GIPSY
59 route Marais, 50430 Lessay
Tel 02 33 46 30 07
This lively club is a favourite with locals from across the Manche for its music policy, which stretches from the 1980s retro tracks that are the staple of French nightlife to more contemporary urban sounds. There are house and techno nights, and a welcoming young team runs the door and bar with friendly efficiency.
🕐 Fri–Sat 11pm–5am

✪ LAITERIE FROMAGERIE DE VAL D'AY
1 rue des Planquettes, 50430 Lessay
Tel 02 33 46 41 33
Before you stock up on the fabulous cheeses, crème fraîche and butter from this dairy, take the guided tour to see how milk is moulded, salted and packaged into

Camembert. A video presentation and visit to the modern production line are complemented by an exhibition of traditional cheese-making tools and a tasting of the finished product.
🕐 Tours: Jul, Aug Mon–Fri 9.15, 10.15, 11.15, 12.15, 1.15; during school terms Fri 2; rest of year by appointment only
💶 Adults €2.25, under-14s free

MONT-ST-MICHEL

✪ ÉCOLE DE CUISINE
La Mère Poulard, 50170 Le Mont-St-Michel
Tel 02 33 89 68 68
www.mere-poulard.fr
The most famous restaurant on Mont-St-Michel now has its

Drinking and dancing at a club

own cookery school. Two-hour classes on preparing classic Norman dishes are followed by a chef's demonstration of Mère Poulard's legendary omelettes, whisked in copper bowls, and the chance to taste this delicious dish with a celebration glass of local cider. Booking is essential.
🕐 Variable 💶 €50 per person 🍴

PÉRIERS

✪ MINI-TRAIN DES MARAIS
Base Touristique Centre Manche-Marchésieux, 50190 Périers
Tel 02 33 05 15 54
www.minitrain.fr
Families squeeze into the carriages of this miniature train, which runs along a track

through a landscape of woods, marshes, lakes and bridges. Built to one-eighth the scale of regular SNCF trains, the locomotive travels around a loop of more than a kilometre (0.6 mile) past model stations and lighthouses.
🕐 Jul, Aug daily 2.30–7; Sep, Oct, Apr–end Jun Sat–Sun 2–7 💶 Adults €2.30, under-13s €1.50

ST-DENIS-LE-GAST

🏛 ANDOUILLERIE DE LA VALLÉE DE LA SIENNE
Pont de la Balaeine, 2 les Planches, 50450 St-Denis-le-Gast
Tel 02 33 61 44 20
Bernard and Jacqueline Boscher are among the last artisanal sausage-makers to create the real *andouille de Vire* in the traditional manner, and all their products are made by hand and cured in authentic smokehouses. The sausages are sold in this shop in St-Denis-la-Gast (between Coutances and Villedieu-les-Poêles) alongside hams, *poitrines fumés* (smoked breast meat) and *rillettes à l'ancienne* (traditional coarse pâtés). Sausage-making demonstrations are held in summer. The opening times may vary, so phone ahead of your visit.
🕐 Jul, Aug daily 10.30–5.30; early Sep–mid-Sep, Easter–end Jun Tue–Sun 10.30–5.30; mid-Sep–Easter Tue–Sat 10.30–5.30. Demonstrations: Jul, Aug Mon–Fri 11, 3.30, 4.30, 5.30, Sat 3.30–5.30 💶 Demonstrations and visits: adults €2.20, under-14s free

ST-LÔ

🎬 LE DRAKKAR
29 rue Alsace-Lorraine, 50000 St-Lô
Tel 02 33 05 16 60
This cinema has four screens showing the latest releases, mainly Hollywood blockbusters but occasionally independent films shown in their original language. Movies for children are shown on Wednesdays.
🕐 Thu–Tue 6pm–10pm, Wed 2.30pm–10pm 💶 Adults €8.50, children around €5.50

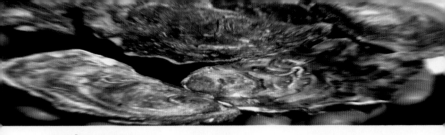

ST-LÔ-D'OURVILLE

✪ LE MANOIR DU PARC

50580 St-Lô d'Ourville
Tel 02 33 94 02 22

Enjoy a medieval feast (booking essential), with original regional recipes served by costumed characters, in the inn of this historic manor house 10km (6 miles) southeast of Barneville-Carteret. Or tour the farm and park to see the Shetland ponies, horses and cows bred here before visiting the big house.
🕐 Manor and farm: mid-Jun–mid-Sep, school holidays daily 2–6. Medieval feast: year-round by reservation 💷 Manor: adults €3, children €2.30. Farm: adults €2.30, children €1.50 🍽

ST-VAAST-LA-HOUGUE

🏢 MAISON GOSSELIN

27 rue de Verrüe, 50550 St-Vaast-la-Hougue
Tel 02 33 54 40 06
www.maison-gosselin.fr

This family-run grocer's store in the main shopping street of St-Vaast is known throughout the region, and its vintage delivery vans are something of a local icon. Besides an excellent range of Norman delicacies, from coarse *rillettes* (pâtés) to cheese, the shop has a superb wine cellar and vast selection of spirits.
🕐 Tue–Sat 9–12.30, 3–7, Sun 9–12.30

🏢 TATIHOU

6 rue des Parcs, 50550 St-Vaast-la-Hougue
Tel 02 33 54 43 04

Buy your oysters from the fishing shed on rue des Parcs on Tatihou island, and learn about the famed seafood, *les huîtres de St-Vaast*, with an exhibition, video presentation and regular tastings. See the freshly caught shellfish being cleaned and packaged. Groups can enjoy escorted trips out to the extensive oysterbeds.
🕐 Mon–Fri 8–noon, 2–6

VALCANVILLE

🏢 LA TRICOTERIE DU VAL DE SAIRE

36 rue Doncanville, 50760 Valcanville
Tel 02 33 54 02 06

Behind the traditional stone walls of this unassuming house is the headquarters of a knitwear company with shops across the Cotentin peninsula. The stylish jumpers and cardigans for men, women and children are firm favourites with the sailing community in the nearby pleasure port of St-Vaast-la-Hougue, and the tailored woollen suits for women are also sought after. A free guided tour of the factory on Thursdays may be booked

by prior arrangement.
🕐 Jul, Aug Mon–Sat 10–noon, 2–6; rest of year Tue–Sat 10–noon, 2–6

VILLEDIEU-LES-POÊLES

🏢 GENEVIÈVE PERRUT

39 rue du Docteur Havard, 50800 Villedieu-les-Poêles
Tel 06 88 31 30 46 / 02 33 90 77 87
www.gene-perrut.com

Geneviève Perrut creates jewellery from glass and paper protected by a clear resin. Her pieces are almost weightless but hard-wearing and come in distinctive designs.
🕐 Mid-May–end Sep Tue–Sun 10–7

VILLIERS-FOSSARD

✪ FERME MINIATURE

1 Hôtel Durant, 50680 Villiers-Fossard
Tel 02 33 57 06 41
www.perso.wanadoo.fr/thierry.durel/Claude.htm

A tiny, perfectly scaled model of a traditional Normandy farm has been the passion of retired gendarme Claude Delaunay, who has been working on his miniature creation for more than 20 years. Farm buildings, animals, equipment and even people are all made at 1:20 scale, and they offer a glimpse into the heritage of the region.
🕐 Mar–end Oct Sun and public holidays 3–7 💷 Free

FESTIVALS AND EVENTS

CARNIVAL

Granville
February
Tel 02 33 91 30 03

Winter is officially on its way out when Granville stages its Mardi Gras carnival. This essential date since the mid-19th century sees parades, live music and merrymaking in the streets of the port, resort and old town, a colourful treat and a great chance to see the townsfolk enjoying themselves to the full outside the holiday season.
🕐 Long weekend closest to Shrove Tue

JAZZ SOUS LES POMMIERS

Coutances
May
Tel 02 33 19 08 10 (tourist office)
www.jazzsouslespommiers.com

France's first major jazz event of the year is the music in the orchards festival at Coutances. It's a packed programme, with plenty of fringe events in the streets and bars of the town.
🕐 One week early in the month

LES TRAVERSÉES TATIHOU

St-Vaast-la-Hougue
August
Tel 02 33 05 95 88

This convivial music festival is

held on the island of Tatihou and in the seafront cafés and restaurants of St-Vaast.
🕐 Third weekend in Aug

VOIX DU MONDE

Across La Manche
September
Tel 02 33 05 95 88

Concerts across the *département* and hikes and rambles to local beauty spots characterise this wide-ranging celebration of music and the great outdoors.
🕐 Second or third weekend in Sep

WHAT TO DO

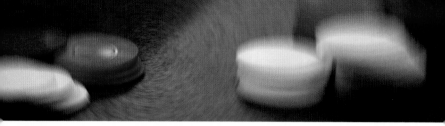

ORNE

Relax with a massage after taking your chances at Bagnoles-de-l'Orne's casino, above

With sausages and strong cider to taste in Orne's country markets, it would be easy to overlook some of the pleasures on offer in the region's towns. But there are theatres, arts venues and nightlife in Alençon and Mortagne-au-Perche, as well as the hedonistic pleasures of the spa resort at Bagnoles-de-l'Orne, 20km (12 miles) southeast of Domfront, whose diversions include healing waters, massage and blackjack in the casino. Enjoy the great outdoors without a car, pedalling a family rail-bike along abandoned train tracks.

KEY TO SYMBOLS

🛍 **Shopping**
🎭 **Entertainment**
🍸 **Nightlife**
🏅 **Sports**
✪ **Activities**
♥ **Health and Beauty**
🧒 **For Children**

ALENÇON

🎭 SCÈNE NATIONALE 61

2 avenue de Basingstoke, 61000 Alençon
Tel 02 33 29 16 96
The national theatre of Alençon, Flers and Mortagne-au-Perche specialises in performance art, world music and puppet shows. The box office in Alençon is open weekday afternoons and a full programme can be found at local tourist offices. There is also a venue at the Château Duhazé in Flers and at Mortagne-au-Perche (▷ 56).
🕐 Box office: Mon–Fri 1–6.30; performance times vary 🎟 Ticket prices vary with performances

🍸 LA LUCIOLE

171 route de Bretagne, 61000 Alençon
Tel 02 33 26 53 72

Whether you're into jungle jazz, hip-hop, heavy metal or accordion music, this is the venue to see contemporary bands and musicians. Events take place on the large or small stages or, during festivals, outside in the grounds.
🕐 Box office: Mon–Fri, performance Sats 2–7

BAGNOLES-DE-L'ORNE

🛍 JEAN-CLAUDE LEBARON

14 rue des Casinos, 61140 Bagnoles-de-l'Orne
Tel 02 33 37 92 10
Come here to discover the Orne's chocolate specialities, such as *étriers normands* and melt-in-the-mouth miniature swans. At the counter, choose from freshly made milk, plain and white chocolates to create your own gift assortment that is then neatly tied up in a smart box, or sit down with a *tarte normande* and glass of green tea in the tearoom.
🕐 Mar–end Jun, Sep, Oct daily 7.15–1.15, 3–8; Jul, Aug Mon–Fri 7.15–1.15, 3–8, Sat–Sun 7.15am–8pm

🍸 LE BILIBI

5 avenue Robert Cousin, 61140 Bagnoles-de-l'Orne
Tel 02 33 37 40 43
www.lebilibi.com
At this lively bar opposite the casino you can hear live music every Friday evening and most Saturday nights in season. Blues and *chanson* are the house speciality on stage, and plates of farmhouse favourites the speciality from the kitchen.
🕐 Jun–end Aug daily 3pm–1am (until 3am on live music nights); Sep–end May daily 5–1

🍸 CASINO DE LAC

6 avenue Robert Cousin, 61140 Bagnoles-de-l'Orne
Tel 02 33 37 84 00
The blackjack table, English roulette wheel and 100-plus slot machines attract the players here, but there is also plenty for non-gamblers: Dancing to a live big band, weekend tea dances, cabaret revues and shows are all on the summer programme.
🕐 Hours vary. Performances usually start at 9pm 🎟 Admission free; €10 charge to play the tables

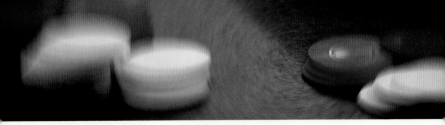

⊙ HOTEL EMERAUDE
Rue des Casinos, 61140 Bagnoles-de-l'Orne
Tel 02 33 38 44 44
www.groupe-emeraude.com
Among the treatments offered here are seaweed and sea-salt baths for a mineral boost, and detox or 'frigi thalgo' chilling sessions to improve circulation. The sauna and steam room are included with all packages. Open to non-residents.
🕐 Daily 7.30–10 💶 Seaweed bath: from €23. Frigi thalgo: €33

CAMEMBERT
✪ FERME PRESIDENT LE BOURG
Le Bourg, 61120 Camembert
Tel 02 33 36 06 60
www.fermepresident.com
In a renovated 18th-century farm, learn about the Pays d'Auge and its most famous product, Camembert cheese. The museum tells the life story of Marie Harel (▷ 56) with an audio-tour, demonstrates cheese-making methods and ends with a tasting session.
🕐 Jun–Aug daily 10–noon, 2–6 💶 Adults €5, children (11–16) €2

DOMFRONT
⊕ CHAIS DU VERGER NORMAND
Rue du Mont-St-Michel, 61700 Domfront
Tel 02 33 38 53 96
Buy and taste cider, Pommeau, Calvados and the famed Domfront Poiré from the town's old cellars. Visitors can see an exhibition of agricultural and distilling equipment. Those taking the one-hour guided tour receive a special gift.
🕐 Mon–Fri 9–noon, 2–6, Sat 9.30–noon

ESSAY
✪ KARTING 61
Circuit du Pays d'Essay, La Barre, 61500 Essay
Tel 02 33 81 97 85
www.karting61.com
A 1.6km (1-mile) karting track 10km (6 miles) southeast of

Sées that has a self-draining surface guaranteeing road-hugging performance in rain.
🕐 Tue–Sun 2–6 💶 €10–28 for 10 mins depending on kart

FLERS
✪ CAP FL'O
Centre Aquatique du Pays de Flers, Les Closet, 61100 Flers
Tel 02 33 98 49 49
www.recrea.fr/flers
Indoor and outdoor swimming pools for all the family, a big bubbling whirlpool bath and, especially for the kids, a huge waterslide for splashing and squealing. For adults, the centre has an aqua-gym and hydrotherapy centre, and the

Beer beats cider at La Poelerie

spa treatment complex is also equipped with a sauna.
🕐 Jul–Aug daily 10–6, 7 or 9; Sep–end Jun daily but shorter hours. Closed one week in Mar and one week in Sep for maintenance 💶 Swimming pools: adults €5, children (4–12) €4. Lockers: €1 coin

JOUÉ-DU-BOIS
⊕ LA POELERIE
61320 Joué-du-Bois
Tel 02 33 37 77 26
As an alternative to the many invitations to taste farmhouse cider, this tiny brewery, 5km (3 miles) east of the town of La Ferté-Macé, has created Normandy beer in apple country since 2001, after the storms

of 1999 damaged local orchards (▷ 12). Traditional-style ales include Norman Gold, a light *bière blonde*, and a stronger, darker *bière brune* called Le Conquérant. The beers are available from shops and bars in and around Alençon, or can be bought from the brewery, which is housed in a traditional farm on the site of an 11th-century forge. Free tastings.
🕐 Thu–Sun 10–6

MARCHAINVILLE
⊕ LA HALTE DE MARCHAINVILLE
Tel 02 33 73 65 66
www.marchainville.com
Marchainville is a tiny village 25km (15 miles) northeast of Mortagne-au-Perche with just 220 inhabitants, and its nightlife, shopping centre and cultural hub are all to be found under one modest roof. The Halte de Marchainville is the village fuel station, bread shop, newsagent, grocery store, bar, café and entertainment centre. Typical of the rural way of life in Normandy, patrons Dominique and her daughter-in-law Virginie sell croissants and newspapers in the morning and supervise entertainment by night. One corner of the small bar has comfy sofas for enjoying karaoke nights, settling down with a good book or challenging the men of the village to a game of tabletop football.
🕐 Shop: Thu–Tue 7.45am–8pm. Café-bar: as long as the villagers require

MORTAGNE-AU-PERCHE
⊕ ART ET PASSIONS
33 place de la République, 61400 Mortagne-au-Perche
Tel 02 33 83 91 71
Art et Passions is home to a picture restorer and frame shop, and has exhibitions of works by local artists. This is a good place to pick up paintings by up-and-coming and respected new talent. Since

1996, the shop has displayed and sold pictures by acclaimed naive artist Prune Bardoux.

🕐 Thu–Sat 10.30–12.15, 3–7

🏛 COUASNON

2 rue Ste-Croix, 61400 Mortagne-au-Perche

Tel 02 33 25 16 20

This family business has been mending clocks, selling watches and providing wedding and engagement rings to the local community for 45 years. Despite the traditional image of the firm, it specialises in smart contemporary jewellery, with modern designs for diamond, ruby, sapphire and emerald pendants, earrings and necklaces.

🕐 Tue–Sat 9.15–12, 2.15–6. Closed one week in Feb

🏛 LE CARRÉ DU PERCHE

23 rue Ferdinand de Boyères, 61400 Mortagne-au-Perche

Tel 02 33 85 23 00

www.lecarreduperche.com

This bright, glass-fronted modern building is part of the Scène Nationale 61 theatre complex, based in Alençon (▷ 52). A varied programme of touring productions from other national theatres around the country and local community performance work alternates with classical concerts.

🕐 Times vary depending on performance 🎟 Ticket prices vary depending on performance

ST-MICHEL-DES-ANDAINES

✪ VILLAGE DU CHEVAL DE BAGNOLES-DE-L'ORNE

61600 St-Michel-des-Andaines

Tel 02 33 38 98 20

There are riding stables and residential equestrian centres across the Orne for horsey weekends and longer holidays. Here, just north of the spa town of Bagnoles-de-l'Orne, you can saddle up and join other riders for a two-hour

weekend ride through the forest. Other options, including riding lessons and stays, are available on request.

🕐 Sun mornings 💶 €17 per hour

ST-PIERRE-DU-REGARD

✪ RAIL-BIKING

Gare du Pont-Erambourg, 61790 St-Pierre du Regard

Tel 02 31 69 39 30

An unusual way to explore the Suisse Normande region is to board a rail-bike, seating up to four passengers, and then pedal along 6.5km (4 miles) of disused railway track between Pont-Erambourg and Berjou stations, just east of the town of Condé-sur-Noireau. Exhibitions in the station buildings and rail carriages suggest sights to look out for on your journey, and explanatory panels line the route.

🕐 Jul, Aug daily 10.30–6; Sep, Oct, Apr–end Jun Sat–Sun and public holidays 10.30–6 💶 €5 per four-seater bike

WHAT TO DO

FESTIVALS AND EVENTS

FESTIVAL DU BOUDIN NOIR

Mortagne-au-Perche

March

Tel 02 33 85 11 18

The celebrated black pudding sausage of the Perche (▷ 56) is fêted with three days of feasting, tasting and merry-making. There are markets and musical entertainment.

🕐 Second or third weekend in Mar

LES MUSICALES DE MORTAGNE

Mortagne-au-Perche

June–July

Tel 02 33 85 11 18

This music festival sees chamber concerts, with local and national musicians, staged across the Perche region.

🕐 Last weekend in Jun and the first two weekends in Jul

Watch my hands: magic fingers at the Autour d'un Piano festival

AUTOUR D'UN PIANO

Château de Carrouges, 61320 Carrouges

July

Tel 02 33 31 16 42

Internationally acclaimed pianists perform in the majestic setting of the historic chateau (▷ 52).

🕐 Second fortnight in Jul

SEPTEMBRE MUSICAL DE L'ORNE

Across Orne

August–September

Tel 02 33 26 99 99

This concert season makes use of such diverse venues as the Haras National du Pin royal stud (▷ 54) and country churches, sites that provide lovely backdrops to evenings of jazz, baroque music, opera and dance. Food tastings usually feature too.

🕐 Late Aug–end-Sep

FOIRE AUX DINDES

Sées

December

Tel 02 33 28 74 79

The annual turkey fair held just outside the town attracts chefs and families travelling from miles around to choose their Christmas bird.

🕐 Second Sat in Dec

CALVADOS

Treading the boards: drinkers at a waterfront bar watch the action on Deauville's promenade

WHAT TO DO

Calvados is a great place for shopping and self-indulgence—not surprising when you remember that it is home to both the regional capital of Caen and the resort of Deauville, which claims to have invented couture and style. Pamper yourself at a spa, then buy some designer clothes and dress up for a night at a casino or club. Or you could always opt for the simpler pleasures of sampling country food in a dairy or distillery and rummaging for bargains in markets, roadside *brocantes* (junk shops) and portside galleries.

KEY TO SYMBOLS	
⊞	**Shopping**
ⓐ	**Entertainment**
ⓨ	**Nightlife**
ⓚ	**Sports**
✪	**Activities**
♡	**Health and Beauty**
✪	**For Children**

BAYEUX

⊞ BAYEUX BRODERIE
39 rue du Bienvenu, 14400 Bayeux
Tel 02 31 51 05 81
www.bayeux-broderie.com
Chantal James demonstrates the techniques of the famous Bayeux stitch and sells tapestry kits. She is happy to help amateur needleworkers with tricky stitches.
⊙ Mid-Apr–mid-Oct Mon 5–6.30, Tue–Sat 10.30–6.30

BLONVILLE-SUR-MER

ⓨ LES PLANCHES
Les Longs Champs, 14910 Blonville-sur-Mer
Tel 02 31 87 58 09
www.lesplanches.com
This nightclub, at a small resort near Deauville, has an outdoor

swimming pool. There are two dance floors, one reflecting current tastes and the other dedicated to reliving the sounds of the past.
⊙ Jul, Aug daily 11pm–5am; rest of year Fri–Sat 10pm–4am 🅟 €16

BRETTEVILLE-SUR-ODON

✪ PARC FESTYLAND
B.P. 50, 14760 Bretteville-sur-Odon
Tel 02 31 75 04 04
www.festyland.com
Normandy's heritage gets the theme-park treatment at this family playground on the outskirts of Caen, where rides and attractions are divided into zones designed around historical periods. There is a choice of dining, from crêpes to sit-down restaurants.
⊙ Jul, Aug daily 10.30–6; Sep, late Mar–end Jun selected days 10–6 (phone for details) 🅟 Adults €11.20, under-12s €9.50 🍽 🛍 🚻 🚗 Follow signs from Caen's Périphérique

LE BREUIL-EN-AUGE

✪ CALVADOS CHÂTEAU DU BREUIL
Les Jourdains, 14130 Le Breuil-en-Auge

Tel 02 31 65 60 00
www.chateau-breuil.fr
Not many distilleries have such an elegant setting. This one is in a 17th-century chateau south of Pont-l'Évêque, where apples are turned into the region's most famous export, the apple brandy Calvados. Take a guided tour and choose from various Calvados vintages or try Pommeau (Calvados and apple juice) or Coeur du Breuil (a Calvados-based liqueur).
⊙ Daily 9–noon, 2–6 (sometimes closed Sun in winter) 🅟 Adults €3, under-18s free

CAEN

⊞ CHARLOTTE CORDAY
114 rue St-Jean, 14000 Caen
Tel 02 31 86 33 25
This city-centre confectioner's may be named after a notorious murderess (▷ 56), but the chocolates on sale are sheer heaven. The delicacies, made from pure cocoa butter, include the local speciality *rochers du château*.
⊙ Tue–Sat 9.30–12.30, 2.30–7
🚋 Tram to Résistance

ZÉNITH DE CAEN
Rue Joseph Philippon, 14000 Caen
www.zenith-caen.fr
The auditorium here can seat up to 7,000 for the comedy, ballet, classical music concerts and other performances that are staged here.
Performances usually start at 8.30pm Ticket prices depend on the performance and can be purchased only at the venue on the night of the performance unless booked beforehand through a ticket agency

6X
7 rue St-Sauveur, 14000 Caen
Tel 02 31 86 36 98
This narrow café-bar in Caen's main commercial street is a firm favourite with locals weighed down with shopping bags seeking mid-afternoon refreshment. On Sundays, the shopping crowd makes way for students enjoying the last late night of the weekend. The back room is rather pokey and smoky, so find a table near the door or outside on the terrace.
Mon–Fri noon–1am, Sat 2pm–1am, Sun 4pm–1am Tram to St-Pierre

LE CARRÉ NEW CLUB
32 quai Vendeuvre, 14000 Caen
Tel 02 31 38 90 90
In Caen's trendy riverside district, this club is a hit with 30-somethings. The music policy is a canny blend of retro hits and the latest sounds. Before the main club opens its doors, the French Bar upstairs offers a welcome from 5pm. Karaoke on Tuesday and Wednesday.
Tue–Wed 9pm–4am, Thu–Sat 10.30pm–5am Tue–Wed often free, Thu–Sat €13 Tram to Résistance

LE CHIC
Place Courtonne, 14000 Caen
Tel 02 31 94 48 72
The dance floor is always packed at this nightclub, which despite its ever-changing programme of theme nights has an irresistible feel of the 1980s. The mixed crowds here include local students, holidaymakers and metropolitan

weekenders from Paris.
Tue–Sun 10.30pm–5am €12; women admitted free before midnight at weekends Tram to Bernières

L'ORIENT-EXPRESS
24 rue du 11 Novembre, 14000 Caen
Tel 02 31 72 81 64
Despite the garish pink awning over its entrance, this bar near the fashionable banks of the Orne is the essential late-night pre- and post-club rendezvous for students and locals. It is also an excellent choice for meeting up in the late afternoon to make restaurant plans for the evening ahead.
Daily 2.30–4 Tram to quai de Juillet

Two green bottles of Calvados

SOUTERROSCOPE DES ARDOISIÈRES
Route de St-Lô, 14240 Caumont-l'Éventé
Tel 02 31 71 15 15
www.souterroscope.com
Seemingly endless underground passages and four vast subterranean chambers are waiting to be discovered in the former slate quarries under the *bocage* landscape of Caumont-l'Éventé. The guided tour (in English or French) explains the mineral treasures and passes underground waterways and even rainbows. Warm clothing is advisable as the average year-round temperature stays below 12°C (54°F).
Jul, Aug daily 10–6; Sep, May, Jun

Mon–Sat 10–5, Sun 10–6; Oct–mid-Dec, mid-Feb–end Apr Tue–Sat 10–5
Adults €9.45, children (4–12) €4.50
Accessible to visitors with disabilities

COURSEULLES-SUR-MER
AUX TROIS MATELOTS
20 rue de la Marine, 14470 Courseulles-sur-Mer
Tel 02 31 97 53 13
You are as likely to meet a poet as a sailor in this wine bar around the corner from the quai des Allies in the port town of Courseulles-sur-Mer, 15km (9 miles) east of Arromanches-les-Bains. Have a rendezvous with the arts over a decent bottle of wine and a platter of cheese or charcuterie. Regular exhibitions of work by local painters, occasional poetry recitals from contemporary Norman writers and a reputation for good live music mark out this place as more than the usual bar or restaurant.
Restaurant: Tue–Sat 12.30–1.45, 7.30–9, Sun 12.30–1.45

CREULLY
PARAPLUIES H2O
Hameau de Creullet, 14480 Creully
Tel 02 31 80 31 35
www.h2oparapluies.fr
The ultimate rainy day diversion: Buy a hand-made umbrella and watch craftsmen at work in this shop, 9km (6 miles) southeast of Arromanches-les-Bains. These are the ultimate in brollies, with prices upwards of €60. Some are personally embroidered; others double as hardwood walking sticks. Special models keep the rain away yet allow the wind to blow through the material.
Mon–Sat 9–noon, 2–7

DEAUVILLE
MARIE LE BAUREC'H
1 rue Désiré le Hoc, 14800 Deauville
Tel 02 31 87 26 44
Normandy's best-dressed brides come to this boutique at the corner of rue Désiré le Hoc and avenue de la

République, but the stunning creations to be found here are not merely for walking up the aisle. Sensational corsetry, eveningwear and cocktail outfits are a reminder that Deauville has always been home to couture, ever since Coco Chanel invented style in the town in 1916.
🕐 Tue–Fri 3–7, Sat 11–1, 3–7

🎰 CASINO DE DEAUVILLE
Rue Edmond Blanc, 14802 Deauville
Tel 02 31 14 31 14
www.lucienbarriere.com
This casino and club is in a beautiful belle époque building on the seafront.
There are slot machines, gaming tables, two bars, three restaurants and a nightclub, and the dress code is formal.
🕐 Slot machines: Mon–Thu 11am–2am, Fri 11am–3am, Sat 10am–4am, Sun 10am–3am 💷 Cover charge for gaming room: €12

⛳ GOLF BARRIÈRE DE DEAUVILLE
Mont Canisy St-Arnoult, 14803 Deauville
Tel 02 31 14 24 24
www.lucienbarriere.com
You'll get beautiful views of the sea and the countryside from this 18-hole golf course on top of Mont Canisy, which offers fast greens and tough rough. After your round of golf, have a drink in the clubhouse or browse in the shop.
🕐 Daily 9–6 💷 Green fee: €34–80

DOUVRES-LA-DÉLIVRANDE

🍰 PÂTISSERIE DE LA BASILIQUE
3 place de la Basilique, 14440 Douvres-la-Délivrande
Tel 02 31 37 29 74
You'll find this small village a stone's throw from the local beaches north of Caen, and the pâtisserie itself in a pretty half-timbered house. For three generations, the Jung family have been making Normandy specials such as *brasillés* (bread made with the local

salted butter) and biscuits similar to Scottish shortbread.
🕐 Wed–Sat 7.45–12.45, 2.15–7.45, Sun 7.45–7.45; Jul–Aug daily, same hours

HÉROUVILLE-ST-CLAIR

🎬 CAFÉ DES IMAGES
4 square du Théâtre
14202 Hérouville-St-Clair
Tel 02 31 45 34 35
A state-of-the-art cinema complex and rendezvous for movie buffs, where English and American films are shown in their original language and there are plenty of themed seasons. There are also comfortable seats, low prices and a friendly café (with discounts for film-goers), all easily

Stick or twist at Deauville casino

reached by tram from central Caen (the last tram back to the city is at 11.50pm).
🕐 Phone for film times. Café: Tue–Fri 11.20–9.30, Sat 9.30–1.30, 3–9
💷 €3.30–5 🚊 Tramway B to Café des Images 🔲 🅿 ❓ Access for visitors with disabilities

HONFLEUR

🏛 ANTIC-DÉCO-ART
4 rue Brûlée, 14600 Honfleur
Tel 02 31 89 42 74
In a change from the heavy, dark furniture so typical of Normandy antiques shops, here you will find knick-knacks (*bibelots*), ivories, cameos, paintings and chandeliers against light walls, on polished tables and on the neatly tiled

floor. It's just the place to buy a special gift or the finishing touch for your favourite room at home.
🕐 Fri–Mon 10–1, 2.30–7, other days according to owner's whim

🎨 LES ARTS DE L'ENCLOS
Quai St-Etienne, 14600 Honfleur
Tel 02 31 89 19 13
www.galeriedaniellebourdette.com
The Danielle Bourdette-Gorzkowski art gallery on the quayside of Honfleur has a constantly changing programme of temporary exhibitions and is the place to buy works by such distinguished Norman painters as Yvonne Guégan and André Lemaitre.
🕐 Daily 10–12.30, 2.30–7

🛒 MARCHÉ TRADITIONNEL
Place de l'Église Ste-Catherine, 14600 Honfleur
This traditional market takes place on a pretty square presided over by a 15th-century church and lined with half-timbered buildings now housing cafés. Treat yourself to the locally caught fish and farm produce on sale here, including fruit, vegetables and dairy products such as the Normandy cheeses Camembert and Livarot. In season, craft stalls often line the streets leading up to the main market.
🕐 Sat 9.30–12.30

L'HÔTELLERIE

🏺 BROCANTE BEAU GEST
Route Nationale 13–Le Bourg, 14100 l'Hôtellerie
Tel 02 31 63 18 16
www.beau-gest.com
On the main road from Évreux to Caen, this treasure trove of a sale-yard has everything from farm tools to furniture, paintings, old clocks and kitchenware. It's well worth a rummage if you are looking for authentic souvenirs. No credit cards.
🕐 Mon, Thu–Sun 10.30–6

ISIGNY-SUR-MER

🏢 COOPÉRATIVE LAITIÈRE D'ISIGNY-STE-MÈRE

2 rue du Docteur Boutrois, 14230 Isigny-sur-Mer
Tel 02 31 51 33 88
www.isigny-ste-mere.com
The produce from this dairy co-operative is famous the world over, and since 1986 use of its name has been controlled, just as with champagne. The dairy is known for its crème fraîche, but it also produces a butter with a particularly distinctive taste, as well as cheeses (Camembert, Mimolette, Pont-l'Évêque), some of which are made from unpasteurised milk. Book in advance if you want to take a guided tour Sep–Jun.
🕐 Guided tours Jul–Aug Mon–Sat at 10, 11, 2, 3, 4 💶 Guided tours: adults €4.50, children €3

LISEUX

🍷 LE GRILLON

80 rue Henry Chéron, 14100 Lisieux
Tel 02 31 62 14 50
A favourite with the student crowd for its reasonable prices and contemporary music policy, this bar comes into its own in summer when tables spill out from behind the smoked-glass windows onto the pavement terrace. There are also occasional live music performances.
🕐 Mon–Thu 8am–10pm, Fri–Sat 8am–1pm

🍷 LE WEB CAFÉ

6 place de la République, 14100 Liseux
Tel 02 31 62 07 62
With bright blue awnings and colourful tables and chairs set outside in a corner of Lisieux's central square, this cybercafé is as much a place to surf the real thoroughfares as the information superhighway from the Internet workstations inside. Karaoke nights provide distraction from emails and downloads.
🕐 Daily 8–8

⚽ BOWLING DE LISIEUX

69 rue de Paris, 14100 Lisieux
Tel 02 31 62 19 30
The high spot—literally above the town—of Lisieux by night is its ten-pin bowling alley, the social hub of the town after the local bars close at 1am.
🕐 Fri–Sat 3pm–4am, Sun–Tue, Thu 3pm–2am, Wed 2pm–2am 💶 €5 per game

LIVAROT

🧀 LE VILLAGE FROMAGER

42 rue du Général-Leclerc, 14140 Livarot
Tel 02 31 48 20 00
www.graindorge.fr
Learn why the Normans call Livarot cheese 'Le Colonel',

Calvados is spa country

discover which red wines are best served with Pont-l'Évêque cheese, and watch commercial cheese-making in action during a free tour of this prettily timbered and flower-decked dairy 20km (12 miles) south-west of Lisieux. There are also occasional Pays d'Auge art exhibitions here.
🕐 Mon–Fri 9.30–noon, 1.30–5, Sat 9.30–noon 💶 Tours: free

OUISTREHAM

🌀 THALAZUR

Avenue de Cdt-Kieffer, 14150 Ouistreham
Tel 02 31 96 40 40
www.thalazur.fr
This is a thalassotherapy sea-water health spa, with hydrotherapy, seaweed treatments, a heated salt-water swimming pool, a Jacuzzi, a sauna and a gym. Health and beauty treatments are offered à la carte or on a residential basis, and there are special weeks for singles.
🕐 Mon–Fri 9–8, Sat 8.30–6, Sun 8.30–5 💶 Hydrotherapy: €38 for one session, €58 for two, €74 for three

PONT-L'ÉVÊQUE

🍴 LES TONNEAUX DU PÈRE MAGLOIRE

Route de Trouville, 14130 Pont-l'Évêque
Tel 02 31 64 65 20
www.lebistrotnormand.fr
Fun for the family, this themed restaurant serves dinner inside huge Calvados barrels from the Père Magloire cellars. Telephone for information on special evenings celebrating Norman heritage, when diners can learn to churn their own butter and join in folk songs and traditional games. You can also take the Père Magloire Calvados cellar tour nearby (tel 02 31 64 30 31).
🕐 Restaurant: daily 12–2.30, 7–10. Cellar tour: May–end Sep 10.30, 11.30, 2.30, 3.30, 4.30, 5.30; Oct, Apr 11, 2.30, 3.30, 4.30 💶 Cellar tour: adults €2.30, children free

PONT-D'OUILLY

🎸 ROCK 'N' ROLL ADVENTURES

Le Relais des Amis, rue de la Liberation, 14690 Pont d'Ouilly
Tel 02 31 69 83 34
www.rocknrolladventures.com
Explore the miles of mountain bike trails in Suisse Normande with English-speaking guides. Hire bikes are available and the operator, based in a farm-house on the river Orne, offers other activities including motocross riding, power boating, paintball, go-karts, rock climbing, kayaking, kite surfing, waterskiing and horse-riding. Packages are inclusive of food, activities and accommodation.
🕐 All year 💶 Weekend full board from £199 per person, including three activities

WHAT TO DO

VILLERVILLE

⊕ MA POMME
Rue du Général Leclerc, 14113 Villerville
Tel 02 31 98 11 42

Ma Pomme, up the coast from Trouville, stocks a range of products all derived from locally grown apples, including cider, Calvados and sparkling Pommeau (a mix of Calvados and apple juice). Other local specialities on offer include caramels, preserved meat and marmalade, all of which you can try before you buy.

🕐 Daily 9–1, 3–7 (sometimes closed Tue–Wed)

VIRE

⊕ GUY DEGRENNE
Route d'Aunay, 14500 Vire
Tel 02 31 66 44 44
www.guydegrenne.com

Guy Degrenne's fame stems from its original range of steel cutlery, and the company's stylish tableware, from glass bowls to children's crockery, is now sold in France's smartest stores. Take a guided tour of the workshops where the famous knives and forks are manufactured, then shop at the factory outlet store on avenue de Bischwiller.

🕐 Tours (75 mins): Tue–Fri by appointment only. Closed Aug
🎟 Tours: adults €3, under-18s €1

⚐ LE TIFFANY
Route de Champ-du-Boult, 14500 Vire
Tel 02 31 68 62 27

This venue is two clubs in one, with one room playing the latest techno and house sounds for a young crowd, and another dance floor for more retro partygoers. The garden outside is a great place for chilling out in the small hours.

🕐 Fri–Sat 11pm–5am 🎟 €9 (includes first drink)

FESTIVALS AND EVENTS

WHAT TO DO

FÊTE DES MARINS
Honfleur
May
Tel 02 31 89 23 30

Across town, this traditional festival blends religious services with folk celebrations. Fishing boats, colourfully decorated for the occasion, sail from the old port to be blessed by the priest, and there is a procession of sailors up to the chapel of Notre-Dame de Grace.

🕐 Whitsun weekend

MARATHON DE LA LIBERTÉ
D-Day beaches
June
Tel 02 31 27 90 30

This mass jog along the 'Freedom' coastline is a commemoration of the Battle of Normandy.

🕐 Weekend closest to 6 Jun

LES JOURNÉES ROMANTIQUES
Cabourg
June
Tel 02 31 91 20 00

Films with a feel-good factor are shown on the big screen as the resort spends a week celebrating full-length and short romantic movies on the theme of love.

🕐 One week in Jun

On the waterfront: famous names at Deauville

FÊTE MÉDIÉVALES
Bayeux
July
02 31 51 28 28

Troubadors, jesters and jugglers take to the streets around the cathedral as the town re-enacts a traditional medieval fair.

🕐 First weekend in Jul

FESTIVAL SWING'IN DEAUVILLE
Deauville
July
Tel 02 31 14 40 00

The big-band sound comes to the fashionable resort, with concerts in the casino theatre and events around town.

🕐 One week in Jul

FÊTE DU FROMAGE
Livarot
July
Tel 02 31 63 47 39

AOC (appellation d'origine contrôllée) cheese from around Normandy and across France, together with some of the nation's best wines, are celebrated with a market. Gastronomy turns to greed with Sunday's Livarot cheese-eating contest.

🕐 Late Jul

FÊTE DE LA MER
Trouville-sur-Mer
July–August
Tel 02 31 14 60 70

Sea-shanties and boat trips characterise the Festival of the Sea, when the port celebrates its fishing tradition with a party on Saturday and a Mass on Sunday.

🕐 Late Jul or late Aug

FESTIVAL DU CINÉMA AMÉRICAIN
Deauville
September
Tel 02 31 14 40 00

Hollywood comes to Normandy as the stars arrive for the American Film Festival, one of Europe's most accessible yet prestigious film festivals.

🕐 First half of Sep

EURE

Seeing the sights of Eure from the Pontaurail vintage train in Pont-Audemer

The Eure is essentially a rural district whose principal attractions are to be found among the farms and forests of its countryside. Shopping opportunities range from foraging for food to buying traditional country craftware. However, the area has a flourishing cultural life, too, in the lively late-night venues and imaginative performance spaces converted from old buildings in towns such as Évreux and Louviers. For those looking for adventure, the Eure valley and the route to the coast may be explored on vintage train journeys, while the river's waters are a magnet for canoeists.

KEY TO SYMBOLS	
🌐	Shopping
🎭	Entertainment
🍸	Nightlife
🏃	Sports
⚙	Activities
❤	Health and Beauty
☺	For Children

AIZIER

⚙ VIKING AVENTURE
27500 Aizier
Tel 02 32 57 24 46
This is a forest adventure park 10km (6 miles) northeast of Pont-Audemer. Take the tree-top trail, swinging from high branches, or perhaps enjoy a morning's paint balling.
🕐 Mid-Jun–mid-Sep daily 10–7; Apr–mid-Jun Wed, Sat–Sun 10–7
💶 Tree-top trail: €10–16. Paint-balling: €14 per hour. Mountain-bike hire: €8 per half-day 🚗 Take the D89 from Bourneville towards Quillebeuf-sur-Seine; after 3 km (2 miles) turn right and follow signs to 'Viking Aventure'

LES ANDELYS

🌐 HÔTEL DES VENTES
15 rue Sadi Carnot, 27700 Les Andelys
Tel 02 32 54 30 04
There is nothing quite like a French provincial auction house. If your command of the language is not up to it, stay very still; if you are confident enough to bid, you could go home with a bargain. In Les Andelys, auctioneer Jacqueline Cousin is in charge as locals sell the family silver. Themed sales of *objets d'art*, jewellery and haute couture are held year-round. Summer, mid-winter and Easter see the best items go under the hammer.
🕐 Sales: Sun 2.30. Viewing: Sat 3.30–6, Sun 10.30–noon

🏃 RACE TRACK
Route de Louviers, Tosny, 27700 Les Andelys
Tel 02 32 69 54 26
Race day in Les Andelys is an old tradition, when eight trotting races are held over a 1,450m (1,586yd) grass course beneath the Château Gaillard (▷ 78). Grandstands are erected and hundreds of spectators make a day of it.
🕐 Four Sun a year (Apr, May, Jul, Sep) 2.30

LE BEC-HELLOUIN

🌐 LES ATELIERS DU BEC
Abbaye du Bec-Helllouin, 27800 Le Bec-Helllouin
Tel 02 32 43 72 60
Originally established in 1034, the Abbey of Bec-Helllouin has been home to a community of Benedictine monks since 1948 (▷ 77). The brothers run a workshop manufacturing fine ceramics (tableware, dishes, vases and candlesticks), which incorporate antique designs.
🕐 Workshops: Mon–Sat 11–11.45, 2.45–5.45. Boutique: Mon–Sat 11–11.45, 2.30–6, Sun 12–1, 2.30–7

BOISEMONT

🏛 LE PRESSOIR D'OR

St-Jean-de-Frenelles, 27150 Boisemont
Tel 02 32 69 41 25

The picturesque setting of a 17th-century farmhouse and its gardens, 6km (4 miles) from Écouis, provides a perfect backdrop to cider buying. The gingham cloth-covered tables in the reception room are stacked with apple *compotes*, cider vinegars and even breakfast preserves created by the award-winning farm.

🕐 Mon–Sat 2–6

CORMEILLES

✪ DISTILLERIE BUSNEL

Route de Lisieux, 27260 Cormeilles
Tel 02 32 57 80 08

Normandy's biggest Calvados manufacturer makes a contrast to the region's homely family-run cider farms. The distillery, 20km (12 miles) southwest of Pont-Audemer, was built in 1910 and is also home to the Maison du Pays d'Auge, so the guided visit not only takes the visitor through the stages of production, but also celebrates local heritage. It's worth a visit, but don't miss out on seeing the farmhouse alternatives.

🕐 Apr–end Oct 10–12.30, 2.30–7
💶 €2, under-12s free

LA COUTURE-BOUSSEY

✪ BRASSERIE HOTTETERRE

12 rue Hotteterre, 27750 La Couture-Boussey
Tel 02 32 36 76 06

This pleasantly surprising farm visit, 4km (2.5 miles) west of Ivry-la-Bataille, promises shopping, drinking, entertainment and even a bed for the night. During the afternoon, guided tours of the brewery provide an opportunity to learn about the local Hotteterre beers, which can then be bought in the shop. On certain evenings (phone for the schedule) the place becomes a live-music venue for jazz and blues concerts. The brasserie also has some lovely *chambre d'hôte* (bed-and-breakfast) rooms

within the farmhouse for overnight stays.

🕐 Brewery tours (by appointment): Wed, Fri–Sun 2–5. Concerts: 9pm
💶 Brewery tours: €4. Concerts: €5–10. Accommodation: from €50 per night

DAMVILLE

✪ CHOCOLATRIUM CLUIZEL

Avenue de Conches, 27240 Damville
Tel 02 32 35 20 75
www.cluizel.com

Master chocolatier Michel Cluizel has been creating truffles in Normandy since the 1940s and his products are sold around the world. The family's Damville chocolate factory, halfway between Évreux and Verneuil-sur-Avre,

Explore cider's subtleties

employs 200 people and has a museum and visitor centre. Tour before you buy.

🕐 Tue–Sat 10–4.45. Closed one week in Apr, four weeks in Jul–Aug 💶 €5, children (6–18) €4, under-6s free

ÉVREUX

🏛 AU JARDIN DE POMONE

15 rue Edouard Féray, 27000 Évreux
Tel 02 32 33 06 81

Whether you are shopping for a family picnic or for gifts, this high-quality grocery shop is worth browsing. Good wine cellars, an excellent cheese counter and mouthwatering hampers of traditional Normandy delicacies are all to be found in one place.

🕐 Tue–Sat 8.30–7.30, Sun 9–1

🏛 BOULANGERIE PÂTISSERIE DE LA VIERGE

5 rue St-Sauveur, 27000 Évreux
Tel 02 32 33 07 83

When faced with the sumptuous crêpes, Cluizel chocolates (see above) and pistachio- and strawberry-flavoured confections at this delicious pastry shop, no one leaves with just a single baguette. It's pure heaven for the sweet-toothed!

🕐 Thu–Tue 7.30–7.30. Closed first week in May and first fortnight in Aug

🏛 FORUM ESPACE CULTURE

18 rue de la Harpe, 27000 Évreux
Tel 02 32 31 20 59

Catch up on your emails in the heart of rural Normandy at this relatively inexpensive cyber-café. The Forum's bookshop/music store is a good place to stock up with CDs for the car. And, if you require it, you can also find a photocopier here.

🕐 Mon 2–7, Tue–Sun 10–7
💻 Internet access: €1 per 15 minutes

🎭 LE P'TIT PARIS

Galerie Chartraine, 27000 Évreux
Tel 02 32 33 21 26

Come here for a big night out. This cabaret, floorshow and old-fashioned dinner-theatre venue has themed nights ranging from Chippendale-style revues to musical nights with cancan girls and magicians. There are two dining rooms, one seating 250 guests for dinner and a show, the other for smaller groups of up to 60.

🕐 Daily; times depend on programme
💶 From €36

🍸 LE MATAHARI

15 rue de la Petite Cité, 27000 Évreux
Tel 02 32 38 49 88

The essential hip haunt of Évreux is a former locksmith's. Bright and cool during the day, it is the ideal place to settle down and linger over the local papers and a coffee. In the evenings, DJs play rock sounds into the night. The waterside terrace is a favourite weekend hangout for students.

🕐 Mon–Sat 2pm–1am, Sun 4pm–8pm

🎵 LE NEW WORLD
15 boulevard de Normandie, 27000 Évreux
Tel 02 32 62 36 43
Always packed, even during the week, this popular club has regular theme nights. The main dance floor tends towards techno sounds, while a smaller disco revives the sounds of the 1980s and 1990s.
🕐 Thu, Sun 10.30pm–4am, Fri, Sat 10.30pm–5am 💰 Thu and Fri: €4. Sat: men €13; women free before midnight, €11 after midnight

🎵 PUB MACLÉOD
47 rue Jean Jaurès, 27000 Évreux
Tel 02 32 33 00 09
Unlike most Continental Irish pubs, this is more a meeting place for the locals than an expat hangout. At the weekend it becomes a tapas bar, and in summer live bands play in the garden once or twice a month as customers tuck into a barbecue. Known in Évreux as Le Mac, it plays Celtic music and serves a variety of beers.
🕐 Tue–Sat 11am–1am, Sun 4pm–1am

🎳 LE PARVIS BOWLING
2 rue Franklin D. Roosevelt, 27000 Évreux
Tel 02 32 62 42 33
This ten-pin bowing alley has eight lanes with electronic scoreboards, plus a pool hall and restaurant. Advance booking is advisable at weekends.
🕐 Mon 7.30pm–midnight, Tue–Thu 2pm–2am, Fri–sat and eve of public holidays 2pm–4am, Sun and public holidays 2.30pm–1am. Restaurant closed Sun–Mon 💰 Dinner and bowling package: €25.50

JOUY-SUR-EURE

🎵 LA GUINGUETTE
49 rue de l'Ancienne Abbaye, 27120 Jouy-sur-Eure
Tel 02 32 36 18 99
Come to Jouy-sur-Eure, 15km (9 miles) east of Évreux, for a traditional Sunday afternoon *guinguette* country tea dance. Favourite waltzes and ballads are played on the accordion as couples of all ages take to the

dance floor. There's no need to dress in your Sunday finery, just don't wear jeans or trainers. If you come on a Saturday evening, however, put on your smartest clothes and phone ahead to book for dinner.
🕐 Fri, Sun 3–7; Fri, Sat 9.30 💰 €10, €28–35 for a dinner dance

LÉRY

🛶 BASE RÉGIONAL DE PLEIN AIR ET DE LOISIRES DE LÉRY-POSES
227690 Léry
Tel 02 32 59 13 13
Some 16km (10 miles) north of Louviers between Léry and Poses are two fabulous lakes between the rivers Seine and

Bowled over in Évreux

Eure. From April to October, two beaches on the Lac des Deux Amants are supervised, and by the lakeside you will find golf courses, volleyball sets and a hire shop. The Lac de Mesnil is busier year-round, with windsurfing, canoeing, rock climbing, caving and rowing on offer.
🕐 Daily 10–7 🅿 €6 per car

LOUVIERS

🎵 LA GARE AUX MUSIQUES
Place des Anciens d'Indochine, B.P. 621, 27406 Louviers
Tel 02 32 25 78 00
In the year 2000, Louviers converted its former railway station into a music venue. A full line-up of concerts is matched by

the station's role as a music maker in its own right, with workshops and recording studios giving the place a soul.
🕐 Mon–Fri 2–midnight, Sat 2–8 💰 Ticket prices: vary with the performance; on first and last Fri of month during school term €5

🎭 LE MOULIN
Rue des Anciens Combattants Afrique du Nord, 27406 Louviers
Tel 02 32 40 22 39
This 18th-century mill has a long and distinguished history. Twice destroyed by fire in the 19th century, bomb-damaged in World War II and finally bought by the town in 1980, Le Moulin reopened as an arts centre in 2000. The venue has two theatres, a café and a bar.
🕐 Times vary with performance
💰 Ticket prices depend on programme
🅿 🍴

☕ GRAIN DE CAFÉ
39 rue du Matrey, 27400 Louviers
Tel 02 32 40 29 22
Despite a choice of a dozen excellent coffees, this address is a firm favourite with lovers of fine teas. Around 70 varieties of tea are always on the menu at this tiny café, which has a few seats on the street and is popular with Louviers' chattering classes.
🕐 Tue–Sat 8.30–7.30 💰 Cup of tea: €2

MISEREY

🍽 LA PASSÉE D'AOÛT
1 rue du Stade, 27930 Miserey
Tel 02 32 67 06 24
Blackberries and figs make excellent jams, but at Miserey, 8km (5 miles) east of Évreux, you can taste not only the fruits you might normally expect to find, but also carrot, prune and rhubarb. The owner, Vivianne, makes and sells her home-made preserves from her parents' fruit farm. You can pop by to pick up a jar of jam or choose to stay the night in one of the simple *chambre d'hôte* bedrooms and taste a selection over breakfast.
🕐 Daily 💰 Rooms: €37–42 per night

MONTFORT-SUR-RISLE

VAL DE RISLE

27290 Montfort-sur-Risle
Tel 02 32 56 37 14
www.ckvalderisle.fr.st
Make your way down the fast-flowing waters of the river Risle in a two-man canoe. You could attempt the 8km (5-mile) journey from Montfort-sur-Risle (15km/9 miles south-west of Pont-Audemer) to Corneville alone, take a guide with you for the half-day 9km (5.5-mile) expedition from upstream Pont-Authou to Montfort, or make a day of it and battle 17km (10.5 miles) of waters with your guide from Pont-Authou all the way to Corneville. A reservation is essential.

🕐 Tue–Sun 9–noon, 2–5 💶 Half-day: €25. Full day: €45. Guide: €20 per half-day

LE NEUBOURG

✪ MUSÉE DE L'ECORCHÉ D'ANATOMIE

Espace Culturel, 54 avenue de la Liberation, 27110 Le Neubourg
Tel 02 32 35 93 95
Little boys will love this eccentric medical museum, dedicated to the work of Dr. Auzoux, who in the early 19th century came up with a technique of making anatomical models from paper and cardboard. Astonishingly realistic re-creations of human bodies, revealing muscles, veins and bones, along with a generous array of internal organs and body parts ranging from eyes to limbs, are on display, some dating back 150 years or more.

🕐 Feb–end Jul, Sep–end Dec Wed–Sun and public holidays 2–6; Aug Wed 10–noon, 2–6 💶 Adults €2.80, children €2.30

PACY-SUR-EURE

✪ CHEMIN DE FER DE LA VALLÉE D'EURE

Place de la Gare, 27120 Pacy-sur-Eure
Tel 02 32 36 04 63
http://cfve.free.fr
With three scenic routes to choose from, a trip on this vintage train, departing from Pacy, east of Évreux, is the ideal way to discover the Eure valley. The century-old Pacy station was completely renovated in 2003 and is the start point for trips to Breuilpont, Chambray and Cocheral. Throughout the year, an imaginative programme of events ranges from dinners aboard the train to country markets on the platforms at Pacy. The train can be hired for private parties.

🕐 Train services: Jul, Aug Wed–Sun 2–6.30; Sep, Easter–end Jun Sun 2–6.30. Ticket office: Easter–end Sep Mon–Fri 8.30–12.30, 2–5.30, Sat 8.30–12.30 💶 Adults from €8, under-16s from €6. Private hire: from €320

Steam travel at Pacy-sur-Eure

PONT-AUDEMER

✪ PONTAURAIL

c/o Office du Tourisme, place Maubert, 27500 Pont-Audemer
Tel 02 32 41 08 21
Take a day-trip to Honfleur on a vintage train along the scenic railway line from Pont-Audemer via the impressive Pont de Normandie. The journey time is 55 minutes, plus a 10-minute bus transfer from the station to the port of Honfleur.

🕐 Late Jun–early Sep Sun and public holidays 9.30, 2, 4.35 💶 Adults €9, children €4

STE-OPPORTUNE-LA-MARE

⊕ MARCHÉ AUX POMMES

27680 Ste-Opportune-la-Mare
Apples, ciders and Calvados from the orchards of the Eure are the principal lure to this monthly farmers' market, 8km (5 miles) north of Pont-Audemer. You will also find foie gras, sausages, cheeses and honeys from local hives.

🕐 Oct–end Apr first Sun morning of the month

VASCOEUIL

✪ PARC DU CHÂTEAU

Château de Vascoeuil, 8 rue Jules Michelet, 27910 Vascoeuil
Tel 02 35 23 62 35
A relaxing afternoon walk through the grounds of the castle at Vascoeuil, 10km (11 miles) from Rouen, is worth a detour, even if you don't visit the museum, with its works by painter Fernand Léger (1881–1955) and film director Jean Cocteau (1889–1963). The river Crevon runs through the 5ha (12-acre) garden, which contains more than 50 contemporary sculptures; here, you can see works by Salvador Dalí (1904–89) and Georges Braque (1882–1963) among the trees and plants.

🕐 Jul–Aug daily 11–6.30; Apr–Jun, end Sep–Oct Wed–Sun 2.30–6. Closed Nov–Mar (phone to check out of season) 💶 Gardens: adults €5, children (10–18) €3. Museum: €2 extra

VERNEUIL-SUR-AVRE

⊕ FONDERIE D'ART CLAUDE ALEXANDRE

3 rue de Gournay, Les Barils, 27130 Verneuil-sur-Avre
Tel 02 32 37 64 70
www.alexandrefigurines.com
Visit the Les Barils foundry, 8km (5 miles) west of Verneuil-sur-Avre, to see Claude Alexandre at work casting and painting France's well-known model soldiers. Alexandre's detailed pewter and lead figurines are the star attraction of his museum, with such scenes from French history as the storming of the Bastille and the Battle of Waterloo. At the museum shop you can buy model soldiers

and chess sets to take home.
🎥 Foundry visits: Jul, Aug daily 11–12.30 2.30–6; rest of year phone to book an appointment. Museum and shop: Jul, Aug daily 11–12.30, 2.30–6, Sep, Oct, mid-Feb–end Jun Wed–Sun 3–5.30 💰 Museum: adults €4, children €3.10. Museum and workshop: adults €5.50, children €4.50 🍴 🅿 Free ♿ Access for visitors with disabilities

🔴 LE BOIS DES AIGLES
Route Nationale 12, Bâlines, 27130 Verneuil-sur-Avre
Tel 02 32 32 14 75
Watch displays of falconry at this 5ha (12-acre) park 5km (3 miles) east of Verneuil-sur-Avre, home to more than 100 birds of prey. Outside show-time, you can see the birds at home in 35 tree-filled aviaries.
🎥 Daily 10–6. Shows: 3, 4.30
💰 Adults €12, children €7

VERNON

🔴 LE CAFÉ DE FRANCE
59 rue d'Albuféra, 27200 Vernon
Tel 02 32 51 16 69
This is a useful address, especially at weekends, for visitors adding Vernon to their Giverny itinerary. Open far longer hours than most bars in the centre of town, the Café de France serves coffee early in the morning before the crowds head off on the Monet trail, and a late-night beer or glass of wine at the end of an exhausting day's sightseeing. You can also eat well for under €15 here, and there is a pleasant pavement terrace for watching the town revive after the working day.
🎥 Daily 7.30am–10.30pm

🔴 ESPACE PHILIPPE AUGUSTE
12 avenue Victor Hugo, 27200 Vernon
Tel 02 32 64 53 16
Vernon's theatre stages a variety of entertainment, from dance to classic theatre, experimental performance and children's shows. It also hosts a spring book fair. This independent arts centre flourishes despite Vernon's proximity to Paris and Rouen. Time a visit so that you arrive for a concert.
🎥 Sep–Jun, performance times vary
💰 Variable

FESTIVALS AND EVENTS

FÊTE DE L'ÉTAMPAGE
Marais-Vernier
May
Tel 02 35 37 23 16
The annual branding of the cattle at Marais-Vernier, 12km (7.5 miles) northwest of Pont-Audemer, brings a whiff of cowboy culture to Normandy. The event is marked with entertainment and plenty of food.
🎥 Beginning of May

JOURNÉES MEDIÉVAL
Les Andelys
June
Tel 02 32 58 28 74
The streets around the chateau are transformed as the town dresses up for its old-style markets, merrymaking and *son et lumière* show.
🎥 Last weekend in Jun

LE ROCK DANS TOUS SES ÉTATS
Évreux
June
Tel 02 32 24 04 43
Three days of live music erupt across town as Évreux stages its annual rock festival.
🎥 Last weekend in Jun

Turn back time at Les Andelys' Journées Mediéval

LES MASCARETS
Pont-Audemer
June–July
Tel 02 32 41 08 21
This three-week summer entertainment festival brings together established performers and street musicians in a programme ranging from concerts to impromptu sets on street corners by buskers from across Europe.
🎥 Late Jun–mid-Jul

FESTIVAL DE LA MARIONNETTE EN PAYS RISLE-CHARENTONNE
Bernay
July
Puppeteers from far and wide gather for the official festival programme and for fringe events held in the streets away from the main stages.
🎥 Four days in early Jul

VIÈVRE, TERRE DES MYSTÈRES
Épreville-en-Lieuvin
July
Tel 02 32 42 09 16
A spectacular *son et lumière* light show 18km (11 miles) south of Pont-Audemer, blending local history with folk tales and legends, begins at sunset.
🎥 Selected evenings throughout Jul

FÊTE DE LA POMME, DU FROMAGE ET DU CIDRE
Évreux
November
Tel 02 32 24 04 43
Great Normandy produce is celebrated with a festival of apples, cheeses and ciders. There are tastings and a chance to buy the best from local farmers.
🎥 First Sun after All Saints' Day (1 Nov)

SEINE-MARITIME

Follow the leader: learner sailors find their sea legs in the harbour at Le Havre

WHAT TO DO

Apart from the more gentle pleasures of touring country villages along the Seine and the Alabaster Coast, visitors to Seine-Maritime may discover the liveliest nightlife to perk up any city break in Rouen, Le Havre and Dieppe. Children can enjoy themselves in town, coast or country, exploring on roller-blades, swinging from the tree-tops in the woods or cuddling newborn animals down on the farm. And there are plenty of opportunities to shop for ornate, handmade jewellery and traditional tableware in craft shops or to indulge your sweet tooth with delicious cakes and chocolates.

KEY TO SYMBOLS	
🛍	**Shopping**
🎭	**Entertainment**
🍸	**Nightlife**
🏃	**Sports**
⭐	**Activities**
❤	**Health and Beauty**
✿	**For Children**

AMFREVILLE-LES-CHAMPS

✿ HAMEAU DE YÉMANVILLE
76560 Amfreville-les-Champs
Tel 02 35 56 41 46
This is a farm visit with a difference: There are donkey rides for the kids and summertime tea parties, as well as a year-round exhibition on the local linen tradition. The farm shop sells ciders, farmyard terrines, honey, cheese and fruit juices.
🕐 Jul, Aug daily 5–7; Sep–end Jun Wed, Fri 2–7, Sat 10–noon, 2–7 🅵 Free
🚍 Amfreville-les-Champs is 22km (14 miles) south of the Alabaster Coast's St-Valery-en-Caux via the D20

ARQUES-LA-BATAILLE

⭐ QUAD DIEPPOIS
76 Rocade d'Arques-la-Bataille, 76880 Arques-la-Bataille
Tel 06 63 41 53 08
Well-matured and planted outdoor trails and tracks characterise this fabulous quad-biking venue, which has a dedicated area for beginners and children. A young adult crowd enjoy the facilities in the week, while families come to have fun here at the weekend.
🕐 Jul, Aug Thu–Mon 2–7; Sep, Oct, mid-Mar–end Jun Fri–Sat 2–7, Sun 10.30–7; Nov–mid-Mar adults only by appointment Sat–Sun 🅵 €8 for 10 minutes

LES AUTHIEUX-RATIÉVILLE

🛍 FERME DES AUTHIEUX CHAPEAU DE PAILLE
76690 Les Authieux-Ratiéville
Tel 02 35 33 56 30
www.chapeaudepaille.fr
Possibly even more fun than a picnic is the chance to pick your own fruit and vegetables direct from the farm. As well as collecting your salad vegetables or fresh berries from the fields here at Les Authieux-Ratiéville, just east of Clères, you can buy cold meats and pâtés from the farm shop.
🕐 Mid-May–end Oct daily 9–noon, 2–7; Nov–mid-May daily 9.30–noon, 2–6

BEAUSSAULT

🛍 JOAILLIER PHILIPPE MARINECHE
350 rue de Serqueux, 76870 Beaussault
Tel 02 35 90 29 90
Many of the pieces at this wonderfully original jeweller are created by Philippe Marineche to his own designs. Creative and imaginative gold and silver brooches, chains and rings, plus some lovely pieces of china and tableware, can be found here as well.
🕐 Fri–Sun 10–noon, 2–7

DIEPPE

⊕ ATELIER COLETTE

3 rue Ango, 76200 Dieppe
Tel 02 35 82 36 97

The traditional Dieppois maritime craft of ivorywork, featuring meticulously carved *objets d'art*, is for sale in this workshop commemorating a disappearing art. Rest assured; these days bone and synthetic ivories are used by today's craftsmen. In the same street, at number 2, the neighbouring Atelier d'Art Ragault (tel 02 35 82 10 50) is open daily by appointment but charges €5 admission.

🕐 Mon–Sat 3–7

⊕ DIEPPE SCÈNE NATIONALE

Quai Bérigny, 76374 Dieppe
Tel 02 35 82 04 43
www.dsn.asso.fr

This modern auditorium, one of France's national theatre stages, hosts a variety of performances, including plays, dance and concerts, and has a cinema showing independent films and classics. There are touring productions from other regional theatres and a year-round programme of festivals and events. The good English-language website posts advance information on performances.

🕐 Daily 2–10 💶 Ticket prices depend on performance

⊕ CASINO DE DIEPPE

Boulevard de Verdun, 76200 Dieppe
Tel 02 32 14 48 00

Play blackjack and roulette at the gaming tables, or settle down with a glass of champagne and some Cole Porter in the Piano Bar. This resort casino has a good restaurant and live cabaret entertainment in the summer season. Smart dress is essential.

🕐 Gaming tables: Mon, Thu 9pm–3am, Fri 9pm–4am, Sat 5pm–4am, Sun 4pm–3am
💶 Admission: €10 worth of non-refundable chips

⊕ GOLF CLUB DIEPPE-POURVILLE

51 route de Pourville, 76200 Dieppe
Tel 02 35 84 25 05
www.golf-dieppe.com

The 18-hole course was landscaped in 1897 by Willie Park Jr. and has spectacular views of the white cliffs of Dieppe, the English Channel and the Pourville valley—bring your camera for the unmissable photo-opportunities at holes 7 and 17. Billed as the closest course in France to England's Sussex Downs, the club is used to English-speaking visitors.

🕐 Mon–Fri 8–7, Sat–Sun 8–7.30
💶 Mid-Jun–mid-Sep €47 weekdays, €52 weekends; Apr–mid-Jun, mid-

Get the blues in Forges-les-Eaux

Sep–end Oct €39 weekdays, €47 weekends; Nov–end Mar €29 weekdays, €36 weekends. Discounts for players arriving late afternoon

ÉTRETAT

✪ LE CLOS ARSÈNE LUPIN

Maison Maurice Leblanc, 15 rue Guy de Maupassant, 76790 Étretat
Tel 02 35 10 59 53
www.arsene-lupin.com

France's answer to A. J. Raffles, the fictional gentleman thief, is Arsène Lupin, created in 1905 by author Maurice Leblanc. Lupin, master of disguise, cat burglar and all-round decent chap, is one of the most popular characters in French fiction. The author's house has been transformed into the home of

Arsène Lupin, where visitors are escorted through the early 20th-century building by the hero's sidekick, Grognard, on an imaginary tour of his life and exploits.

🕐 Apr–end Sep daily 10–6; Oct–end Dec, Feb, Mar Fri–Sun 11–5. Closed Jan and two weeks in Nov 💶 Adults €6, over-60s €5, children (6–16) €3.50

✪ VILLAGE ÉQUESTRE D'ÉTRETAT

248–50 rue de la Sauvagère, 76790 Le Tilleul
Tel 02 35 27 04 22
www.village-equestre.cjb.net

This equestrian venue, which welcomes beginners, is south of Étretat at Le Tilleul. It offers guided rides through the beautiful surrounding countryside of forest and sea cliffs. There's a maximum of eight per group.

🕐 Fri–Wed 💶 €23 per hour

FORGES-LES-EAUX

⊕ AUX DEUX GOUTTES D'EAU

Place de l'Ancienne Gare Thermale, 76440 Forges-les-Eaux
Tel 02 35 09 61 53

This shop sells excellent reproductions of old-style blue and white Rouenware pottery, including plates, tureens, vases and lamps. Visit the workshops and see the kilns where traditional earthenware and glazing techniques are resurrected and re-created by Alexandre Audel and his fellow potters.

🕐 Daily 10–12.30, 3–7.30

LE HAVRE

⊕ LA GALERNE

148 rue Victor Hugo, 76600 Le Havre
Tel 02 35 43 22 52

More than just the biggest and best bookshop in town, with 100,000 books to choose from, La Galerne is a literary and artistic hangout. The café is a great place to eavesdrop or chat with fellow shoppers, and the various cultural spaces within the building have a packed programme of talks, debates and performances.

🕐 Mon–Sat 10–7

WHAT TO DO

🎵 L'AGORA

Espace Oscar Niemeyer,
76600 Le Havre
Tel 02 32 74 09 70
www.infoceane.com/agora
Expect hip-hop and jazz
among other types of music at
this venue. The bar plays
extracts of the music to be per-
formed on stage to get you in
the mood.
🕐 Sep–Jun (performance times vary)
💷 From €9

🎵 DEL RIO

Espace Oscar Niemeyer, 76600 Le
Havre
Tel 02 35 43 35 55
This late-night bar, slap bang in
the heart of the Espace Oscar
Niemeyer, has an unabashed
global culture feel to its décor
and ambience: Buddhas,
scented candles, leopard-skin
hangings and Southeast Asian
carvings combine to create a
sense of the exotic. This makes
Del Rio the perfect venue for
monthly live-music events,
from reggae to salsa, world
music and rock.
🕐 Tue–Sun 10pm–4am. Closed
alternate Sun

🎵 TRANSEPT

75, rue Guillemard, 76600 Le Havre
Tel 02 35 19 02 11
Rue Guillemard is better
known to locals as rue de la
Soif (thirsty street), since it is
the place to go for a final late-
night tipple before a summer
sunrise. This venue hovers
between the informality of a
bar and the pulse of a nightclub with the DJ spinning discs
until late.
🕐 Mon–Sat 6pm–4am

🎵 LE FLOSTON CLUB

34 rue Eugène Mopin, 76610 Le Havre
Rouelles
Tel 02 35 51 41 17
Dominique and David are the
weekend hosts at this nightclub, which is popular with gay
men and their straight friends.
The décor changes with the
legendary party programme,
and there are two dance floors

to choose from. Sunday night
is karaoke time.
🕐 Fri–Sun 11pm–4am 💷 Fri and Sun
free, Sat €10 (includes first drink)

🎵 LE MUSIC BAR

28 rue François Arago, 76600 Le Havre
Tel 02 35 53 14 59
It could be so easy just to walk
past this tiniest of bars, but the
seductive sounds from within
lure passersby inside. Crowds
packed into the split-level
venue enjoy the eclectic art
collection on the walls of what
looks like an elderly aunt's
spare bedroom, and the music,
which ranges from reggae to
punk via karaoke.
🕐 Daily 2–2 💷 Drinks from €2

It's a jazz thing: you can enjoy a
live jam in Rouen's music bars

MASSY

✪ ARTMAZIA

25 route de Neufchâtel, 76270 Massy
Tel 02 35 93 17 12
Just 5km (3 miles) from the
cheese centre of Neufchâtel en
Bray is the world's longest permanent natural hedge maze,
with some 3,500 copper beech
trees and 3.5km (2 miles) of
pathways. This eccentric instal-
lation is also an art centre with
works to be found amid the
twists and turns of the
labyrinth and a full summer
programme of art and crafts
workshops and exhibitions
🕐 May–late Sep daily 2.30–6.30
💷 Adults €4, children €2

ROUEN

🏬 GLOBO LOCO CLUB

59 rue Jeanne d'Arc, 76000 Rouen
Tel 02 35 15 00 58
Not a club, but a shop that is a
major meeting point for Rouen
youth. Pick up the coolest
streetwear here (such as the
Comète label), as well as
accessories and skateboards.
🕐 Mon 10–noon, Tue–Sat 10–noon,
2–7 🚇 Palais de Justice

🏬 MARCHÉ DU PLACE ST-MARC

Place St-Marc, 76000 Rouen
A splendid open-air market in
the heart of old Rouen. Pick up
vintage magazines, old jewellery and classic kitchenware
at the flea-market stalls and
stock up on country fare from
the food stalls. There are lots
of ciders and cheeses, but also
some delicious loaves of bread
and pain d'épices, a moist
gingerbread-style cake. On
Sunday mornings, the butcher
shops and ethnic food stores
in the streets around the
marketplace are also open.
🕐 Tue, Fri–Sat 8–6.30, Sun 8–1.30

🏬 MONASTÈRE DES BÉNÉDICTINES

14 rue Bourg-l'Abbé, 76000 Rouen
Tel 02 35 71 92 60
Come here for delicious cakes
and biscuits, including light
and fluffy madeleines, baked
and sold by the Benedictine
nuns who work in the little
cake shop at the side of St-
Ouen abbey church.
🕐 Daily 10.15–11.45, 2.15–5.15
🚇 Boulingrin

🏬 PÂTISSERIE DU PALAIS

37 bis, rue Jeanne d'Arc, 76000 Rouen
Tel 02 35 71 02 98
www.cirette-traiteur.com
This pâtisserie makes
Calvados-filled chocolates and
caramels using Isigny butter.
For a great souvenir, buy an
assortment of sweets packed
in a Rouen earthenware box.
The delicious cakes are irresistible, so take a break from
your city tour, relax in the

tearoom and pamper your tastebuds.

🕐 Mon–Sat 9–7 🚇 Palais de Justice

🎵 EXO 7
13 place Chartreux, 76140 Petit Quevilly
Tel 02 35 03 32 30

On the opposite side of the Seine to central Rouen, in the residential district of Petit Quevilly, discover this popular club for live gigs, with a year-round line-up of local and national bands. There is also a good calendar of theme nights, plus a play list that includes lots of dance-floor-pulling 1970s and 1980s tracks.

🕐 Fri–Sat 11pm–5am; closed Aug
💶 €10 (includes first drink), free for students before midnight 🚇 Jean Jaures

🎵 CYBERNÉTICS
59 place du Vieux-Marché, 76600 Rouen

Tel 02 35 07 02 77

Catch up with your emails in the heart of old Rouen. This cybercafe boasts 31 computers with flat screens and a warm welcome from the friendly team behind the counter. .

🕐 Daily 11am–midnight 💶 €6 per hour of surfing

🎵 LE CHAKRA
4 bis, boulevard Ferdinand de Lesseps, 76000 Rouen

Tel 02 32 10 12 02

A predominantly gay crowd packs itself into this newest incarnation of the former Traxx club in Rouen's port district. DJs play house and techno sounds until late, with a mellower music policy at the weekend 'afters club' that keeps the party mood swinging until breakfast time.

🕐 Fri–Sat and eve of public holidays 11pm–4am. Sat and Sun afters club: 5am–9am 💶 Fri €8, Sat €10 (prices include first drink) 🅿 Free parking nearby

🎵 LE KIOSQUE
43c boulevard de Verdun, 76000 Rouen
Tel 02 35 88 54 50

This is not the biggest or flashest club in Normandy, but it is an essential late-night rendezvous for the over-25s once the city-centre bars close their doors at 2am. Le Kiosque welcomes a mixed crowd of gays and straights, students and 30-somethings. The big plus is that it is safely within walking distance of the centre of town, a rarity in France where most nightclubs seem to be designed for motorists.

🕐 Thu–Sat 11pm–5am 💶 €14 (includes first drink), students €9
🚇 Boulingrin

🎵 LE TRIO
5 rue Ecuyère, 76000 Rouen
Tel 02 35 70 02 97

Let's roll: you can hire roller blades in Rouen

Between the Église Jean-d'Arc and the Gros Horloge in old Rouen, and within staggering distance of most city-centre hotels, is this young cocktail bar. Prices for the 40-plus house drinks start at €5.50, but only the very hardy order the speciality la Piscine: a litre (2 pints) of a heady alcoholic mix, poured into a vast glass to be shared with a good half-dozen friends. If you are driving, Le Trio also serves non-alcoholic drink combinations.

🕐 Wed–Mon 6pm–2am 🚇 Palais de Justice

🎵 LE SAXO
11 place Saint Mark, 76000 Rouen
Tel 02 35 98 24 92

A fine chill-out zone by the weekend marketplace, this haunt of musicians, students and the laidback is a great place to enjoy an inexpensive drink and regular live performances. The accent is on jazz and blues. Early evening or daytime, sit outside on the terrace; around midnight find a table inside and enjoy the mellow sounds.

🕐 Mon–Sun 9pm–2am

⭐ ROLL' BROTHERS SHOP
14 rue Jacques Lelieur, 76000 Rouen
Tel 02 35 70 65 82

Hire in-line skates and find out about roller-blading itineraries and events in and around the city at this skate shop and unofficial meeting place of young skaters.

🕐 Mon 2.30–7.30, Tue–Fri 10.30–12.30, 2.30–7.30, Sat 10.30–7.30
🚇 Théâtre des Arts

ST-MARTIN-DE-BOSCHERVILLE

⚡ ESPACE NORMANDIE AVENTURE
Val St-Lénard, 76840 St-Martin-de-Boscherville
Tel 06 71 17 36 03
www.espaceaventure.com

Try acrobranching (swinging from tree to tree) at this forest adventure centre. There is a choice of three kids' routes and one adult trail to suit various levels of skill and fitness.

🕐 Mid-Mar–mid-Sep Wed, Sat–Sun and school holidays 10–7, Mon–Tue, Thu–Fri 2–6 💶 Adults €19, children €15

ST-MICHEL-D'HALE-SCOURT

🍷 DOMAINE FOUGERAY-DUCLOS
76440 St-Michel-d'Halescourt
Tel 02 35 90 61 39

This typical 18th-century farm in the Pays de Bray makes traditional ciders, Calvados and the fortified aperitif Pommeau. In the 16ha (40 acres) of

orchards around the farm-house, various varieties of apple tree are cultivated in the time-honoured manner.

🕐 Jul–Aug Mon–Sat 9–12.30, 2–7; rest of year 2–6 except Wed, Sun

SASSEVILLE

⊕ CHÈVRERIE DU VIEUX MANOIR

76450 Sasseville
Tel 02 35 57 29 62

This organic farm shop, 13km (8 miles) inland from the Alabaster Coast's St-Valery-en-Caux, has a fine range of ciders, jams and apple juices, but best of all is its full-flavoured goat's cheese, made using milk from the alpine goats raised on the farm itself. Children will love visiting in springtime, when the newborn kids are on the farm and the milk and cheese are at their sweetest. Arrive at 5pm to see the milking.

🕐 Mar–end Dec daily 5pm–7pm

LE TRÉPORT

⊕ PERLERIE ENTRÉ EN MATIÈRE

5 quai Francois 1er, 76470 Le Tréport
Tel 02 35 86 84 97

Madame Piskadio makes striking costume jewellery from sticks of coloured glass beading worked with a blowtorch. Pick up some original earrings or a stylish necklace from the selection in her shop, or commission something special for a birthday or anniversary present. You can watch the artist at work in her studio.

🕐 Jul, Aug daily 10–7; Sep–end Jun Wed–Sun 10–noon, 2–6

VEULES-LES-ROSES

⊕ J. C. CLAIRE

78 voie Charles de Gaulle, 76980 Veules-les-Roses
Tel 02 35 97 61 10

Find top-quality cast-ironware, trivets, candlesticks, ornaments and fire irons, as well as attractive ceramics and pottery, are to be found at this old forge on the Alabaster Coast west of St-Valery-en-Caux. You can also watch the craftsmen at work before you buy.

🕐 Wed–Mon 10.30–noon, 2.30–6.30; Jul–Aug daily, same hours

FESTIVALS AND EVENTS

FOIRE AUX MOULES

Le Tréport
May
Tel 02 35 86 05 69

Seafood tastings and much merrymaking are to be had during this springtime mussel fair.

🕐 Whitsun weekend

FÊTES JEANNE D'ARC

Rouen
May
Tel 02 32 08 13 90

A medieval market and commemorative ceremonies are held by the river and at sites associated with Joan of Arc.

🕐 Weekend closest to 30 May

MARCHÉ DE TERROIR

Yvetot
June
Tel 02 35 95 08 40

A country market of traditional food, drink and local crafts.

🕐 Mid-Jun

LES PUCES ROUENNAISES

Rouen
September
Tel 02 35 18 28 28

Rouen's autumn flea market

Living history: Fêtes Jeanne d'Arc celebrate the heroine

and antiques fair is an opportunity for bargain-hunting in the streets of the old city.

🕐 Second weekend in Sep

FÊTE DU CIDRE

Caudebec-en-Caux
September
Tel 02 35 96 10 82

The Pays de Caux cider festival coincides with the area's apple harvest. There are music performances, tastings and markets.

🕐 Third or fourth weekend in Sep

FÊTE DU VENTRE

Rouen
October
Tel 02 35 18 28 28

A one-day food fair and produce market, with things to eat and drink from across the region.

🕐 Late Oct

FÊTE DU HARENG

Étretat
October
Tel 02 35 27 05 21

The annual herring festival is a celebration of Étretat's seafaring past and present, with folk traditions and plenty of food to eat.

🕐 End of Oct

MARCHÉ DE NOËL

Rouen
December
Tel 02 35 18 28 28

In the weeks leading up to Christmas Eve, wooden chalets appear in the centre of town, selling warm, spicy mulled wine, savoury cakes and Christmas nativity scene figurines.

🕐 Most of Dec

WHAT TO DO

This chapter describes four driving tours and five walks that explore Normandy. The locations of the walks and drives are marked on the map on page 134. It is advisable to buy a detailed map of the area before you set out on any walk.

Out and About

The map below shows the starting points of the driving and walking tours featured in this section of the book.

le Tréport

Dieppe

St-Valery-en Caux

Fécamp

Étretat **7**

Neufchâtel-en-Bray

Montivilliers Bolbec Yvetot

le Havre Lillebonne

Honfleur Deauville Rouen **8** Gournay-en-Bray

Cabourg Rouen **9**

Pont-Audemer Elbeuf Gisors

Cherbourg-Octeville

Valognes

Carentan Bayeux

St-Lô Caen **4** Lisieux le Neubourg Louviers les Andelys

Coutances **3** **5** St-Pierre-sur-Dives Gaillon Vernon **6**

Bernay Évreux

Villedieu-les-Poêles Condé-sur-Noireau Falaise Vimoutiers Conches-en-Ouche

Granville **1** Vire Verneuil-sur-Avre

Argentan l'Aigle

Flers

Avranches la Ferté-Macé

Pontorson Domfront Sées

St Hilaire Alençon **2** Mortagne-au-Perche

KEY TO THIS MAP

2 Drive   ■ Capital City

4 Walk   ■ City / Town

KEY TO ROUTE MAPS IN THIS CHAPTER

★ Start point   **6** Featured sight along route

— Route   ● Place of interest in Sights section

= = Alternative route   ● Other place of interest

▶ Route direction   ☀ Viewpoint

2 Walk start point on drive   621▲ Height in metres

OUT AND ABOUT

1. Walk
Granville Port and Town
(▷ 135)

2. Drive
Circling the Perche
(▷ 136–137)

3. Walk
Historic Caen (▷ 138–139)

4. Drive
Along the D-Day coast
(▷ 140–143)

5. Drive
Suisse Normande and the
Orne Valley (▷ 144–145)

6. Walk
Giverny (▷ 146–147)

7. Walk
Étretat (▷ 148–149)

8. Drive
Lower Seine Valley
(▷ 150–151)

9. Walk
Rouen (▷ 152–153)

War and peace: 5 June 1944, D-Day, is part of the fabric of Normandy

GRANVILLE PORT AND TOWN

This circuit takes in the ports and waterfront of Granville (▷ 45), as well as the ramparts and steep streets of the old town, with the opportunity to break the journey in attractively landscaped parks and gardens. Comfortable walking shoes are essential.

THE WALK

Distance: 5km (3 miles)
Allow: 2 hours, excluding visits
Start/end at: Place d'Orléans

HOW TO GET THERE

Arriving at Granville from the south on the D911, follow boulevard des Amiraux Granvillais through place Albert Godal to place d'Orléans. You can park in place d'Orléans, place Guepratte or in Granville's main port

The walk begins at place d'Orléans, looking out over the sailing port. Follow the quai d'Orléans to your left and the turn left again onto rue d'Orléans. At a crossroads, turn right along boulevard des Amiraux Granvillais to reach the Station Nautique.

❶ The Station Nautique is Granville's principal pleasure port, and is the perfect place for hiring all types of boat, from kayaks to catamarans. A sailing school offers long courses or half-day lessons, and boat-hire outlets and tour operators run excursions to the Îles Chausey.

At the square de la Bisquine, turn left, climbing up to rue St-Gaud. On your right, around 50m (55yd) along the road, is the chemin de la Huguette. At the top of this road turn left onto rue St-Paul, then take the second road on your right, rue Ste-Marie. A further 50m (55yd) on your left, take rue Tardif, then follow the passage Gautier on your right. At the end of the passage, cross the main road (rue Couraye) and follow the gently curving chemin de Val des Fleurs into the Parc de Val des Fleurs.
    Pause for a stroll under the trees in the park, which provide welcome shade on a sunny day, then leave via the winding allée des Daimes. Turn right along boulevard Girard Desprairies past the Catholic school and turn left on rue de la Croix de Lude. Cross over avenue de la Libération onto rue d'Estoutville.

Turrets and towers: a building in Granville's old town

❷ The Musée de Christian Dior is on your right in the Villa les Rhumbs. The childhood home of one of the most influential fashion designers of the 20th century hosts enthralling exhibitions and is a perfect example of a 1920s domestic villa. A tearoom in the museum's gardens provides refreshment.

Follow chemin du Noroit, then bear right onto rue de la Falaise. Turn right when you come to rue Michelet. Cross place Maréchal Foch, taking the steps by the casino to place de l'Isthme.

❸ Place de l'Isthme provides a perfect photo-opportunity: From here you look out over the town itself, and have a superb panorama over the sea to the north and south, with clear views of the Îles Chausey.
    While you are in place de l'Isthme, check out the modern art collection at the Musée Richard Anacréon (▷ 45), which includes works by Pablo Picasso, Raoul Dufy and Paul Signac. There are often interesting temporary exhibitions here, and the museum library has an acclaimed collection of original manuscripts and photos of key literary figures of the early 20th century, among them Jean Genet and Colette.

Walk along the ramparts that follow rue du Nord. Turn left on rue Platriers and right along rue St-Jean. The Montée du Parvis leads to place Notre-Dame and its church.

❹ The 15th-century Église Notre-Dame may have an austere granite exterior, but appearances can be deceptive. Inside, modern stained-glass images of Old Testament characters illuminate the chancel.

From the church, follow boulevard du 2ème and 202ème de Ligne to the Grand'Porte, original gateway to the fortified town.

❺ The Musée du Vieux Granville (▷ 45), above the gateway, has displays of traditional maritime costumes and tells the story of the port from the days of pirates to the golden age of seaside holidays.

Follow rue des Juifs from the Grand'Porte. Steps on your right lead to place Pleville and the start point on place d'Orléans.

PLACES TO VISIT

Station Nautique
Centre Régional de Nautisme, 260 boulevard des Amiraux, 50400 Granville
☎ 02 33 91 22 60. Sailing school: 02 33 91 83 72

Musée de Christian Dior
Villa les Rhumbs, 50400 Granville
☎ 02 33 61 48 21
🕐 Late May–end Sep daily 10–6.30
🎫 Adults €5, children €4

WHEN TO GO

The walk is best undertaken from spring to September, when the sights are open and the weather—and hence the views—are most likely to be at their best. Note that the stairs along the route may become slippery in rain.

WHERE TO EAT

La Citadelle
▷ 159

OUT AND ABOUT

CIRCLING THE PERCHE

Although this tour passes through a handful of towns with fine churches, it is a discovery of Normandy at its most rural. Vast forests, rolling hills, meandering rivers and timbered manor houses are reminders that the Perche is the land of the horse and the hiker, and that motorists are mere visitors.

OUT AND ABOUT

THE DRIVE

Distance: 221km (137 miles)	
Allow: 1 day	
Start/end: Alençon	

HOW TO GET THERE

Alençon is reached from junctions 18 and 19 of the A28 autoroute

Start your journey at the town of Alençon, the southern gateway to Normandy and boasting several fine gabled timber houses. The town's tradition of lace-making is remembered with two museums (▷ 52), and the numerous gift shops are also testament to the craft.

Leaving town, ignore the signs towards the direct N138 road to Sées and instead take the scenic D26 route out into the Fôret d'Écouves, which forms part of the Parc Naturel Régional Normandie-Maine.

❶ Parc Naturel Régional Normandie-Maine (▷ 55) encompasses four forests, the largest of which is Écouves. The temptation here is to pull over and set off on a forest walk, but before you do so ensure you pick up a map from the information centre at Carrouges (▷ 52) and stick to marked trails. The park is home to deer as well as snakes and wild boar.

As you drive along the D26, follow road signs for the Rochers du Vignage.

❷ The Rochers du Vignage are granite rocks next to a stream a little way from the roadside. Walkers can hike from here to la Croix Madame to the west, with panoramic views, then take the GR36 hiking route to the Signal d'Écouves further north (see below).
This rural setting played a part in the Battle of Normandy. After Général Leclerc liberated Alençon on 12 August 1944,

Allied soldiers encountered German troops in the forest at Rochers du Vignage. On the left-hand side of the road here is a tiny war cemetery with 19 French graves, while a little further on, on the right, is a monument to Roger Remy, an 18-year-old soldier of the 2nd Armoured Division.

Continue on the D26 to the Croix de Médavy crossroads, easily seen thanks to the Sherman tank standing in tribute to the 2nd Armoured Division. Before continuing, consider stopping at the crossroads and following the walking trail up to the Signal d'Écouves, at 417m (1,368ft) the highest point in Normandy. Turn right at the crossroads onto the D226, following the road until you can bear right onto the D908 into Sées.

❸ Sées sits on the banks of the river Orne and is famous for its magnificent cathedral (▷ 56), which is illuminated at night in summer. If you are passing through on a summer Sunday, take a break here to enjoy live music by the waterside.

From Sées, take the N158 to Mortrée, turning right onto the D26 to reach the Château d'O.

A Percheron horse at the Haras National du Pin stud. The breed originated in the Perche

❹ The fairytale Château d'O is surrounded by water and imbued with political history (▷ 53). There are lovely gardens and a restaurant in one of the farm buildings on the estate.

Follow the D26 until it becomes the D16, then follow signs for Le Pin-au-Haras to reach the Haras National du Pin.

❺ The Haras National du Pin, known as the Versailles of the Horse, is a royal stud farm that was built by King Louis XIV. The elegant 17th-century buildings are worth breaking your journey to discover, especially if you can visit during one of the musical displays of horsemanship (▷ 54).

Follow the N26 east beside the river Risle towards the country town of l'Aigle.

❻ L'Aigle has typical half-timbered buildings and a weekly livestock market, and is dominated by the clock tower of its 11th–15th-century Église St-Martin. Admire the stained glass in the church and visit the Musée Juin 1944, devoted to the Battle of Normandy.

Drive south on the D930 to the Abbaye de la Trappe.

❼ The Abbaye de la Trappe is set in beautiful, tranquil surroundings, which makes it worth stepping out of the car for even though the buildings themselves are not particularly impressive. It is easy to understand that it was here, in the 17th century, that the Abbot de Rance instigated the famous Trappist vow of silence and abstinence.

Continue on the D930 to Mortagne-au-Perche.

❽ Mortagne-au-Perche is home to the region's most

famous black pudding, the *boudin noir* (▷ 56), although it is equally proud of the area's celebrated Percheron horses—the breed is honoured with a statue in the public gardens. Don't miss the 13th-century crypt of St-André church.

Head south on the D938 to Bellême. From here, you can take a detour around the manor houses that lie to the southeast: Taking the D920, D9, D277 and D7, loop around the manors of Courboyer, l'Angenardière and Les Feugerets, then return to

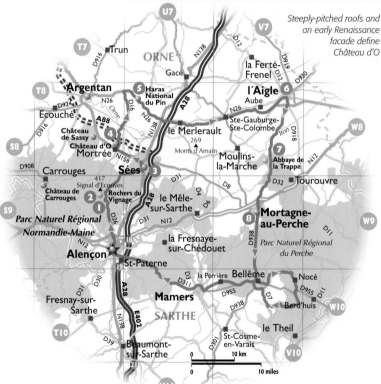

Steeply-pitched roofs and an early Renaissance facade define Château d'O

Bellême to continue the drive.
Take the D955 west from Bellême to the D21. Follow this road through La Perrière, with its splendid view of the Butte de Montgaudry, a strategic hill in medieval times, and skirt the border between Normandy and Sarthe as you take the D311 from Mamers back to Alençon.

WHEN TO GO
Spring, summer and autumn are the times to see the forest at its best.

PLACES TO VISIT
Musée Juin 1944
Place Fulbert de Beine, 61300 l'Aigle
☎ 02 33 24 19 44
🕐 Jul, Aug Tue–Wed, Sat–Sun 2–6; early Sep, late Apr–end Jun Wed, Sat–Sun 2–6
🎫 Adults €3.30, children €1.60

Abbaye de la Trappe
61380 Soligny-la-Trappe
☎ 02 33 84 17 00

WHERE TO EAT
Île de Sées
61500 Macé
☎ 02 33 27 98 65
🕐 Tue–Sat noon–1.45, 7.30–8.45, Sun noon–1.45. Closed Jan–end Feb
Between Sées and the Château d'O.

Le Genty-Home
4 rue Notre-Dame, 61400 Mortagne-au-Perche
☎ 02 33 25 11 53
🕐 Mon–Sat noon–2.30, 7–9, Sun noon–2.30

HISTORIC CAEN

This trek through the oldest parts of the city follows in the footsteps of William the Conqueror, crossing from the King's Abbaye-aux-Hommes to Queen Mathilde's Abbaye-aux-Dames via a regal chateau and attractive cobbled streets.

THE WALK

Distance: 2.5km (1.5 miles)
Allow: 2 hours excluding visits to sights
Start: esplanade de l'Hôtel de Ville
End: place Courtonne

HOW TO GET THERE

From the Périphérique ring road, follow signs for 'centre ville' then 'Hôtel de Ville'. Park on place Louis Guillouard. To return to the car park after the walk, take bus 10 from place Courtonne to Hôtel de Ville

Start the walk at the esplanade de l'Hôtel de Ville.

❶ The Abbaye St-Étienne (▷ 63) is also known as the Abbaye-aux-Hommes (Men's Abbey). This is the final resting place of William the Conqueror (died 1087), although a thigh bone is all that remains of the King's body after his grave was looted by Huguenots.

Return along the landscaped esplanade Jean Marie Louvel to place Fontette, home to the law courts with their imposing classical columns. Cross the square and walk through place St-Sauveur, past rows of dignified and well-proportioned townhouses, towards the war-damaged Église Vieux St-Sauveur. To the right of the church, follow rue St-Sauveur, turning right into rue Froide and then left onto bustling rue St-Pierre to reach the Église St-Sauveur.

❷ Lively rue St-Pierre is a good place for a mid-walk sugar boost, as *crêperies* and *chocolatières* number among its shops. At no. 52 is the Musée de la Poste, whose exterior alone is worth a photograph since the 16th-century timbered building is one of the best preserved in town. Inside you'll find a wonderful slice of nostalgia, courtesy of France's la Poste, with its simple, old-fashioned celebration of the history of Normandy's postal and telephone service, with informative displays.

Point of reference: use Église St-Pierre's spire as a landmark

Continue to the end of the street and cross rue St-Jean to reach the Église St-Pierre.

❸ The Église St-Pierre's 72m (236ft) spire is a comforting town centre landmark should you ever get lost in Caen. Step inside the church to admire some unexpected carvings on the columns of the north side of the nave, including depictions of Arthurian legends.

From rue Montoir outside the church, follow signs to the entrance to the Château.

❹ The Château was founded by William the Conqueror and now houses two museums, the Musée des Beaux Arts and Musée de Normandie (▷ 62). The original keep was destroyed during the French Revolution and more damage was inflicted on the castle during World War II. Despite this, the ramparts make a fine diversion on a sunny day.

Leave the Château by the meandering drawbridge pathway to reach rue Vaugeux, which twists as it crosses the avenue de la Libération below the castle walls. Take your time on rue Vaugeux to read the mouthwatering menus displayed in the restaurant windows and plan your evening meal. As you cross rue Poissonnière, the road becomes rue Buquet. Turn right onto rue Basse, then take the second turning on your left, rue Manissier, continuing up to place de la Reine Mathilde and the Abbaye de la Trinité.

❺ At the Abbaye de la Trinité (▷ 63), also called Abbaye-aux-Dames (Women's Convent), round off your homage to William and Mathilde by paying your respects at the Queen's modest black marble tomb.

From the abbey and its gardens, retrace your steps along rue Manissier, turning right to regain rue Basse. Take the next left down into rue Samuel Bochard to arrive at place Courtonne.

❻ Place Courtonne is a large open square linking Caen's waterways to the city centre. At one end is a pleasure port where yachts are moored, while opposite is the Tour Guillaume-le-Roy, situated on a busy traffic island. There are plenty of cafés and restaurants on place Courtonne with outdoor tables where you can take a well-earned rest.

PLACES TO VISIT

Musée de la Poste
52 rue St-Pierre, 14000 Caen
☎ 02 31 50 12 20
🕐 Mid-Jun–mid-Sep Tue–Sat 10–noon, 2–6; mid-Sep–mid-Jun Tue–Sat 1.30–5.30
💶 Adults €2.50, children €1

WHEN TO GO

This is a year-round walk but Caen is at its best from spring to autumn, outside August.

OUT AND ABOUT

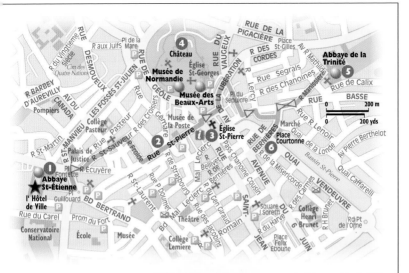

WHERE TO EAT

Au Bureau
21 place St-Sauveur, 14000 Caen
☎ 02 31 85 74 34
🕐 Mon–Sat noon–midnight
Traditional fare.

Restaurant Alcide
▷ 161
There are several crêperies and cafés on the walk for snacks.

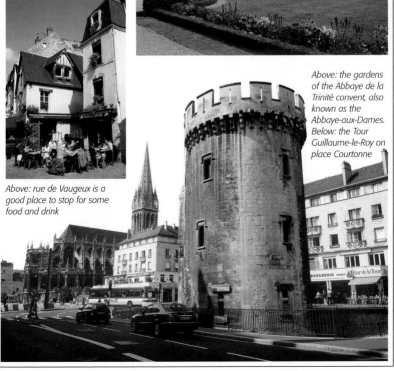

Above: the gardens of the Abbaye de la Trinité convent, also known as the Abbaye-aux-Dames. Below: the Tour Guillaume-le-Roy on place Courtonne

Above: rue de Vaugeux is a good place to stop for some food and drink

OUT AND ABOUT

ALONG THE D-DAY COAST

This evocative drive through many of the key sites associated with D-Day begins at the first piece of French soil liberated in the Battle of Normandy and continues along the beaches and villages of the *départements* of Calvados and La Manche. Dozens of museums and cemeteries large and small line the route, and cafés, restaurants and shops along the coast have their own personal memories of 5 and 6 June 1944.

THE DRIVE

Distance: 160km (100 miles)	
Allow: 1–2 days	
Start: Ranville–Bénouville	
End: Quinéville	

HOW TO GET THERE

The drive begins at Pegasus Bridge, 10km (6 miles) northeast of Caen on the D515, between Ranville and Bénouville

Pegasus Bridge was the landing site of Captain John Howard and his gliders, the first Allied arrivals on D-Day. The wartime bridge, seized and held by the British troops, was dismantled in 1993 owing to heavy traffic and a larger replica now crosses the Caen canal. The original bridge can be visited a few metres away in the grounds of the Mémorial Pegasus, an inspiring museum of the 6th Airborne Division that has strong relationships with veterans and is the perfect starting point for a D-Day tour. Across the bridge, the Café Gondrée was the first place in France to be liberated by Allied troops. It is still open as a café in summer, it is adorned with memorabilia.

Follow the D514 and well-signposted D84 to Ouistreham.

1 At Ouistreham, visit the Musée du Mur de l'Atlantique (▷ 73) and the Musée du Débarquement no. 4 Commando (▷ 73) to learn the story of the first dawn landings on Sword Beach.

Continue on the D514 out of Ouistreham and along Sword Beach, passing small resorts. At Luc-sur-Mer, turn left onto the D83 for Douvres-la-Délivrande.

2 Douvres-la-Délivrande is the site of a former German station with twin bunkers and is now home to the Musée Radar, which looks at the history of radar.

Waving the flag: Café Gondrée was the first building to be liberated after D-Day began

Take the D7 back towards the sea and turn left onto the D514 coast road towards Courseulles at Bernières-sur-Mer.

3 In Courseulles, at the very spot where Canadian soldiers came ashore on 6 June 1944, is the Centre Juno Beach, which showcases Canada's role in World War II and the country's contemporary culture.

Continue along the D514 via Ver-sur-Mer (where the Musée America Gold Beach is worth a visit) to reach Arromanches-les-Bains.

4 Arromanches-les-Bains affords panoramic views over the Mulberry Harbour and has two very different museums telling the story of the prefabricated port and the D-Day landings (▷ 58). This is a good point on the drive to stretch your legs and take a breath of bracing sea air.

Head south from Arromanches on the D87 to Ryes, stopping at the British and Commonwealth Cemetery, with its 4,868 graves and memorial to 1,837 missing servicemen. Follow signs to

Bayeux, taking the D12 into the centre of the town.

5 Bayeux may attract busloads of visitors to see its tapestry, but its other claim to fame is as the first town in occupied France to be liberated in 1944. The Musée Mémorial de la Bataille de Normandie (▷ 61) has films and displays recalling the events. A lesser-known museum in the town is devoted to General de Gaulle.

Drive north out of town on the D6 to reach the coast at Port-en-Bessin, where you can visit the Musée des Épaves Sous-Marines du Débarquement, a museum devoted to 15 years of underwater diving expeditions to rescue items from D-Day wrecks sunk off the coast. Continue along the D514 parallel to Omaha Beach.

6 Omaha Beach is the site of several D-Day reminders, the most poignant of which is the American Cemetery, with 9,386 neat white crosses, at Colleville-sur-Mer. The Musée Omaha—6 Juin 1944, just metres from the beach itself at St-Laurent-sur-Mer, displays uniforms, weapons and other items from the battlefield. A little further along the coast at Vierville-sur-Mer is the Musée D-Day Omaha, which looks at the technological advancements made during the war that still affect daily life today.

Continue to Pointe du Hoc.

7 Pointe du Hoc is the very symbol of the courage of Colonel Rudder's young American Rangers, who stormed its steep cliff face on D-Day (▷ 73). Stop here first before driving a further 5km (3 miles) to the Musée des Rangers at Grandcamp-Maisy, where you can learn the full story (▷ 73).

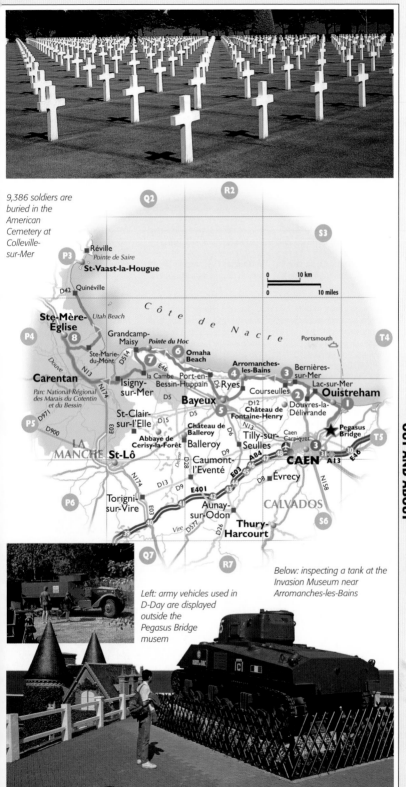

9,386 soldiers are buried in the American Cemetery at Colleville-sur-Mer

R2

Q2

S3

Réville
Pointe de Saire
P3
St-Vaast-la-Hougue

D42 Quinéville

0   10 km
0   10 miles

Côte de Nacre

Ste-Mère-Église
P4
Grandcamp-Maisy
Utah Beach
8
Pointe du Hoc
Ste-Marie-du-Mont
7 E46
6 **Omaha Beach**
Portsmouth
T4

Carentan
Parc National Régional des Marais du Cotentin et du Bessin
Isigny-sur-Mer
la Cambe
Bessin-Huppain
Port-en-Bessin-Huppain
4 **Arromanches-les-Bains**
Ryes
Bermières-sur-Mer
3
Bernières-sur-Mer
Lac-sur-Mer
N13
D5
Courseulles
2 **Ouistreham**
1

Douve
N174
Bayeux
5
D12
Château de Fontaine-Henry
Douvres-la-Délivrande

P5 D971
St-Clair-sur-l'Elle
D15
D5
★ **Pegasus Bridge**
T5

D900
Abbaye de Cerisy-la-Forêt
Château de Balleroy
Balleroy
Tilly-sur-Seulles
Caen Carpiquet
3
CAEN A13
48 E46
LA MANCHE
St-Lô
D9
D28
Caumont-l'Eventé
E03
45
44
D8
Évrecy
N158

P6
N174
D13
D9
E401 42
43
Aunay-sur-Odon
CALVADOS
S6

Torigni-sur-Vire
E03
40
Vire D577
D26
Thury-Harcourt

Q7
R7

Below: inspecting a tank at the Invasion Museum near Arromanches-les-Bains

Left: army vehicles used in D-Day are displayed outside the Pegasus Bridge musem

A monument at Omaha Beach: German defences were unaffected by bombing and 2,400 US soldiers died within hours of landing

From Grandcamp-Maisy, take the D199 south, turning left onto the D113 and left again onto the D613 to reach La Cambe, where black crosses mark 21,500 graves in the German Cemetery. Continue on the D613 to join the N13, heading towards Cherbourg. Follow this for 29km (18 miles) before turning onto the D67 to Ste-Mère-Église.

8 Ste-Mère-Église is still dominated by two images of D-Day: the mannequin of an American parachutist hanging from its church tower and the parachute-shaped Musée des Troupes Aéroportées, housing a Douglas C-47 aircraft (▷ 49) which dropped paratroopers.

Take the D523 out of town for 0.5km (0.3 miles), then turn left onto the D423 and left again on the D70 to reach Ste-Marie-du-Mont and the Musée du Débarquement d'Utah Beach. The beach itself is signposted from the D319. The trail of memorial milestones that mark the path of liberation stretches from here to Belgium. You can continue driving along the beach road until you reach Quinéville and its modest little Musée de la Liberté, depicting scenes from daily life in occupied France.

PLACES TO VISIT

Mémorial Pegasus
Avenue de Major Howard, 14860 Ranville
☎ 02 31 78 19 44
🕐 May–end Sep daily 9.30–6.30; Oct–mid-Dec, Feb–end Apr daily 10–1, 2–5.30. Closed mid-Dec–end Jan
💶 Adults €5.50, children (8–25) €4.40

Musée Radar
Route de Basly, 14440 Douvres-la-Délivrande
Enquiries through Caen Memorial Museum (www.memorial-caen.fr)
☎ 02 31 06 06 45
🕐 Jul, Aug daily 10–6

Centre Juno Beach
Voie des Français Libres, B.P. 104, 14470 Courseulles-sur-Mer
☎ 02 31 37 32 17
🕐 Apr–end Sep daily 9.30–7; Oct–end Dec daily 10–1, 2–6; Feb, Mar daily 10–1, 2–5. Closed Jan
💶 Adults €6.50, children (8–18) €5

Musée America Gold Beach
2 place Admiral Byrd, 14114 Ver-sur-Mer
☎ 02 31 22 58 58
🕐 Jun–end Oct daily 10.30–12.30, 2.30–5.30
💶 Adults €4, children (5–21) €2.40

Mémorial du Général de Gaulle

OUT AND ABOUT

10 rue Bourbesnour, 14400 Bayeux
☎ 02 31 92 45 55
⏰ Jul, Aug daily 9.30–12.30, 2–6.30; Sep–end Nov, Mar–end Jun daily 10–12.30, 2–6. Closed Dec–end Feb
💶 Adults €3.50, children (5–21) €2.50

Musée des Épaves Sous-Marines du Débarquement
Route de Bayeux, Commines, 14520 Port-en-Bessin
☎ 02 31 21 17 06
⏰ Jun–Sep daily 10–noon, 2–6
💶 Adults €6, children (7–16) €3

Musée Omaha–6 Juin 1944
Avenue de la Libération, 14710 St-Laurent-sur-Mer
☎ 02 31 21 97 44
⏰ Jul, Aug daily 9.30–7.30; early–mid-Sep, mid-May–end Jun daily 9.30–7;

mid-Sep–mid-Nov, mid-Mar–mid-May daily 9.30–6.30; mid-Feb–mid-Mar daily 10–12.30, 2.30–6. Closed mid-Nov–mid-Feb
💶 Adults €5.20, children (7–15) €2.80

Musée D-Day Omaha
Route de Grandchamp, 14710 Vierville-sur-Mer
☎ 02 31 21 71 80
⏰ Easter–end Sep daily 9.30–7.30; Oct–Easter daily 10–12.30, 2–6
💶 Adults €5.30, children (2–25) €3

Musée du Débarquement d'Utah Beach
50480 Ste-Marie-du-Mont
☎ 02 33 71 53 35
⏰ Jun–end Sep daily 9.30–7; Apr, May, Oct daily 10–6; Nov, Dec Sat–Sun 10–12.30, 2–5.30; Feb–end Mar daily 10–12.30, 2–5.30. Closed Jan
💶 Adults €4.80, children €2

Musée de la Liberté
Avenue de la Plage, 50310 Quinéville
☎ 02 33 21 40 44
⏰ Jul, Aug daily 9.30–7.30; Sep, Jun daily 9.30–7; Oct–mid-Nov, mid-Mar–end May daily 10–6. Closed mid-Nov–mid-Mar
💶 Adults €5.30, children €4

The remnants of war exhibited at the Musée du Débarquement on Utah beach

The American Army landed here: a memorial on Utah Beach

WHEN TO GO
Spring onwards is the best time for this drive, since many of the museums close during the winter months.

WHERE TO EAT
Le Lion d'Or
▷ 161

Le Bistrot d'à Côté
10–12 rue Michel-Lefournier, 14520 Port-en-Bessin
☎ 02 31 51 79 12
⏰ Thu–Mon noon–1.30, 7–9.15. Closed Jan–mid-Feb

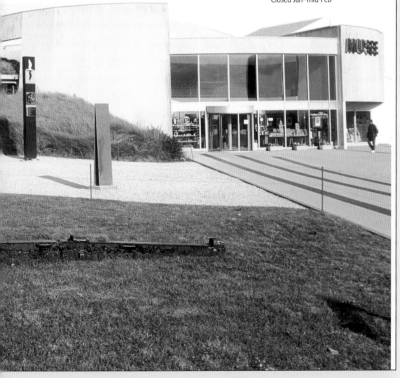

OUT AND ABOUT

SUISSE NORMANDE AND THE ORNE VALLEY

This tour takes in some of the high points of the Suisse Normande, a
pretty, hilly region south of Caen and bounded by the river Orne. The river runs
beside the road for much of your drive. The roads are narrow, single track in places,
always winding and sometimes steep, so high speeds are not advisable.
The route takes in attractive towns and villages and some good viewpoints.

THE DRIVE

Distance: 110km (68 miles)

Allow: 1 day

Start/end: Caen

HOW TO GET THERE

The drive starts in Caen

Caen (▷ 62–64) is the ancient
capital of the Norman dukes
and is full of interest. Sights
include the castle, the
Mémorial de Caen and the two
abbeys —the Abbaye-aux-
Hommes, built by William the
Conqueror, and the Abbaye-
aux-Dames, built by his wife,
Mathilde.

Leave from below the castle, in
the heart of town, and follow the
'Toutes Directions' signs, then
signs for Rennes-Granville as far
as the racecourse at La Prairie.
From there, pick up the D8,
signed for Évrecy and Aunay-sur-
Odon, and follow this road to
Évrecy.

❶ At Évrecy you will pass a
small group of World War II
memorials on the left. The
countryside around Caen is full
of memorials to the bitter
fighting of 1944; this one is
dedicated to the men of the
43rd (Welsh) Division. There is
a Churchill tank and a monument to Hill 112, declaring
'Whoever holds Hill 112 holds
all of Normandy'.

Turn left at the church in Évrecy
onto the D41. At Amayé-sur-
Orne, turn right at the outskirts of
the village onto the D212, signed
for Thury-Harcourt. Turn left at
the hamlet of Le Hom, crossing
the river and an old railway track
into the town of Thury-Harcourt.

❷ Thury-Harcourt (▷ 74) is a
market town and visitor base
for the Suisse Normande and
the Vallée de l'Orne. It is a
pretty and prosperous town
with a ruined moated chateau
and a park. Two gatehouses

*Le Lande viaduct bridges the
river Orne near Clécy, where you
can rock climb or go kayaking
under its arches*

with beehive-shaped roofs,
one wing and a bricked-up
façade are all that can be seen
of the chateau today. A plaque
on the park wall pays tribute to
British forces.

Follow the D562 along the river
for 13km (8 miles) then, at a
large roadside cross, take the
D133A down into the middle of
Clécy.

❸ Clécy (▷ 66) is set in one
of the most attractive parts of
the Orne valley, at a point
where the river is overlooked
by high cliffs, and is popular as
a base for walking and touring.
It's a good place to stop for
lunch and a stroll—follow signs
to the Pont du Vey, passing
Clécy's miniature railway
museum. Don't cross the
bridge, but admire the watermill on the other side. There
are fine views and walks along
the Orne valley from the Pont
du Vey. The best way to see
the river is from the footpath
or the road that runs alongside
it, overlooking the riverside
hotels, the canoeists and the
climbers who scramble on the
cliffs by the old viaduct.

Follow the main road, signed for
Le Lande, round past a little art
gallery on your right and several
riverside cafés and restaurants on
your left. Drive through Le Bô
and Cossesseville, with their
lovely churches. (These roads
may be flooded in winter.) With
the river on your right, continue
along the D167 through Pont-
d'Ouilly. At Le Bâteau, take the
D18E towards the parking and
picnic area by the viaduct. At the
end of the viaduct turn sharp
right under the arches on the
D18A, signed St-Philbert, continuing to the top of hill and the
viewpoint at Roches d'Oëtre.

❹ The Roches d'Oëtre viewpoint overlooks the river
Rouvre. This 118m (387ft)
precipice has no barrier, so
observe the warning signs, be
extra careful on wet or windy
days, and keep control of small
children.

Return the way you came, under
the viaduct. Turn right back onto
the D18 through Le Mesnil-
Villement. At the T-junction turn
left onto the D511, then right
onto the D43. It's then a left turn
onto the D241 to Tréprel.
Continue on the D241 through
farming country north to
Bonnoeil and Angoville, then left
onto the D6 to Meslay. Turn right
onto the D23 to Bretteville-sur-
Laize. Cross the river Laize and
turn left onto the D132, following
the Laize valley to the D562.
Turn right here to return to Caen
through small suburban towns.

WHEN TO GO

Some roads on this tour may
be flooded in winter.

WHERE TO EAT

Au Site Normand

1 rue des Châtelets, 14570 Clécy

☎ 02 31 69 71 05

🕓 Closed early Dec–end Feb

Le Moulin du Vey

▷ 161

OUT AND ABOUT

MUSÉE du CHEMIN de FER MINIATURE

Rural retreat: the Suisse Normande landscape

The museum at Clécy is home to the last of the old-fashioned steam-powered trains

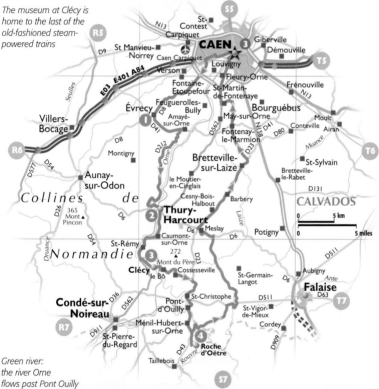

R5 S5 CAEN 3 T5 R6 T6 R7 4 T7 S7

CALVADOS

Collines de Normandie

Green river:
the river Orne
flows past Pont Ouilly

OUT AND ABOUT

GIVERNY

The lovely riverside village of Giverny (▷ 84–85), spread across a hillside near Vernon, is the most visited place in Normandy. Crowds of art- and garden-lovers flock to see the home of Claude Monet and the world's most famous lily pond, immortalised in some of the artist's best-known paintings.

THE WALK

Distance: 9km (5.5 miles)
Allow: 2.5 hours
Start/end: Maison de Claude Monet

HOW TO GET THERE

Giverny is near Vernon, off the D5, west of Paris (and possible as a day-trip from the capital)

Start outside the Maison de Claude Monet. In 1883 the artist moved into this pastel-pink house with grass-green shutters, where he had worked with Auguste Renoir, Alfred Sisley and Édouard Manet for a number of years. He designed the gardens himself and created his famous water garden with its lilies and Japanese bridge. The main garden, with its 12 resident gardeners, still keeps to Monet's design and is a palette of changing hues from spring to autumn. Near the house, Monet's enormous studio is filled with huge copies of his works.

Head along rue Claude Monet, towards the Musée d'Art Américain. Take the lane to the right, called chemin Blanche-Hoschéde, then go right again almost immediately up the narrow rue Hélène-Pillon, which curves left before becoming a dirt track. Follow this path along the backs of houses, running parallel to rue Claude Monet below, until you reach the end of the village. Turn left (signposted GR2 and marked with red and white paint markers) up a steep path, then turn right at the first intersection. The path snakes across open meadowland towards the woods, with sweeping views over the Epte valley below.

At the next crossing of footpaths, go left and climb up through oak woods. At this point you leave the GR2 and the path is now marked in yellow. At the next crossroads, go right. At the edge of the woods, take the grassy path on the left, passing alongside pastureland then more

Above: Claude Monet is buried in the family vault near the church in Giverny, his home for 43 years. Right: the bridge in the gardens

woodland. As you reach the woods, turn right towards a small road. Turn left onto the road, which runs steeply downhill. After 50m (55yd), bear right, then right again along a track bordering the woods of La Réserve on the right, and flanked by fields on the left. When you come to a crossroads level with a small yellow house on the left, continue straight, then go left along the fringe of the Garenne woods.

Turn to the right in the woods, once again following the red and white signs of GR2. Soon you will come to a promontory marked by a large cross, with a magnificent view of the Seine.

Continue down a steep, narrow path leading to the hamlet of Manitaux; it comes out on a small lane bordered by cottages. Turn left, following the course of a former railway track until you reach the edge of Giverny. Go along the grassy path behind the first houses in the village, until the path joins the Sente des Grosses Eaux and, soon afterwards, rue Claude Monet.

Back on the main street of the village, proceed past the church, where Monet lies buried, to the Restaurant Baudy.

❶ The Restaurant Baudy was once a boarding house and the rendezvous of various painter friends of Monet, including Auguste Rodin, Alfred Sisley, Auguste Renoir, Paul Cézanne, Camille Pissarro and various visiting American artists. It was also the site of the first studio and the first art exhibitions in the village.

Continue along the main street to the Musée d'Art Américain.

❷ The Musée d'Art Américain houses a permanent collection of works by Monet's American contemporaries in France, as well as temporary exhibitions.

Continue along rue Claude Monet, filled with galleries and artists' workshops, before returning to Monet's house and garden at the far end of the village.

PLACES TO VISIT
Maison de Claude Monet
and
Musée d'Art Américain
▷ 84

Restaurant Baudy
▷ 85

WHEN TO GO

Monet's house and gardens are closed on Mondays and from November to April.

WHERE TO EAT
Moulin de Fourges
▷ 163

OUT AND ABOUT

ÉTRETAT

The Côte d'Albâtre (Alabaster Coast) stretches 100km (60 miles) from Dieppe to Étretat and beyond. It is a formation of imposing white cliffs that seem to mirror the white cliffs of Dover across the Channel. At Étretat the seascape is at its most spectacular, with sheer cliffs pierced by massive arches and a solitary needle rock soaring to 70m (230ft) a little way offshore. This coastal walk can be rough in places (wear sturdy, non-slip shoes or walking boots), but the breathtaking panoramas make it worthwhile.

THE WALK

Distance: 6.5km (4 miles)	
Allow: 2.5 hours	
Start/end: Étretat	

HOW TO GET THERE

Étretat is on the Côte d'Albâtre, between Le Havre and Fécamp

Étretat (▷ 94) was a modest, obscure fishing village until the mid-19th century, when the writers Guy de Maupassant and Alexandre Dumas discovered its lovely pebbled beach enveloped by cliffs, and the great artists of the day began to paint the dramatic scenery. Fashionable visitors arrived from Paris and elsewhere, lured by the views reproduced by Eugène Boudin, Eugène Delacroix and Claude Monet. In town, visit place du Maréchal Foch, with its wooden covered market built in 1926 amid a cluster of 16th-century townhouses. For golfers, the 18-hole clifftop course is France's highest golf links, with views guaranteed to put you off your stroke.

Start on the promenade. Walk to the eastern end, then turn right, up a flight of 83 brick steps that opens out onto a grassy clifftop pathway. Continue past a children's theme park and up to the top of the Porte (or Falaise) d'Amont.

❶ Falaise d'Amont affords spectacular views of the western Falaise d'Aval across the

Lost at sea: a memorial at Étretat to the aviators Charles Nungesser and François Coli

bay, where a 70m (230ft) rock stack known as the Aiguille d'Étretat (Étretat Needle) stands in the sea beyond the cliffs. Stop at the Chapelle Notre-Dame de la Garde, a sailors' chapel, then turn inland to a carved monument commemorating the lost French aviators Charles Nungesser and François Coli,

Dedicated to seafarers, the Chapelle Notre-Dame de la Garde stands close to the cliffs of Étretat

whose plane, *L'Oiseau Blanc*, was last seen crossing these cliffs in 1927 on its ill-fated bid to fly from Paris to New York. The aviators were presumed drowned in the Atlantic and their bodies were never recovered.

Continue along the cliff edge, past the chapel, and go down some steps leading to the arch of Amont. A steep, slippery and narrow pathway, cut into the chalky stack, offers wonderful views of the alabaster cliffs to the east. A wooden handrail and a ladder assist in the final descent to a small beach. Retrace your steps, past the chapel and back down the brick steps. Proceed along the promenade, an unbroken curve of café-lined concrete above the steep shingle beach. At the far end, another flight of steps, followed by a steep, well-trodden, flint-filled path, leads up beside a scenic golf course to Porte d'Aval. Bear right along the cliff edge, crossing a narrow bridge and onto the top of the cliff arch—not for those with a fear of heights!

❷ The cliff arch offers stunning vistas over Étretat's slate roofs and to the Porte d'Amont beyond. Legend has it that many centuries ago three beautiful sisters were imprisoned by an evil lord in a cave at the foot of these cliffs.

Continue along the windswept cliff edge, admiring the wildflowers, yellow gorse and purple sea cabbage, and on to a second arch, La

A model of the airplane used for Nungesser and Coli's transatlantic attempt

Right: Étretat is protected by headlands

Manne-Porte, with breathtaking views stretching as far as the port of Le Havre-Antifer. Just beyond the next headland, Pointe de la Courtine, follow a track inland (the GR21, marked with a red and white stripe). Branch left, where two paths meet, to Valaine. At the next intersection, leave the GR21 and head straight on down a narrow country lane, through the attractive brick and stone farm buildings of Ferme la Valaine.

❸ Ferme la Valaine is a lovely old farmhouse selling delicious home-produced cider, Calvados and goat's cheese.

Follow the road as it winds gently downhill, past grazing goats, until you reach the D940. Turn left back into the middle of Étretat and left again to return to the waterfront.

WHEN TO GO
Check weather reports before starting the cliff walk, as the wind may be strong and the steps slippery. Hardy visitors might like to join the locals for the traditional New Year's Day swim!

WHERE TO EAT
Dormy House
▷ 172

Stop for a snack at a café in Étretat

The Falaise d'Aval cliff arch offers superb views of the town

OUT AND ABOUT

LOWER SEINE VALLEY

The Seine is at its most flamboyant as it pours out of the city of Rouen and rushes seawards. Taking in an exuberant serpentine swoop of the river that encompasses a landscape of pretty villages and grand abbeys, this drive leads its followers from the city out into the Pays de Caux.

THE DRIVE

Distance: 72km (45 miles)	
Allow: at least an afternoon	
Start: Rouen	
End: Caudebec-en-Caux	

HOW TO GET THERE

The drive starts in Rouen, capital of Normandy

Rouen (▷ 99–103) is an inspirational place of martyrs and artists, of kings and of powerful bishops. The centre of the city has half-timbered buildings and magnificent churches, its unmissable sights including the cathedral, the Gros Horloge clock tower and a fine arts museum.

Leave the spires of Rouen behind you, taking the industrial quayside roads that become the D982, and following signs for St-Pierre-de-Mannerville and Route de l'Abbaye. Turn left onto the D267 to arrive at St-Martin-de-Boscherville.

❶ St-Martin-de-Boscherville's large central square is dominated by the stark white 12th-century abbey church of St-Georges, and it has plenty of parking spaces as well as a bar and an inn. The abbey gardens are open to the public, and contain a discovery trail and shop. The church itself is light and airy, with some interesting capitals inside that feature scenes of medieval jousting.

Return to the D982 and follow the road past the small but pretty riverside resort of Duclair, with its ferry crossing, tubs of flowers and waterfront restaurants. Here, or perhaps further along the route at Jumièges, you can take a ferry across to the opposite bank of the Seine. At Yainville, turn left onto the D143 towards Jumièges.

❷ The Abbaye de Jumièges (▷ 89) was largely destroyed

Steps in the garden lead to the Abbaye de Jumièges, which hosts evening shows in summer

in the 17th century, but its ruins are still majestic and stand in well-maintained parkland. The roofless 11th-century abbey church and the neighbouring 10th-century Église St-Pierre in particular are perfect photographic subjects. If you fancy extending this gentle drive into a two-day event, try to stop off here for a summer evening's *son et lumière* entertainment.

Back on the D143, turn left onto the D982 and left again along the D22 to reach picturesque St-Wandrille-Rancon.

❸ The Abbaye de St-Wandrille (▷ 90) dominates the higgledy-piggledy houses and shops of the village. Its fortunes have taken it from a 13th–16th-century abbey to a mill and a private residence, then back again to a religious community, the result being a mixture of the palatial and the rustic. A church, in a converted barn, and the cloisters are open to the public. Buy a jar of fruity home-made jam from the Benedictine monks in their shop or listen to their moving chants in the church.

Return to the D982, driving under the stark and imposing Pont de Brotonne before reaching Caudebec-en-Caux.

❹ Caudebec-en-Caux is best visited in time for its bustling Saturday morning market, held beneath the beautiful late-Gothic church of Notre-Dame, with its fine stained-glass windows (▷ 90). However, you may have to park some way from the church on market day. Sitting on one of the prettiest stretches of the Seine, Caudebec is a three-star Ville Fleurie (Flower Town) with plenty of attractive picnic spots down by the water's edge.

Follow the river on the D81, passing through Villequier, where, in 1842, the treacherous tidal currents claimed the daughter and son-in-law of the writer Victor Hugo. The quayside family home of Charles Vacquerie, Hugo's son-in-law, is now a museum (▷ 91). Keep on the same road until you reach Norville. Here, take the D281 to the extravagant Gothic Château d'Etelan.

❺ The private Château d'Etelan, a contemporary of Rouen's Palais de Justice (▷ 152), is a listed monument, principally for its beautiful Ste-Madeleine chapel, with Renaissance stained glass, frescoes and statuary. The 15th-century chateau was built for Louis Picard, chamberlain to King Louis XII (ruled 1498–1515). It was here that Catherine de Medici, as regent, famously proclaimed the succession of her son King Charles IX in 1560. Other illustrious guests at the castle have included King Henri IV and the writer and philosopher Voltaire, known to his parents as François-Marie Arouet.

Return to Caudebec-en-Caux via the D81 and D281.

OUT AND ABOUT

Château d'Etelan

76330 Saint-Maurice-d'Etelan

☎ 02 35 39 91 27

🕐 Mid-Jun–end Sep Sat–Tue 11–1,
3–7. Easter–end Oct by appointment

🎫 E4, under-10s free

WHEN TO GO

Late spring and summer is the
best time, when the Pays de
Caux is at its prettiest, the window boxes are blooming and
you can dance by the river at
Caudebec-en-Caux (see La
Marine below).

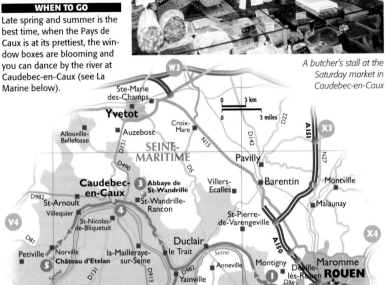

*A butcher's stall at the
Saturday market in
Caudebec-en-Caux*

*Right: Abbaye de
St-Wandrille*

WHERE TO EAT

Le Cheval Blanc

Place René Coty, 76490 Caudebec-en-
Caux

☎ 02 35 96 21 66

🕐 Mon–Sat 12–1.30, 7.30–9, Sun
12–1.45. Closed 22–31 Dec

Regional dishes.

La Marine

18 quai Guilbaud, 76490 Caudebec-en-
Caux

☎ 02 35 96 20 11

🕐 Mon–Thu 12.30–2, 7.30–9, Fri–Sat
7.30–9, Sun 12–2

Traditional country cooking on
the banks of the Seine. There
is dancing on the restaurant's
terrace on Sundays.

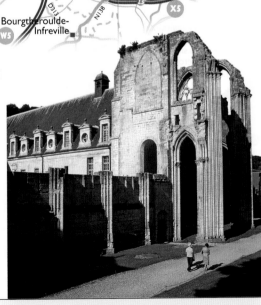

OUT AND ABOUT

An escorted tour is the perfect way of tapping into local knowledge and allows you to enjoy the best views. Normandy is ideally seen from the water and boat trips offer new perspectives on the rivers and coast. Discover the area on horseback, in a jeep or from a floating restaurant. Or explore it on foot—walking tours of Caen and Rouen may be booked at tourist offices.

LA MANCHE

ACCUEIL TATIHOU

Quai Vauban, 50550 St-Vaast-la-Hougue
Tel 02 33 23 19 92

An amphibious craft takes visitors from St-Vaast-la-Hougue's quayside to the island of Tatihou, its museum and tower. Reservation is essential in summer since there is a daily limit of 500 visitors. Dogs are not allowed on Tatihou.

🕒 Jul, Aug daily 10–7; Sep, Apr–end Jun daily 10–6. Departures every 30 mins at high tide, hourly at low tide 💶 Crossing only: adults €4.60, children (4–11) €1.50. With museum and tower visit: adults €7.60, children €3.05

LA GRANVILLAISE

43 boulevard des Amiraux Granvillais, 50400 Granville
Tel 02 33 90 07 51
www.lagranvillaise.org

Head out to sea under sail aboard *La Granvillaise*. It is usually hired out for three-day cruises in the Channel Islands, but the boat keeps several days each month free for day trips and half-day excursions.

🕒 Dates and times vary; see website for current details 💶 Half-day: €35. Full day: €50. Family tickets available

MONT-ST-MICHEL VOYAGES

4 rue de la Métairie, 50170 Boucey
Tel 02 33 60 68 00

Discover Mont-St-Michel's bay in a horse-drawn carriage, taking in marshlands and the old quarter of Pontorson.

🕒 Depend on weather and tides 💶 €99–144 for 5–9 passengers

ORNE

LE VAL D'ORNE

Rue de la Forge, 61210 Putanges
Tel 02 33 39 30 30
www.valdorne.com

Explore the Lac de Rabodanges on the river Orne with a cruise. Afternoon excursions last 1.25 hours, while lunch and dinner trips last 2.5 hours and offer a range of menus to suit most budgets and tastes.

🕒 Mar–end Jun, Sep–end Dec daily lunch and dinner cruises according to demand, Sun excursion 4pm 💶 4pm trip: €7. Lunch/dinner cruises: €39–56

A cruise boat on the river Seine

VILLAGE DU CHEVAL DE BAGNOLES-DE-L'ORNE

61600 St-Michel-des-Andaines
Tel 02 33 37 12 79

Two-hour horse-riding trips in the forest around Bagnoles. Horses may also be hired by the day on request.

🕒 Sun mornings all year 💶 €17/hour

CALVADOS

BATEAU L'HASTINGS

Quai Vendeuvre, 14018 Caen
Tel 02 31 34 00 00, 02 31 38 88 22
http://perso.wanadoo.fr/bateau.lhastings

This boat offers sightseeing along the canal from Caen, past Pegasus Bridge, to the sea at Ouistreham. Trips last 2.5 hours and have a commentary in French. The 12.15 and 7pm departures are dining cruises with menus costing from £19.50 to £25.50.

🕒 Jun–end Aug daily 9, 12.15, 3.15, 7 💶 Adults €12, under-12s €6.50 🚋 Tram A or B to Résistance ♿ Access for visitors with disabilities

BATTLE BUS TOURS

16 rue Maitrise, 14400 Bayeux
Tel 02 31 22 28 82

Expert escorted tours around the D-Day sites for individual travellers in groups of up to eight people. Tour themes, routes and anecdotes are adapted for each party. The 'Band of Brothers' tour, taking in sites from the television series, is a less expensive option.

🕒 Dates and times to suit 💶 €75. Band of Brothers tour: €45

COLONEL RUDDER

Quai Nord, 14450 Grandcamp-Maisy
Tel 02 31 21 42 93

Approach the scene of the Allied landings on Omaha Beach from the sea, on a boat trip from Grandcamp-Maisy. The 65-seat tour boats have toilets and bar facilities.

🕒 Apr–end Sep; departures vary according to tides 💶 One-hour trip: adults €10, children (4–12) €6.50. 2.5-hour trip: adults €16, children €10

NORMANDY TRAVEL

B.P. 13114, 14400 Bayeux
Tel 02 31 51 89 99
www.normandy-travel.com

Full-day tours for groups of four or more. Visitors are met at their hotels in Bayeux or Caen and taken around key sites, from Ste-Mère-Église to D-Day landing beaches. During the afternoon, participants join a three-hour tour of the *bocage* (hedgerows) by jeep.

🕒 Daily 9–6 💶 From €143 per person

EURE

RIVES DE SEINE CROISIÈRES

Cale du Bac, 27740 Poses
Tel 02 35 78 31 70

Sunday lunch on the Seine on board the riverboat *Guillaume le Conquérant* takes in a stretch of river beloved by the Impressionists, passing watermills and such sights as Château Gaillard. The price includes food and wine. Board at the port of Poses. Trips to Vernon and Les Andelys may be available midweek.

🕒 May–end Aug Sun 11am 💶 €59

SEINE-MARITIME

BELCINAC

Quai Guilbaud, 76490 Caudebec-en-Caux
Tel 02 32 70 46 32

Venture out from Caudebec-en-Caux to discover the rich heritage of the Seine. Two short trips take in the best sites: The early departure goes to Jumièges; the later excursion visits Aizier-Vieux-Port.

🕒 Jul, Aug Tue–Sun 3, 5; Sep, Jun Wed, Fri–Sun 3, 5 💶 Adults €10, children (3–12) €8, visitors with disabilities €6

This chapter lists places to eat and stay, broken down regionally, then alphabetically by town.

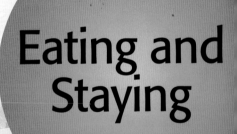

Eating and Staying

EATING OUT IN NORMANDY

Food fads may come and go, but this is a region where hearty eating has never fallen out of fashion. Normandy even has its own way of helping you squeeze in a bit more—the *trou normand* (literally 'Norman hole'), taken to clear the digestive system. Traditionally a shot of potent farmhouse Calvados, the *trou* is now often an alcoholic sorbet or granita.

You can dine outside at gourmet restaurants in Normandy. Oysters, right, are a regional speciality

THE FLAVOURS OF NORMANDY

'Although I did not realise it at the time, it was by way of Norman cookery that I first learned to appreciate French food.' So said Elizabeth David, one of many visitors seduced by Normandy's *crème fraîche* and *beurre d'Isigny*, its rich cheeses, coarse *rillette* pâtés and Mont-St-Michel omelettes. Fresh fish and farmyard fare dominate menus across the region, with cream and apples finding their way into most dishes. The same fruit used to make cider, Pommeau and Calvados often accompanies meat dishes and appears in the ubiquitous *tarte tatin* apple tart. The cheeseboard is a key course. Camembert, Livarot and Pont-l'Évêque are served with every meal.

Each corner of Normandy has its own special dishes. Normans declare that they could be led blindfolded around the region and know each place by its food: tripe in Caen, *andouille* sausage in Vire, sole in Dieppe and the distinctive flavour of the lamb and mutton reared on the salty pastures around the bay of Mont-St-Michel.

WHERE TO EAT

Cafés, bars, brasseries, bistros and restaurants make up a confusing array of establishments, each with its own rules and traditions. Many cafés and bars will offer a *plat du jour* lunch, which is less expensive than a restaurant, and an excellent way of enjoying unpretentious home cooking.

Bistros offer a choice of simple country dishes, cooked from old family recipes, and again provide good value with their set menus. Brasseries are a halfway point between the informality of the bistro and the formality of a restaurant. They may be more flexible about opening hours. Restaurants themselves range from simple or specialist tables to grander gastronomic establishments.

MENUS

Restaurants typically offer the choice of dining *à la carte* or opting for a set menu. The set menu, or *prix fixe*, has a selection of two or three courses at a fixed price. At the top end of the scale is the *menu dégustation*, or *menu gastronomique*, which may cost anything from £30 to £80.

The daily specials (*plats du jour*) will usually make use of the freshest seasonal ingredients. The best-value set menus are served midweek lunchtimes only, and are a good way of sampling food at top restaurants without going over budget.

WHAT TO DRINK

When choosing a wine, be guided by your waiter. Waiters in France are professionals and will be adept at selecting the best accompaniment to your meal. Let the waiter know your budget, and always consider the house wines, as in a good establishment these should reflect the taste of the restaurateur. If you are dining on traditional country food in a bistro, try a farmhouse cider.

WHEN TO EAT

Restaurant opening hours in Normandy are generally from noon to 2.30pm for lunch and from 7.30pm in the evening for dinner. However, in quiet rural areas out of season, arrivals after 1.30pm for lunch or 9pm in the evening may sometimes be turned away. Conversely, people may dine later in resorts during the summer. It is always advisable to reserve a table in advance. Since the introduction of the 35-hour working week, some restaurateurs have been flexible with their opening hours, closing early on Monday to Friday to accommodate weekend demand. Many establishments also close Saturday and Monday lunchtimes and Sunday evenings.

EATING

DINING ETIQUETTE

● Dress smartly if dining in a gastronomic restaurant. A meal is treated as a special event in such places, and dressing well shows respect for the food, the establishment and other diners.
● Switch off mobile phones in smart restaurants.
● Address serving staff as Monsieur, Madame or Mademoiselle.
● Smoking is the norm in most restaurants. Non-smoking tables may be token gestures in corners.
● Service charges are now included in the price listed on the menu, so the traditional 10–15 per cent tip is no longer expected.

VEGETARIAN FOOD

Normandy is not the most enlightened corner of France when it comes to vegetarian options. In towns and resorts, ethnic North African and Asian restaurants, chains such as Bistrot Romain and pizzerias are the best bets for meatfree meals.

PRICES

In the restaurant listings that follow, these abbreviations are used within price information:
L—lunch (2 courses for 1 person, without drinks); D—dinner (3 courses for 1 person, without drinks); Wine—the least expensive bottle of wine.

Rustic restaurants serve country dishes such as apple tart, but you can also find haute cuisine here

MENU READER

COOKING STYLES

…à la Deauvillaise a cream and onion sauce, served with white fish
…à la meunière a method of serving fish, which is panfried and topped with butter, lemon juice and parsley
…à la Normande a white sauce made with crème fraîche, served with variety of dishes

MEATS AND POULTRY

agneau lamb
andouille de Vire lightly smoked chitterling sausage
boeuf beef
boudin black sausage from Mortagne-au-Perche
canard duck
caneton duckling
dinde turkey
jambon ham
lapin rabbit
lardons bacon pieces
lièvre hare
oie goose
porc pork
poulet roast chicken
poussin baby chicken
pré-salé lamb reared on the salt marshes of Mont-St-Michel
sanglier wild boar
veau veal
venaison venison
volaille chicken

FISH

bar sea bass
brochet pike
cabillaud cod
carpe carp
carrelet plaice
coquilles St-Jacques scallops
crabe crab
crevettes shrimps or prawns
fruits de mer seafood
hareng herring
homard lobster, best from Barfleur or la Hague
huîtres oysters
maquereaux mackerel
moules mussels
palourdes clams
raie skate
rouget red mullet
sole sole
truite trout
turbot turbot

SAVOURY DISHES

caneton à la Rouennais pressed duckling (▷ 13)
côtes de porc vallée d'Auge pork cutlets fried in butter, then flambéed with Calvados and served with a cider sauce
escalopes Cauchoise veal with cream, apples and Calvados
faisan à la Cauchoise roast pheasant flambéed in Calvados and served with sautéed apples
marmite Diéppoise a fish stew

poule au pot stewed chicken
poulet vallée d'Auge chicken in a cream and onion sauce
sole à la Diéppoise sole with white wine and seafood
sole en Matelote sole cooked in cider with mussels
tripes à la mode de Caen tripe cooked with cows' hooves, cider, Calvados and stock

DESSERTS

pommes au beurre slices of apple fried in sugar and butter
tarte aux pommes apple tart
tarte tatin upside-down tart
tergoule rice pudding

DAIRY PRODUCTS

beurre d'Isigny the finest butter in France (▷ 13)
Camembert the round creamy cheese sold from farmhouses
crème fraîche the other famed product of Isigny is a rich cream, sold in tubs or ladled from bowls
fromage frais young farmhouse cream cheese, often eaten as a yoghurt-style dessert with sugar
Livarot strong smelling and recognisable by its straw bands
Neufchâtel eaten within a fortnight of being made or as a three-month-old mature variety
Pont-l'Évêque farmhouse cheese of the Pays d'Auge

EATING

LA MANCHE

Seafood and fish are the staples of many menus along the Cotentin peninsula, but by their abundance the inns and seafront restaurants offer a variety of approaches to the catch of the day. You will find young chefs with new approaches to local produce, including oysters being prepared in a variety of sauces. Yet this is a country of tradition, and the owners of many family-run restaurants will offer the same recipes served up by their parents and grandparents.

AVRANCHES

CROIX D'OR

83 rue de la Constitution, 50300 Avranches
Tel 02 33 58 04 88

This 17th-century coach house is built in the timbered style of the area. Chef Franck Baulieu is passionate about using the best local produce and freshly caught fish. A favourite among diners eating à la carte is the *bavaroise de tourteaux et marinade de coquillages au jus de langoustines* (crab marinated shellfish bavarois with a langoustine sauce). The Croix d'Or has a well-judged wine list and specialises in bottles from the Loire valley. Service is smart and efficient.
🕓 Apr–end Sep daily noon–1.45, 7.15–9.15. Closed Sun eve Oct–Mar, Jan
🍷 L €15, D €23, Wine €15

BARNEVILLE-CARTERET

LA MARINE

11 rue de Paris, 50270 Barneville-Carteret
Tel 02 33 53 83 31
www.hotelmarine.com
This family-run hotel restaurant overlooks the sea. Savour the local catch in the dining room, which is decorated with pastel colours and cane chairs. Apart from the obvious fish dishes,

try the appetising *mille-feuille de saumon cru* (raw salmon pastry) or the *carré d'agneau en croûte de niora* (rack of lamb). Service is attentive.
🕓 Tue, Wed Fri–Sat noon–2, 7–9.30, Sun noon–2; Mon, Thu 7–9.30. Closed mid-Nov–Feb
🍷 L €30, D €45, Wine €25

CÉAUX

AU P'TIT QUINQUIN

9 Les Forges, 50220 Céaux
Tel 02 33 70 97 20
www.au-petit-quinquin.com
This modest service station restaurant is a perfect place to stop for a good-value meal on the road to Mont-St-Michel. Enjoy honest and basic *cuisine de terroir* (local food) on the regularly changing menu, with dishes such as *gigot d'agneau de pays* (leg of lamb). Allow enough time to appreciate the meal and the friendly service.
🕓 Tue–Sat noon–2, 7–9.30, Sun noon–2. Closed early Jan–mid-Feb
🍷 L €12, D €30, Wine €15

CHERBOURG

FIFTY'S DINER

Place de Gaulle, 50100 Cherbourg
Tel 02 33 43 58 20
Come to this 1950s American-style diner for a quick bite. The kids will love the Hollywood design theme, and it is a great place for a one-course refuelling stop for the family. Friday night is karaoke night.
🕓 Mon–Sat 8am–1am, Sun 10am–1am (food served noon–2.30, 7–11)
🍔 Burger, coffee and drink: €10

LA RÉGENCE

42 quai de Caligny, 50100 Cherbourg
Tel 02 33 43 05 16
www.laregence.com
La Régence overlooks the port of Cherbourg and its fishing fleet. Inside, the fine bistro-style furniture and tableware give the place a touch of class. The menu includes regional specials, especially seafood. There is a children's menu.
🕓 Daily noon–2.30, 7.30–10. Closed Christmas and New Year
🍷 L €17, D €17, Wine €15

RESTAURANT CAFÉ DE PARIS

40 quai de Caligny, 50100 Cherbourg
Tel 02 33 43 12 36

The current owners of this long-standing brasserie, facing the fishing port of Cherbourg, pay particular attention to food quality. The imaginative menu features such local specialities as *huîtres pochées en habit vert* (poached oysters) and *filet de st-pierre rôti* (roast fillet of John Dory), attracting attention from locals and weekenders.
🕓 Mon–Sat noon–2, 7–10. Closed mid-Jan–early Feb, early Nov–end Nov
🍷 L €25, D €30, Wine €15

COURTILS

MANOIR DE LA ROCHE TORIN

34 route de la Roche, 50220 Courtils
Tel 02 33 70 96 55
www.manoir-rochetorin.com
This lovely old manor house facing Mont-St-Michel is set in beautiful parkland, with a dining room that has stone walls and wood beams. It is famed for its local lamb dishes.
🕓 Tue–Fri 7–8.30, Sat–Sun noon–1.30. Closed Jan–mid-Feb, mid-Nov–mid-Dec
🍷 L €32, D €49, Wine €15

EATING

COUTANCES

LE CLOS DES SENS

55 rue Geoffroy-de-Montbray, 50200 Coutances

Tel 02 33 47 94 78

The new owners of this old restaurant have injected a modern and lively feel to the menu while maintaining the traditional approach to good food which has served it well.

🕐 Mon–Tue, Thu–Sat 12–1.30, 7.30–9.30, Wed noon–1.30

🍽 L €25, D €37.50, Wine €17

ÉQUEURDREVILLE-HAINNEVILLE

LA GOURMANDINE

24 rue Surcouf, 50120 Équeurdreville-Hainneville

Tel 02 33 93 41 26

Regarded by local foodies as one of the best choices in the Cherbourg area, this restaurant is run by Stéphanie and Sylvain Lebas. Regular diners suggest the *bouillon de volaille aux champignons et langoustines* (chicken soup with mushrooms and langoustines) as a starter, and like to finish with one of the renowned desserts. There is access for visitors with disabilities; dogs are allowed.

🕐 Tue–Sat noon–2.15, 7.15–9.15. Closed mid-Jul–early Aug, late Dec–early Jan

🍽 L €35, D €35, Wine €16

GRANVILLE

LA CITADELLE

34 rue du Port, 50400 Granville

Tel 02 33 50 34 10

www.restaurant-la-citadelle.com

La Citadelle, a seafood restaurant opposite the port, has a pretty dining room, or you can relax and enjoy your food on a veranda. Oysters with a Camembert cream are praised.

🕐 Thu–Tue noon–2, 7–9.30. Closed Dec, late Feb–early Mar

🍽 L €17, D €21, Wine €16

LA GENTILHOMMIÈRE

152 rue Couraye, 50400 Granville

Tel 02 33 50 17 99

Franck Baumert has cooked at this restaurant for more than 25 years. His cooking is a mix of contemporary and regional style, the *citron vert avec la côte de veau au beurre demi-sel* (veal ribs with lime and salted butter) being a terrific example. The interior is as trendy as the food.

🕐 Wed–Sat noon–2, 7–9, Tue–Wed 7–9

🍽 L €16, D €21, Wine €12

LE GUÉ DU HOLME

14 rue des Estuaires, 50220 Ducey

Tel 02 33 60 63 76

www.le-gue-du-holme.com

Anne and Michel Leroux offer you a friendly welcome at the restaurant of their family-run hotel. The two dining rooms provide a perfect backdrop to the dishes prepared by chef Guillaume Leroux. The owners are proud of their 'Bonne Table 2003' award, earned through the kitchen's flair with fresh fish and seafood, ranging from springtime sea bass with asparagus to the complex truffle-infused ravioli of lobster *en capuccino*.

🕐 Tue–Fri 12.30–1.30, 7.30–9; Sat 7.30–9; Sun 12.30–1.30 and evenings Jul–Aug. Closed mid–end Nov and Feb school holidays

🍽 L €27, D €58, Wine €16

MONT-ST-MICHEL

DU GUESCLIN

Grande Rue, 50170 Le Mont-St-Michel

Tel 02 33 60 14 10

Set on Mont-St-Michel's main street, Du Guesclin has wonderful panoramic views across the bay. There's plenty of seafood and the fresh grilled local lamb is recommended. There is also a children's menu.

🕐 Thu–Mon 12–2, 7–9; Tue 12–2; Aug open daily; closed Nov–mid-Mar

🍽 L €17, D €34, Wine €16

ST-GERMAIN-DES-VAUX

LE MOULIN À VENT

Hameau Danneville, 50440 St-Germain-des-Vaux

Tel 02 33 52 75 20

The rough exterior of the building contrasts with the fine dining room inside. The interior design is traditional and matched by the fresh produce served. Chef Michel Briens believes in good, honest food, such as marinated organic salmon served with a *tartare d'algues* (seaweed tartar). Meals are complemented by a comprehensive wine list.

🕐 Tue–Sat noon–2, 7–9, Sun noon–2. Closed Jan

🍽 L €26, D €26, Wine €17

ST-LÔ

LA GONIVIÈRE

1 rue d'Alsace-Lorraine, 50180 St-Lô

Tel 02 33 05 15 36

www.restaurant-goniviere.fr

Chef Gilles Plasse follows the traditional style of French and Norman cuisine and likes to use local meat and game produce. Here, you can savour *filet de boeuf en cocotte et au soja* (beef stew with soya).

🕐 Mon–Sat noon–2, 7–9.30. Closed early Jan

🍽 L €18, D €34, Wine €20

ST-PIERRE-DE-SEMILLY

LA FLEUR DE THYM

Le Calvaire, 50810 St-Pierre-de-Semilly

Tel 02 33 05 02 40

www.lafleurdethym.com

The décor may hint at Norman tradition, yet all is not what it seems—Yann Auger's cuisine is refreshingly different. Having travelled widely, Auger has infused his dishes with a distinct Mediterranean flavour, as you will taste in the calamari stuffed with fennel. The restaurant's location between Bayeux and St-Lô makes it ideal for a lunch stop. Service is attentive and there is a classic wine list.

🕐 Tue–Fri noon–2, 7–9.30, Sat 7–10, Sun noon–2

🍽 L €18, D €36, Wine €18

ST-VAAST-LA-HOUGUE

RESTAURANT LES FUCHSIAS

20 rue du Maréchal-Foch, 50550 St-Vaast-la-Hougue

Tel 02 33 54 42 26

www.france-fuchsias.com

Under the supervision of the same family for 50 years, this restaurant got its name from the fuchsias around the building. The colours continue into the air conditioned dining room. Or you can dine on the terrace. The chef uses local fish and shellfish in his menus, and his *choucroute de la mer* (seafood sauerkraut) is famous. There is access for wheelchair-users, and bedrooms (▷ 167).

🕐 Daily Jul–Aug noon–2, 7–9.45. Closed Mon rest of year, Tue Nov–Mar, Jan, Feb

🍽 L €18, D €25, Wine €12

EATING

ORNE

The green heartland of Lower Normandy promises hearty farmyard fare, with home-made foie gras, traditional frogs' legs and seasonal game nudging the region's regular hallmark fish dishes into second position on menus. You can find simple but memorable bistro meals in town or head out into the countryside for indulgent feasts in opulent surroundings.

PRICES AND SYMBOLS

The restaurants are listed alphabetically (excluding The) by town or area, then by name. The prices given are for a two-course lunch (L) and a three-course dinner (D) for one person, without drinks. The wine price is for the least expensive bottle. See page 2 for a key to the symbols.

L'AIGLE

LE DAUPHIN

Place de la Halle, 61300 L'Aigle
Tel 02 33 84 18 00
The arrival of Régis Ligot in this unpretentious family-run hotel restaurant revitalised the menu. His dishes are prepared with flair, and his signature creation, *galettes de socca aux légumes et homard décortiqué* (chickpea galettes with vegetables and lobster), tempts gourmets. The wine list is fair, but has not evolved as far as the menu.
🕐 Mon–Sat noon–1.30, 7.15–9.30, Sun noon–1.30
🍴 L €35, D €35, Wine €25

ALENÇON

LE BISTROT

21 rue de Sarthe, 61000 Alençon
Tel 02 33 26 51 69

This cosy venue has the blackboard menus and chequered tablecloths of a Parisian bistro. Honest, good-value food—such as marinated fresh anchovies and a hearty sausage dish—is waiting to be enjoyed at this warm, friendly eatery. There is a reasonably priced wine list.
🕐 Tue–Sat noon–2, 7–9.30. Closed Aug
🍴 L €12.50, D €15, Wine €11

ARGENTAN

HOSTELLERIE DE LA RENAISSANCE

20 avenue de la 2e D.B., 61200 Argentan
Tel 02 33 36 14 20
www.hotel-larenaissance.com
Arnaud Viel is passionate about his cuisine, and has been as innovative in creating modern dishes as at retaining regional traditions. A particular Viel approach to the classics is the plate of *cuisses de grenouilles croûtées à la farine de pois chiche* (frog's legs cooked in a chickpea-flour crust). The dining room's black-and-white-tiled floor offsets the timber, and elegant candlesticks grace each table. Cecilia Viel selects wines from her very fine cellar.
🕐 Tue–Sat noon–2, 7–9.15, Sun noon–2. Closed early Aug, late Feb
🍴 L €21, D €45, Wine €20

BAGNOLES-DE-L'ORNE

LE MANOIR DU LYS

Route de Juvigny, 61140 Bagnoles-de-l'Orne
Tel 02 33 37 80 69
www.manoir-du-lys.fr
This country-house hotel is in the heart of a park (▷ 168), and its elegant dining room leads onto a terrace overlooking the gardens. The Quinton family have refined the menus here to produce a *cuisine bourgeoise* fit for a king; the wild hare '*à la royale*' is a good example. The wine list reflects all the major regions. There is wheelchair access.
🕐 Daily 12.15–2, 7.30–9.30 Apr–Oct. Closed Sun eve, Mon Nov–Mar; Jan–Feb
🍴 L €29, D €60, Wine €18
🅿 Parking service

FLERS

AU BOUT DE LA RUE

60 rue de la Gare, 61100 Flers
Tel 02 33 65 31 53
The retro design at this bistro includes old photos that reflect the owner's passion for jazz. An open dining room allows you to see into the kitchen. As diners settle on the banquettes, Jacky Leboulleux suggests house specialities, including *agneau en croûte de pain d'épices* (gingerbread-wrapped lamb).

SPECIAL IN BAGNOLES

BOIS JOLI

12 avenue Philippe-du-Rozier, 61140 Bagnoles-de-l'Orne
Tel 02 33 37 92 77
www.hotelboisjoli.com

This 19th-century Norman villa is now an hotel (▷ 168), and with its wooden beams and carved fireplace it is an idyllic setting. Chef Loic Malfilatre creates menus that woo a wide-ranging clientele. His *rosace de sole et langoustines aux pommes de terre écrasée* (sole and langoustine with crushed potato), has won much praise. Service is efficient. The wine list includes a good selection from the Bordelais region.
🕐 Daily noon–2, 7–9.30. Closed mid-Feb–end Mar
🍴 L €19, D €29, Wine €15
🅿 Private parking

🕐 Mon–Tue, Thu–Fri noon–2, 7.30–9.30, Wed noon–2, Sat 7.30–9.30. Closed Aug
🍴 L €20, D €25, Wine €17

ST-VICTOR-DE-RÉNO

AUBERGE DE BROCHARD

Le Brochard, 61290 St-Victor-de-Réno
Tel 02 33 25 74 22
A young team has converted a country house into an intimate restaurant. They have focussed on the menu, which offers a good *terrine maison* (house terrine). A dessert highlight is the *tarte tatin*. The wine list is adequate, and the welcome compensates for any shortfalls.
🕐 Tue–Sat noon–1.30, 7.30–9.15, Sun noon–1.30. Closed Nov
🍴 L €21, D €31, Wine €15

EATING

CALVADOS

Strung along Normandy's D-Day coast are numerous simple, old-fashioned seaside resorts whose brasseries and restaurants offer inexpensive dining with panoramic views. Away from the shore, head inland to the Pays d'Auge for country-house dining and atmospheric inns, or to the regional capital of Caen, whose waterfront area has fashionable tables to suit all budgets.

SPECIAL IN AUDRIEU

CHÂTEAU D'AUDRIEU

14250 Audrieu
Tel 02 31 80 21 52
www.chateaudaudrieu.com
Three adjoining dining rooms grace this chateau (▷ 169). Fresh flowers enhance carved fireplaces, wood panelling and crystal chandeliers. The food, prepared by Cyril Haberland, is presented on fine china bearing the crest of the chateau. His signature dishes marry contemporary panache with Norman flavour, as in such main course delicacies as *pigeon en cocotte* (pigeon casserole) with apples. To accompany your meal, choose from some superb vintage wines.
🕐 Tue–Fri 7–9.30, Sat–Sun noon–2, 7–9.30. Closed mid-Dec–end Jan
🍴 L €35, D €50, Wine €25

BAYEUX

LE LION D'OR

71 rue St-Jean, 14400 Bayeux
Tel 02 31 92 06 90
www.liondor-bayeux.fr
This former coach house, dat-

ing back to the 18th century, provides a lovely setting for a meal after a long day's drive. Chef Patrick Mouilleau cooks reliable regional dishes—try his rabbit confit with sage and a *mille-feuille* of carrots, or the salmon steak pan-sautéed in olive oil and thyme and served with thick slices of potato.
🕐 Tue–Fri, Sun noon–2.30, 7.30–10, Sat, Mon 7.30–10. Closed mid-Dec–mid-Jan
🍴 L €20, D €46, Wine €16

PRICES AND SYMBOLS

The restaurants are listed alphabetically (excluding The) by town or area, then by name. The prices given are for a two-course lunch (L) and a three-course dinner (D) for one person, without drinks. The wine price is for the least expensive bottle. See page 2 for a key to the symbols.

LE PAVÉ D'AUGE

Place du Village, 14430 Beuvron-en-Auge
Tel 02 31 79 26 71
www.lepavedauge.com
A meal here will be a satisfying experience. The restaurant is in the village's marketplace and original markethall features have been retained. Menus are updated regularly but one old favourite is escalope of warm salt cod, which is served with a home-made chutney.
🕐 Jul, Aug Tue–Sun noon–1.45, 7.30–9.30; Sep–end Jun Wed–Sun noon–1.45, 7.30–9.30; closed 24 Nov–26 Dec, 1–8 Jul
🍴 L €30, D €41, Wine €23

CAEN

LE PRÉSSOIR

3 avenue Henry-Chéron, 14000 Caen
Tel 02 31 73 32 71
Yvan Vautier has taken over as chef at this reputable eatery, which is popular among local businessmen. Its location close to Caen's Périphérique makes it accessible to travellers going to Cotentin or the Pays d'Auge. Dishes include the house speciality *le ris de veau au homard et huile truffée* (veal sweetbreads with lobster and truffle oil). The wine list will improve with time.
🕐 Tue–Fri 12.30–1.30, 7.30–9.30, Sat 7.30–9.30, Sun 12.30–1.30. Closed Aug
🍴 L €44, D €66, Wine €30
🅿 Private parking

RESTAURANT ALCIDE

1 place Courtonne, 14000 Caen
Tel 02 31 44 18 06
The city's most famous dish, *tripes à la mode de Caen* (Caen-style tripe), and other regional specialities are on the menu at this lively venue on place Courtonne.The legendary restaurant has been given a facelift. Happily, the food policy is unmodernised, and reliable fare—some say the best in town—keeps the place busy.
🕐 Sun–Fri noon–2, 7–10
🍴 L €20, D €20, Wine €9.50

CAMBREMER

CHÂTEAU LES BRUYÈRES

Route du Cadran, 14340 Cambremer
Tel 02 31 32 22 45
www.chateaulesbruyeres.com
Dine on the veranda, where the chef will invite you to sample some of his original recipes based on traditional regional cuisine, including an interesting 'sea and sand' plate of scallops with foie gras. Among the desserts is a dramatic flambée of strawberries in Pays d'Auge Calvados. The chateau has accommodation (▷ 169).
🕐 Tue–Sun noon–1.30, 7.30–9. Closed Jan
🍴 L €45, D €50, Wine €12

CLÉCY

LE MOULIN DU VEY

Le Vey, 14570 Clécy
Tel 02 31 69 71 08
www.moulinduvey.com
Enjoy free-spirited summer dining on a riverfront terrace in the shade of willow trees, or the cosiness of winter eating in a luxurious dining room with a log fire. The menus change with the seasons, enabling the chef to produce innovative and traditional dishes from the freshest local produce. There are guest rooms in the mill (▷ 170) for overnight stays.
🕐 Daily 12.30–2, 7.30–9. Closed Dec, Jan, Sun D and Mon L Feb–Mar
🍴 L €24.50, D €48, Wine €15

CRÉPON

FERME DE LA RANÇONNIÈRE

Route d'Arromanches, 14480 Crépon
Tel 02 31 22 21 73
www.ranconniere.com
The dining room in this 18th-century farmhouse hotel (▷ 169), has a rustic authenticity. Relax under beamed ceilings, as you settle down to

EATING

a platter of fresh seafood served at linen-draped tables.

🕐 Daily noon–1.30, 7–9. Closed Jan

🍴 L €15, D €26, Wine €14

CRESSERONS

LA VALISE GOURMANDE

7 rue de Lion-sur-Mer, 14440 Cresserons

Tel 02 31 37 39 10

This 18th-century priory, with its courtyard, luxurious gardens and pristine dining room, sets the scene for an intimate *dîner à deux*. The food here is classic Norman fare, such as *poitrine de cochon braisée au cidre fermier* (pork braised in farm-house cider), at a surprisingly reasonable price. The balanced wine list also offers value for money. The restaurant is only a few minutes from the coast.

🕐 Wed–Sat noon–2, 7.30–9, Sun 12–2, Tue 7.30–9. Closed early Mar, mid-Sep–end Oct

🍴 L €30, D €40, Wine €24

CREULLY

HOSTELLERIE ST-MARTIN

Place E. Paillaud, 14480 Creully

Tel 02 31 80 10 11

www.hostelleriesaintmartin.com

This restaurant lies beneath the vaulted ceilings of Creully's original 16th-century market. Monsieur Legrand, the owner and chef, is justifiably proud of the regional country fare he produces as well as his more complex speciality dishes. The house foie gras with apples, or a duck steak with honey sauce, will stimulate the palate of any gourmet. These dishes are at their best when accompanied by wine from Monsieur Legrand's extensive cellars.

🕐 Daily noon–2, 7–9.30. Closed end Dec–mid-Jan

🍴 L €14, D €20, Wine €12

DEAUVILLE

AUGUSTO

27 rue Désiré le Hoc, 14800 Deauville

Tel 02 31 88 34 49

At Augusto, a chic bistro, the staff claim to be the 'kings of lobster'. The house special is lobster served with fresh pasta, while other incarnations of the crustacean include lobster mousse and broth. There are also fish and meat dishes. Eat outside or in a marine-inspired dining room. Choose from *prix fixe* menus or eat *à la carte*.

🕐 Thu–Mon noon–2.30, 7–10.30, open daily Jul, Aug until midnight

🍴 L €27, D €50, Wine €23

DIVES-SUR-MER

CHEZ LE BOUGNAT

27 rue Gaston-Manneville, 14160 Dives-sur-Mer

Tel 02 31 91 06 13

Traditional family favourites are the secret of this restaurant's success. French comfort food, including the classic winter warmer *pot au feu*, appeal to young and old alike. Locals like this unpretentious seaside eatery for its reliable food and ambience. Dogs are welcome.

🕐 Daily 12–2, Thu–Sat 7–10, Sun–Wed 7–10. Closed Jan

🍴 L €19, D €19, Wine €14

FALAISE

L'ATTACHE

Rond-point Nord de l'Attache, 14700 Falaise

Tel 02 31 90 05 38

Housed in an old coaching inn, this small restaurant has an excellent wine list—nurturing the cellar is the passion of the patron, Alain Hastain. Service in the dining room is attentive and friendly. The use of local fish, fresh herbs and spices makes the menu interesting.

🕐 Thu–Mon noon–2, 7–9, Tue noon–2. Closed late Sep–early Oct

🍴 L €18, D €18, Wine €10

GOUPILLIÈRES

AUBERGE DU PONT DE BRIE

Halte de Grimbosq, 14210 Goupillières

Tel 02 31 79 37 84

www.pontdebrie.com

Frédérique and Thiérry Cottarel's *auberge* has an enchanting dining room with a stone fireplace and pastel tableware, and has much to offer with its seasonal fare. For a typical taste of Normandy, consider the pork cooked in cider.

🕐 Wed–Sun 12.15–1.30, 7.15–9. Closed mid-Nov–early Jan, late Feb–early Mar

🍴 L €18, D €28, Wine €16

HONFLEUR

FERME ST-SIMÉON

Rue Adolphe Marais, 14600 Honfleur

Tel 02 31 81 78 00

www.fermesaintsimeon.fr

Produce from the Ferme St-Siméon's kitchen garden adds to the flavours when you lunch either in the dining room with its vaulted ceiling, or on the terrace. This hotel could rely on its association with art celebrities (▷ 170), but its restaurant has earned a fine reputation as one of the finest in Normandy. Savour *homard façon Tourville* (Tourville-style lobster) or opt for *langoustines sur gêlée de crustacés* (langoustines in a shellfish aspic).

🕐 Wed–Sun 12.30–2, 7–9, Tue 7–9

🍴 L €85, D €120, Wine €30

HOULGATE

HÔTEL RESTAURANT 1900

17 rue des Bains, 14510 Houlgate

Tel 02 31 28 77 77

www.hotel-1900.fr

Dine in style at the restaurant of Houlgate's small Hôtel 1900. It specialises in fish, its signature dish a turbot fillet served *à la Houlgataise* with baby vegetables infused with fragrant rosemary.

🕐 Daily noon–2.30, 6.30–10

🍴 L €18.50, D €24.50, Wine €17

THURY-HARCOURT

LE RELAIS DE LA POSTE

7 rue de Caen, 14220 Thury-Harcourt

Tel 02 31 79 72 12

This old post house has an old-fashioned dining room with a beamed ceiling and walls adorned with copper items. It boasts a fine wine cellar, which complements the chef's classic dishes. Try the terrine of foie gras, which is partnered with apple chutney—a favourite with guests and regulars.

🕐 Daily noon–2, 7–9 Jun–Sep. Closed Fri, Sat L, Sun D rest of year, mid-Dec–end Jan

🍴 L €18, D €25, Wine €16

EURE

Country-house hotel restaurants, with their award-winning chefs, are ideal for special occasions or as a reward after a day's driving, but the back country of Upper Normandy also has a good range of mid-priced restaurants offering regional cuisine on a sensible budget.

PRICES AND SYMBOLS

The restaurants are listed alphabetically (excluding The) by town or area, then by name. The prices given are for a two-course lunch (L) and a three-course dinner (D) for one person, without drinks. The wine price is for the least expensive bottle. See page 2 for a key to the symbols.

CONCHES-EN-OUCHE

RESTAURANT ET HÔTEL DU CYGNE

2 rue Paul Guilbaud, 27190 Conches-en-Ouche
Tel 02 32 30 20 60
Tucked away in a cottage that was once a coach house, this dining room has a tiled floor and beamed ceiling. The menu changes seasonally, but always reflects good, local produce. Foie gras is usually an option.
🕐 Tue–Sat noon–2.30, 7.30–9.30, Sun noon–2.30. Closed Oct
🍴 L €15, D €28, Wine €15

LES DAMPS

AUBERGE DE LA POMME

44 rue de l'Eure, 27340 Les Damps
Tel 02 35 23 00 46
Here you can choose from interesting fish dishes, all served up in russet-toned surroundings. Occasional events are organised on the terrace and gardens.
🕐 Mon, Thu–Sat noon–2, 7–9, Tue, Sun noon–2. Closed Aug
🍴 L €24, D €33, Wine €22
🅿 Good parking facilities

ÉVREUX

LA GAZETTE

7 rue St-Sauveur, 27000 Évreux
Tel 02 32 33 43 40

This lovely bistro has much to offer. Chef Xavier Buzieux creates some unexpected flavours; for example, a red mullet fillet is served with the southern salt-cod speciality *brandade de morue* and a pistachio vinaigrette. Round off the meal with the powerfully refreshing eucalyptus sorbet.
🕐 Mon–Fri noon–2, 7–9.30, Sat 7–9.30. Closed Aug
🍴 L €20, D €30, Wine €17

FOURGES

MOULIN DE FOURGES

38 rue du Moulin, 27630 Fourges
Tel 02 32 52 12 12
www.moulin-de-fourges.com
This beautiful mill stands just a couple of miles from Giverny but it is a relaxing sanctuary away from the crowds on the Monet trail. The food makes innovative use of local produce. You can stay the night here.
🕐 Tue–Sat noon–2.30, 7.30–10, Sun noon–2.30; closed Nov–Mar
🍴 L €35, D €40, Wine €21

MONTREUIL-L'ARGILLÉ

AUBERGE DE LA TRUITE

5 rue Grande, 27390 Montreuil-l'Argillé
Tel 02 32 44 50 47
Jacky, the owner of this Norman *auberge*, has a warm and often musical greeting for guests. Relax to background sounds from his collection of vintage barrel organs while you dine. Large portions of regional food are served with good humour.
🕐 Mon–Tue noon–2, Thu–Sun noon–2, 7–9. Closed Jan
🍴 L €17, D €17, Wine €10.50

PONT-AUDEMER

BELLE-ISLE SUR RISLE

112 route de Rouen, 27500 Pont-Audemer
Tel 02 32 56 96 22
www.bellile.com
Chef Gaston Grenier produces such specialities as the famous *croustade chaude aux trois fromages Normands* (pastry of three Normandy cheeses). A blend of business lunchers and hedonists sets this manor house (▷ 171) apart.
🕐 Daily 7.15–9.30, Thu–Sun 12–2. Closed mid-Nov–mid-Mar
🍴 L €29, D €60, Wine €21

SPECIAL IN VERNEUIL

HOSTELLERIE LE CLOS

98 rue de la Ferté-Vidame, 27133 Verneuil-sur-Avre
Tel 02 32 32 21 81
www.hostellerieduclos.fr
Set in a 12th-century village, this fairy-tale manor house nestles in parkland. The grand dining room, with *trompe l'oeil* decoration, leads onto a sunny terrace. The chef prepares seasonal dishes, which can be accompanied by wines from a mature list that includes some fine Calvados.
🕐 Daily noon–2, 7.30–9. Closed mid-Dec–late Jan
🍴 L €32, D €78, Wine €25

PONT-ST-PIERRE

L'HOSTELLERIE LA BONNE MARMITE

10 rue René Raban, 27360 Pont-St-Pierre
Tel 02 32 49 70 24
www.la-bonne-marmite.com
The dining room in this former coaching inn (▷ 171), has a romantic atmosphere. Dishes celebrate the local turbot, lobster and duck. The chef-patron, Maurice Amiot, has won many culinary awards. The wine list has 800 vintages dating back as far as 1858.
🕐 Wed–Sat noon–2.15, 7–9.15, Sun noon–2.15. Closed late Feb–late Mar, late Jul–mid-Aug
🍴 L €17, D €25, Wine €13

VERNON

LES FLEURS

71 rue Carnot, 27200 Vernon
Tel 02 32 51 16 80
In this half-timbered house in the heart of Vernon, Michel Graux creates evolving menus that will enchant any palate. When asparagus comes into season, regular diners adore the arrival of Graux's delicious blend of the vegetable with lightly pan-fried scallops. The restaurant's attention to detail in the kitchen is matched by the service and presentation.
🕐 Tue–Sat noon–2, 7.30–9.15, Sun noon–2. Closed early Mar, early Aug
🍴 L €33, D €33, Wine €21

EATING

SEINE-MARITIME

In the historic ducal capital of Rouen, visitors are spoilt for choice. Here, trendy contemporary eateries line up alongside classic tables preparing old-style gastronomic gems, such as the famous pressed duckling (▷ 13). Along the coast, lobster, turbot and sole are the highlights of many a menu on port-side tables from Dieppe to Le Havre. Harbour tables are ideal for a cheap meal of mussels and oysters, while the region's country inns serve foie gras and veal dishes.

PRICES AND SYMBOLS

The restaurants are listed alphabetically (excluding The) by town or area, then by name. The prices given are for a two-course lunch (L) and a three-course dinner (D) for one person, without drinks. The wine price is for the least expensive bottle. See page 2 for a key to the symbols.

DIEPPE

RESTAURANT DE L'HÔTEL WINDSOR

18 boulevard de Verdun, 76200 Dieppe
Tel 02 35 84 15 23
www.hotelwindsor.fr

The restaurant at the Hôtel Windsor has panoramic sea views and serves local specialities, with an emphasis on seafood, to a loyal market of holidaymakers. The fresh shellfish platter and the foie gras are both highly recommended.
🕐 Daily noon–2.30, 7.30–9.30
🍴 L €14, D €49, Wine €24

EU

RESTAURANT MAINE

20 avenue de la Gare, 76260 Eu
Tel 02 35 86 16 64
Sitting in this family-run restaurant, you will be fascinated by the eccentric variety of items on display. The owner, Jean Claude Maine, will always take time for a chat. Surf and turf are both represented on the menu, and among the desserts is a chocolate and strawberry *mille-feuille* pastry with a lip-smacking raspberry coulis. A good selection of Bordeaux

SPECIAL IN DIEPPE

BISTROT DU POLLET

23 rue Tête-de-Boeuf, 76200 Dieppe
Tel 02 35 84 68 57
In the old fishing quarter of Dieppe, you will discover this

bistro, which is far more used to serving locals than daytrippers from the ferry port. The cosy restaurant has a huge selection of locally caught fish, and although the cooking is simple without any sauces, it is exquisite in flavour. One of the dishes is whole sea bass served with fresh spinach and mashed potato with black olives. Both the service and atmosphere are good yet relaxed.
🕐 Tue–Sat noon–2, 7–9.30. Closed mid–end Aug
🍴 L €12, D €15, Wine €14

and burgundy wines is offered.
🕐 Daily 12–1.30, 7.30–9
🍴 L €15, D €24, Wine €13

FÉCAMP

AUBERGE DE LA ROUGE

Route du Havre, 76400 Fécamp
Tel 02 35 28 07 59
Relax in the family atmosphere of this *auberge*. Chef Paul-Aymeric Durel has added his own touch to the menu since he took over in 2003, a fact that is apparent on tasting his *pavé de gros turbot roti à la sariette* (roasted turbot cutlets). There are some inventive vegetarian dishes too. The service is attentive.
🕐 Tue–Sat noon–2, 7–9, Sun noon–2. Closed early Feb
🍴 L €18, D €28, Wine €16

JUMIÈGES

AUBERGE DES RUINES

17 place de la Mairie, 76480 Jumièges
Tel 02 35 37 24 05

Facing the ruins of the abbey across the street, this restaurant has elegant table settings to complement its equally lovely food. The chef has opted for lighter dishes, including *ris de veau rôti jaune d'oeuf cru* (roast veal sweetbreads with raw egg yolk) served in its smoked spicy jus, and uses the finest local ingredients, which is reflected in the *à la carte* prices. Since Jumièges is half an hour from Rouen, the *auberge* has proved popular with city-break weekenders.
🕐 Mon, Thu–Sat noon–2, 7–9, Tue, Sun noon–2. Closed late Aug–early Sep, mid-Dec–mid-Jan
🍴 L €18, D €45, Wine €26

ROUEN

LE CATELIER

134 bis, avenue des Martyrs de la Résistance, 76100 Rouen
Tel 02 35 72 59 90
www.lecatelier-restaurant.fr
Dine on local delicacies in this Norman house close to the botanical garden. The dining room is elegant yet convivial. Chef Marie-France Atinault specialises in seafood—try scallops from Dieppe, turbot in a white wine sauce or lobster salad with cider-butter and fried apples. Her husband, Daniel, will help you choose the best wine to go with your meal. There are several fixed-price menus.
🕐 Tue–Sat noon–2, 7–9; closed first 3 weeks of Aug
🍴 L €35, D €50, including wine

EATING

LA VILLA DU HAVRE

66 boulevard Albert-ler, 76600 Le
Havre

Tel 02 35 54 78 80

This is a gastronomic experience not to be missed. Enter the world of a master chef, where the contemporary art on the walls complements the food on the table. Look out for the *bonbons de foie gras en coque de légumes* (a daintily presented plate of foie gras and vegetables). In addition to the gastronomic paradise, service is excellent, and the sommelier will advise the best wine for each course. The icing on the cake is an ever-changing view of the sea from the restaurant.

🕐 Tue–Sat noon–2, 7.30–10. Closed early Jan, Jul

🍴 L €32, D €45, Wine €30

L'ÉCAILLE

26 Rampe-Cauchoise, 76000 Rouen

Tel 02 35 70 95 52

This acclaimed fish restaurant is one of the finest in the area. The chef, Marc Tellier, who deals directly with local fishermen and selects only the best catches, is also a keen fisherman himself. As well as the classic choices, the menu features a fresh special such as a salad of whole lobster with a *vinaigrette*. Service is friendly and the wine list is very good.

🕐 Tue–Fri noon–2, 7–9.30, Sat 7–9.30

🍴 L €30, D €44, Wine €45

LA PÊCHERIE

29 place de la Basse Vieille Tour, 76000 Rouen

Tel 02 35 88 71 00

www.lapecherie.fr

At this friendly brasserie staff serve generous platters of fish and shellfish, as well as less common combinations such as lobster in a cider reduction.

A couple of meat dishes and some memorable desserts, including a spicy pineapple *carpaccio* and an Earl Grey tea-scented *crème brulée*, finish the line-up. You can sit outside on the small terrace.

🕐 Mon–Fri 12–2.30, 7.30–9.30, Sat 7.30–10

🍴 L €25, D €38, Wine €16

LE P'TIT ZINC

20 place du Vieux Marché, 76000 Rouen

Tel 02 35 89 39 69

The restaurant is tiny and the service can be hurried, yet the atmosphere and the food are great. It is difficult to imagine how dishes like *entrecôte à la moelle et son gâteau de champignons* (marrowbone steak with a mushroom cake) can be produced so beautifully from such a small kitchen. Alain, the patron, recommends appropriate wines from his exceptional wine list and considers Le P'tit Zince more a wine cellar than a restaurant.

🕐 Mon–Fri noon–2, 8–10, Sat noon–2. Closed Aug

🍴 L €25, D €25, Wine €15

RESTAURANT DUFOUR

67 bis, rue St-Nicolas, 76000 Rouen

Tel 02 35 71 90 62

This is a typical Norman restaurant close to the cathedral. The menu has a traditional feel, and as the restaurant is popular with both local and tourists, advance booking is advised. A speciality is the famous *caneton à la Rouennaise*, pressed duckling served with a flourish at your table (▷ 13).

🕐 Tue–Sat noon–1.30, 7–9.30, Sun noon–1.30

🍴 L €20, D €28, Wine €12

TOURVILLE-LA-RIVIÈRE

LE TOURVILLE

12 rue Danielle-Casanova, 76410 Tourville-la-Rivière

Tel 02 35 77 58 79

The walls of this long-standing restaurant are hung with many fine paintings. Today's menus may have retained traditional dishes, but they are presented in a contemporary manner, and are described with such florid Gallic phrases as *'un peu de gêlée et de la salade avec le foie gras'* (prosaically, foie gras with aspic and salad).

🕐 Tue–Sun 12–2, Fri–Sat 7.30–9.30

🍴 L €45, D €45, Wine €16.50

VEULES-LES-ROSES

LES GALETS

3 rue Victor-Hugo, 76980 Veules-les-Roses

Tel 02 35 97 61 33

This restaurant, on the Côte d'Albâtre, has a conservatory-style room where locals and visitors explore a menu rich in fish. Chef Gilbert Plaisance has combined timeless classics with new ideas. For those with the budget and the appetite, the *menu découverte* is worth trying. Look out for the oysters served with a terrine of baby leeks. The wine list has a good selection available by the glass.

🕐 Thu–Mon 12.30–2.30, 7.30–9. Closed mid-Nov–mid-Dec

🍴 L €33, D €50, Wine €18

YVETOT

AUBERGE DU VAL AU CESNE

Croix Mare, 76190 Yvetot

Tel 02 35 56 63 06

www.valaucesne.fr

This 17th-century farmhouse sits in the heart of the countryside. Within the half-timbered *auberge* (▷ 173), chef Jerome Carel attracts seekers of culinary perfection. Among his various specialities is sole stuffed with a langoustine mousse, which has become a local legend. The rustic dining room has an open fireplace, and the service is friendly. You can take a postprandial stroll.

🕐 Wed–Sun noon–2, 7–9. Closed 3 weeks Jan, 2 weeks Aug

🍴 L €35, D €45, Wine €22

EATING

STAYING IN NORMANDY

From chateau luxury to simple country hospitality, Normandy has a welcome for all visitors whatever their budget, inland or along the coast. Norman hotels in are inspected and categorised with a nationally approved star rating, ranging from four stars at the top end, down to no stars for the most basic. Arguably the most authentic taste of Norman life comes through the *chambre d'hôte* (bed-and-breakfast) experience.

In Normandy's hotels you can enjoy swimming pools, luxury bedrooms and à la carte meals

PRICING

Detailed prices are posted in the front windows of hotels and are always quoted per room and not per person, except in the case of full- or half-board accommodation, when the price is per guest. While many chain hotels offer no-smoking rooms, not every hotel provides this option. Check before booking if you require one.

LUXURY

Normandy's most luxurious hotels are deep in the countryside, around the Côte d'Albâtre (▷ 91) and in the Orne. Here you will find gastronomic treats in the dining room. Pampering of a different sort is to be enjoyed at coastal or spa resorts.

MID-RANGE

In the middle price range are comfortable city-centre hotels, often air conditioned in summer, and traditional seafront hotels. Inns and family-run hotels bearing the Logis de France symbol (www.logis-de-france.fr) are independent establishments renowned for their hospitality and home-cooked meals. All Logis are regularly inspected and are of a high standard. Some offer themed fishing and hiking packages.

ON A BUDGET

Chain hotels and motels are the least expensive touring option, offering basic rooms at the lowest prices. But they do not reflect the character of the region. Simple one-star hotels, often close to railway stations, can be good value if you overlook dated décor. Youth hostels (*auberges de jeunesse*) are open to visitors of all ages, provided that they are members of the Youth Hostelling Federation of their home country. Discover more online at www.fuaj.org.

BON WEEKEND

The Bon Weekend en Ville promotion gives you two nights' accommodation for the price of one on Fridays and Saturdays at a range of hotels, together with two-for-one discounts at local visitor sights and attractions. You have to reserve your hotel through the tourist office at Le Havre.

BED-AND-BREAKFAST

While many roadside signs advertise *chambre d'hôte*, it is best to select one through the Gîtes de France organisation (see below). You can stay in a farmhouse or a watermill, a converted barn or manor house. Rooms often have ensuite facilities. Breakfast will include a home-made element, such as fresh-baked bread. Many establishments are situated in rural locations and *table d'hôte* evening meals may also be offered, when you dine with the family at a very low price.

SELF-CATERING

Purpose-built holiday homes, ranging from resort complexes in towns such as Deauville to basic VVF holiday parks, are widely availble. However, the Gîtes de France organisation (www.gites-de-france.fr) offers a more authentic local flavour. Note that linens and towels are rarely supplied in French self-catering properties.

CAMPSITES

Camping and caravanning are part of French life. Excellent sites where you can pitch your own van or tent, or rent tents, chalets or static caravans, are found across the region. Regional tourist offices supply listings brochures. Book in advance in summer. Sites may close in winter. Do not park motorhomes by the roadside or on beaches, and note that casual camping may be forbidden.

STAYING

LA MANCHE

The sweep of coastline taking in D-Day beaches, family resorts and the Bay of Mont-St-Michel is home to a full range of traditional seaside hotels. Country inns in quieter villages and the occasional grand retreat away from the sea offer comfortable options at all budgets.

AGNEAUX

LE CHÂTEAU D'AGNEAUX
Avenue Ste-Marie, 50180 Agneaux
Tel 02 33 57 65 88
This fairy-tale turreted chateau, restored to its former glory, has spacious bedrooms with whitewashed stone walls that are furnished with four-poster beds. The lounge has views of the garden through wooden-shuttered windows. There is wheelchair access and dogs are welcome. A playground and tennis are some of the leisure activities on site.
🅖 Closed mid-Jan
🛏 €91–196, excluding breakfast (€13)
🚪 12

BARNEVILLE-CARTERET

HÔTEL DES ORMES
13 promenade Barbey-d'Aurevilly, 50270 Barneville-Carteret
Tel 02 33 52 23 50
www.hoteldesormes.fr

An ivy-covered *maison bourgeoise*, facing the port on one side and a garden on the other, this hotel is ideal for a romantic break. The upgrading of the bedrooms blends the antique and modern. Enjoy golf, tennis, horse-riding and water sports.
🅖 Open all year
🛏 €75–145, excluding breakfast (€11)
🚪 10

SPECIAL IN AVRANCHES

LA RAMADE
2–4 rue de la Côte, Marcey-les-Graves, 50300 Avranches
Tel 02 33 58 27 40
www.laramade.fr
A three-star, family-run hotel between the sea and the countryside, the Ramade is close to Mont-St-Michel. There is a separate granite

guesthouse for up to three people. After a winter walk you can enjoy a drink by the open fireplace in the lounge. Madame Morvan can organise trips for her guests. As it has no restaurant, try the Croix d'Or in town (▷ 158).
🅖 Closed mid–end Nov, Jan
🛏 €61–112, excluding breakfast (€8)
🚪 10, 1 guesthouse (non-smoking)

BRÉVILLE-SUR-MER

LA BEAUMONDERIE
20 rue de Coutances, 50290 Bréville-sur-Mer
Tel 02 33 50 36 36
www.la-beaumonderie.com
La Beaumonderie is a smart country house on the bay of Mont-St-Michel, overlooking a nearby harbour. Spacious bedrooms are classically furnished, with large beds. The restaurant is open to non-residents.
🅖 Year-round
🛏 €90–150, excluding breakfast (€10)
🚪 15

DUCEY

AUBERGE DE LA SÉLUNE
2 rue St-Germain, 50220 Ducey
Tel 02 33 48 53 62
www.selune.com
This family-run hotel is close to Mont-St-Michel. An award-winning garden and idyllic countryside are the main reasons to choose this Logis de France hideaway. Bedrooms are modestly furnished and a restaurant serves traditional food. The owner is happy to instruct guests in the art of fly fishing on the Sélune river.
🅖 Closed late Nov–mid-Dec, late Jan–mid-Feb, Mon Oct–Mar
🛏 €54–57, excluding breakfast (€8)
🚪 20

MONT-ST-MICHEL

AUBERGE ST-PIERRE
Grande Rue, 50170 Mont-St-Michel
Tel 02 33 60 14 03
www.auberge-saint-pierre.fr
This 15th-century auberge is on the main street of Mont-St-Michel. Despite a picture-book exterior, it has modern fittings. This is an ideal spot for visiting the Mount, especially late at night and early in the morning, when the place is deserted.
🅖 Year-round
🛏 €85–160, excluding breakfast (€12)
🚪 21

QUINÉVILLE

LE CHÂTEAU DE QUINÉVILLE
18 rue de l'Église, 50310 Quinéville
Tel 02 33 21 42 67
www.chateau-de-quineville.com
Château de Quinéville, once home to King James II of England, has extensive grounds and a heated swimming pool. The dining room and bedrooms are exquisitely furnished.
🅖 Year-round
🛏 €62–130, excluding breakfast (€11)
🚪 24
🏊 Outdoors 🎾

ST-VAAST-LA-HOUGUE

HÔTEL DE FRANCE
20 rue du Maréchal-Foch, 50550 St-Vaast-la-Hougue
Tel 02 33 54 42 26
www.france-fuchsias.com
This popular hotel is near the harbour. Rooms are tastefully furnished and most look onto an exotic garden, the setting for chamber-music concerts in August. Cookery courses in Les Fuchsias restaurant (▷ 159) are offered out of season.
🅖 Closed Jan, Feb, Mon out of season
🛏 €29–98, excluding breakfast (€9)
🚪 33 rooms, 1 suite

STAYING

ORNE

The spa town of Bagnoles-de-l'Orne has all the pampering palaces one would expect. Away from the resort, Orne is very much a rural retreat and its forests are sprinkled with manor houses. This is *chambre d'hôte* country and staying in private homes is the perfect way of discovering it.

BAGNOLES-DE-L'ORNE

BOIS JOLI

12 avenue Philippe-du-Rozier, 61140 Bagnoles-de-l'Orne
Tel 02 33 37 92 77
www.hotelboisjoli.com

The lovely family-run Bois Joli manor house, hiding in a 3,000sq-m (3,600sq-yd) park, was built in the Anglo-Norman style. Relax in the gardens with an aperitif, then move indoors to the dining room (▷ 160) and pretty bedrooms. Sports can be enjoyed in the vicinity.

🔘 Open all year
🛏 €86–136, excluding breakfast (€10)
🛈 20

MACÉ

L'ÎLE DE SÉES

Vandel, 61500 Macé
Tel 02 33 27 98 65
www.ile-sees.fr

This country-house hotel, in chateau country, is surrounded by beautiful grounds. A dining room leads onto large terraces, for al fresco meals. The simple bedrooms are decorated in pastel colours, and the hotel is an ideal stopover for visitors.

🔘 Closed Nov–end Feb
🛏 €53–62, excluding breakfast (€8)
🛈 16
🅿 50 cars

NONANT-LE-PIN

LE PLESSIS

61240 Nonant-le-Pin
Tel 02 33 35 59 02

This pretty half-timbered home offers bed-and-breakfast in large bedrooms with high ceilings. Guests are fiercely loyal to the place, which has won its favour by word of mouth. The hosts are very welcoming and an excellent evening meal is shared with the family. Golf

SPECIAL IN BAGNOLES

LE MANOIR DU LYS

La Croix Gauthier, 61140 Bagnoles-de-l'Orne
Tel 02 33 37 80 69
www.manoir-du-lys.fr

The Manoir du Lys stands on the edge of the Andaine forest. Some bedrooms, each designed differently, look out onto the orchard; others have a lovely view of the gardens. Beside the main house are seven family-friendly cabins on stilts, each with a living room, bedroom and bathroom. There are bicycles for rent, and a restaurant (▷ 160).

🔘 Closed Jan
🛏 €60–190, excluding breakfast (€13)
🛈 23 rooms, 7 cabins
🏊 Outdoor heated

and horse-riding are popular local leisure pursuits.

🔘 Year-round
🛏 €40, including breakfast. Evening meal: €15, including drinks
🛈 3

RÂNES

HOTEL SAINT-PIERRE

6 rue de la Libération, 61150 Rânes
Tel 02 33 39 75 14
www.hotelsaintpierreranes.com

This lovely stone-built mansion has a warm, friendly atmosphere. An elegant dining room will tempt you to savour the delicacies of the area, and well-appointed bedrooms are cosy. This ideal base for touring the area also welcomes dogs.

🔘 Year-round
🛏 €48–65, excluding breakfast (€7)
🛈 12

SÉES

LE DAUPHIN

31 place des Anciennes Halles, 61500 Sées
Tel 02 33 80 80 70

A former coaching inn, Le Dauphin is a Logis de France hotel, in a quiet area of Sées. Attractive bedrooms with four-poster beds are among its features. Dogs are welcome in the bedrooms and restaurant, and you can eat on the terrace. Various activities are offered.

🔘 Closed late Nov, mid–end Jan, Sun eve, Mon Oct–May except public hols
🛏 €57–105, excluding breakfast (€11)
🛈 6

SILLY-EN-GOUFFERN

LE PAVILLON DE GOUFFERN

61310 Silly-en-Gouffern
Tel 02 33 36 64 26
www.pavillondegouffern.com

Once a 16th-century hunting lodge, this imposing residence is surrounded by a deer park. The large bedrooms have polished wood floors, and the furnishings are a blend of the classic and the contemporary. Vast windows make the main restaurant feel airy. A lake is filled by natural springs that meander through the forests.

🔘 Closed Christmas
🛏 €95–150, excluding breakfast (€8)
🛈 19 rooms, 1 suite

STAYING

CALVADOS

A selection of chateau hotels are hideaways in the hinterland, but Calvados is prime seaside holiday country. Cabourg and Deauville offer traditional resort hotels, from the casino and spa addresses of Deauville to the grandeur of Cabourg. The old ports have splendid guesthouses.

ARROMANCHES-LES-BAINS

HÔTEL VICTORIA
24 chemin de l'Église, 14117 Arromanches-les-Bains
Tel 02 31 22 35 37
www.hotelvictoria-arromanches.com
This manor house-style hotel, close to the D-Day beaches, is decorated with period furniture and paintings. Bedrooms range in style from large and vibrantly decorated to intimate with beamed ceilings, and either overlook the gardens or the flower-filled courtyard.
🕙 Closed Oct–end Mar
💶 €88–125, excluding breakfast (€10)
🛏 14
🅿 Enclosed parking area

AUDRIEU

CHÂTEAU D'AUDRIEU
14250 Audrieu
Tel 02 31 80 21 52
www.chateaudaudrieu.com

In the middle of a park sits this 18th-century chateau. Rooms range from attic apartments to standard family rooms. The lavish Louis XV and art deco suites are superior options, and there are salons, drawing rooms and a classy restaurant (▷ 161). In the gardens is a heated swimming pool.
🕙 Closed mid-Dec–early Jan
💶 €120–425, excluding breakfast (€17)
🛏 25 rooms, 4 suites
🏊 Outdoor heated

BAYEUX

CHÂTEAU DE BELLEFONTAINE
49 rue de Bellefontaine, 14400 Bayeux
Tel 02 31 22 00 10
www.hotel-bellefontaine.com
This family-run hotel is near the centre of Bayeux yet surrounded by water and set in

PRICES AND SYMBOLS
The hotels below are listed alphabetically (excluding The) by town or area, then by name. Prices are for a double room for one night, including breakfast. All the hotels listed accept credit cards unless otherwise stated. See page 2 for a key to the symbols.

beautiful grounds. The high-ceilinged rooms are spacious and tastefully furnished. Enjoy coffee and croissants in the vaulted breakfast room or on the veranda. In addition, there are facilities for guests with disabilities. This makes a good base for those visiting the Bayeux Tapestry as well as the D-Day landing beaches.
🕙 Closed Jan
💶 €92–110, excluding breakfast (€11)
🛏 14 rooms, 6 suites
🅿 Private parking

CABOURG

GRAND HÔTEL
Promenade Marcel Proust, 14390 Cabourg
Tel 02 31 91 01 79
www.cabourg-web.com/grandhotel
As you walk through this magnificent building, where novelist Marcel Proust holidayed up until World War I, you will feel transported back into the belle époque. The renovated, bright and sunny bedrooms have either sea or garden views, and sports and leisure activities are available. The hotel is popular for exhibitions, seminars and concerts.
🕙 Year-round
💶 €150–296, excluding breakfast (€16)
🛏 70
🏊 Indoor

CAEN

LE DAUPHIN
29 rue Gémare, 14000 Caen
Tel 02 31 86 22 26
www.le-dauphin-normandie.com
A former priory in the centre of Caen, this refurbished building has interconnecting family rooms of a good standard. Traditional Norman specialities are served in the restaurant.
🕙 Closed mid-Feb–early Mar, late Oct–early Nov
💶 €70–142, excluding breakfast (€11)
🛏 32 rooms (12 non-smoking), 5 suites (3 non-smoking)
🏊 Indoor 🧖 Sauna
🅿 Private parking
🚊 Tram to St-Pierre

HÔTEL DU HAVRE
11 rue du Havre, 14000 Caen
Tel 02 31 86 19 80
www.hotelduhavre.com
It is great to find simple budget accommodation in the centre of the city. The basic rooms here have ensuite bathrooms.
🕙 Year-round
💶 €48–54, excluding breakfast (€6)
🛏 19
🅿 Private parking
🚊 Tram to Résistance

CAMBREMER

CHÂTEAU LES BRUYÈRES
Route du Cadran, 14340 Cambremer
Tel 02 31 32 22 45
www.chateaulesbruyeres.com
Follow the tree-lined drive to this magnificent chateau, an inspiration to many famous writers. Each room is beautifully personalised, with ornate furnishings. Savour the delights of the restaurant, which uses garden-grown food (▷ 161). Themed weekends are available, including cider tasting.
🕙 Open all year
💶 €105–195, excluding breakfast (€12)
🛏 13
🏊 Outdoor

CRÉPON

FERME DE LA RANÇONNIÈRE
Route d'Arromanches, 14480 Crépon
Tel 02 31 22 21 73
www.ranconniere.com
Now a welcoming hotel, this 13th–15th-century fortified farmhouse has been restored

STAYING

to its former architectural glory. You enter the courtyard via a crenellated archway. Inside are exposed beams, stonework and fireplaces. Large bedrooms are furnished with antiques. Dogs are welcomed. There are facilities for guests with disabilities, and a restaurant (▷ 161). Guests can visit D-Day sites at the wheel of the hotel's jeep.

🕐 Closed Jan
💶 €45–128, excluding breakfast (€10)
🛏 34

DEAUVILLE

L'AUGEVAL

15 avenue Hocquart de Turtot, 14800 Deauville
Tel 02 31 81 13 18
www.augeval.com

In the centre of Deauville, this lovely gabled house is perfect for a seaside break. Enjoy food of the region in the elegant dining room, on the terrace or by the swimming pool. Among the extra facilities are a gym and table tennis, and horse-riding can be arranged.

🕐 Year-round
💶 €58–138, excluding breakfast (€11)
🛏 32
🏊 Outdoor 💧

HOSTELLERIE DE TOURGÉVILLE

Chemin de l'Orgueil Tourgéville, 14800 Deauville
Tel 02 31 14 48 68
www.hostellerie-de-tourgeville.fr
Originally built as a country estate by film director Claude Lelouch, this complex of country houses is full of character. You have a choice of rooms or split-level apartments fit for any Hollywood diva. Facilities and sports available include tennis, golf, swimming and horse-riding.

🕐 Closed mid-Feb–early Mar
💶 €120–230, excluding breakfast (€16)
🛏 25 rooms, 19 apartments
🏊 Outdoor 💧 Sauna

SPECIAL IN CLÉCY

LE MOULIN DU VEY

Le Vey, 14570 Clécy
Tel 02 31 69 71 08
www.moulinduvey.com
The intimate bedrooms of this old flour mill, on the banks of the river Orne, are decorated in traditional Norman style. Breakfast can be served in your room in winter or on the terrace in the summer. The annexe restaurant overlooks the river and dishes up fine local cuisine (▷ 161). The hotel offers excursions to explore Suisse Normande.

🕐 Closed Dec–Jan, Sun evenings
💶 €75–105, excluding breakfast (€11)
🛏 12

HONFLEUR

FERME ST-SIMÉON

Rue Adolphe Marais, 14600 Honfleur
Tel 02 31 81 78 00
www.fermesaintsimeon.fr
The Ferme St-Siméon was practically a clubhouse for the artists of the Honfleur school: the guest list has included Jean Baptiste Corot, Claude Monet, Eugène Boudin, and Alfred Sisley. Today, the cider press has been converted into a spa. Follow in the footsteps of the Impressionists and stay in one of the softly furnished bedrooms. Terraces, where you can try classic regional cuisine (▷ 162), overlook the sea. Among the organised tours is a trip to Étretat (▷ 94).

🕐 Year-round
💶 €220–450, excluding breakfast (€20)
🛏 38 rooms and apartments
🏊 Indoor 💧 Spa

LES MAISONS DE LÉA

Place Ste-Catherine, 14600 Honfleur
Tel 02 31 14 49 49
www.lesmaisonsdelea.com
Nestling in the old part of Honfleur, this former salt warehouse has been turned into a unique hotel and cottage. The antiques and colourful fabrics add to the other-wordly atmosphere. You can relax by the fireside in the library, or unwind in the privacy of your bedroom, appreciating the hotel's tranquillity.

🕐 Year-round
💶 €95–170, excluding breakfast (€12)
🛏 27 rooms, 1 suite, 1 cottage

LISIEUX

HÔTEL DE LA COUPE D'OR

49 rue Pont Mortain, 14100 Lisieux
Tel 02 31 31 16 84
www.la-coupe-d-or.com
This budget hotel in the heart of Lisieux has bedrooms that, although not large, are pleasantly decorated in a country style. The restaurant's vast, rustic dining room serves regional dishes. This is a good place to recover after a long drive.

🕐 Year-round
💶 €53–58, excluding breakfast (€7)
🛏 14 (3 non-smoking)

NOTRE-DAME-D'ESTRÉES

AU REPOS DES CHINEURS

Chemin de l'Église, 14340 Notre-Dame-d'Estrées
Tel 02 31 63 72 51
www.au-repos-des-chineurs.com
In the 17th century, this hotel and tearoom was a coaching inn, and it retains its beamed ceilings. *Chineurs* means 'antiques hunters', which is appropriate as everything here is for sale, from the furniture to the fine china cups. The rooms (some with whirlpool tubs) look out across meadows.

🕐 Closed Jan, Feb
💶 €78–150, excluding breakfast (€10)
🛏 10

PORT-EN-BESSIN

LA CHENEVIÈRE

Escures-Commes, 14520 Port-en-Bessin
Tel 02 31 51 25 25
www.lacheneviere.com

This 18th-century chateau has rooms decorated in classical style but with modern amenities such as TV and a mini-bar. Additional facilities include a laundry service, babysitting and Internet access. You can even order fresh flowers for your bedroom. The restaurant, serving seasonal foods, is run by chef Claude Esprabens.

🕐 Closed Dec–end Apr
💶 €180–270, excluding breakfast (€19)
🛏 22

EURE

Eure may have the occasional grand hotel, but its true charm comes from the many traditional coaching inns dotted around the countryside. Rooms are typically just a rickety staircase away from candle-lit restaurants, allowing guests to indulge themselves before staggering to bed.

LES ANDELYS

LA CHAINE D'OR

27 rue Grande, le Petit Andely, 27700 Les Andelys
Tel 02 32 54 00 31
www.lachainedor.com

La Chaine d'Or has kept the original name it used when it was a coaching inn where tolls were collected in the 18th century. But the décor is more stylish at this *auberge* today. In the summer, enjoy your breakfast on the terrace. Dishes at the restaurant, overlooking the river Seine, are prepared from local, seasonal produce.
🕐 Closed Jan
💶 €75–129, excluding breakfast (€12)
🛏 11

ÉVREUX

HÔTEL DE FRANCE

29 rue St-Thomas, 27000 Évreux
Tel 02 32 39 09 25
www.hoteldefrance-evreux.com
A large townhouse with lots of character, the Hôtel de France has attractive bedrooms, some with exposed beams and all with satellite TV. Owner-chef Jean-Luc Wantier serves fine cuisine in the restaurant.
🕐 Year-round
💶 €46–52, excluding breakfast (€6.50)
🛏 15 rooms, 1 apartment
🅿 Private parking

SPECIAL IN PONT-ST-PIERRE

L'HOSTELLERIE LA BONNE MARMITE

10 rue René Raban, 27360 Pont-St-Pierre
Tel 02 32 49 70 24
www.la-bonne-marmite.com
Tucked in a pretty village, this one-time coaching inn is now an inviting hotel that combines plenty of character with modern comforts. Wine and dine by candlelight (▷ 163), then retire to a bedroom lavishly furnished in the Louis XVI style with canopy beds.
🕐 Closed late-Feb–late Mar, late Jul–mid-Aug
💶 €62–93, excluding breakfast (€8)
🛏 9

GAILLON

CHÂTEAU CORNEILLE

17 rue de l'Église, Vieux Villez, 27600 Gaillon
Tel 02 32 77 44 77
www.chateau-corneille.fr
This 18th-century chateau is set in beautiful grounds, and its original barn houses a convivial restaurant. Bedrooms, meanwhile, have been modernised and furnished to suit current tastes. Summer guests enjoy relaxing on the veranda.
🕐 Year-round
💶 €100–130, excluding breakfast (€10)
🛏 19

LYONS-LA-FORÊT

LA LICORNE

La Licorne, B.P. 4, 27480 Lyons-la-Forêt
Tel 02 32 49 62 02
www.licorne-hotel-restaurant.com
Surrounded by Europe's largest beech forest, this 17th-century inn stands in a pretty village. Behind a half-timbered façade are tastefully decorated guest rooms furnished with antiques. The inviting dining room serves regional specialities.
🕐 Closed late Dec–mid-Jan
💶 €68–95, excluding breakfast (€12)
🛏 19 (2 non-smoking)

LES LIONS DE BEAUCLERC

7 rue de l'Hôtel de Ville, 27480 Lyons-la-Forêt
Tel 02 32 49 18 90
www.lionsdebeauclerc.com

Very much a *maison bourgeoise*, the Lions de Beauclerc offers an antiques shop within the hotel itself. All bedrooms have antique furnishings. Nearby you will find tennis, swimming and horse-riding.
🕐 Year-round
💶 €54–69, excluding breakfast (€9)
🛏 6

NASSANDRES

LE SOLEIL D'OR

Fontaine la Sôret, La Rivière Thibouville, 27550 Nassandres
Tel 02 32 45 00 08
www.domainedusoleildor.com
The exterior of this building is typical of the local architecture, so prepare for a surprise—the bedrooms are uncompromisingly modern. The hotel has a café with themed musical evenings and the lovely village is close to the river Risle.
🕐 Year-round
💶 €52–90, excluding breakfast (€12)
🛏 12 rooms, 2 apartments

PONT-AUDEMER

BELLE-ISLE SUR RISLE

112 route de Rouen, 27500 Pont-Audemer
Tel 02 32 56 96 22
www.bellile.com

This 19th-century mansion is in a landscaped, rose-filled park. Each bedroom is individually decorated and named. Some have balconies overlooking a garden. Not only is there an indoor sea-water pool, but also an outdoor pool. Other activities include rowing, canoeing, golf and riding. There is a good restaurant (▷ 163).
🕐 Closed mid-Nov–mid-Mar
💶 €112–220, excluding breakfast (€14)
🛏 20
🌊 Outdoor and indoor

SEINE-MARITIME

Le Havre and Rouen may be ringed by chain hotels, but it is worth driving into town to discover the convenience of a room in the city centre. The Côte d'Albâtre has fabulous seaside hotels. Discover charming inns and superb manor houses tucked away in the Pays de Caux.

AUMALE

LA VILLA DES HOUX
6 avenue du Général de Gaulle, 76390 Aumale
Tel 02 35 93 93 30
www.villa-des-houx.com
Convenient for the beaches at Le Tréport, this country house was once a local *gendarmerie*. You will be greeted by Alain and Michelle Mauconduit. The conservatory-style dining room is light and airy, with views over the gardens. Breakfast can be served on the terrace. Bedrooms are attractively furnished and have satellite TV, and there is also a lift for guests with disabilities.
🄲 Closed Jan; Oct–end Mar Sun eve
🛏 €62–75, excluding breakfast (€7)
🄸 22

BEZANCOURT

CHÂTEAU DU LANDEL
76220 Bezancourt
Tel 02 35 90 16 01
www.chateau-du-landel.fr
In the peaceful Forêt de Lyons, this palatial retreat is ideal for a weekend break. The chateau was once a staging post on the pilgrim route to Santiago de Compostela. Until 1870 it was owned by the Guild of Glass-makers, which explains the ornate chandeliers. The dining room has brick walls bearing stag heads, and the hotel can cater for private family parties.
🄲 Closed mid-Nov–mid-Mar
🛏 €80–170, excluding breakfast (€10)
🄸 17
🏊 Outdoor

DIEPPE

LES ARCADES DE LA BOURSE
1–3 arcade de la Bourse, 76200 Dieppe
Tel 02 35 84 14 12
www.lesarcades.fr

PRICES AND SYMBOLS
The hotels below are listed alphabetically (excluding The) by town or area, then by name. Prices are for a double room for one night, including breakfast. All the hotels listed accept credit cards unless otherwise stated. See page 2 for a key to the symbols.

This historic building in the heart of town takes its name from its covered arcade. The guest rooms, all of which have TV, are simply furnished and some have balconies with views of the harbour. Facilities include Internet access and a renowned seafood restaurant.
🄲 Year-round
🛏 €58–75, excluding breakfast (€8)
🄸 21
🧖 Sauna

ÉTRETAT

LE DONJON
Chemin St-Clair, 76790 Étretat
Tel 02 35 27 08 23
www.ledonjon-etretat.fr
Le Donjon is dramatically set in a 19th-century Anglo-Norman-style chateau overlooking the village and cliffs of Étretat. Some rooms have a spa bath-tub and all have satellite TV, yet they retain individuality. There is an on-site restaurant.
🄲 Year-round
🛏 €90–250
🄸 21

FÉCAMP

HÔTEL NORMANDY
4 avenue Gambetta, 76400 Fécamp
Tel 02 35 29 55 11
www.normandy-fecamp.com
This former post house has spacious, comfortable yet basic modern rooms, all with satel-lite TV, which is a bonus at these prices. The interior of the restaurant, La Brasserie Maupassant, evokes the early 19th century.
🄲 Year-round
🛏 €49–60, excluding breakfast (€6.50)
🄸 30 (5 non-smoking)
🅿 For hotel guests

SPECIAL IN ÉTRETAT
DORMY HOUSE
B.P. 2, route du Havre, 76790 Étretat
Tel 02 35 27 07 88
www.dormy-house.com

Perched on top of the cliffs of Étretat, this mansion has panoramic views from several bedrooms. Some rooms mix period furniture with bright tones, while others are more country style, with floral bed-spreads and wooden chests of drawers. The elegant restaurant has large bay win-dows overlooking the sea.
🄲 Year-round
🛏 €85–155, excluding breakfast (€10)
🄸 61

LE HAVRE

VENT D'OUEST
4 rue Caligny, 76600 Le Havre
Tel 02 35 42 50 69
www.ventdouest.fr

Vent d'Ouest is between the heart of the city and the sea. Several bedrooms have a nau-tical look, while others have rural themes. The hotel doesn't have a restaurant but there is a tearoom that serves snacks.
🄲 Year-round
🛏 €75–100, excluding breakfast (€9)
🄸 33
🅿 Private parking

JUMIÈGES

LE CLOS DES FONTAINES

191 rue des Fontaines, 76480 Jumièges
Tel 02 35 33 96 96
www.leclosdesfontaines.com

Features of this village property facing the Abbey de Jumièges include an orchard and an impressive pool. From here, you can follow Normandy's fruit, cider and cheese-touring routes. It is also within reach of Giverny (▷ 84–85). Breakfast can be had on a terrace. Guests with a disability have access.

🕐 Year-round
💶 €70–160, excluding breakfast (€8)
🛏 6
🏊 Outdoor

MONTIGNY

LE RELAIS DE MONTIGNY

Rue du Lieutenant Aubert, 76380 Montigny
Tel 02 35 36 05 97
www.relais-de-montigny.com

This modern hotel, a couple of miles outside Rouen, looks onto a pleasant garden. The bedrooms, all with satellite TV, are comfortable and some have terraces. Local dishes are served in the restaurant and you can dine outside.

🕐 Closed end Dec–early Jan
💶 €75–85, excluding breakfast (€10)
🛏 22

ROUEN

HÔTEL DES CARMES

33 place des Carmes, 76000 Rouen
Tel 02 35 71 92 31
www.hoteldescarmes.com

Situated in the middle of this medieval city, famous for its 100 bell towers, the Hôtel des Carmes makes an ideal base. Vivid prints make these rooms very individual, and surprisingly, for the budget, it also offers Internet access. Babysitting can be arranged. The hotel doesn't have a restaurant, but there are plenty in the city (▷ 164).

🕐 Year-round
💶 €45–61, excluding breakfast (€7)

🛏 12
🅿 Secure parking
🚌 Palais de Justice

LE VIEUX CARRÉ

34 rue Ganterie, 76000 Rouen
Tel 02 35 71 67 70
www.vieux-carre.fr

This is part of an 18th-century building, restored in the year 2000 to give it the feeling of a private residence. A restaurant opens out onto an exquisite courtyard. Some of the rooms look down onto the courtyard; others overlook the gardens.

🕐 Year-round
💶 €55–57, excluding breakfast (€6)
🛏 14
🅿 Nearby 🚌 Palais de Justice

ST-VALÉRY-EN-CAUX

LES HÊTRES

24 rue des Fleurs, 76460 St-Valéry-en-Caux
Tel 02 35 57 09 30
www.leshetres.com

This authentic Norman house, dating back to 1627, has much to offer if you love nature, golf, food and fishing. Interior design ranges from sharply modern to rustic, timbered hideaways. Dogs are welcome and some rooms have easy access for guests with disabilities.

🕐 Closed Jan–mid-Feb
💶 €90–160, excluding breakfast (€17)
🛏 5

SASSETOT-LE-MAUCONDUIT

CHÂTEAU DE SASSETOT

76540 Sassetot-le-Mauconduit
Tel 02 35 28 00 11
www.chateau-de-sassetot.com

This magnificent 18th-century chateau was once the summer residence of the Austrian Empress Sissi (1837–98). It stands in the centre of a large private estate, allowing you to appreciate the architecture among tranquil surroundings. From the bedrooms through to the dining and reception rooms, you will experience the elegance of the period. There is a helipad on site for those wanting to arrive in style.

🕐 Closed early Jan–mid-Feb
💶 €78–314, excluding breakfast (€10)
🛏 26 rooms, 2 apartments

LE RELAIS DES DALLES

6 rue Elisabeth d'Autriche, 76540 Sassetot-le-Mauconduit
Tel 02 35 27 41 83
www.relais-des-dalles.fr

The gardens at this enchanting inn are well maintained and sport an abundance of colourful flowers in summer. Inside, soft fabrics blend with wooden floors, panelling and beams, with a roaring fire in winter adding to the cosiness. The bedrooms are very spacious, with lovely furnishings, beamed ceilings, tiled floors and traditional rugs, and the inn has an on-site restaurant.

🕐 Closed early Jan, mid-Dec–mid-Jan
💶 €68–130, excluding breakfast (€10)
🛏 4

LE TRÉPORT

LE SAINT YVES

Place Pierre Sémart, 76470 Le Tréport
Tel 02 35 86 34 66

This friendly family-run hotel is perfect for a beach holiday—it is situated at the edge of the port only 30m (35yd) from the sea. The comfortably furnished bedrooms all have satellite TV. It is also convenient for visiting the local crafts shops, the casino and the fishing port.

🕐 Year-round, except Christmas period
💶 €50–65, excluding breakfast (€7)
🛏 20 rooms, 3 suites

L'AUBERGE DU VAL AU CESNE

Croix-Mare, 76190 Yvetot
Tel 02 35 56 63 06
www.valaucesne.fr

Val au Cesne is a typical Pays de Caux *auberge*. Waiting in the garden to welcome new arrivals is a party of hens, ducks and cats. Inside, the cottage-style bedrooms have floral furnishings and their own private terraces leading onto the grounds, and a large brick fireplace dominates the intimate restaurant (▷ 165). Close by, huge white cliffs tower over the tiny fishing villages strung along the coast.

🕐 Closed early Jan–end Jan, mid-Aug–early Sep, late Nov–early Dec
💶 €80, excluding breakfast (€9)
🛏 5

HOTEL GROUPS

Name of hotel group	Description	Website	Phone number
BB Hotels	Superior budget hotels with branches on the edge of towns and near airports with manned reception desks and hot buffet breakfast.	www.hotel-bb.com	00 33 08 92 78 29 29
Best Western	The biggest hotel franchise in the world has eight establishments in Normandy.	www.bestwestern.com	00 33 08 00 90 44 90
Campanile	A budget chain with hotels and grill restaurants on the outskirts of towns around the region.	www.envergure.fr	00 33 08 25 00 30 03
Chateau and Hotels de France	An affiliation of luxury and historic hotels and chateaux.	www.chateauxhotels.com	00 33 08 92 23 00 75
Comfort Inn	An above-average budget chain that includes the Comfort Inn and Comfort Hotel brands.	www.choicehotels.com	00 33 08 00 91 24 24
Etap Hotels	Basic yet smart budget out-of-town hotels with a double and single bed in each room and ensuite facilities.	www.etaphotel.com	00 33 08 92 68 89 00
Formule 1	Inexpensive simple motels on the outskirts of towns. The rooms sleep up to three guests and there is a self-service check-in by credit card at night.	www.hotelformule1.com	00 33 08 92 68 56 85
Holiday Inn	This chain includes a stylish city-centre hotel in Caen, with 40 no-smoking rooms and its own gym, bar and restaurant.	www.holiday-inn.com	00 33 08 00 90 59 99
Ibis	An inexpensive chain of hotels, each often with a restaurant, bar and 24-hour manned reception desk.	www.ibishotel.com	00 33 08 92 68 66 86
Kyriad	Reasonably priced comfortable hotels in and around larger cities.	www.envergure.com	00 33 08 25 00 30 03
Logis de France	Dozens of these independent, family-run inns and hotels are found across Normandy(▷ 166). The full directory is available free from French tourist offices.	www.logis-de-france.fr	00 33 01 45 84 83 84
Mercure	This chain has 21 hotels in the region, ranging from simple yet comfortable to more luxurious accommodation.	www.mercure.com	00 33 08 25 88 00 00
Novotel	Comfortable hotels with large bedrooms, often offering free accommodation and breakfast for children sharing with their parents. There are five in Normandy.	www.novotel.com	00 33 08 25 88 00 00
Premiere Classe	Basic, budget hotels in out-of-town retail/hotel parks. Check in with a credit card and code at night. Rooms sleep three.	www.envergure.fr	00 33 01 64 62 46 46
Relais & Chateau	Smart country houses, chateaux and palatial hotels, usually with gastronomic restaurants.	www.relaischateaux.com	00 33 08 25 32 32 32
Relais du Silence	An association of lovely hotels offering peace and quiet and good food. There are seven member establishments in Normandy.	www.silencehotel.com	00 33 01 44 49 90 00

STAYING

Planning

BEFORE YOU GO

CLIMATE

● Normandy has a generally mild, dampish climate tempered by sea breezes. Some sheltered areas bathed by the Gulf Stream, enjoy a microclimate benign enough for vines and subtropical plants to flourish.

● Extremes of temperature are rare, but the weather is always unpredictable, and can change very quickly. Rain may occur at any time of year, but is most prevalent in autumn and winter. Short-lived bursts of frost and snow occasionally shock the flowering mimosa in winter, and gales assail the ocean coastline from time to time. Mist and fog periodically obscure winter views and threaten shipping off Finistère's reefstrewn shores.

● Summer temperatures average just over 20º C (70ºF), and are highest in August. In Haute Normandie the climate is very similar to that in the south of England, while the Cotentin peninsula feels more like the Channel Islands. But the Channel coast receives just 1,700 hours of sunlight a year, compared with 2,200 hours in southern areas of neighbouring Brittany.

● The interior, whose gentle hills are high enough to puncture Atlantic rain-clouds, is generally wetter than low-lying coastal zones, and has wider temperature variations.

● For up-to-date weather information on Normandy, look up www.meteo.fr.

WHEN TO GO

● In July and August, the beaches and campsites of the popular coastal resorts overflow with French families taking their traditional summer break. Prices soar, and traffic clogs the roads. It can be difficult to find a bed for the night, or a restaurant table. But the resorts are at their liveliest, providing a seamless round of happenings—regattas and boat-trips, open-air concerts, fireworks and son-et-lumière shows. The biggest festivals attract huge gatherings.

● The advice to go in spring or autumn is trite but true, though you may find many other visitors have had exactly the same idea. To miss the crowds, try to avoid school holidays (British or French), and check whether your destination plans any major festivals or events during your visit.

● Spring is always lovely in Normandy, when the cider orchards froth into blossom, hillsides are ablaze with gorse, and local markets display cornucopias of top-quality early vegetables and Normandy's cattle make the most of fresh pasture. Autumn is a season of mellow fruitfulness, of apple-picking and mushroom-hunting. Late hydrangeas and geraniums still glow in gardens and window-boxes. Huge equinoctial tides continually reshape coastal views, and migrant birds stream through the skies.

TIMES ZONES

City	Time difference	Time at 12 noon French time
Amsterdam	0	12 noon
Berlin	0	12 noon
Brussels	0	12 noon
Chicago	-7	5am
Dublin	-1	11am
Johannesburg	+1*	1pm
London	-1	11am
Madrid	0	12 noon
Montréal	-6	6am
New York	-6	6am
Perth, Australia	+7*	7pm
Rome	0	12 noon
San Francisco	-9	3am
Sydney	+9*	9pm
Tokyo	+8*	8pm

Clocks in France go forward one hour on the last Sunday in March, until the last Sunday in October.
* One hour less during Summer Time.

● Normandy has a longer and steadier holiday season than Brittany, boosted by short-break trade from Paris if there's good weekend weather.

● The enticing tropical appearance of Norman and Breton beaches can be deceptive. The shallow seas of Morbihan warm up a little by September, but in general sea temperatures stay cool all year.

● Many monuments and museums in France close on key national holidays (1 January, 1 May, 1 November, 11 November, 25 December), and bus and train services are much reduced.

WHAT TO TAKE

● The key things to remember are travel and health insurance documents, money, credit cards and any medication you'll need. If you plan to drive in France, take your driving licence and, if using your own car, the vehicle registration and insurance certificates.

● A small rucksack or shoulder bag is useful for sightseeing. Bear in mind that these are attractive to pickpockets, so keep your money tucked away and an eye on your bag when you're in restaurants and other crowded places, especially in cities.

● Take the addresses and phone numbers of emergency contacts, including the numbers to call if your credit cards are stolen.

PLANNING

CHERBOURG
TEMPERATURE
■ Average temperature per day
■ per night
°C / °F chart: 30/86, 20/68, 10/50, 0/32
J F M A M J J A S O N D

ROUEN
TEMPERATURE
■ Average temperature per day
■ per night
°C / °F chart: 30/86, 20/68, 10/50, 0/32
J F M A M J J A S O N D

RAINFALL
■ Average rainfall
mm: 160, 120, 80, 40, 0 / in: 6, 4.5, 3, 1.5, 0
J F M A M J J A S O N D

RAINFALL
■ Average rainfall
mm: 160, 120, 80, 40, 0 / in: 6, 4.5, 3, 1.5, 0
J F M A M J J A S O N D

FRENCH EMBASSIES AND CONSULATES ABROAD		
Country	Address	Website
Australia	31 Market Street, St. Martin Tower, Level 26, Sydney, NSW 2000 Tel (02) 92 61 57 79	www.consulfrance-sydney.org
Canada	1 place Ville Marie, Bureau 2601, Montréal, Québec, H3B 4S3 Tel 514 878-4385	www.consulfrance-montreal.org
Ireland	36 Ailesbury Road, Ballsbridge, Dublin 4. Tel 01 260 1666	www.ambafrance.ie
New Zealand	34–42 Manners Street, Wellington, 12th floor, PO Box 11-343 Tel 644 384 25 55	www.ambafrance-nz.org
UK	21 Cromwell Road, London, SW7 2EN. Tel 020 7073 1200	www.frenchembassy.org.uk
US (Los Angeles)	10990 Wilshire Boulevard, Suite 300, Los Angeles, CA 90024 Tel 310/235-3200	www.consulfrance-losangeles.org
US (New York)	934 Fifth Avenue, New York, NY 10021. Tel 212/606-3600	www.consulfrance-newyork.org

Make photocopies of your passport, insurance documents and tickets, in case of loss. Keep a separate note of your credit card numbers in case you need to report a theft to the police.

● Visitors from the UK and US will need adaptors for electrical equipment (▷ 178).

● There is a language guide on pages 189–194 of this book, but if you are keen to communicate in French you may find a separate phrasebook helpful.

● A first aid kit may be useful.

● If you wear glasses, take a spare pair and your prescription.

● Don't forget your camera!

● The strength of the sun can be masked by coastal breezes; take sunscreen and sunglasses during the holiday season.

● Much of your time may be spent outdoors, so take wet-weather gear, some warm, windproof clothing, and robust footwear. Save room in your suitcase for some of Brittany's stylish all-weather marine clothing and knitwear.

● In all but the swankiest places, smart casual clothing is perfectly acceptable for any occasion just about anywhere in Normandy. One or two dressier outfits may be appropriate for the evenings.

● When visiting churches or cathedrals, wear suitably modest clothing—beachwear and shorts are not acceptable.

● A lightweight pair of binoculars is worth packing, and possibly a bird or flower identification guide.

● You'll find English-language books and newspapers in the main towns, but it's cheaper to bring your own reading matter.

PASSPORTS/VISAS

● UK, US and Canadian visitors need a passport, but not a visa, for stays of up to three months. You should have at least six months' validity remaining on your passport. Citizens of EU countries that have National Identity cards need either a passport or National Identity card.

● For more information about visa and passport requirements, look up the French tourist office website (www.franceguide.com).

● Before you travel, check visa and passport regulations since these are subject to change.

● Take a photocopy of the relevant pages of your passport to carry around with you, so you can leave your actual passport in your hotel safe. Always keep a separate note of your passport number and a photocopy of the page that carries your details, in case of loss or theft.

Longer stays

● UK and other EU citizens who want to stay longer than three months should apply for a carte de séjour from the Préfecture de Police. US and Canadian visitors need a carte de séjour and a visa. For information call the Immigration Department of the French Consulate (see chart).

TRAVEL INSURANCE

● Buy full health and travel insurance before you set off.

● EU citizens (plus nationals of Iceland, Liechtenstein, Norway and Switzerland) are entitled to receive reduced-cost emergency health care within any member state if they have the relevant documentation. For Britons, this is the European Health Insurance Card (EHIC), which was introduced in 2006 to replace the E111. Canadian nationals may use the French health system in the same way as EU residents, but comprehensive travel insurance is still strongly advised for all visitors, whether from Europe or beyond.

● Check that your insurer has a 24-hour helpline.

CUSTOMS

From another EU country

Below are the guidelines for the quantity of goods you can take in to France from another EU country, for personal use:

- 3,200 cigarettes
- 400 cigarillos
- 200 cigars
- 3kg of smoking tobacco

- 110 litres of beer
- 10 litres of spirits
- 90 litres of wine (of which only 60 litres can be sparkling wine)
- 20 litres of fortified wine (such as port or sherry)

From a country outside the EU

You are entitled to the allowances shown below only if you travel with the goods and do not plan to sell them.

- 200 cigarettes or 100 cigarillos or 50 cigars or 250gms of tobacco
- 60cc/ml of perfume
- 250cc/ml of eau de toilette

- 2 litres of still table wine
- 1 litre of spirits or strong liqueurs over 22% volume; or 2 litres of fortified wine, sparkling wine or other liqueurs
- Up to €175 of all other goods

PRACTICALITIES

Hiring a car is the best way for many visitors to see Normandy. Book online before you leave for the best rates

CAR RENTAL
- The absence of satisfactory public transport makes driving the only practical way to explore the rural villages and remote countryside of Normandy in depth, though it affords little pleasure in the larger cities. Congestion and parking can be a real headache in popular coastal areas in high season.
- It is often best to reserve a car in advance, making sure that full insurance is included in the package. You can also arrange car rental through some travel agents when you book your travel arrangements.
- See pages 29–31 for information on driving.

CHILDREN
- Look out for service stations (selling food and fuel, with play areas) or *aires* (scenic pull-ins with WCs and space to run around) on *autoroutes* and expressways, where restless children can stretch their legs.
- Most restaurants welcome children, although not many have highchairs and children's menus are not common outside family-friendly tourist resorts, so it's probably best to aim for family-style bistros where facilities are better and staff are more helpful.
- If you need special facilities in your hotel, such as a cot, or a child seat in your rented car,

reserve them in advance.
- For baby-changing facilities while out and about, try the restrooms in department stores and the larger museums.
- Supermarkets and pharmacies sell nappies (diapers) and baby food, although they are often closed on a Sunday so make sure you stock up.
- Entrance to museums is often free to young children.

ELECTRICITY
- Voltage in France is 220 volts. Sockets take plugs with two round pins. UK electrical equipment will need an adaptor plug, which you can buy at airport and Eurostar terminals. American appliances using 110–120 volts will need an adaptor and a transformer. Equipment that is dual voltage should need only an adaptor.

LAUNDRY
- There are two options if you need a laundry service—a *laverie automatique* (laundrette) and a *pressing/nettoyage à sec* (dry-cleaners). Dry-cleaners are easier to find, but are more expensive. Some have an economy service, but this is not recommended for your best silk jacket.

LOCAL WAYS
- Greetings are often quite formal in France. Offer to shake

CONVERSION CHART		
From	**To**	**Multiply by**
Inches	Centimetres	2.54
Centimetres	Inches	0.3937
Feet	Metres	0.3048
Metres	Feet	3.2810
Yards	Metres	0.9144
Metres	Yards	1.0940
Miles	Kilometres	1.6090
Kilometres	Miles	0.6214
Acres	Hectares	0.4047
Hectares	Acres	2.4710
Gallons	Litres	4.5460
Litres	Gallons	0.2200
Ounces	Grams	28.35
Grams	Ounces	0.0353
Pounds	Grams	453.6
Grams	Pounds	0.0022
Pounds	Kilograms	0.4536
Kilograms	Pounds	2.205
Tons	Tonnes	1.0160
Tonnes	Tons	0.9842

hands when you are introduced to someone, and use *vous* rather than *tu*. When speaking to people you don't know, it is polite to use *Monsieur or Madame,* or *Mademoiselle* for young women and girls.
- The continental kiss is a common form of greeting between friends, and the number of times friends kiss each other on the cheek varies from region to region.
- Address waiters and waitresses as *Monsieur, Madame* or *Mademoiselle* when you are trying to attract their attention. Never use *garçon.*
- Communicating in French is

French shopkeepers appreciate a greeting from customers

always the best option, even if you can manage only *bonjour, s'il vous plaît* and *merci* (hello, please and thank you). The French are protective of their language and your efforts to speak it will be appreciated. If your knowledge of French is limited, ask the fail-safe *Parlez-vous anglais?* and hope the answer is *oui*.

● Remember that it is traditional to say hello as you enter a shop, bar or café, particularly in small towns and villages, and that you are greeting your fellow customers as well as the proprietor. For a mixed audience, a *Bonjour Messieurs Dames* is the appropriate phrase. When it is your turn to be served, greet the server with *Bonjour Madame* or *Bonjour Monsieur*, then don't forget to say *merci* and *au revoir* or *bonne-journée* as you leave.

MEASUREMENTS

● France uses the metric system. Road distances are measured in kilometres, fuel is sold by the litre and food is weighed in grams and kilograms.

PLACES OF WORSHIP

● Some of France's greatest architectural treasures are the magnificent Gothic cathedrals of Normandy.
● They have become so popular as visitor attractions that it's easy to forget that they are still active places of worship. It's important to respect these churches and worshippers by dressing appropriately. Men should wear long trousers rather than shorts and should avoid sleeveless shirts. Women should keep their

knees and shoulders covered and men should remove hats on entering the building.
● Take photos only if it is permitted and don't forget to turn off your mobile phone.

SMOKING AREAS

● Smoking is banned in public places such as cinemas, buses and metro stations.
● By law restaurants and cafés should provide a non-smoking section, although in reality it can be difficult to find a dining room, bar or café that is smoke-free. However, France is stepping up the pressure on smokers. Smoking is slowly becoming less prevalent in public places, not least because of the recent draconian tax-rise in the price of cigarettes, and more places are willing to risk the unpopularity of banning smoking completely.
● Some taxis display a no-smoking sign.

TOILETS

● Today's modern unisex public lavatories are a vast improvement on previous facilities. Coin-operated and self-cleaning, you can find them in most large cities.
● In smaller towns and villages, free public lavatories can normally be found by the market square or near tourist offices, although cleanliness varies.
● Facilities in museums and other visitor attractions generally reach a good standard, so take advantage of them while you can. Restaurants and cafés provide WCs for their customers—at least buy a drink if you intend using them.
● Ask for *les toilettes* or WC (pronounced *vay, say*).

Automated lavatories are a common sight in towns

CLOTHING SIZES

Use the clothing sizes chart below to convert the size you use at home.

UK	Metric	US	
36	46	36	SUITS
38	48	38	SUITS
40	50	40	SUITS
42	52	42	SUITS
44	54	44	SUITS
46	56	46	SUITS
48	58	48	SUITS
7	41	8	SHOES
7.5	42	8.5	SHOES
8.5	43	9.5	SHOES
9.5	44	10.5	SHOES
10.5	45	11.5	SHOES
11	46	12	SHOES
14.5	37	14.5	SHIRTS
15	38	15	SHIRTS
15.5	39/40	15.5	SHIRTS
16	41	16	SHIRTS
16.5	42	16.5	SHIRTS
17	43	17	SHIRTS
8	36	6	DRESSES
10	38	8	DRESSES
12	40	10	DRESSES
14	42	12	DRESSES
16	44	14	DRESSES
18	46	16	DRESSES
20	46	18	DRESSES
4.5	37.5	6	SHOES
5	38	6.5	SHOES
5.5	38.5	7	SHOES
6	39	7.5	SHOES
6.5	40	8	SHOES
7	41	8.5	SHOES

VISITORS WITH DISABILITIES

● France has made some headway in recent years in providing access and facilities for visitors with disabilities. All new buildings must take the needs of people with special requirements into account, and, where possible, existing buildings such as town halls, airports and train stations must be adapted with ramps and automatic doors. But the cobbled, hilly streets of many historic towns and villages in Brittany and Normandy can be a trial for wheelchair-users.
● Some visitor offices, museums and restaurants that are in old, protected buildings are still not fully accessible. A telephone call before going to a restaurant is a good idea to organise a more easily accessible table.
● For organisations that give further advice, see page 36.

PLANNING

MONEY MATTERS

THE EURO
● France is one of 12 European countries that has adopted the euro as the official currency. Euro notes and coins were introduced in January 2002, replacing the former currency, the French franc.

BEFORE YOU GO
● It is advisable to use a combination of cash, traveller's cheques and credit cards rather than relying on only one means of payment during your trip. Bear in mind that the number of banks and other outlets offering exchange facilities has plummeted since the introduction of the euro, so organise some euros in advance and take a credit card with you.
● Check with your credit and/or debit card company that your card can be used to withdraw cash from Automatic Teller Machines (ATMs) in France. It is also worth checking what fee will be charged for this and what number you should ring if your card is stolen.

● Try to avoid using higher denomination notes when paying taxi drivers and when buying low-cost items in smaller shops.
● Never carry money or credit cards in back pockets, or other places that are easy targets for thieves.
● Keep your spare money and traveller's cheques in your hotel safe (coffre-fort) until you need them.
● Check the exchange rates for traveller's cheques and cash offered in post offices as well as in banks, as banks do not always offer the best rate.
● In France, Mastercard is sometimes known as Eurocard and Visa is known as Carte Bleue.
● Some smaller hotels and inns don't accept credit cards, so find out before you check in.

TRAVELLER'S CHEQUES
● Traveller's cheques are a safer way of bringing in money as you can claim a refund if they are stolen—but commission can be high when you cash them.

ATMS
● Your card issuer will almost certainly charge you for withdrawing cash.
● ATMs are common in France, often with on-screen instructions in a choice of languages. Among the cards accepted are Visa, MasterCard and Diners Club. You'll need a four-digit PIN number.
● Some British credit cards are still not accepted in certain automatic machines in France because the 'smart' technology doesn't match. It is hoped that the new wave of chip and pin cards will be more compatible.

BANKS
● Hours vary, but usual opening hours are Monday to Friday 8.30 or 9–12 and 2–5, although

BANKNOTES AND COINS

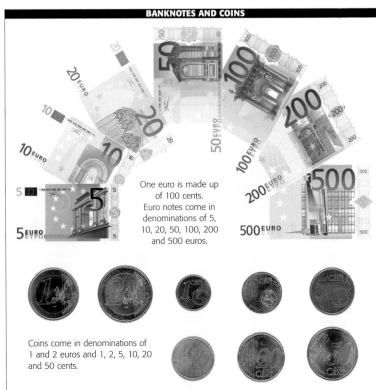

One euro is made up of 100 cents. Euro notes come in denominations of 5, 10, 20, 50, 100, 200 and 500 euros.

Coins come in denominations of 1 and 2 euros and 1, 2, 5, 10, 20 and 50 cents.

PLANNING

Above and below: with the right cards you can use bank facilities

banks in cities may not close for lunch.

● In smaller towns and villages banks often close on Mondays but open on Saturday mornings instead.

● Banks close at noon on the day before a national holiday, as well as on the holiday itself. Only banks with *change* signs change traveller's cheques or foreign currency and you'll need your passport to do this.

BUREAUX DE CHANGE

● Bureaux de Change have longer opening hours than banks, but the exchange rates may not be so good. You'll find them at airports, ferry terminals, large railway stations and in major cities.

● Avoid changing large amounts of traveller's cheques at hotels as the rates may not be competitive.

CREDIT CARDS

● Most restaurants, shops and hotels accept credit cards, although some have a minimum spending limit.

TAXES

● Non-EU residents can claim a sales tax refund *(détaxe)* of 12 per cent on certain purchases, although you must have spent more than €175 in one shop, at one time. Ask the store for the relevant forms, which the trader should complete and stamp. Give these forms to customs when you leave the country, along with the receipts, and they will be stamped. Post the forms back to the shop and they will either refund your credit card account or send you a cheque.

● Remember that you may have to show the goods to Customs when you leave France, so keep them within easy reach.

● Exempt products include food and drink, medicine, tobacco, unset gems, works of art and antiques.

● The company Global Refund offers a reimbursement service (tel: 01 41 61 51 51; www.globalrefund.com).

WIRING MONEY

● In an emergency, you can have money wired to you from your home country, but this can be expensive (as agents charge a fee for the service) and time-consuming.

● You can send and receive money via agents such as Western Union (www.westernunion.com) and Travelex (www.travelex.fr).

● Money can be wired from bank to bank, which takes up to two working days, or through Travelex and Western Union, which is normally faster.

CONCESSIONS

● If you are a student or teacher, apply to the International Student Travel Confederation

(www.isic.org) in your own country for an International Student Identity Card (ISIC). This entitles you to various reductions during your visit.

● Seniors often get reduced-rate tickets on public transportation and on admission to museums and sights by showing a valid identity card or passport.

● Small children often have free entry to sights.

POST OFFICES

● Some larger post offices may provide ATMs.

● Cards accepted are listed on each dispenser and instructions are available in English.

● Money can be wired, through Western Union, via most post offices, and generally takes only a few minutes to receive.

● International Money Orders can be sent from all post offices (for a fee).

● Some larger post offices offer exchange services in the following currencies: American, Australian and Canadian dollars, yen, British pounds sterling, Swiss francs and Swedish kronor, and Danish and Norwegian kroner.

PRICES OF EVERYDAY ITEMS		
Takeout sandwich		€2.50–€3.50
Bottle of mineral water	(from a shop, 0.5 litre)	€0.25–€0.45
Cup of coffee	(from a café, espresso)	€1.10–€2
	(Crème, larger cup with milk)	€2–€2.40
Beer	(*Un demi,* half a litre)	€2–€2.75
Glass of house wine		€2–€2.40
French national newspaper		€1–€1.20
International newspaper		€1.50–€2.30
Litre of fuel	(98 unleaded)	€1.15
	(diesel)	€0.90
Metro ticket	(single)	€1.30
	(per ticket, if you buy a *carnet*)	€1
Camera film	(36 pictures)	€7.50–€8.50
20 cigarettes	(on average)	€6.30

PLANNING

HEALTH

BEFORE YOU GO
● EU citizens receive reduced-cost healthcare in France with the relevant documentation. For UK citizens, this is the European Health Insurance Card (EHIC), which must be stamped by the post office before you travel. Take a photocopy with you as well as the original, as this will be kept by the hospital or doctor if you need treatment. Full health insurance is still strongly advised. For all other countries full insurance is a must.
● Make sure you are up to date with anti-tetanus boosters. Bring any medication you need with you and pack a first-aid kit. In summer, always bring sun-protection cream.

IF YOU NEED TREATMENT
● The French national health system is complex. Any salaried French citizen who receives treatment by a doctor or public hospital can be reimbursed by up to 70 per cent. The same is true if you are an EU citizen and have a valid EHIC.
● If you are relying only on EHIC, rather than travel insurance, make sure the doctor you see is part of the French national health service (a *conventionné*), rather than the private system, otherwise you may face extra charges. In any case, you will have to pay up front for the consultation and treatment. To reclaim part of these costs, send the *feuille de soins* (a statement from the doctor) and the form supplied with your EHIC to the Caisse Primaire d'Assurance-Maladie (state health insurance office) before you leave the country. Call 0820 904 175 to find the nearest office. You should also attach the labels of any medicine you have to buy.
● If you have to stay overnight in a public hospital, you will have to pay 25 percent of the treatment costs, as well as a daily charge (*forfait journalier*). These are not refundable. It is far better to have full health insurance than to rely solely on the EHIC.
● Citizens of non-EU countries must have full health insurance.
● If you are hospitalised and have insurance, ask to see the *assistante sociale* to arrange reimbursement of the costs directly through your insurers.

USEFUL NUMBERS
Emergency medical aid/ambulance
15
General emergencies
112
Police
17
Fire (Pompiers)
18

● In an emergency, dial 15 for Service d'Aide Médicale d'Urgence (SAMU) unit (ambulance). They work closely with hospital emergency units and are accompanied by trained medical personnel.
● If you are able to get yourself to a hospital, make sure it has a casualty or emergency department (*urgences*).

FINDING A DOCTOR
● In a medical emergency, your hotel should be able to help find a hospital or an English-speaking doctor. The number of the regional SOS Médecins (a duty-rota of doctors on call) is in the phonebook, also listed in local newspapers; otherwise call 15 for an ambulance. Main hospitals with casualty (emergency) units are located in all major cities—ask for the nearest *centre hospitalier* or *services des urgences*.
● Any pharmacy should be able to direct you to a doctor (look for the green cross sign—if it is closed, a card in the window will tell you where the nearest one is). Pharmacists are trained to deal with minor medical problems and can provide first aid as well as over-the-counter medication.

Pharmacies in France sell a wide range of medications

FINDING A HOSPITAL
● Hospitals are listed in the phone book under *Hôpitaux*, and round-the-clock emergency services are called *urgences*.
● Private hospitals are a lot more expensive than public ones and treatment is not necessarily better. If you choose a private hospital, check that you are covered for the costs before receiving treatment.

DENTAL TREATMENT
● EU citizens can receive reduced-cost emergency dental treatment with their EHIC, although insurance is still advised. The reclaim procedure is the same as for general medical treatment.
● Other visitors should check that their insurance covers dental treatment. It's a good idea to have a dental check-up before your trip.

PHARMACIES
● A pharmacy (*pharmacie*) will have an illuminated green cross outside. Most are open Mon–Sat 9–7 or 8, but when closed they usually post details on the door of another pharmacy that is open later (called the *pharmacie de garde*).
● Pharmacists are highly qualified and provide first aid, as well as supplying medication (some drugs are by prescription, or *ordonnance*, only). But they cannot dispense prescriptions written by doctors outside the French health system, so bring sufficient supplies of any prescribed drugs you need.
● Some pharmacists speak English and can direct you to local doctors or specialists.

Look for the neon green cross

- They also sell a range of health-related items, although it is less expensive to go to the supermarket for items such as soap, toothbrushes and razors.
- Some commonly used medicines sold in supermarkets at home (such as aspirins and cold remedies) can only be bought in pharmacies in France.

TAP WATER
- Tap water is safe to drink and restaurants will often bring a carafe of water to the table, although most French people opt instead for bottled water.
- In public places look for the sign *eau potable* (drinking water). Don't drink from anything marked *eau non potable*.

SUMMER HAZARDS
- The sun can be strong in Normandy between May and September, so pack a high-factor sun block. You may also like to take an insect repellent, although the insect bites you get in northwestern France are more likely to be irritating than dangerous.
- The likelihood of contracting food poisoning from shellfish is greater in the summer when ambient temperatures are higher. Toxic algal blooms (sudden proliferations of microscopic sea organisms) can sometimes affect fish—watch out for, and heed, local warnings.

ALTERNATIVE MEDICAL TREATMENT
- Alternative medicine, such as homeopathy, is generally available from most pharmacies.

HEALTHY FLYING

- If you are visiting France from the US, Australia or New Zealand, you may be concerned about the effect of long-haul flights on your health. The most widely publicised concern is Deep Vein Thrombosis, or DVT. Misleadingly named economy class syndrome, DVT occurs when a blood clot forms in the body's deep veins, particularly in the legs. The clot can move around the bloodstream and could be fatal.
- Those most at risk include the elderly, pregnant women and those using the contraceptive pill, smokers and the overweight. If you are at increased risk of DVT see your doctor before departing. Flying increases the likelihood of DVT because passengers are often seated in a cramped position for long periods of time and may become dehydrated.

To minimise risk:

Drink water (not alcohol).

Don't stay immobile for hours at a time.

Stretch and exercise your legs periodically.

Do wear elastic flight socks, which support veins and reduce the chances of a clot forming.

A small dose of aspirin may be recommended; this thins the blood before the flight.

EXERCISES

1 ANKLE ROTATIONS	2 CALF STRETCHES	3 KNEE LIFTS

Lift feet off the floor. Draw a circle with the toes, moving one foot clockwise and the other counterclockwise.

Start with heel on the floor and point foot upward as high as you can. Then lift heels high keeping balls of feet on the floor.

Lift leg with knee bent while contracting your thigh muscle. Then staighten leg pressing foot flat to the floor.

Other health hazards for flyers are airborne diseases and bugs spread by the plane's air-conditioning system. These are largely unavoidable, but if you have a serious medical condition seek advice from a doctor before setting off.

- Alternative treatment is available, although chiropractics and reflexology are not widespread. Useful websites include www.chiropratique.org (the Association Française de Chiropratique), www.aea-org.com (Association Europe Acupuncture) and www.naturosante.com (a website listing alternative medical services and products).

OPTICIANS

It's always a good idea to pack a spare pair of glasses or contact lenses and your prescription, in case you lose or break your main pair.

Name	Website
Opticiens Krys	**www.krys.com**
Lissac Opticien	**www.lissac.com**
Alain Afflelou	**www.alainafflelou.com**
Optical Center	**www.optical-center.com**
Optic 2000	**www.optic2000.fr**

There are several types of police force in France

Most visits to northwestern France are trouble-free, but make sure you have adequate insurance to cover any health emergencies, thefts or legal costs that may arise. If you do become a victim of crime, it is most likely to be at the hands of a pickpocket, so always keep your money and mobile phones safely tucked away.

PERSONAL SECURITY

● Take a note of your traveller's cheques numbers. Keep them separate from the cheques, as you will need them to make a claim in case of loss.
● Don't keep wallets, purses or mobile phones in the back pockets of trousers, or anywhere else that is easily accessible to thieves. Money belts and bags worn around the waist are targets, as thieves know you are likely to have valuables in them. Always keep an eye on your bags in restaurants, bars and on the metro, and hold shoulder bags close to you, fastener inwards, when you are walking in the streets.
● Thieves and pickpockets are especially fond of crowded places, such as rush-hour buses and trains, busy markets or popular festivals. Beware if someone bumps into you—it may be a ploy to distract you while someone else snatches your money.
● If you are the victim of theft, you must report it at the local police station *(commissariat)* if you want to claim on your insurance. Keep hold of the

statement the police give you. You must also contact your credit card company as soon as possible to cancel stolen cards.
● Keep valuable items in your hotel safe *(coffre-fort)*.
● Theft of cars and theft from cars are significant problems in France. When you park your car, don't leave anything of value inside. It's even risky leaving anything at all in view that may attract the interest of a thief. Carry your belongings with you or leave them behind.
● On trains, try to keep your luggage where you can see it. There are usually racks at the ends of the carriages.

EMERGENCY NUMBERS

General emergencies	**112**
Ambulance	**15**
Police	**17**
Fire	**18**
Directory enquiries (national)	**12**
Directory enquiries (international)	**3212**

LOSS OF PASSPORT

● Always keep a separate note of your passport number and a photocopy of the page that carries your details, in case of loss or theft. You can also scan the relevant pages of your passport and then email them to yourself at an email account that you can access anywhere.
● If you do lose your passport or it is stolen, report it to the police and then contact your nearest embassy or consulate.

POLICE

● There are various types of police officer in France. The two main forces are the Police Nationale, who are under the control of the local mayor, and the Gendarmerie Nationale, who you often see at airports.
● You are likely to encounter the armed CRS riot police only at a demonstration or protest.
● In France, the police have wide powers of stop and search. It is wise to carry your passport in case a police officer stops you and requests your ID.

FIRE

● The French fire brigade deals with a number of emergencies in addition to actual fires. These range from stranded cats to road accidents and gas leaks. They are trained to give first aid.

HEALTH EMERGENCIES

See pages 182–183.

EMBASSIES AND CONSULATES IN PARIS

● Most national embassies are in the capital (see chart). There is no UK consular assistance anywhere in Normandy.

EMBASSIES AND CONSULATES IN PARIS

Country	Address	Website
Australia	4 rue Jean-Rey, 75724; tel 01 40 59 33 00	www.france.embassy.gov.au
Canada	35 avenue Montaigne, 75008; tel 01 44 43 29 00	www.amb-canada.fr
Germany	13–15 avenue Franklin Roosevelt, 75008; tel 01 53 83 45 00	www.amb-allemagne.fr
Ireland	4 rue Rude, 75116; tel 01 44 17 67 00	
Italy	51 rue de Varenne, 75007; tel 01 49 54 03 00	www.amb-italie.fr
Spain	22 avenue Marceau, 75008; tel 01 44 43 18 00	www.amb-espagne.fr
UK	35 rue du Faubourg-St-Honoré, 75008; tel 01 44 51 31 00	www.amb-grandebretagne.fr
US	2 avenue Gabriel, 75008; tel 01 43 12 22 22	www.amb-usa.fr

COMMUNICATION

TELEPHONING

French numbers All numbers in France have 10 digits. The country is divided into five zones, indicated by the first two digits of the number (see chart below). You must dial these two digits even if you are calling from within the zone. Numbers in Normandy begin with 02.

International calls To call France from the UK dial 00 33, then drop the first zero from the 10 digit number. To call the UK from France, dial 00 44, then drop the first zero from the area code.

Call charges For calls within France, peak period is from 8am to 7pm, Monday to Friday. You'll save money if you call outside this time. Numbers beginning with 08 have special rates. 0800 or 0805 numbers are free. 0810 and 0811 numbers are charged at local rate. Other 08 numbers cost more than national calls; the prefixes 0893, 0898 and 0899 are particularly expensive.

PAYPHONES

● Nearly all public payphones in France use a card (*télécarte*) rather than coins. You can buy these at post offices, *tabacs*, newsagents and France Telecom shops. Some phones also accept credit cards, although this may

GUIDE PRICES		
Type of Call	**Initial charge**	**Each further minute**
Local, peak	€0.091 (1 min)	€0.033
Local, off-peak	€0.091 (1 min)	€0.018
National, peak	€0.112 (39 sec)	€0.091
National, off-peak	€0.112 (39sec)	€0.061
Calling the UK, off-peak	€0.11 (15 sec)	€0.12
Calling the US, off-peak	€0.11 (27 sec)	€0.15

make the calls more expensive. You do not need to pay if you are calling an emergency number.
● The phone gives instructions in various languages. If the phone displays the blue bell sign, you can receive incoming calls.
● Phones in restaurants and cafés tend to be more expensive than public payphones. Also, check the rates for hotel phones.

MOBILE PHONES

You can usually use your own mobile, but there are a few points to check before leaving:
● Contact your Customer Service department to find out if you have any restrictions on making calls from France and to check the charges for making and receiving calls abroad.
● Check if you need an access code to listen to your voice mail.

SENDING A LETTER

● You can buy stamps (*timbres*) for a letter (*lettre*) or a postcard (*carte postale*) at post offices and *tabacs*. Write *par avion* (by air) on the envelope or postcard.
● If you want registered post, ask for the letter to be sent *recommandé*. For a parcel (*colis*), choose either *prioritaire* (priority) or the slower *économique*.
● Mailboxes are yellow. In larger cities, some have two sections, one for the local *département*, and another for national and international mail (*autres départements/étranger*). Mail sent from France should take between two and five days to arrive, but can take longer.

POST OFFICES

● Post offices (*bureaux de poste*) are signposted. The postal service is known as *La Poste*.
● Opening hours are generally Monday to Friday 8–5 or 6, Saturday 8–12. Queues tend to be worst during lunch hours and in the late afternoon.
● Facilities usually include phone

booths, photocopiers, fax (*télécopieur*) and access to the Minitel directory. *Poste Restante* services are available for a fee.

INTERNET ACCESS

● Most main towns have Internet cafés. Look for the Cyberposte sign in larger post offices, or see www.cyberposte.com. You buy a card at the counter, which can be recharged if you need more connection time. Certain hotels, libraries (or *mediathèques*, as they are often called these days), supermarkets, bars and tourist offices also have Internet terminals, many operated by France Telecom using a *télécarte* (look for the word Borne). Public internet access in France is relatively expensive compared with services in the UK or US.

LAPTOPS

● Most mid-range hotels and above provide modem points. You can easily connect to the Internet providing this service is supported by your ISP (Internet Service Provider). Local telephone charges will apply. Remember that you may need a modem plug adaptor.
● Laptops should be compatible with the 220V current in France; otherwise you will need both a converter and an adaptor, or a French modem lead. A global modem should work in France. Protect your machine against voltage surges—modem testers will check the line. WiFi access points are becoming widespread.

COUNTRY CODES FROM FRANCE	
Australia	00 61
Belgium	00 32
Canada	00 1
Germany	00 49
Republic of Ireland	00 353
Italy	00 39
Monaco	00 377
Netherlands	00 31
New Zealand	00 64
Spain	00 34
Sweden	00 46
UK	00 44
US	00 1

PREFIXES	
00	International
01	Île-de-France (including Paris)
02	Northwest France
03	Northeast France
04	Southeast France
05	Southwest France
06	Mobile telephone numbers
0800/0805	Toll-free
08	Special-rate numbers

POSTAGE RATES FOR LETTERS	
Within France	€0.53
To Western Europe	€0.55
To Eastern Europe	€0.75
To America	€0.90
To Africa	€0.75
To Asia	€0.90
To Australia	€0.90

TOURIST INFORMATION

Be quick to get the best deals

TICKETS

● Popular tourist towns, such as Rouen, may provide a reduced-rate pass for entry to the main sights and museums, or packages including free entry to some attractions and accommodation. Some schemes include low-cost transport, a free guided tour, a boat-trip or a *petit-train* ride. Ask the tourist office for details of any inclusive deals, but be realistic about how much use you are likely to make of them.

● Students with an International Student Identity Card (ISIC) and seniors get reduced-price entry at some museums.

● For information on show and concert tickets, see page 107.

TOURIST OFFICES

● France has a complex but generally very efficient tourist information system. At the top end of the scale is the centralised regional office known as Comité Régional de Tourisme. In Normandy, the head office is in Évreux, in Brittany it is in Rennes. These and their subordinate Comités Départemental (one in each *département*) mostly handle postal, fax or telephone enquiries, some from overseas, rather than face-to-face.

● Visitors are much more likely to have direct contact with the *offices de tourisme* or *syndicats d'initiative* in individual towns and villages, where you can collect all sorts of maps, leaflets and brochures on the attractions of the local area. Just about everywhere you may want to visit in France has some kind of tourist office (often on the main square). If you can't see one, ask

at the local *mairie* (town hall).

● A useful document is a *Guide Pratique*, an informative listing of more or less everything a town has to offer from dentists to DIY shops. Accommodation brochures and public transport timetables are usually published separately, however. Make sure you get the current edition.

● Most promotional information is free, but you may have to pay for guidebooks, detailed touring maps or walks guides. Some brochures are available in English (though occasionally the translation can be more baffling than the *version originale*).

● Tourist offices can book accommodation for you, and sometimes sell tickets for excursions or events. Some have Internet points, or provide exchange facilities.

● A sign with a letter 'i' ('information' logo) on it may simply denote a display board with a local map and other information such as hotel listings, rather than an office.

● If you arrive when a tourist office is closed, a local hotel may be able to provide a guide or map of the town, or information leaflets. These are sometimes available at museums or tourist attractions, and passers-by may be only too happy to tell you about their home town.

● Other kinds of tourist office include small seasonal *Points d'Information*, commercially operated *Maisons du Tourisme* and *Pays d'Acceuil Touristiques*, which provide excellent regional information by post or email but are not open to the public.

● If you are travelling through Paris, La Maison de la Bretagne, at 203 Boulevard St-Germain, Paris 75007 (Metro Rue du Bac) can help organise your trip.

● The French government tourist

offices overseas are generally called Maisons de la France. The UK's office is at 178 Piccadilly, London, W1J 9AL (premium rate telephone information line: 09068 244 123).

● Regional representation sometimes exists abroad too, for example at the UK's Normandy Tourist Board, The Old Bakery, 44 Bath Hill, Keynsham, Bristol BS31 1HG (fax for brochures on 0117 986 0379).

● Increasingly, information for visitors overseas is provided online rather than in printed form (see Websites on page 188).

OPENING TIMES

● Most museums in Normandy are closed on Monday in the off-season and some national museums close on Tuesday. In the high season they are generally open every day, sometimes without closing for lunch. If you are planning to visit a special museum, telephone in advance to check that it is open; sometimes public holidays, festivals or renovation may cause unexpected closures.

● Restaurants generally take at least one day off a week (often Sunday or Monday), except in high season (July and August), when they stay open longer hours. Except in larger towns, many restaurants close completely from November to Easter. Lunch is generally served from 12–2 or 2.30 and dinner from 7.30–10 or 11. Brasseries may serve food all day.

● Most banks close at noon on the day before a national holiday, as well as on the holiday itself. Usual opening hours are from 9–12 and 2–5 but may vary.

● Shops typically open from 8am–6.30pm or 7.30pm. On Saturday and Sunday they may open mornings only.

TOURIST INFORMATION IN NORMANDY		
Town/City	**Telephone**	**Website**
Barfleur	02 33 54 02 48	www.ville-barfleur.fr
Bayeux	02 31 51 28 28	www.bayeux-tourism.com
Caen	02 31 27 14 14	www.caen.fr/tourisme
Cherbourg	02 33 93 52 02	www.ot-cherbourg-cotentin.fr
Deauville	02 31 14 40 00	www.deauville.org
Dieppe	02 32 14 40 60	www.dieppetourisme.com
Giverny	02 32 51 39 60	www.giverny.org
Honfleur	02 31 89 23 30	www.ot-honfleur.fr
Le Havre	02 32 74 04 04	www.lehavretourisme.com
Rouen	02 32 08 32 40	www.rouen.fr

PLANNING

MEDIA

TELEVISION

● France has five non-cable television stations, the nationally owned and operated channels 2 and 3, the privately owned 1 and 6, and the Franco-German ARTE (channel 5). Almost all the shows are in French. There are commercials on all channels.

● TF1 has news, recent American and French films, soaps and shows.

● France 2 has news, recent French and foreign films, soaps, shows and documentaries.

● France 3, a regional and national channel, has regional and national news, regional shows, documentaries, mostly French films and, once a week, a film in its original language.

● ARTE is a Franco-German channel with shows in French and German. International films are shown in their original language and there are also cultural documentaries.

● M6 shows a lot of low-budget films and past American sitcoms and soaps. There are also some interesting documentaries.

● Digital television has now taken off in France. More than 100 channels are on offer either through satellite or cable.

● If the TV listings mention VO (*version originale*), the show or film will be in the language in which it was made, with French subtitles (channel 3 usually screens a good VO film every Sunday at around midnight).

● Note that French television channels do not always keep exactly to schedule.

● Many hotels provide a basic cable service; this may include Sky or Eurosport, BBC World and CNN. Cable channels now offer multilingual versions of some shows. Ask at your hotel how to use this option. The commercial-free ARTE usually offers a choice between French and German for its cultural shows.

RADIO

● French radio stations are available mainly on FM wave lengths, with a few international stations on LW. All FM stations are in French.
Stations (with their Paris frequencies) include:

● Chérie FM: 91.3 FM; French mainstream pop, news, reports.

● France Infos: 105.5 FM; news

bulletins every 15 minutes.

● France Musique: 91.7 FM; classical and jazz music, concerts, operas, news.

● NRJ: 100.3 FM; French and international pop, techno, R'n'B.

● Radio Classique: 101.1 FM; classical music.

● Skyrock: 96 FM; rap, R'n'B.

● BBC Radio 4 198 kHz MW; news, current affairs, drama.

● BBC Five Live 909 kHz MW; news and sport, (reception is patchy in northwestern France).

● BBC World Service 648 kHz LW.

NEWSPAPERS

● In tourist areas and the major cities you can buy the main English dailies, sometimes a day old, at a price premium.

● *The Economist*, *USA Today* and *The Wall Street Journal* can be found at news-stands in cities, along with *The European*, which presents a pan-European perspective, and the *International Herald Tribune*, which reports news from a US standpoint.

● Most cities and regions have their own newspapers. In Brittany, you'll find the popular daily *Ouest France* and the Morlaix-based *La Télégramme*, plus regional periodicals. Normandy has its own regional paper, *Paris-Normandie*.

● Leading local newspapers play an active part in pressure politics in their area, though the issues of some may seem parochial to the outsider.

● One of the most widespread chain newsagents is Maison de la Presse, found in virtually every

community of any size.

● If you want to find out what's happening in a French city, consult the 'what's on' supplements which are issued with some newspapers.

● Listings magazines in Normandy include Rouen's *L'Agenda Rouennais* and *Le Cyber Noctambule*. You'll often see these distributed free of charge in tourist offices, music stores, cafés and hotels.

● Weekly news magazines include *Le Nouvel Observateur*, *Le Point* and *L'Express*.

NEWSPAPERS

French daily newspapers have clear political leanings.

Le Monde
This stately paper, left-of-centre, refuses to run photos and uses illustrations

Libération
This lively youth-focused paper is more clearly leftist

L'Humanité
Left wing

Le Figaro
Mainstream conservative daily

Ouest France
A popular daily newspaper covering Brittany, Lower Normandy and Pays de la Loire

Journal du Dimanche
Sunday newspaper

CABLE TV

Depending on what cable option your hotel has, you may have some of the following channels:

BBC World	A global news service with magazine-style reports
Canal+	Shows recent films (some in the original language)
MTV	Contemporary music channel
MCM	The French version of MTV
Eurosport or Infosport	For major sporting events
Planète	Nature and science documentaries
RAI Uno	Italian
TVE 1	Spanish
Euronews	A European all-news channel
LCI	All news in French
Canal Jimmy	Shows some British and American shows like *Friends* and *NYPD Blue* in English or multilingual versions
Paris Première	A cultural channel with some films in English
Canal J	With children's shows until 8pm
Téva	A women's channel that runs English-language shows

PLANNING

MEDIA   187

USEFUL WEBSITES

www.aeroport.fr
Information on all of France's airports. (French)

www.fodors.com
A comprehensive travel-planning site that lets you research prices, reserve air tickets and put questions to fellow visitors. (English)

www.franceguide.com
Practical advice from the French Tourist Office on everything from arriving in France to buying a property. The site also has features on holidays and attractions. (French, English, German, Spanish, Italian, Dutch, Portuguese)

www.francetourism.com
The official US website of the French Government Tourist Office. (English)

www.lemonde.fr
Catch up on current events on the site of *Le Monde* newspaper. (French)

www.meteo.fr/meteonet
Weather forecasts for France. (French, English and Spanish)

www.monum.fr
Find out more about some of France's most historic monuments, on the site of the Centre des Monuments Nationaux. (French and English)

www.pagesjaunes.fr
France's Yellow Pages online. (French and English)

www.radio-france.fr
News, music and sport. (French)

www.theAA.com
The AA website contains a route planner, helpful if you are driving in France. You can also order maps of the country. (English)

www.tourist-office.org
Lists details of tourist information offices in France. (French)

Other websites are listed alongside the relevant sights and towns in the Sights section, and in the On the Move section. Important ones include:
www.normandy-tourism.org
www.franceguide.com
www.fncrt.com
www.tourisme.fr
www.fco.gov.uk
www.cdt-eure.fr
www.calvados-tourisme.com
www.manchetourisme.com
www.ornetourisme.com
www.seine-maritime-tourisme.com
www.abbayes-normandes.com

FILMS AND BOOKS

FILMS
● Watching a French film is a good way to get the feel of the place before you visit.
● For a classic, try *Les Enfants du Paradis* (1945) directed by Marcel Carné. For *nouvelle vague* (new wave) cinema—often filmed with a hand-held camera—try *Jules et Jim* (1962), directed by François Truffaut and starring Jeanne Moreau, or *À Bout de Souffle* (1959), directed by Jean-Luc Godard. The surreal *Belle de Jour* (1967), starring Catherine Deneuve, caused a scandal at the time due to its erotic subject matter. The 1987 weepie *Au Revoir les Enfants* tells the story of a Jewish boy in occupied France in World War II.
● No reference to French movies would be complete without mentioning Gérard Depardieu, the actor who conquered France and then Hollywood. His best-known works include *Cyrano de Bergerac* (1990) and *Jean de Florette* (1986). The sequel to this, *Manon des Sources* (1986), stars a young Emmanuelle Béart,

one of France's leading actresses.
● Jean-Pierre Jeunet's *Delicatessen* (1991) turns the controversial subject of cannibalism into a black comedy.
● For a French feel with a Hollywood budget, watch a film directed by Luc Besson, such as *The Fifth Element* (1997), *Léon* (1994), with an understated performance by Jean Reno, or the more patchy *Unleashed* (2005), starring Jet Li.
● Normandy's lush countryside has inspired many film-makers. *Les Parapluies de Cherbourg*, Jacques Demy's romantic 1964 comedy starring Catherine Deneuve, is an answer to *Singing in the Rain*, still fondly remembered by the umbrella-makers of the Cotentin.
● More familiar in the English-speaking world are Roman Polanski's *Tess*, filmed on location in Normandy and Brittany, *Un Homme et une Femme*, *Jules et Jim* and the unforgettable *Babette's Feast*.
● War-film fans hark back to *The Longest Day,* though Steven

Spielberg's more recent take on D-Day, *Saving Private Ryan,* was not actually shot in Normandy due to high production costs.

BOOKS
● Normandy's writers, or adopted writers, read like a roll-call of France's literary giants. From the romantic poets of the Middle Ages such as Robert Wace (*The Romance of the Rose*), through Pierre Corneille (*Le Cid*), to Emile Zola, Guy de Maupassant, Stendhal, Victor Hugo—all have achieved fame.
● A lifelong resident of Rouen, Gustave Flaubert's lasting contribution was *Madame Bovary*, while Marcel Proust penned parts of *À la Recherche du Temps Perdu* in Cabourg.
● Jean-Paul Sartre (*Nausea*) and Simone de Beauvoir both taught at Rouen university.
● For some modern novels, try *Flaubert's Parrot*, by Julian Barnes, a wander by the Seine in Rouen, or *Odo's Hanging*, by Peter Benson, about the creation of the Bayeux Tapestry.

WORDS AND PHRASES

Even if you're far from fluent, it is always a good idea to try to speak a few words of French while in Normandy. The words and phrases on the following pages should help you with the basics, from ordering a meal to dealing with emergencies.

CONVERSATION

What is the time?
Quelle heure est-il?

When do you open/close?
A quelle heure ouvrez/fermez-vous?

I don't speak French.
Je ne parle pas français.

Do you speak English?
Parlez-vous anglais?

I don't understand.
Je ne comprends pas.

Please repeat that.
Pouvez-vous répéter (s'il vous plaît)?

Please speak more slowly.
Pouvez-vous parler plus lentement?

What does this mean?
Qu'est-ce que ça veut dire?

Write that down for me please.
Pouvez-vous me l'écrire, s'il vous plaît?

Please spell that.
Pouvez-vous me l'épeler, s'il vous plaît?

I'll look that up (in the dictionary).
Je vais le chercher (dans le dictionnaire).

My name is…
Je m'appelle…

What's your name?
Comment vous appelez-vous?

This is my wife/husband.
Voici ma femme/mon mari.

Voici ma fille/mon fils.
This is my daughter/son.

This is my friend.
Voici mon ami(e).

Hello, pleased to meet you.
Bonjour, enchanté(e).

I'm from …
Je viens de …

I'm on holiday.
Je suis en vacances.

I live in …
J'habite à …

Where do you live?
Où habitez-vous?

Good morning.
Bonjour.

Good evening.
Bonsoir.

Goodnight.
Bonne nuit.

Goodbye.
Au revoir.

See you later.
A plus tard.

How much is that?
C'est combien?

May I/Can I?
Est-ce que je peux?

I don't know.
Je ne sais pas.

You're welcome.
Je vous en prie.

How are you?
Comment allez-vous?

I'm sorry.
Je suis désolé(e).

Excuse me.
Excusez-moi.

That's all right.
De rien.

USEFUL WORDS

Yes **Oui**	There **Là-bas**	Who **Qui**
No **Non**	Here **Ici**	When **Quand**
	Where **Où**	Why **Pourquoi**

How **Comment**	Open **Ouvert**	Please **S'il vous plaît**
Later **Plus tard**	Closed **Fermé**	Thank you **Merci**
Now **Maintenant**		

Could you help me, please?
(Est-ce que) vous pouvez m'aider, s'il vous plaît?

How much is this?
C'est combien?/Ça coûte combien?

I'm looking for …
Je cherche …

When does the shop open/close?
A quelle heure ouvre/ferme le magasin?

I'm just looking, thank you.
Je regarde, merci.

This isn't what I want.
Ce n'est pas ce que je veux.

This is the right size.
C'est la bonne taille.

Do you have anything less expensive/smaller/larger?
(Est-ce que) vous avez quelque chose de moins cher/plus petit/plus grand?

I'll take this.
Je prends ça.

Do you have a bag for this, please?
(Est-ce que) je peux avoir un sac, s'il vous plaît?

Do you accept credit cards?
(Est-ce que) vous acceptez les cartes de crédit?

I'd like ….grams please.
Je voudrais …grammes, s'il vous plaît.

I'd like a kilo of …
Je voudrais un kilo de …

What does this contain?
Quels sont les ingrédients?/ Qu'est-ce qu'il y a dedans?

I'd like … slices of that.
J'en voudrais … tranches.

Bakery
Boulangerie

Bookshop
Librairie

Chemist
Pharmacie

Supermarket
Supermarché

Market
Marché

Sale
Soldes

1 un	6 six	11 onze	16 seize	21 vingt et un	70 soixante-dix
2 deux	7 sept	12 douze	17 dix-sept	30 trente	80 quatre-vingts
3 trois	8 huit	13 treize	18 dix-huit	40 quarante	90 quatre-vingt dix
4 quatre	9 neuf	14 quatorze	19 dix-neuf	50 cinquante	100 cent
5 cinq	10 dix	15 quinze	20 vingt	60 soixante	1000 mille

Where is the nearest post office/mail box?
Où se trouve la poste/la boîte aux lettres la plus proche?

How much is the postage to…?
A combien faut-il affranchir pour …?

I'd like to send this by air mail/ registered mail.
Je voudrais envoyer ceci par avion/en recommandé.

Can you direct me to a public phone?
Pouvez-vous m'indiquer la cabine téléphonique la plus proche?

What is the number for directory enquiries?
Quel est le numéro pour les renseignements?

Where can I find a telephone directory?
Où est-ce que je peux trouver un annuaire?

Where can I buy a phone card?
Où est-ce que je peux acheter une télécarte?

Please put me through to…
Pouvez-vous me passer …, s'il vous plaît?

Can I dial direct to …?
Est-ce que je peux appeler directement en …?

Do I need to dial 0 first?
Est-ce qu'il faut composer le zéro (d'abord)?

What is the charge per minute?
Quel est le tarif à la minute?

Have there been any calls for me?
Est-ce que j'ai eu des appels téléphoniques?

Hello, this is …
Allô, c'est … (à l'appareil)?

Who is speaking please …?
Qui est à l'appareil, s'il vous plaît?

I would like to speak to …
Je voudrais parler à …

Monday **lundi**	January **janvier**	August **août**	spring **printemps**	morning **matin**	day **le jour**
Tuesday **mardi**	February **février**	September **septembre**	summer **été**	afternoon **après-midi**	month **le mois**
Wednesday **mercredi**	March **mars**	October **octobre**	autumn **automne**	evening **soir**	year **l'année**
Thursday **jeudi**	April **avril**	November **novembre**	winter **hiver**	night **nuit**	
Friday **vendredi**	May **mai**	December **décembre**	holiday **vacances**	today **aujourd'hui**	
Saturday **samedi**	June **juin**		Easter **Pâques**	yesterday **hier**	
Sunday **dimanche**	July **juillet**		Christmas **Noël**	tomorrow **demain**	

HOTELS

Do you have a room?
(Est-ce que) vous avez une chambre?

I have a reservation for … nights.
J'ai réservé pour … nuits.

How much each night?
C'est combien par nuit?

Double room.
Une chambre pour deux personnes/double.

Twin room.
Une chambre à deux lits/ avec lits jumeaux.

Single room.
Une chambre à un lit/pour une personne.

With bath/shower/lavatory.
Avec salle de bain/ douche/WC.

Is the room air-conditioned/ heated?
(Est-ce que) la chambre est climatisée/chauffée?

Is breakfast/lunch/dinner included in the cost?
(Est-ce que) le petit déjeuner/le déjeuner/le dîner est compris dans le prix?

Is there a lift in the hotel?
(Est-ce qu')il y a un ascenseur à l'hôtel?

Is room service available?
(Est-ce qu')il y a le service en chambre?

When do you serve breakfast?
À quelle heure servez-vous le petit déjeuner?

May I have breakfast in my room?
(Est-ce que) je peux prendre le petit déjeuner dans ma chambre?

Do you serve evening meals?
(Est-ce que) vous servez le repas du soir/le dîner?

I need an alarm call at…
Je voudrais être réveillé(e) à… heures.

I'd like an extra blanket/pillow.
Je voudrais une couverture/ un oreiller supplémentaire, s'il vous plaît.

May I have my room key?
(Est-ce que) je peux avoir la clé de ma chambre?

Will you look after my luggage until I leave?
Pouvez-vous garder mes bagages jusqu'à mon départ?

Is there parking?
(Est-ce qu') il y a un parking?

Where can I park my car?
Où est-ce que je peux garer ma voiture?

Do you have babysitters?
(Est-ce que) vous avez un service de babysitting/garde d'enfants?

When are the sheets changed?
Quand changez-vous les draps?

The room is too hot/cold.
Il fait trop chaud/froid dans la chambre.

Could I have another room?
(Est-ce que) je pourrais avoir une autre chambre?

I am leaving this morning.
Je pars ce matin.

What time should we leave our room?
A quelle heure devons-nous libérer la chambre?

Can I pay my bill?
(Est-ce que) je peux régler ma note, s'il vous plaît?

May I see the room?
(Est-ce que) je peux voir la chambre?

Swimming pool.
Piscine.

No smoking.
Non fumeur.

Sea view.
Vue sur la mer.

Where is the tourist information office, please?
Où se trouve l'office du tourisme, s'il vous plaît?

Do you have a city map?
Avez-vous un plan de la ville?

Where is the museum?
Où est le musée?

Can you give me some information about…?
Pouvez-vous me donner des renseignements sur …?

What are the main places of interest here?
Quels sont les principaux sites touristiques ici?

Please could you point them out on the map?
Pouvez-vous me les indiquer sur la carte, s'il vous plaît?

What sights/hotels/restaurants can you recommend?
Quels sites/hôtels/restaurants nous recommandez-vous?

We are staying here for a day.
Nous sommes ici pour une journée.

I am interested in…
Je suis intéressé(e) par…

Does the guide speak English?
Est-ce qu'il y a un guide qui parle anglais?

Do you have any suggested walks?
Avez-vous des suggestions de promenades?

Are there guided tours?
Est-ce qu'il y a des visites guidées?

Are there organised excursions?
Est-ce qu'il y a des excursions organisées?

Can we make reservations here?
Est-ce que nous pouvons réserver ici?

What time does it open/close?
Ça ouvre/ferme à quelle heure?

What is the admission price?
Quel est le prix d'entrée?

Is there a discount for senior citizens/students?
Est-ce qu'il y a des réductions pour les personnes âgées/ les étudiants?

Do you have a brochure in English?
Avez-vous un dépliant en anglais?

What's on at the cinema?
Qu'est-ce qu'il y a au cinéma?

Where can I find a good nightclub?
Où est-ce que je peux trouver une bonne boîte de nuit?

Do you have a schedule for the theatre/opera?
Est-ce que vous avez un programme de théâtre/ d'opéra?

Should we dress smartly?
Est-ce qu'il faut mettre une tenue de soirée?

What time does the show start?
A quelle heure commence le spectacle?

How do I reserve a seat?
Comment fait-on pour réserver une place?

Could you reserve tickets for me?
Pouvez-vous me réserver des billets?

ILLNESS AND EMERGENCIES

I don't feel well.
Je ne me sens pas bien.

Could you call a doctor?
(Est-ce que) vous pouvez appeler un médecin/un docteur, s'il vous plaît?

Is there a doctor/pharmacist on duty?
(Est-ce qu') il y a un médecin/docteur/une pharmacie de garde?

I feel sick.
J'ai envie de vomir.

I need to see a doctor/dentist.
Il faut que je voie un médecin/docteur/ un dentiste.

Please direct me to the hospital.
(Est-ce que) vous pouvez m'indiquer le chemin pour aller à l'hôpital, s'il vous plaît?

I have a headache.
J'ai mal à la tête.

I've been stung by a wasp/bee/jellyfish.
J'ai été piqué(e) par une guêpe/abeille/méduse.

I have a heart condition.
J'ai un problème cardiaque.

I am diabetic.
Je suis diabétique.

I'm asthmatic.
Je suis asmathique.

I'm on a special diet.
Je suis un régime spécial.

I am on medication.
Je prends des médicaments.

I have left my medicine at home.
J'ai laissé mes médicaments chez moi.

I need to make an emergency appointment.
Je dois prendre rendez-vous d'urgence.

I have bad toothache.
J'ai mal aux dents.

I don't want an injection.
Je ne veux pas de piqûre.

Help!
Au secours!

I have lost my passport/ wallet/purse/handbag.
J'ai perdu mon passeport/ portefeuille/porte- monnaie/sac à main.

I have had an accident.
J'ai eu un accident.

My car has been stolen.
On m'a volé ma voiture.

I have been robbed.
J'ai été volé(e).

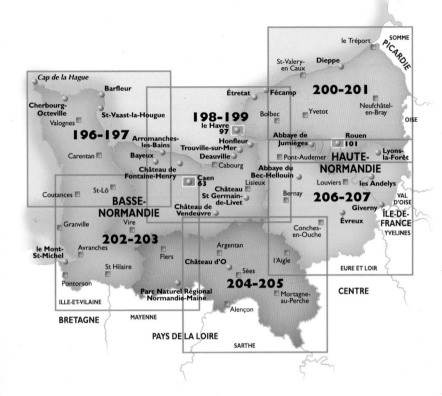

196-207

| 0 | | | 50 km |
| 0 | | | 40 miles |

Toll motorway

Motorway

Motorway junction with
and without number

National road

Regional road

Other road

Railway

Administrative region boundary

Département boundary

City

Town / Village

National park

Featured place of interest

Airport

621 ▲ Height in metres

Ferry route

Maps

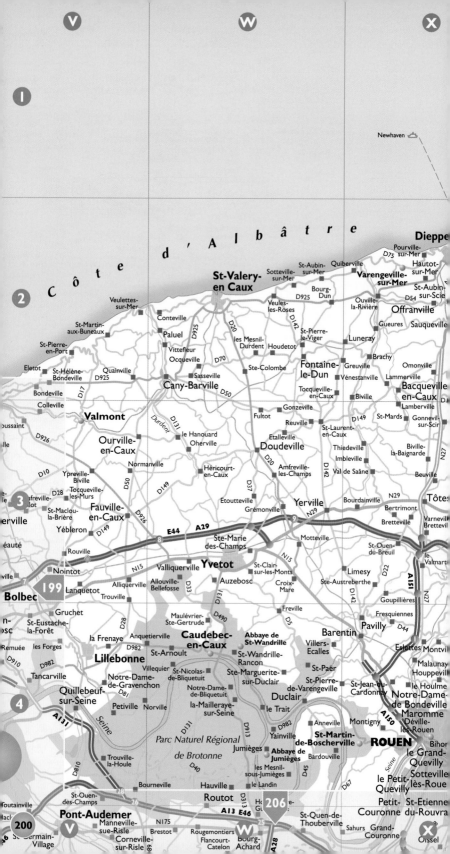

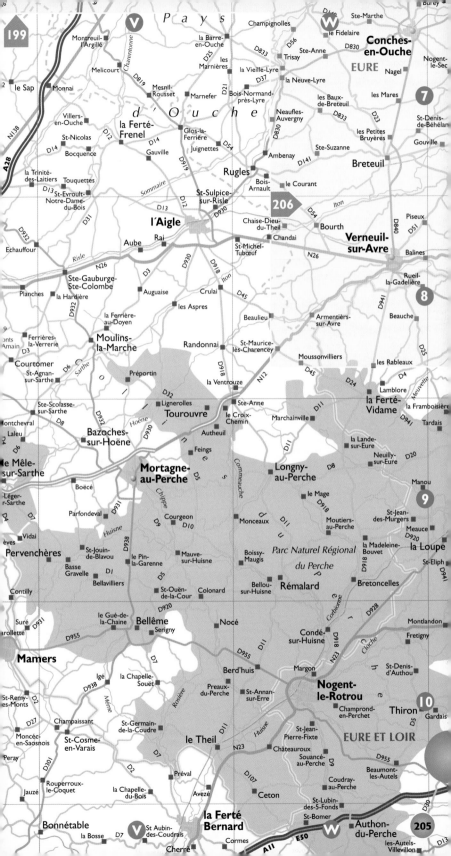

ACKNOWLEDGMENTS

Abbreviations for the credits are as follows:
AA = AA World Travel Library, t (top), b (bottom), c (centre), l (left), r (right), bg (background)

UNDERSTANDING NORMANDY

5lc AA/C. Sawyer; 5b © Peter Turnley/CORBIS; 5c AA/C. Sawyer; 5rc AA/R. Moore; 7lc AA/C. Sawyer; 7c AA/P. Bennett; 7rc AA/I. Dawson; 7b AA; 8tr AA/R. Moore; 8rac AA/I. Dawson; 8rc AA/R. Moore; 8rbc AA/P. Bennett; 8br AA/C. Sawyer; 8bl AA; 9tl AA/P. Bennett; 9lac Paul Painter; 9c AA/I. Dawson; 9lbc AA/C. Sawyer; 9br AA/R. Moore; 9bl AA/R. Moore; 10tl AA/R. Moore; 10bl Corbis; 10tr AA/P. Bennett; 10rac Dave Austin; 10c AA/B. Smith; 10rbc AA/R. Moore; 10abr AA/R. Moore; 10br AA/P. Bennett

LIVING NORMANDY

11 AA/I. Dawson; 12tl AA/R. Moore; 12lc AA/R. Moore; 12bl AA; 12tr Courtesy Le Manoir du Lys; 12rc AA/R. Moore; 12/13bg AA/R. Moore; 13tl AA/R. Moore; 13cl AA/R. Moore; 13tc Courtesy Le Brewery; 13tr AA/R. Moss; 13rc AA/R. Moore; 14tl Rex Features Ltd.; 14cl AA/R. Moore; 14bl AA/R. Moore; 14tc AA/I. Dawson; 14/15 © Raul Benegas/CORBIS; 14/15bg AA/R. Moore; 15tl Rex Features Ltd; 15tr AA/I. Dawson; 15c © Eric Fougere/CORBIS SYGMA; 15cr AA/R. Moore; 16tl AA/P. Bennett; 16cl AA/P. Bennett; 16bl AA/C. Sawyer; 16tr AA/I. Dawson; 16cr AA/P. Bennett; 16bg AA/R. Moore

THE STORY OF NORMANDY

17 AA/R. Moore; 18bl AA/C. Sawyer; 18/19b English Heritage; 18/19bg AA; 19lc AA; 19c AA/R. Moore; 19rc © Trustees of the Royal Watercolour Society, London/Bridgeman Art Library, London; 19br Musee Dobree, Nantes/Bridgeman Art Library, London; 19bc AA/R. Moore; 20bl Musee Lambinet, Versailles/Lauros/Giraudon/Bridgeman Art Library, London; 20/21b ILN; 20/21bg AA/I. Dawson; 20rc Private Collection/Bridgeman Art Library, London; 21lc © Peter Turnley/CORBIS; 21c & br Roger Viollet/Topfoto.co.uk; 21bc Musee Marmotton, Paris/Giraudon/Bridgeman Art Library, London; 22tl Hulton-Deutsch Collection/CORBIS; 22lc © Transmanche Ferries; 22bl © Thomas Jouanneau/CORBIS SYGMA; 22br © Yves Forrestier/CORBIS; 22bg Martin Sparenberg;

ON THE MOVE

23 AA/P. Bennett; 24t DigitalVision; 25t AA/R. Moore; 26t AA/R. Moore; 26cr AA/ W. Voysey; 27t AA/C. Sawyer; 27cr AA/C. Sawyer; 28 AA/C. Sawyer; 29t AA. P. Kenward; 29rc AA/P. Bennett; 30/31t AA/P. Kenward; 30c AA/P. Bennett; 32/3t AA/P. Kenward; 32cl AA/M. Adelman; 33c AA/J. Tims; 34/35t AA/P. Bennett; 34l AA/R. Moore; 34r © Walter Bibikow, Jon Arnold Images/Alamy Images; 35 AA/R. Moore; 36 AA/C. Sawyer

THE SIGHTS

37 AA/R. Moore; 39tl AA/P. Bennett; 39tr AA/C. Sawyer; 40l AA/I. Dawson; 40t AA/I. Dawson; 40bl AA/R. Moore; 41tl AA/C. Sawyer; 41tr ImagesFrance.com; 42tl AA/C. Sawyer; 42tr AA/P. Bennett; 42bc AA/C. Sawyer; 43t AA/C. Sawyer; 43rc AA/I. Dawson; 43br AA/R. Moore; 44t AA/R. Moore; 45tl AA/B. Smith; 45tr AA/C. Sawyer; 45bc AA/J. Tims; 46 AA/I. Dawson; 47t AA/C. Sawyer; 46/7c AA/I. Dawson; 47c

AA/ R. Moore; 47cr AA/C. Sawyer; 48tl AA. C. Sawyer; 48tr AA/I. Dawson; 48bl AA/C. Sawyer; 49tl AA/R. Moore; 49tr AA/C. Sawyer; 49br AA/R. Moore; 50tl AA/I. Dawson; 50tr AA/C. Sawyer; 52tl AA/S. Day; 52tr AA/R. Moore; 52bl AA/C. Sawyer; 53t AA/C. Sawyer; 53cr AA/R. Moore; 53br AA/R. Moore; 54tl AA; 54tr AA/R. Moore; 54bc AA/R. Moore; 55t AA/P. Bennett; 55br AA/P. Bennett; 56tl AA/R. Moore; 56tr AA/C. Sawyer; 56br AA/C. Sawyer; 58cl AA/I. Dawson; 58t AA/C. Sawyer; 58bl AA/I. Dawson; 59tl AA/R. Moore; 59tr AA/R. Moore; 59cr AA/R. Moore; 60 © Martin Beddall/Alamy Images; 61t AA; 61cl AA/I. Dawson; 61c AA/B. Smith; 61cr AA/I. Dawson; 62t AA/I. Dawson; 62cl AA/C. Sawyer; 62c AA/R. Moore; 62cr AA/I. Dawson; 63t AA/C. Sawyer; 63br AA/I. Dawson; 64tl AA/I. Dawson; 64cl AA/R. Moore; 65tl AA/R. Moore; 65tr AA/I. Dawson; 66tl AA/C. Sawyer; 66tr AA/P. Bennett; 67tl AA/R. Moore; 67tr AA/P. Bennett; 68t AA/I. Dawson; 68lc AA/C. Sawyer; 69tl AA/R. Moore; 69tr AA/R. Moore; 70t AA/C. Sawyer; 70cl AA/C. Sawyer; 70/71b AA/I. Dawson; 71tr AA/I. Dawson; 72rc AA/C. Sawyer; 72bl AA/I. Dawson; 73tl AA/I. Dawson; 73tr AA/R. Moore; 73c AA/R. Moore; 74tl AA/P. Bennett; 74tr AA/C. Sawyer; 74c AA/R. Moore; 75t © Agence Images/Alamy Images; 75rc International Photobank/Jeanetta Baker; 75br AA/R. Moore; 77t AA/R. Moore; 77cr AA/R. Moore; 78t AA/C. Sawyer; 78lc AA/C. Sawyer; 78c AA/R. Moore; 78r AA/R. Moore; 78bl AA/R. Moore; 79t AA/R. Moore; 79rc Robert Harding Picture Library; 80/82 AA/P. Bennett; 83t © Franz-Marc Frei/CORBIS; 83cr AA/C. Sawyer; 84t AA/I. Dawson; 84lc AA/R. Moore; 84c AA/I. Dawson; 84rc AA/C. Sawyer; 84bl AA/C. Sawyer; 85t AA/C. Sawyer; 85rc AA/I. Dawson; 86t AA/R. Moore; 86rc AA/R. Moore; 86bl AA/C. Sawyer; 87tl AA/C. Sawyer; 87tr AA/P. Bennett; 89t AA/I. Dawson; 89rc AA/I. Dawson; 90tl AA/C. Sawyer; 90tr AA/R. Moore; 90bl AA/R. Moore; 91tl AA/R. Moore; 91tr AA/R. Moore; 92/3 AA/C. Sawyer; 93tr AA/C. Sawyer; 93cr AA/R. Moore; 93br AA/R. Moore; 94t AA/C. Sawyer; 94lc AA/I. Dawson; 95tl ImagesFrance.com; 95tr AA/C. Sawyer; 96t © Andy Arthur/Alamy Images; 96lc © Florian Monheim, Bildarchiv Monheim GmbH/Alamy Images; 96cr Pictures Colour Library; 96bl © Frederic Carnuccini/HEKA/Alamy Images; 97t © Andy Arthur/Alamy Images; 97rc AA/I. Dawson; 98 © Jochen Helle, Bildarchiv Monheim GmbH/Alamy Images; 99t AA/R. Moore; 99lc AA/R. Moore; 99c AA/R. Moore; 99rc AA/I. Dawson; 99br R. Moore; 100 AA/I. Dawon; 101l AA/B. Smith; 101c AA/R. Moore; 101r AA; 102t AA/R. Moore; 102b AA/R. Moore; 103 AA/I. Dawson; 104tl AA/P. Bennett; 104tr AA/R. Moore

WHAT TO DO

105 AA/P. Bennett; 106t AA/C. Sawyer; 106cr AA/P. Bennett; 106cl AA/S. Day; 107t DigitalVision; 107cl DigitalVision; 107cr AA/I. Dawson; 107cr AA/I. Dawson; 108t AA/R. Moore; 108cl Brand X Pictures; 109 AA/I. Dawson; 110t Photodisc; 110b AA/R. Moore; 111t AA/N. Setchfield; 111c AA/R. Moore; 112/13t AA/N. Setchfield; 112c AA/ P. Bennett; 113c AA/R. Moore; 114t AA/N. Setchfield; 115t Photodisc; 115c AA/C. Sawyer; 116/17t Photodisc; 116c Courtesy Le Brewery; 117c DigitalVision; 118/19t AA/R. Moore; 118c AA/R. Moore; 119c AA/R. Moore; 120/21t AA/R. Moore; 120c AA/R. Moore; 121c Image 100; 122t AA/R. Moore; 122c AA/I. Dawson; 123c AA/P. Bennett; 123t AA/S. Day; 124/25t AA/S. Day; 124c AA/I. Dawson; 125c Photodisc; 126/27t AA/S. Day; 126c

AA/P. Bennett; **127c** AA/C. Sawyer; **128/29t** AA/I. Dawson;
128c AA/R. Moore; **129c** AA/R. Moore; **130/31t** AA/I. Dawson;
130c DigitalVision; **131c** Photodisc; **132t** AA/I. Dawson; **132c**
AA/R. Moore

OUT AND ABOUT

133 AA/P. Bennett; **133** AA/ B. Smith; **134** AA/R. Moore; **136**
AA/R. Moore; **137** AA/C. Sawyer; **138** AA/R. Moore; **139l** AA/I.
Dawson; **139cr** AA/R. Moore; **139b** AA/I. Dawson; **140** AA/R.
Moore; **141t** AA/C. Sawyer; **141cl** AA/R. Moore; **141b** AA/R.
Moore; **142tl** AA/C. Sawyer; **142/43b** AA/I. Dawson; **143tr**
AA/C. Sawyer; **144** AA/C. Sawyer; **145tl** AA/R. Moore; **145tr**
AA/I. Dawson; **145b** AA/R. Moore; **146** ImagesFrance.com;
147cr AA/R. Moore; **148t** AA/I. Dawson; **148b** AA/I. Dawson;
149tr AA/I. Dawson; **149cr** AA/I. Dawson; **149b** AA/R. Moore;
150 AA/R. Moore; **151tr** AA/I. Dawson; **151br** AA/R. Moore;
152 AA/R. Moore; **153tr** AA/R. Moore; **153b** AA/I. Dawson;
154 AA/P. Bennett

EATING AND STAYING

155 Courtesy Dormy House Hotel; **156l** AA/P. Bennett; **156c**
AA/P. Bennett; **156r** Photodisc; **157l** AA/R. Moore; **157c** AA/R.
Moore; **157r** AA/C. Sawyer; **158l** AA/J. Tims; **158c** AA/P.
Bennett; **158r** AA/P. Bennett; **159** AA/J. Tims; **160/65** AA/P.
Bennett; **166c** Courtesy Hostellerie de Tourgeville; **166r**
Courtesy Dormy House Hotel; **167l** AA/P. Bennett; **167c** AA/J.
Tims; **168/171** AA/P. Bennett; **172c** AA/P. Bennett; **172r**
Courtesy Dormy House Hotel; **173t** AA/P. Bennett; **173b** AA/P.
Bennett

PLANNING

175 AA/P. Bennett; **178** AA/P. Kenward; **179** AA/P. Bennett;
181t AA/R. Strange; **181b** AA/C. Sawyer; **182** AA/R. Strange;
183t AA/J. Tims; **184** AA/P. Bennett; **186** AA/C. Sawyer; **188**
AA/C. Sawyer

Project editor
Robin Barton

Design work
Bob Johnson, Keith Russell

Picture research
Kathy Lockley

Internal repro work
Susan Crowhurst, Ian Little, Michael Moody

Production
Lyn Kirby, Helen Sweeney

Mapping
Maps produced by the Cartography Department of AA Publishing

Main contributor
Laurence Phillips

Copy editor
Susi Bailey

Published by AA Publishing, a trading name of Automobile Association Developments Limited, whose registered office is Fanum House, Basing View, Basingstoke, Hampshire RG21 4EA. Registered number 1878835.

A CIP catalogue record for this book is available from the British Library.

ISBN-10: 0-7495-4820-7
ISBN-13: 978-0-7495-4820-9

Key Guide is a registered trademark in Australia and is used under license. Binding style with plastic section dividers by permission of AA Publishing.

Colour separation by Keenes
Printed and bound by Leo, China

Find out more about AA Publishing and the wide range of travel publications and services the AA provides by visiting our website at www.theAA.com/bookshop

A02404
Maps in this title produced from mapping © MAIRDUMONT / Falk Verlag 2005
Relief map images supplied by Mountain High Maps ® Copyright © 1993 Digital Wisdom, Inc
Weather chart statistics supplied by Weatherbase © Copyright (2005) Canty and Associates, LLC
Transport map © Communicarta Ltd, UK

We believe the contents of this book are correct at the time of printing. However, some details, particularly prices, opening times and telephone numbers do change. We do not accept responsibility for any consequences arising from the use of this book. This does not affect your statutory rights. We would be grateful if readers would advise us of any inaccuracies they may encounter, or any suggestions they might like to make to improve the book. There is a form provided at the back of the book for this purpose, or you can email us at Keyguides@theaa.com

COVER PICTURE CREDITS
Front cover and spine: AA World Travel Library/Ian Dawson, AA World Travel Library/Ian Dawson, AA World Travel Library/Rob Moore, AA World Travel Library/Rob Moore
Back cover, top to bottom: AA World Travel Library/Clive Sawyer, AA World Travel Library/Clive Sawyer, AA World Travel Library/Pete Bennett, AA World Travel Library/Pete Bennett

Dear Key Guide Reader

──────●──────

Thank you for buying this Key Guide. Your comments and opinions are very important to us, so please help us to improve our travel guides by taking a few minutes to complete this questionnaire.

You do not need a stamp (unless posted outside the UK). If you do not want to cut this page from your guide, then photocopy it or write your answers on a plain sheet of paper.

Send to: **Key Guide Editor, AA World Travel Guides FREEPOST SCE 4598, Basingstoke RG21 4GY**

Find out more about AA Publishing and the wide range of travel publications the AA provides by visiting our website at **www.theAA.com/bookshop**

ABOUT THIS GUIDE

Which Key Guide did you buy? _____

Where did you buy it? _____

When? _ _ month/ _ _ year

Why did you choose this AA Key Guide?
- ❏ Price ❏ AA Publication
- ❏ Used this series before; title _____
- ❏ Cover ❏ Other (please state) _____

Please let us know how helpful the following features of the guide were to you by circling the appropriate category: very helpful (**VH**), helpful (**H**) or little help (**LH**)

Size	**VH**	**H**	**LH**
Layout	**VH**	**H**	**LH**
Photos	**VH**	**H**	**LH**
Excursions	**VH**	**H**	**LH**
Entertainment	**VH**	**H**	**LH**
Hotels	**VH**	**H**	**LH**
Maps	**VH**	**H**	**LH**
Practical info	**VH**	**H**	**LH**
Restaurants	**VH**	**H**	**LH**
Shopping	**VH**	**H**	**LH**
Walks	**VH**	**H**	**LH**
Sights	**VH**	**H**	**LH**
Transport info	**VH**	**H**	**LH**

What was your favourite sight, attraction or feature listed in the guide?

Page _____ Please give your reason _____

_____

Which features in the guide could be changed or improved? Or are there any other comments you would like to make?

_____

_____

ABOUT YOU

Name (*Mr/Mrs/Ms*) _____

Address _____

_____

Postcode _____ Daytime tel nos _____
Please *only* give us your mobile phone number if you wish to hear from
us about other products and services from the AA and partners by text or mms.

Which age group are you in?
Under 25 ❑ 25–34 ❑ 35–44 ❑ 45–54 ❑ 55+ ❑

How many trips do you make a year?
Less than 1 ❑ 1 ❑ 2 ❑ 3 or more ❑

ABOUT YOUR TRIP

Are you an AA member? Yes ❑ No ❑

When did you book? _ _ month/_ _ year

When did you travel? _ _ month/_ _ year

Reason for your trip? Business ❑ Leisure ❑

How many nights did you stay? _____

How did you travel? Individual ❑ Couple ❑ Family ❑ Group ❑

Did you buy any other travel guides for your trip? _____

If yes, which ones? _____

Thank you for taking the time to complete this questionnaire. Please send it to us as
soon as possible, and remember, you do not need a stamp (*unless posted outside
the UK*).

Titles in the Key Guide series:
Australia, Barcelona, Britain, Brittany, Canada, Costa Rica, Florence and Tuscany, France, Germany,
Ireland, Italy, London, Mallorca, Mexico, New York, New Zealand, Normandy, Paris, Portugal, Prague,
Provence and the Côte d'Azur, Rome, Scotland, South Africa, Spain, Venice, Vietnam.
To be published in November 2006:
Thailand